ARMY
DIPLOMACY

Battles and Campaigns

The Battles and Campaigns series examines the military and strategic results of particular combat techniques, strategies, and methods used by soldiers, sailors, and airmen throughout history. Focusing on different nations and branches of the armed services, this series aims to educate readers by detailed analysis of military engagements.

Series editor: Roger Cirillo

An AUSA Book

ARMY
DIPLOMACY

American Military Occupation
and Foreign Policy after
World War II

WALTER M. HUDSON

 UNIVERSITY PRESS OF KENTUCKY

Scholarly publisher for the Commonwealth,
serving Bellarmine University, Berea College, Centre College of Kentucky,
Eastern Kentucky University, The Filson Historical Society, Georgetown
College, Kentucky Historical Society, Kentucky State University, Morehead
State University, Murray State University, Northern Kentucky University,
Transylvania University, University of Kentucky, University of Louisville,
and Western Kentucky University.
All rights reserved.

Editorial and Sales Offices: The University Press of Kentucky
663 South Limestone Street, Lexington, Kentucky 40508-4008
www.kentuckypress.com

Library of Congress Cataloging-in-Publication Data

Hudson, Walter M., (Judge advocate)
  Army diplomacy : American military occupation and foreign policy after
World War II / Walter M. Hudson.
    pages cm. — (Battles and campaigns)
  Includes bibliographical references and index.
  ISBN 978-0-8131-6097-9 (hardcover : alk. paper) —
  ISBN 978-0-8131-6099-3 (pdf) — ISBN 978-0-8131-6098-6 (epub)
  1. World War, 1939–1945—Occupied territories. 2. United States—Foreign
relations—1933–1945. 3. United States—Foreign relations—1945–1953.
4. Military occupation—History—20th century. 5. Military government—
History—20th century. I. Title.
  D802.A2H83 2015
  355.4'9097309044—dc23   2014047967

This book is printed on acid-free paper meeting
the requirements of the American National Standard
for Permanence in Paper for Printed Library Materials.
∞

Manufactured in the United States of America.

Member of the Association of
American University Presses

To my wife, Laura,
to my mother, Elizabeth Anne (née Muller) Hudson,
and to the memory of my father, William Augustus Hudson,
  Colonel of Infantry, US Army, 1928–2011,
    a soldier of two wars who saw the need to win the peace

Contents

Photographs follow page 200

Illustrations

Introduction

In the immediate aftermath of World War II, the US Army became the principal executor of American postwar governance policy throughout the world. It administered the military occupations of not only the defeated Axis powers of Germany and Japan but also of Austria, Korea, and many nations liberated by American military forces in their drives across Europe and the Pacific. At the height of the army's responsibilities, more than three hundred million people around the world were under some form of US military government authority.[1] According to Cold War scholar Melvyn Leffler, of all the services, the army had the most influence over early Cold War policy, primarily because of its occupational duties in Germany, Japan, and elsewhere.[2] Generals such as Lucius Clay in Germany, Douglas MacArthur in Japan, Mark Clark in Austria, and John Hodge in Korea presided over occupied territories as American viceroys. And because of these occupational responsibilities, the army's influence over American foreign policy in the early Cold War period was profound, though in ways not usually understood.

American military government was looked upon apprehensively by many civilians, and even senior army leaders voiced concerns. President Franklin D. Roosevelt had deep misgivings about the army running postwar occupations. And Roosevelt was not alone: many inside and outside his administration also opposed military governance. George Kennan said: "The ruling of distant peoples is not our dish. . . . There are many things we Americans should beware of, and among them is the acceptance of paternalistic responsibility to anyone, be it even in the form of military occupation, if we can possibly avoid it."[3] An article in the October 1943 issue of *Harper's* magazine asked: "Somehow the job [postwar occupation] must be done. But why should it be done by the Army? The Army is specialized in destroying enemy armies. Why should it be presumed to be specialized in the most complex and gigantic task of reconstruction the world has ever seen?"[4] Even Gen. George C. Marshall worried that presiding over the governance of people throughout the world could send the wrong signal to the American people. In a discussion with the chief of the Civil Affairs Division, Maj. Gen. John Hilldring, Marshall said: "Our countrymen, our fellow citizens, are not afraid of us. They don't harbor any ideas that we intend to alter the government of the country or the nature of this government. . . . And I don't want to permit the enormous corps of military governors that you are in the process of training and that you are going to dispatch all over the world, to damage this high regard in which the professional soldiers in the Army are held by our people, and it could happen . . . if you don't understand what you are about."[5]

Marshall's caution and circumspection reflected the army's overall unease. But this unease itself vacillated. True, the army was concerned about assuming postwar occupation responsibilities. Indeed, it often seemed to want to get out of such duties as quickly as possible. On the other hand, the army fought for the sole responsibility, during the first postwar phase, of administering postwar governance. That underlying tension found expression in how the army would interpret and execute its occupation tasks. And despite such resistance and skepticism, at war's end the US Army administered the occupation of both liberated and conquered countries, and that administration would have major implications for the United States in the postwar world.

The literature on the postwar occupations, particularly of Germany and Japan, is vast and deep, ranging from major works of synthesis to detailed monographs focused on specific locations or issues. But these studies tend to focus on the specific occupation experiences themselves, and they do not reach either back in time, to reveal how the army conceived those occupations, or do not extend outward in scope, to reveal how the army's particular doctrine, leadership, and implementation of occupation policy had larger foreign policy consequences.[6] There is also a significant body of literature on the high diplomacy of the war years, especially the Allied conferences at Yalta and Potsdam. Undoubtedly these meetings of the Allied national leaders resulted in many of the key decisions that led to the construction of the postwar world.[7] But these high-level conferences provided broad and often rather unclear guidance that required interpretation by on-the-ground administrators. Furthermore, the notion of a grand strategy delivered from on high can warp one's sense of how history, even military history, unfolds. As the American intellectual Randolph Bourne pointed out when he lamented the "collapse" of American strategy that led to the US entry into World War I, the American case (for Bourne the legal, rational, and nonjingoistic basis) for war hung on a "perfect working partnership of ideals, strategy, and morale."[8] High policy, in other words, has to be contextualized and seen as part of a larger process. In a democratic, bureaucratized form of government, it particularly has to be placed in a framework where governmental agencies and organizations operate and interact.

As the evidence indicates, the army became the dominant US government actor in postwar occupation policy due to a variety of factors and circumstances that go beyond diplomatic documents or even the apparent national interests of the United States. This study attempts to examine the factors and circumstances within the army's own institutional culture, including its historical understanding of how postwar military governance was conducted prior to World War II; its creation and implementation of doctrine, training, and organization; and its ability as a governmental agency to represent its interests in the bureaucratic realm with not only other US governmental organizations but with organizations in Allied governments as well. As the chapters on the particular occupations in Germany, Austria, and Korea reveal, these occupations were not simply driven by policymaking decisions from the US government that reflected a unified "national interest." They were driven just as much if not more by the army's understanding of how postwar governance should be conducted in a multinational environment that included America's postwar superpower rival, the Soviet Union.

It should be pointed out that the occupation of Japan is excluded from this study. Germany was a conquered nation, Korea was ostensibly liberated, and Austria was in an unusual gray area in-between in that it was considered to have been illegally annexed and to some degree victimized by Germany but also responsible for the crimes its leaders and people had committed as part of the Third Reich. Given that each country's status was different, each brought something different to the dynamic of occupation. In this context, Japan was the same as Germany: a conquered nation. Even more important, a major focus of this study is not simply upon the occupations themselves but how they shaped Cold War outcomes, particularly vis-à-vis the Soviet Union. The US-Soviet dynamic was absolutely critical in Germany, Austria, and Korea, though almost completely absent in Japan. Much of that on-ground dynamic at the military level contrasted with early Cold War hostility at higher levels. In Japan that dynamic simply did not exist: the Soviets occupied none of Japan and were thus nonplayers in the day-to-day aspects of occupation there.

The Army's Strategic Outlook prior to and during World War II

To understand the American army's approach to postwar governance during and after World War II, one must first understand the army's traditional distinction between warfare and politics. Commentators have noted that at least for much of its history, the army did not view war as a *gestalt*—as a whole comprising concrete and abstract elements. Rather, it traditionally looked at war in a more linear way, with "ends, ways and means arranged hierarchically and linked to discrete levels of command."[9] At the risk of generalization, the pre–World War II army's view reflected an approach far more "Jominian" than "Clausewitzian" in its extreme rationalization of conflict and in its desire to delineate carefully between what did and did not constitute conflict.[10] According to this understanding of high-level policymaking (what could also be termed grand strategy), the army operated in an instrumental fashion, with such strategy dictating and directing and the army serving as the instrument to enact that strategy. This Jominian approach stressed a maximum amount of order and control, often in the form of rules and laws, including laws that regulated armed conflict.

A 1936 lecture to officers at the army's Command and General Staff College highlighted this separation of the military and political spheres: "Politics and strategy are radically and fundamentally things apart. Strategy begins where politics ends. All that soldiers ask is that once the policy is settled, strategy and command shall be regarded as something in a sphere apart from politics. . . . The line of demarcation must be drawn between politics and strategy, supply, and operations. Having found this line, all sides must abstain from trespassing."[11] Warfare was seen as a method of last resort after "politics" had failed. War had a starting point that indicated such failure, usually a formal declaration and an end point, usually formal surrender terms and/or a peace treaty. Furthermore, war in the traditional American understanding was conventional conflict between nation-states. During wartime the military took over. In order to achieve victory, decisive and overwhelming force was required, and military requirements, as opposed to political ones, predominated.

Such a notion of the separateness of war and politics as a fundamental part of pre–Cold War US military culture has been subject to debate and challenge. Recently much has been written about American participation in so-called small wars in the late nineteenth and early twentieth centuries, and some have taken those experiences as evidence to show that the American military deliberately used force that interacted with political goals.[12] But even the foremost practitioner of small wars during that period, the US Marine Corps, itself did not consider a small war as war in its true form. As its *Small Wars Manual* stated, "small wars vary in degrees, from simple demonstrative operations to military intervention *in the fullest sense, short of war*" (my emphasis).[13]

The political/military separation characterized what is sometimes termed the "American way of war," in which the requirements of absolute military victory are paramount, even over longer-range political objectives. This same separation also characterized what might be called an American way of *post*war, in which the requirements of securing that victory dominated political concerns.[14] As Secretary of War Henry Stimson wrote about World War II planning, "even in diplomatic questions . . . the major consideration was almost always the advancement of American victory."[15] Similarly, army chief of staff General Marshall wrote to Gen. Dwight Eisenhower as the war ended on the subject of a British recommendation to capture Prague. He said that he was "loath to hazard American lives for purely political purposes."[16] Eisenhower remarked that Berlin was nothing but a "geographical location" and that "military plans . . . should be devised with the single aim of speeding victory."[17]

This focus on military objectives by senior army leaders, a reflection of its strategic culture at the time, had consequences relevant to postwar governance policy. A narrow focus on military goals, for example, actually made certain army officials *less* likely than State Department officials to perceive a long-range Soviet threat—such a perception being considered overly "political." Averell Harriman, who served as wartime ambassador to the Soviet Union, commented that he believed that both Marshall and Eisenhower were the slowest to recognize that there would be future difficulties with the Soviet Union, because to them Stalin had kept his military commitments, and that, according to Harriman, "neither [was] involved in [the] political phase."[18] And among several senior US military leaders, the alliance with the Soviet Union remained fairly strong after the war ended. Even during the early occupation period, key American military leaders were not predisposed toward an anti-Soviet viewpoint. In 1946 Lucius Clay, for example, protested the establishment of Radio Liberty in Munich, which provided anticommunist broadcasts, refused to offer support for conservative or moderate parties during the crucial elections in heavily communist Berlin, and was "appalled" by George Kennan's famous 1946 cable that set forth the containment strategy.[19] In January of the same year, Eisenhower addressed Congress on the slow pace of demobilization. Noting that there were still over six hundred thousand soldiers assigned to the European theater, he justified their presence based on the "primary and continuing mission of occupation duties" and listed the army's responsibilities for "supervising all the headaches of a changeover from war to peace, with the added directive that we must make certain these people are so disarmed, both economically and in a military sense, that they cannot make war again." Yet not once did he reference the Soviet Union: there was no word of any threat beyond that of the defeated enemies themselves.[20]

The army did not remain in total control of the occupations following World War II. As both V-E Day and V-J Day receded from view, the State Department in particular began to reassert its authority to conduct foreign policy. After years of neglect or indifference by Roosevelt, President Harry S. Truman insisted that the State Department become a much more forceful agency. Assistant Secretary of War John McCloy, who played a major role in assuring the army's dominance in postwar governance planning, himself saw as early as October 1945 that US policy had been too immediately focused on the "immediate debris of active warfare" and that there needed to be greater emphasis and consultation with native leaders on "matters relating to their social, economic, and political restoration."[21] And in the spring of 1946, the State Department established the position of assistant secretary of state for occupied areas, charged with the responsibility "for coordinating the formulation of policy for Occupied Areas" and tasked to "assure that fully coordinated United States Government policies are developed by the State Department and supplied the Army, as executive agent."[22] According to the new assistant secretary of state, the establishment of the position was a first step in reorienting the relationship between State and War.[23] Yet by the time the State Department began to reassert its traditional role in foreign policy matters in the latter years of the 1940s, US military government doctrine, organization, and leadership had already deeply influenced the environments where that foreign policy would operate. The Cold War began during the post–World War II occupations, and some of its most contentious issues were framed by preceding military government planning and policies and by early decisions of military government officials, many of whom did not necessarily contemplate the worldwide struggle that the Cold War would become.

Understanding the Army's Institutional Culture prior to and during World War II

In addition to understanding army strategic culture, there must be a further understanding of the army's own particular institutional culture and how that culture informed thinking and practice when it came to planning and conducting postwar military government. The strategic understanding that viewed military goals as predominating over longer-term political goals connected powerfully with the army culture that also saw the need for specifically *military* government, with uniformed officials serving as commanders, high commissioners, and governors of occupied territories. That culture developed internally and through time, through a series of internal decisions that led to changes in institutional doctrine, education, training, and organization. The paradoxical result was a military force dispensing political rule, and the paradox was resolved by the military government focused fundamentally on the accomplishment of shorter-term military goals and objectives.

Understanding how the army gained predominance in post–World War II governance requires a close inspection of its doctrine, education, training, and organization before and during the war. Such a detailed study has been done of other armies. In her book *Absolute Destruction: Military Culture and the Practices of War in Imperial Germany,* historian Isabel Hull refers to the "continuities in military practices, doctrines, and micrologics" that in the case of the German army led to a cultural climate that permitted it to transgress legal and moral boundaries before and during World War I. Specifically, despite the presence of internationally agreed-upon norms in the late nineteenth and early twentieth centuries, a set of particular circumstances unique to the German army led to the acceptance and practice of atrocity both during and after conflict, circumstances that included its experiences fighting French partisans during the 1870–1871 Franco-Prussian War, its understanding of "military necessity," and its view that battles of "annihilation" were the preferred way to achieve absolute victory. Hull's study points out how the particular German army's culture, and not only the experiences of "total war" or other external phenomena, conditioned it to accept and justify atrocity.[24]

The same level of detailed analysis into the interior practice of the American army before, during, and after World War II reveals a culture that formed its own unique conception of postwar occupations, notably different from Germany's. For example, the army's 1863 Lieber Code, which provided a basic set of rules for the treatment of civilians, was an internally created document. It actually preceded the Hague and Geneva Conventions (and influenced them) by several decades. "Military necessity," a phrase used in the Lieber Code, was, as in the German army, a concept of overriding importance but was qualified with restraints that, at least in theory and doctrine, did not allow warfare to be practiced without limits against civilian populations. Furthermore, the primary historical experience that shaped the American army's conception of post–World War II governance was not brutal guerrilla warfare (even though the army had had its share, particularly during the insurgency in the Philippines) but the relatively peaceful Rhineland occupation that followed World War I. The Rhineland occupation was in fact atypical of the army's experience. Most of its occupations followed conflicts that were not conventional wars on such a total scale. Nonetheless, the Rhineland occupation was central to the army's understanding of postwar occupations in large part because it best fit the paradigmatic conventional-war mission that army leaders believed was the army's essential function.

Additionally, the army's cultural understanding of war did not occur in a vacuum but in an interactive environment where the army, along with other governmental institutions, fought for primacy in administering the postwar occupations. In this institutional domain, the army competed with other agencies in the Roosevelt and Truman administrations and, because of a variety of factors, became the dominant agency in postwar planning. Fully examining internal practice and the army's interactions with other agencies also helps to reveal the overlooked connection between the military objectives of post–World War II occupations and their political consequences during the early Cold War. Politics and ideology do not necessarily control a nation's policies or even determine the nation's interests. Those policies and interests are often shaped, if not fundamentally determined, by subordinates making decisions in the immediacy of events and guided by doctrine and policies that reflect a particular agency's outlook and culture.

Reconstructing the historical milieu in which this competition arose requires understanding the American army's nature, not only as an armed force that fought the nation's wars but also as a bureaucratic organization, as a professionalizing force, and as an agency of the American federal government interacting with other agencies. In doing so, I have relied on insights from institutional and military sociology as well as international relations theory, particularly the theory of so-called political constructivism.[25] I acknowledge that history's contingencies should not be bound by theory. Nonetheless, the work in these fields helps frame and clarify crucial parts of the story of the dominant role the army played in post–World War II occupations.

Like other industrial-era institutions, the American army moved toward a more bureaucratic ordering and control in the late nineteenth and early twentieth centuries. According to Max Weber, modernity was characterized by the steady march of nearly all public and private institutions and organizations toward such bureaucratization, as greater and more sophisticated rationally devised procedures and regulations became established. Weber contended that bureaucracy was inescapable and inevitable in all societies, the notable distinction between modern and past bureaucratic models being that modern bureaucracy, in its rationality, technical specialization, and training, was far more encompassing and absolute than its predecessors. Additionally, modern organizations especially found their legitimacy through conformity with legal norms and a readiness to conform with formal rules that were imposed by common procedures, as opposed to the older legitimizing forms—those of tradition, of effectual attitudes, or of beliefs in absolute values, even though Weber recognized that an organization's patterns of submission and obedience could be premised on a combination of the older and new forms.[26] Modern militaries were themselves part of this bureaucratizing process. Rather than setting militaries apart as unique organizations not subject to the principles of bureaucracies, Weber saw commonalities between military and civilian organizations, noting the discipline and human cooperation demanded of bureaucracy in the "army, office, workshop and business."[27] Weber also saw comparative advantages between them—"differential advantages which favor[ed] one type over another"—and he contended that the modern military was the ultimate form of bureaucracy and that it had developed the most effective method in ensuring bureaucratic success in the form of "rationally ordered discipline."[28]

The processes of centralization and bureaucratization described by Weber did not take place smoothly but in fits and starts. In America in the late nineteenth and early twentieth centuries, these processes arose as a result of industrialization, the close of the frontier, the rise of the city, and the emergence of the United States as a global power, as federal government bureaucracy arose in the form of a variety of centralizing agencies, laws, and regulations to the diminishment of more particularized forms of power. The army's reformers during this period likewise sought to achieve a rational, legalistic reordering of its internal structures and significant training and educational reforms. Secretary of War Elihu Root, a corporate lawyer, was perhaps the most influential of those reformers at the beginning of the twentieth century. Such reforms continued into the century's interwar period, even if during then the army was isolated from society in general and from other governmental organizations. All the while, the army's traditions and hierarchies bound it together in a way that made it more cohesive and homogenized.[29]

The move toward rationalizing, bureaucratizing reform corresponded with a professionalization of the army's officer corps. In *The Soldier and the State,* Samuel Huntington explored the development of this professionalization, defined by a strong distinction between military and civilian roles and ultimately by civilian control. The American military remained autonomous and independent within its own sphere of expertise in order to retain its professional capability. At the same time, according to Huntington, what occurred was an internalization, as part of its professional ethos, of the idea of not challenging civilian control of the military. Part of the army's identity as a "profession" derived from this concept. In return, civilians largely permitted the army autonomy in its area of expertise.[30] (Indeed, especially in the period between the world wars, civilians ignored or even disdained the army outright.) Huntington's emphasis on military professionalization helps one understand how the army developed its own professional standards, particularly during the late nineteenth and early twentieth centuries. It is especially useful in understanding the way the army approached postwar occupation after World War II. It clarifies the army's reconciliation of the political and military dimensions of occupation. It also illuminates the interagency disputes between it and other civilian governmental agencies during World War II. Clearly military government fell into a grayer area than more purely military issues such as campaign strategy or battlefield tactics. Military government bridged, often uncomfortably, the military/political divide that the army's strategic culture emphasized.

Huntington's analysis also assists in focusing on relevant historical evidence. Army doctrine, education, and training provided officials with an expert body of knowledge that thereby provided the basis on which to implement military government. Yet it did so in a way that nonetheless emphasized the military/civilian (and hence political) division. Specifically, by relying on numerous examples through its history, the army's theory of military government rested on two overarching principles that, while quite basic, were of great importance not only because of the repeated emphasis placed upon them by senior military leaders but also because they were a logical corollary to American strategic thinking about the subordination of political to military ends.

First, during the initial phases of occupation, "military necessity" meant that military objectives were paramount and more "political" objectives subsidiary. Given the totality of World War II and the subordination of political ends to military ones throughout the war, it was uncontroversial to conclude that the army should have primary "wake-of-battle" responsibilities to ensure victory was lasting. But there was also a second overarching principle in US Army military government doctrine: the desire to return to local civilians control of the occupied area as quickly as possible. The army had internalized the idea that prolonged occupations were clearly beyond its ability and expertise. To depart from this concept would be just as professionally contradictory as it would be to attempt to usurp the notion of civilian control. In so doing, American military government essentially harmonized military interests in absolute victory with civilian concerns about military takeovers of foreign policy. In particular, public statements of trusted agents such as Marshall and Eisenhower during and after World War II provided reassurances that no such takeovers would occur, and they did not. Though the army was extremely influential and even the dominant foreign policy actor for the first postwar year, the State Department, as the traditional US civilian policy actor, in all cases eventually took over the army's authority.

Military sociology provides a way to understand how military government emerged the way it did before, during, and after World War II.[31] Institutional sociology, especially so-called new institutionalism, provides a way to understand more fully how the army transformed as a result of various societal influences and how it interacted with other governmental institutions. In contrast to theories that tend to posit institutions as static entities or are based on rational-actor models, new institutional theory looks to institutions as not only dynamic and changing entities but also as themselves independent variables that have cultural significance and that influence individuals within them and the societies in which they are located. As Walter Powell and Paul DiMaggio state, "institutions do not just constrain options: they establish the very criteria by which people discover their preferences."[32] It is therefore necessary not simply to look at the "state interests" or even national strategy or perceived threats of the United States in determining why the postwar occupations were army-executed.[33] It is also necessary to look *within* an influential institution such as the army to determine what the institution did to influence policy.

Using a typology of social organizations, one can examine the interwar and World War II army in a number of ways. It can be analyzed as an institution from the point of view of its unique *structural nature*— the emphasis on formality, specialized functions, rules, records, and routines. The army was both a rule-bound and rule-creating entity, and its formulation of military government doctrine was of key importance in understanding how the army was successful in gaining control over postwar occupation. The army can also be examined as an *organizational type,* such as a business, bureaucracy, or profession.[34] Its continuing professionalization, especially in the period between the world wars at its premier educational institution, the Army War College, reveals how the institution established the procedures that would govern postwar occupation practice. It can also be analyzed as an *interacting* organization that competes with and negotiates space with other organizations.[35] The army was an intensely bureaucratic organization that worked alongside other governmental organizations whose interests and viewpoints sometimes harmonized, yet also frequently clashed, with its own. Finally, the army can be viewed as an *organizational culture,* which consists of "taken-for-granted values, underlying assumptions, expectations, collective memories, and definitions present in an organization," and these derive from either explicit or implicit unwritten "rules."[36] Much post–World War II military government practice was grounded both in international rules and internal military rules and regulations. However, these rules and regulations were not simply external. They were interpreted and mediated by cultural and institutional practices that were based in the army's culture, a culture not only controlled by coercive mechanisms compelling obedience but also informed by normative constructions of rules, regulations, and modes of behavior.[37] Particularly revealing are not only the actions and opinions of high-ranking officials, such as Secretary of War Henry Stimson, Assistant Secretary of War John McCloy, and the military governors of occupied territories such as generals Clay, Clark, and Hodge, but also of lesser-known officials, such as provost marshal of the army Maj. Gen. Allen Gullion, Military Government Division director Col. Jesse Miller, and others. These acts and opinions were shaped by powerful assumptions about the separation of military objectives from political ones and about the absolute primacy of military necessity, particularly in wartime operations. Indeed, the concept of "military necessity" would achieve nearly totemic status that, virtually by its evocation, would override all other concerns.

In addition to military and institutional sociology, constructivist political theory provides useful insights into how army cultural imperatives led to its control of the postwar occupations. In recent years, this theory of international relations has challenged traditional "realist" notions about how nations interact and how organizations in nations influence those nations' behaviors. Traditional realist notions have posited nations as autonomous entities that interact with each other based on exogenous "interests" and typically downplay or ignore altogether questions about the identities, norms, and values that those nations, or organizations within those nations, possess.[38] The central theme of constructivist theory is that the *identities* of the organizations and domestic societies of states in turn powerfully influence the identities, and hence the policies and the interests, of those states.[39] State actors bring identities to the table of international relations, and those identities are formed through the interaction of organizations within those states, including the interplay of ideas, social structures, and patterns of behavior.[40] These identities may be consciously formed or not, may arise spontaneously, or be planned.[41] As political theorist Bill McSweeney points out, "actors acquire identities defined as 'relatively stable, role-specific understandings and expectations about self' by participating in collective meanings. Identity is inherently relational and identity is the basis of interests."[42]

The constructivist approach is useful as a hermeneutic tool in separating actors' intentions from the events and interpreting the latter in light of often overlooked factors. Philosopher Hans-Georg Gadamer has pointed out that one can neither confuse the meaning of a literary work with its author's intent nor the meaning of historical events by the intentions of historical actors.[43] One should not be put off by constructivism's theoretical language. Its essential tenets were grasped by one of the most pragmatic and astute insiders of the Vietnam War, Robert Komer, who helped design and who initially led the Civil Operations and Revolutionary Development Support (CORDS) program. Komer noted that the declassified Pentagon Papers made it clear that while the United States *meant* what it said in Vietnam, it did not *do* what it said. He pointed out that the US military's actions there were bound by "institutional constraints—doctrine, tactics, training, equipment [that] made it difficult to do anything else." Bureaucracy in Vietnam, particularly military bureaucracy, in Komer's words "did its thing"—it caused policy to bend to its demands and its internal imperatives rather than the opposite.[44]

Constructivist theory helps one to understand how government bureaucracies shape national interests. For as it makes evident, governmental institutions, and especially military ones, are not simply instruments that the state uses to pursue national interests. As French military historian Elizabeth Kier points out, what a "military perceives to be in its interests is a function of its culture."[45] Those interests shape, even if indirectly, military doctrine and policy and, as a result, strategy. This does not discount that states and their militaries take into account enemy threats in determining interests. But enemy threats are one factor among many within a military culture. Kier points out that determining what a particular military culture looks like, and determining what possible interaction the military culture may have with outside agencies, requires close examination of material such as curricula at military academies, internal bureaucratic communications, and professional military publications. Examining these sources reveals the interplay of forces that shape internal policy as well as influence external behaviors.[46]

Constructivism therefore allows a closer review of conceived propositions. Why did the United States not seek other ways to conduct the post–World War II occupations? The particular form of military government used by the United States in occupied territories was not the inevitable solution. Roosevelt himself frequently stated he did not think the military was appropriate to conduct such operations. Many influential members of his cabinet openly and vigorously opposed a military-run postwar occupation scheme. It is at least arguable that while military forces could have executed postwar policy, it would have better served the national interest to have senior-level civilian executors take over leadership as soon as possible in the occupied territories, especially given that one of the main reasons for fighting the war was to end militarist authoritarianism.

Why and How the Army Became the Lead Agency

Such theoretical tools help to answer essential questions. How and why did the army become the lead agent in occupation responsibilities? How did it become so important in postwar foreign affairs? There were several interrelated reasons that require close analysis of the army as an institution and the context in which it operated. Upon close analysis, it is clear that the army vigorously asserted its postwar governance prerogatives and prevailed in interagency disputes with civilian organizations. This runs counter to some current scholarship. Recent studies have contended that during FDR's presidency and throughout World War II, civilian predominance in civil-military disputes was never in doubt. Political scientist Michael Desch lists twenty-eight separate US civil-military conflicts between 1938 and the early 1940s and indicates that civilian leadership prevailed in each instance. The United States, according to Desch, was a "model" of military subordination to civilian authority and control during World War II.[47] Yet Desch's list is selective, and when it comes to wartime control of civilians and postwar occupation policy and implementation, a very different set of outcomes is revealed (see table I.1). As this study shows, and as the figure highlights, in a series of civil-military disputes related to the establishment of military control over civilians during and after the war, the army again and again emerged as the "victor" over its civilian interagency "rival." In each of these cases, the army's imperatives prevailed. Ironically, those imperatives prevailed not over wartime operations but over control of *civilians* in either wartime or postwar settings, when military imperatives should at the very least have been integrated into, and even subordinated to, a larger geopolitical viewpoint.

Because FDR was in the center of so many of these civil-military

Dispute/Conflict/Competition	Rivals	Resolved in Favor of:
Martial Law Imposed in Western Continental Zone (1941–42)	Dept of War/ Dept of Interior	Dept of War
Military Rule in Hawaii (1941–44)	Dept of War/ Dept of Interior/ Justice	Dept of War
School of Military Government Controversy (1941–42)	Dept of War/ Dept of Interior	Dept of War
Japanese-American Internment (1942)	Dept of War/ Dept of Justice	Dept of War
Civil Affairs in North Africa (1942–43)	Dept of War/ Dept of State	Dept of War
US Position at European Advisory Commission (1943–45)	Dept of War (Civil Affairs Division)/ Dept of State and Other Actors	Dept of War (Civil Affairs Division)
Morgenthau Plan (1944)	Dept of War/ Dept of Treasury	Dept of War
Preference of Occupation Zone in Germany (1944–45)	Dept of War/FDR	Dept of War
Dominant Organization at State-War-Navy Control Commission (1944–45)	Depts of War and Navy/Dept of State	Depts of War and Navy
Choice of German Military Governor (1945)	Dept of War/FDR Others in FDR's Cabinet	Dept of War
Decision to Divide Korea at Thirty-eighth Parallel (1945)	Military Decision	US Military
Ultimate Implementation of JCS 1067 (1946–47)	Amer Mil Govt in Germany (Clay)/ Dept of State	Amer Mil Govt in Germany (Clay)

Table I.1. US civil-military disputes over wartime control of civilians and postwar planning and implementation. (Created by the author.)

disputes, his role was of great significance. During World War II, he saw himself as a war president. He assembled a so-called war cabinet that contained lifelong Republicans such as Henry Stimson and staunch New Dealers such as Harold Ickes in order to conduct a war that would require unity across the political spectrum. Some historians argue Roosevelt was a masterful strategist who deliberately forged consensus at times and at other times allowed friction and debate, all with the view of ultimately leading the country in a united effort to win the war.[48] According to this view, FDR deliberately deferred key decisions about who should run the postwar occupations as a way to avoid fracturing consensus. Others have contended that FDR's motives were not so pure and his actions not so brilliantly calculated—that in fact he was an inept manager of the executive branch, and therefore the decision fell to the army virtually by default. The historical record suggests that the president was *both* a shrewd strategist and a poor manager—and the end result of the army running the postwar occupations was partially influenced by both FDR's strategic and managerial abilities.

But focusing on executive management style or such a "team of rivals" is too reductive and ignores significant institutional imperatives. There were deeper reasons why postwar governance occurred the way it did. The first has to do with the aforementioned professionalization of the army that had been occurring throughout the nineteenth and early twentieth centuries, a professionalization that was driven by reformers such as Elihu Root and that was realized in its educational institutions, such as the Army War College, founded by Root in 1903. In *The Soldier and the State,* Huntington asserts that professionalism allows for the maximization of "objective" civilian control—that is, by allowing the officer corps to develop a separate, independent sphere of expertise, it essentially becomes depoliticized, making it easier for civilians to assert their supremacy. As opposed to "subjective" control, which relies on a governmental agency (such as the executive branch), social class, or form of government to control the military by suppressing it as needed, objective control achieves civilian supremacy structurally—by permitting a specific domain for the military to operate in with expertise and even dominance, which satisfies the military's need to control and at the same time bounds it within the military sphere exclusively.[49] Yet professionalization may cause the sphere of military expertise to expand into areas that would previously be considered beyond its competence and thereby to encroach on areas that may be considered "civilian"—and when that occurs, professionalization of the military may give it a competitive advantage over other civilian organizations. This is what occurred before America's entry into World War II. The army gained a certain expertise in postwar occupation matters, subsequently developed upon that expertise in doctrine, organization, and education, and thereby gained comparative advantage over other far less organized civilian agencies competing in the same domain. Particularly at the Army War College, students began researching and proposing strategic ideas that went far beyond the normal province of campaigns and battles and ventured into civil-military realms, such as the occupation of territories after the termination of conflict. These ideas were often elementary and were usually considered peripheral in relation to other Army War College studies—generally they were appendices to other studies that dealt with more traditional warfighting tasks. Nevertheless, there was an undeniable influence in what these studies proposed, as seen in the policies and procedures later adopted.

This professionalization was closely linked with a second reason—the creation of a body of law in the late nineteenth and early twentieth centuries regarding the rules of armed conflict. The US Army's own famous Lieber Code of 1863 remarkably forecast many of the rules of conduct later embodied in international law, especially in the Geneva and Hague Conventions. The American army came to link the concept of military government with the rules of such government from Lieber to Hague, and it also expanded on those notions. For example, it crafted an interpretation of the fundamental principle of "military necessity," a notion also encoded within the laws of armed conflict, and turned it into a powerful, overriding concept, as evidenced by its use not only abroad but at home, as seen in the sweeping powers given to the army in Hawaii and on the West Coast (within the purview of the Western Defense Zone) during the war.

A third key factor was the army's development and creation of internal doctrine and its conversion of that doctrine into practice. The army took these rules and encoded them within itself. It used the concepts of international law for postwar occupation and created a specific doctrine for its forces. Embodied in *Field Manual* (*FM*) *27-5* (itself part of a set of doctrinal publications that represented the army's collective thinking on a vast number of tactical, operational, and strategic tasks), the army established a series of principles for its internal use. It used this doctrine to establish schools for military government, to pro-

mulgate studies of all potentially occupied countries, to shape planning
and operation, and to train and organize units for military government,
setting up a program years before any conquest of enemy territories
occurred. The army further established within the War Department
the Civil Affairs Division, largely supplanting or making unnecessary
many of the civilian agencies that were or could have been involved
in the postwar governance in occupied territories. Roosevelt, in other
words, was able to turn to the army in large part because it had mechanisms at hand to deal with the requirements that lay ahead.

In contrast, civilian organizations offered ineffective opposition
to the army over primary responsibilities in postwar matters—a final
reason why the army became dominant. Whereas it was able to organize, train, and plan according to a coherent set of doctrinal principles,
civilian agencies could not. Throughout the early years of America's
involvement in World War II, Roosevelt and others in his cabinet set
up multiple agencies, boards, and committees, and all had roles and
responsibilities that were meant to be at least equal if not more important than the army's. Yet these bodies simply lacked the fundamental
cultural underpinnings and coherent internal doctrines that the army
had. Nearly as important, they were essentially ad hoc, put together
in a seemingly rushed and incomplete manner, and they often lacked
a clear direction, especially in relation to corresponding War Department purposes. Often such organizations were at cross purposes and
wracked with internal dispute. The practical failing of civilian organizations in the governance of territories, especially during the North
African campaign of 1942–1943, was especially evident and helped to
ensure the army's ultimate prevalence.

The issue of the military's, and in this case especially the army's,
influence within the government and in foreign affairs is, as this study
attempts to show, a complex and multifaceted one. It was not simply a uniformed "power elite" subtly manipulating events to achieve
its ends or inchoate militarism insinuating itself into the structure of
government and achieving a "militarized" outcome. A complex set
of historically contingent events occurred that required specific decisions by actors as well as decisions not to act. The army, for example,
was hardly an "elite" in the US governmental structure in the interwar
years. It was relatively marginalized and excluded from strategic think-

ing. Nonetheless, it acted within its own sphere to develop an approach to postwar governance that became codified into doctrine. The army *did* during the war years rise to preeminence, but it relied on thinking during its earlier, more isolated history to establish its concept of postwar governance.

The Postwar Occupations, the Cold War, and Their Subsequent Influence

How did the specifically military character of these occupations influence foreign policy outcomes during the post–World War II period, especially the first years of the Cold War? The result of the army's domination of early postwar governance policy led to political configurations in US-occupied countries that reflected military-oriented approaches and solutions. This book focuses on occupations in three countries: one country was conquered and its central government destroyed (Germany), another was severed from a former enemy (Austria), and a third was liberated (Korea). In each case, military governance meant that policy would orient around military organizational structures, reflect military doctrine, and be led, at least in the occupied countries themselves, by military officers. While undoubtedly other US agencies, particularly the State Department, asserted the right and authority to set American strategic policy in those nations, any policy enacted occurred via US Army military government organization, doctrine, and leadership.

The period from the surrenders in Europe and the Pacific (May and September 1945) to mid-to-late 1946—approximately a year to a year and a half—was one of profound uncertainty. Relationships between the Soviet Union and the United States were straining but had not yet broken down. In Germany, Austria, and Korea, where the United States and the Soviet Union were occupiers, what were often crucial were not necessarily the political or ideological constructions that would later be seen as defining the Cold War—the various pronouncements, doctrines, and agendas from strategic leaders. During the 1945–1946 period, many of those statements were yet to be made. Rather, on-the-ground interpretations of policy and even on-the-ground decisions made by military leaders themselves shaped the political landscapes in those occupied nations for years to come.

Germany was central to US postwar strategy, and its integration into an international order was of the highest significance for US civilian policymakers. During the war, however, military planning about postwar governance dominated US policy. Any detailed planning was closely linked with wartime military goals. In a series of postwar occupation plans, from Rankin to Talisman to Eclipse, an emphasis on military objectives was paramount. Within the US government, controversy did erupt over the publication of an army handbook that set forth the army's conceptions of what postwar Germany would look like. The famous "Morgenthau Plan," which called for Germany's pastoralization, was one outcome of perceived army "softness" toward Germany. There was significant resistant to Morgenthau's proposals, especially from Secretary of War Stimson, and the influential document that ultimately provided the initial guidance on Germany's occupation, known as Joint Chiefs of Staff Directive 1067 (JCS 1067), was essentially in keeping with army conceptions of what the occupation should be. Even more important than the wartime planning was the implementation of postwar governance by the de facto American military governor, Gen. Lucius Clay. Clay's establishment of military government units and directorates as stand-alone executors of US policy meant that all such policy would be refracted through the army's understanding of postwar governance. Furthermore, his own understanding and implementation of JCS 1067 meant that the document would far more reflect the army's own doctrinal approach to military government. This was nowhere better revealed than in his emphasis on returning power to Germans as quickly as possible, especially his efforts to decentralize and federalize the German government in the US zone in the elections of 1946–1947. The American efforts to denazify also revealed the clash between the aspirations of US policy and the institutional imperatives of the army. The result was a denazification program but one largely run by the Germans themselves.

Austria was of course far less significant in the postwar international order to the United States than Germany and a focus of far less policy attention. Apart from the 1943 Moscow Declaration that stated that Austria would be treated as a liberated, rather than a conquered, country, no US agency other than the army spent any significant time planning for Austria's postwar occupation. Accordingly, regardless of the Moscow Declaration, the US military government model for Austria was essentially the same as Germany's: zonal division largely determined by the troop movements into the country and the US military government model established in *FM 27-5* as the template for occupation. Of all the occupations, the conditions in Austria most resembled those of the post–World War I Rhineland. The first American military high commissioner, Gen. Mark Clark, also served a highly significant role in securing Austria's future, even over significant Allied resistance. Clark's insistence on recognizing the Karl Renner government early in the occupation was a key factor in reestablishing Austrian autonomy and ultimately in reducing Soviet authority in the eastern half of the country. Even though Renner was a socialist and had communists in his provisional cabinet, Clark's willingness to accept someone who just a few years later might be viewed highly suspiciously was consistent with American military government thinking about returning power quickly. The quick recognition of the Renner government would later be seen as one of the primary reasons Austria was unified and neutralized nearly a decade later.

Finally, Korea provided the most complex set of conditions for American military government to operate, conditions furthest removed from the historical template established by the Rhineland occupation and doctrinally promulgated by *FM 27-5*. American policy toward Korea, derived from vague notions of an independent Korean state announced at the 1943 Cairo Conference, was enacted according to standard military government imperatives. Occupying forces were sent to Korea based upon their proximity to the peninsula. The military government mission was premised on the wartime goals of disarming the hundreds of thousands of Japanese soldiers in the country. But standard military government policy—that of leaving local civil administrators in charge—foundered against the political reality that many civil administrators were Japanese, which ran counter to the professed goal of Korean autonomy and ultimate independence. Perhaps the most momentous decision in postwar Korean history, its division along the thirty-eighth parallel, was done by US military planners entirely for military reasons. The American military governor, Lt. Gen.

John Hodge, was given a tremendously difficult task, even more so than either Clay's or Clark's. Yet he lacked any significant civil-military experience, and while decent and fair-minded, he could not manage the political complexities of postwar Korea. His military government units, placed in an environment far different from the relatively placid occupations in Western Europe, grappled with a slew of political parties. Failing to understand the Korean language, culture, and political landscape adequately, Hodge and his subordinates were often themselves pawns of certain Korean politicians who had English-language skills and an understanding of the West, especially Syngman Rhee, who would ultimately dominate South Korea after the Americans' departure. Hodge admitted that the Joint US-Soviet Commission established to unify the country soon failed, and ultimately the thirty-eighth parallel hardened into a militarized border. Korea remained divided, highly turbulent, and unstable after the US Army departed in 1948 and shortly thereafter plunged into war.

As the occupations of Germany, Austria, and Korea reveal, the actions of the citizens of the countries the Americans occupied interacted with and influenced postwar governance as well. Military government doctrine, organization, and the actions of army leaders sometimes clashed, and sometimes were in conformity, with the needs and desires of the local populations. It is evident from these three occupations that American military government was most successful when the military government doctrinal and organizational model, largely a product of the army's own culture, was best suited to the locale of occupation and where the military government leadership responded most fully to local actors, as in Austria. It was least successful when the model was poorly suited to local conditions and where military leadership was less responsive to local needs, as in Korea.

In the postwar years, the army studied its postwar occupation role and institutionalized civil governance to a limited degree. Surveys of former military government officers showed the mixed results of the army's attempt at postwar governance. Those surveys and other studies especially showed the frequent gap between higher-level occupation policy and on-the-ground implementation of that policy. The army established some institutional structures and promulgated certain doctrinal principles but organizationally largely forgot what it had learned about governing civilian populations. Ironically, while the State Department and the US Agency for International Development led the first efforts at civilian pacification in Vietnam, arguably the most successful program, Komer's CORDS, did so *after* Komer successfully had it placed under military control, though Komer admitted that even the CORDS effort was insufficient. And in the post–Vietnam War years, the army continued to struggle to come to terms with governance of civil populations, culminating in the attempts at governance in Iraq after the 2003 invasion.

What the post–World War II occupations reveal is that postconflict governance is a complex, multifaceted problem that defies standard doctrinal solutions. New ways of thinking about such problems should be welcome, and at the end of this study I examine systemic operational design as well as insights from philosophical hermeneutics to provide ways of thinking about postwar problems and to help sort through the various traps and fallacies that may lay in wait for military and civilian planners and executors of postconflict policies.

This is a study focused primarily but not exclusively on military institutions and military bureaucracy. Similar institutional and bureaucratic studies were more popular in the wake of the Vietnam War. Certain of those histories' conclusions aligned with Komer's contention that bureaucracy forced the United States into making very poor decisions about Vietnam.[50] An objection to such studies is that they deprive individuals of choice, agency, and, in the end, responsibility. While there is some merit to this objection, to ignore or to downplay institutional and bureaucratic forces is to overrate significantly the ability of policymakers to act as purely rational agents and thereby to singularly control historical events. Rather, embedding such actors in institutions and bureaucracies provides context to their choices and very often shows how their choices are intensely constrained. High-level policy and ideology, as this study intends to reveal, do not necessarily control a nation's actions or even determine its interests. Those interests are profoundly influenced, if not determined, by subordinates within bureaucratic structures making decisions in the immediacy of events and guided by doctrine and on-the-ground planning and implementation that reflect a particular agency's outlook and culture.

This study makes no claim about which agency ultimately was

the correct one to conduct America's post–World War II occupations. What is clear, however, from the historical evidence is that the army was able to achieve an internal consensus and to a large degree provide a coherent training and organizational model for postwar occupation (though with clear limitations, as the Korean occupation revealed). Civilian agencies failed to do so. I also do not suggest that the post–World War II occupations represent models that current and future military strategists and civilian policymakers should strive to match. Rather, I intend to show that those occupations represented the culmination of over a century of practice, training, education, and doctrinal development within the army itself. The planning and implementation of those occupations further represented the height of the army's power and influence, during the years of World War II and immediately following when military imperatives predominated over ostensibly "political" ones. Those occupations are often viewed as civil-military accomplishments unrivalled in modern times, in which strategy and on-the-ground execution resulted in conditions largely favorable to the United States. The reality was far more complex.

1

Military Government Planning prior to 1940

The army's dominance in the planning and execution of post–World War II governance has its origins in practices dating back to the mid-nineteenth century, including its internal adoption of laws regulating treatment of civilians and its acceptance and application of laws of international conflict, in particular the Geneva and Hague Conventions. The army had gained practical experience throughout the nineteenth and early twentieth centuries with occupations in Mexico, the Reconstruction South, the Philippines, Puerto Rico, and Cuba. And while army officers often lauded their own achievements, in reality the long-lasting achievements of American occupations were ambiguous in almost every case. Political scientist David Edelstein has rated the army's 1898–1902 and 1906–1909 occupations of Cuba as well as the Marine Corps's 1915–1934 occupation of Haiti and 1916–1924 occupation of the Dominican Republic as failures, since the countries were left in a state of instability and disorder. The army's Philippines occupation also had mixed results. It prevailed but only after a brutal, controversial counterinsurgent struggle. Military leaders were subject to public criticism for their treatment of civilians, and the US actions there looked to many Asians as no different from European imperialism, contributing to subsequent Japanese claims of "Asia for Asians."[1] By far, however, the army's most significant postwar experience was the Rhineland occupation following World War I. That occupation in particular led to the development of occupation methods and concepts at the Army War College in the 1920s and 1930s. Those methods and concepts in turn formed the basis of military government doctrine to be used in World War II.

It is especially important to point out that this methodological and conceptual development occurred within the army *itself,* with no guidance from other US governmental agencies. Whatever subsequent policy determinations were made by the president and other high-level officials regarding military government during and after World War II, the template for that government had already been developed, a template constructed according to the army's own culture and its own understanding of how to conduct postwar occupations. The consequences were far-reaching and would culminate in the army administering the post–World War II occupations of liberated and conquered territories around the globe and greatly influencing American foreign policy during the early years of the Cold War.

Legalizing Armed Conflict

The army's handling of civilian populations dated back to the Mexican War of 1846–1848.[2] Gen. Winfield Scott, for example, issued a general order throughout conquered Mexican territory that provided for martial law and the establishment of provost courts and military commissions. In order to ensure good order after victory and to minimize the need for large-scale occupation, he was mindful of the need for good civic relations. He directed his soldiers to salute priests and magistrates, and though a Protestant he regularly attended Mass in Vera Cruz and even marched in a religious procession. Scott's military government rested on two fundamental principles that would ultimately be elaborated and fully developed during World War II. First, the primary function of military government was to ensure the accomplishment of the military mission. Scott had no directive to rebuild or to reorder Mexican society; his fundamental goal was to ensure that that battlefield success was not undermined in the wake of victory. Second, military necessity was nonetheless premised on providing for basic needs of the civilian society. Allowing for wholesale pillaging and devastation only undermined battlefield gains.[3]

Two decades later, in the middle of the Civil War, the Union army promulgated its famous Lieber Code of 1863, also known as General

Orders No. 100. It was arguably the first attempt by a fighting force to encode a set of rules regarding the treatment of prisoners, the protection of civilians, and the application of "military necessity"—that is, determining when military requirements could overrule otherwise legal restrictions.[4] German American jurist Francis Lieber had convinced Union general in chief Henry Halleck that because the Civil War was fought largely by relatively inexperienced and amateurish militaries, a code of rules was necessary to control and guide behavior.[5] The code's purpose was simultaneously idealistic and pragmatic. Lieber wrote to Halleck on its publication that it was a "contribution by the United States to the stock of common civilization." At the same time, he saw the code's need to control the widespread destruction of property in practical terms: "[Such damage] does incalculable injury. It demoralizes our troops; it annihilates wealth irrecoverably, and makes a return to the state of peace more and more difficult."[6]

The Lieber Code did not specifically mention military government. However, it did place the actions of the federal troops within the framework of the related legal construct of martial law. The opening paragraph of the code conflated martial law and military government by asserting that "a place, district, or country occupied by an enemy stands, in consequence of the occupation, under the martial law of the invading or occupying army." The power of martial law was seemingly absolute, since it included "the suspension by the occupying military authority of the criminal and civil law, and of the domestic administration and government in the occupied place or territory." But the Lieber Code also mitigated the apparent unlimited nature of martial law. It stated that such authority "disclaimed all cruelty and bad faith." And it had language that stressed that the conquered/occupied populace should attempt to carry on life in as normal a fashion as possible—civilians could not be forced into the service of the victorious army, private property was generally to be respected, and civil servants would continue to be paid.[7] As noted, the rationale for this was as pragmatic as it was benevolent. In the words of historian Geoffrey Best, the Lieber Code was an example "close to perfection" of the "arch-occupier" model. The arch-occupier model stressed that the population needed to stay at work and to continue life as normally as possible and thereby cause minimal interference with military operations.[8]

As military historian Brian McAllister Linn points out, the code was the legalized manifestation of an American military mindset prevalent in the nineteenth century that arose during the Civil War and the army's frontier constabulary duties. Specifically, army leaders formed a contractual relationship with conquered populations: on the one hand, military forces would attempt to treat the civilians humanely; for their part, civilians had to abide by rules of good behavior in order to allow those forces to achieve their mission.[9]

The American army inculcated the Lieber Code's basic principles—and in later wars worked within its ambiguities. Certain of the code's provisions were open-ended enough to suit whatever requirements were on hand. Its assertions of "military necessity," for example, were also used as a defense by officers accused of torturing Filipino insurgents during the 1899–1902 Philippine Insurrection.[10] Its vagaries notwithstanding, and partly because the code was internally generated (in the form of a general order, no less) and not imposed by international requirement, it was a source of some pride among the officer corps. It was praised by George B. Davis, judge advocate general of the army and a delegate plenipotentiary to the Geneva and Hague Conferences, for being a generation ahead of its time and for influencing much of the later Geneva and Hague Conventions and Regulations.[11]

The Lieber Code anticipated late nineteenth- and early twentieth-century codifications of what would be known as the law of armed conflict. The Geneva Conventions of 1864 and 1868, the St. Petersburg Conventions of 1868, and the Brussels Convention of 1874 all provided increasing control over what states could and could not do during and after hostilities.[12] Most significantly, the Hague Conventions and Declarations of 1899 and 1907 provided the fullest treatment of military occupation. Prompted by Russian foreign minister Count Mouravieff in 1898 and then later by President Theodore Roosevelt following the Russo-Japanese War, the Hague Conventions not only dealt with rules about weapons and treatment of prisoners and noncombatants, but they also specifically addressed military authority over hostile territory, the military's responsibilities while conducting an occupation, and civilian rights in occupied territory.

The Hague Conventions' treatment of occupations was similar in many ways to the Lieber Code's. Fifteen articles stated the responsibilities of occupying armies. Article 43, for example, required the occupying power to restore public order, and Articles 44 and 45 asserted that inhabitants could not be forced to provide information about their nation's military or be required to swear allegiance to the occupying power. Article 47 prohibited pillaging, and Article 49 only permitted levying the population for military purposes if military necessity required it. The conventions also implied a contractual relationship between occupier and occupants. Article 55, for example, allowed the occupying force to be a usufructuary for the territory it occupied, and at the same time it required that force to safeguard public buildings and agricultural and real property so that they would be in sufficient working condition when the occupation ended.[13] Ultimately the Lieber Code's influence on the law of armed conflict came full circle when the Hague Conventions and other international legal conventions became incorporated into army policy and doctrine. In 1914 the War Department published *Rules of Land Warfare,* which incorporated "everything vital in [General Orders No.] 100," noting also that "during the past 50 years, many of these rules have been reduced to writing by means of conventions or treaties." Accordingly, *Rules of Land Warfare* referenced the Geneva and Hague Conventions, along with a variety of other works, including opinions of the judge advocate general and United States Supreme Court cases. *Rules of Land Warfare* would subsequently be updated twice, in 1934 and in 1940, as *FM [Field Manual] 27-10,* which was even more expansive and included interpretations of post-Hague treaties to which the United States was a signatory.[14]

A Professional Force

Efforts to legalize armed conflict and, as part of that effort, to define responsibilities of an occupation during the late nineteenth and early twentieth centuries paralleled efforts to professionalize the American army. Many officers wanted to turn the army into a more capable organization that could wage wars against more powerful adversaries.[15] These reformers sought to move it from a constabulary force that had largely confined itself to patrolling the frontier and manning coastal defenses to a force capable of asserting American power on a global scale. To do this required making the officer corps more sophisticated and knowledgeable.[16] In particular, the work of military intellectuals such as Emory Upton sought to improve army leadership, especially through education and the creation of military journals to elaborate reformist ideas. At Fort Leavenworth Kansas, for example, the army established schools beginning in 1880. Officers began publishing more widely in journals and forming professional associations.[17] Military reformers such as Upton and Arthur L. Wagner also studied past battles and campaigns as a way to draw lessons from the past.[18]

Other officers looked beyond the battlefield. An 1892 work by 1st Lt. William E. Birkhimer titled *Military Government and Martial Law* focused on the army's postwar responsibilities. It was a lengthy treatise that fully explored the application of legal concepts of postwar occupation.[19] Birkhimer was a soldier-scholar who had participated in much of the nineteenth-century American military experience. Born in 1848, he entered the Civil War as a private in the Union army and ultimately rose to the rank of brigadier general in 1906. His post–Civil War service began with his graduation from West Point in 1870. He later served as judge advocate for the Department of the Columbia from 1886 to 1890, and he won the Medal of Honor while in the Philippines in 1899 fighting insurgents. His service in constabulary duties formed the basis of his book, which was, in the words of Gen. George B. Davis, "the most complete treatise on the subject in the English language."[20]

In his work, Birkhimer asserted that the Lieber Code was the most "successful attempt" to codify law of war principles. Comparing it to the 1880 Brussels Code, he noted that because the Lieber Code was written in the midst of conflict when there was a need for practicality, it was set apart from the more abstract formulations found in the Brussels document. Birkhimer set forth in detail the legal foundations of military government. He cited both legal opinions and historical examples, showing how the various occupations during the Mexican and Civil Wars were justified and ratified by opinions in American common law.[21] Distinguishing the occupation of foreign nations (military government) from the imposition of military control within one's own country (martial law), Birkhimer placed the notion of military government within a highly legalistic understanding of both the role of states and the role of contemporary international law.[22] States could lawfully engage in war, and military government's prerogatives and responsibilities came from that lawful right. But Birkhimer further noted that while throughout most of history victory gave a conqueror unlimited authority over a conquered nation and the property therein, the increasing regulation of the nation-state system in the nineteenth century had set limits upon the conqueror's ability to do as he chose.

Birkhimer also distinguished between the form of a particular military government and the substance of the fundamental laws and principles that military government had to follow. As long as the laws and principles were complied with, the form could be left open to the occupying power. Proclamations, for example, although advisable, were not legally necessary. He barely touched upon specific and practical questions of command and control and the organization of military government itself—for example, whether there needed to be specialized staffs or units devoted exclusively to occupation responsibilities. He left little doubt, however, about the need for an occupation to be completely run by military officers. Military government depended upon "swiftness of action, impartiality in meting out justice . . . and overwhelming force." Therefore, the qualities of such a government "attach peculiarly to a government of military power conducted alone by military officers."[23]

Birkhimer's work came out in 1892 and was part of a growing body of professional works by American military officers. The army continued to make efforts at increasing professionalization within its own ranks through the application of scientific and managerial concepts and procedures, through study of past successes and failures, and through broadening the intellectual horizons of the officer corps by exploring areas beyond wartime strategies and battlefield tactics. But major professionalizing and reform required a galvanizing event. It was only after the colossal planning and logistical failures of the Spanish-American War in 1898 that Secretary of War Elihu Root and similar reformers sought to fully turn the army into a more capable, modern organization. The Root reforms shifted the army from a "heroic" command model to a modern corporate and managerial one. Determined to apply business principles to military problems, Root approached the army as if it were another form of public administration. A strong believer in scientific progress and advancement, and aligned with the

Progressive movement's ideas of social advancement, Root had three main goals in reforming the army. First, he sought a clearer line of authority to the president and the secretary of war from subordinate commands, which would thereby eliminate the more traditional commanding-general role and link the army with broader strategic designs. Second, he urged the creation of a standing peacetime army that would plan and prepare for war against major powers: the army was to fight other large-scale forces; it would compete upon the world scale with the other armies of great powers and empires. Last, he sought a more corporate and professionalized force and, accordingly, a more educated officer corps.[24]

Many officers likewise believed that the application of business principles would produce a more efficient and better run military. They looked with great admiration at the successes of American industrialists in creating massive organizations that reaped enormous profits.[25] The large-scale industrial corporation, just coming into being, sought to organize large numbers of workers into coordinated and regimented labor forces as a way to maximize output and profits. Military officers sought to do the same.[26] A "managerial" mindset arose in the military that went far beyond improving close-order drill and basic tactics. As Brian McAllister Linn points out, many army officers began to study matters that might not be considered the essence of warfare and battle.[27] Professionalism thereby meant doing more than wartime soldiering. It brought responsibilities *before* and *after* fighting. Effective management of war meant being able to manage what occurred after fighting had stopped. And just as doctrinal principles were helping to define the nature of conflict, the application of law would help to do the same both during and after combat. Required were not simply brave soldiers and officers but also effectively organized and trained ones capable in both war and peace.[28]

Root directed a 1902 report by Charles E. Magoon, a law officer in the War Department's Division of Insular Affairs, titled "The Law of Civil Government in Territory Subject to Military Occupation by the Military Forces of the United States." Root wanted all of the various reports on military occupation matters following the Spanish-American War to be compiled and studied, and the length and detail of the report, responding to actual problems in current occupation matters, was in keeping with Root's desire to achieve practical results in his reforms. Citing Lieber, Birkhimer, and other treatises, Magoon ranged over numerous topics, from monetary claims made against American forces to complaints by shipowners being restricted from trading. And while such topics may appear to be particular and even arcane, Magoon's report advanced important notions about the need for military predominance during postwar occupations.

Grounding his understanding of military government in numerous legal precedents, Magoon noted that military government existed differently in the three locations where American forces had defeated the Spanish. In Puerto Rico military government served not as a substitute for civil government but as the representative form of American government because the island was the legal possession of the United States following the 1898 Treaty of Paris. In Cuba, on the other hand, military government was a substitute form of government because the United States did not take lawful possession there. Finally, in the Philippines military government existed in its most fundamental form. There, because hostilities continued, such government proceeded as military operations continued. As the three modes of occupation indicated, military government could have various forms during and after fighting. Just as important, Magoon highlighted that military government should not be subject to congressional control. Furthermore, the foundational premise of military government was military necessity: "If Congress has the authority and shall exercise it and make martial rule the subject of legislation, then the justification of the acts of persons enforcing martial law becomes a question of law and not of necessity."[29] "Law" as understood in its fullest sense—of statutes passed by legislators, and of civil judges interpreting and ruling based upon those laws—was a cumbersome mechanism to enact and to enforce military government, which presupposed the exigencies of military necessity. It stood to reason, therefore, that while military necessity predominated, the military should be the principal governing force.

Army officers in the late nineteenth and early twentieth centuries likewise argued that they should be given postwar duties. The final report in 1899 of Maj. Gen. John Brooke, the military governor of Cuba, set forth the wide-ranging tasks that he believed had been successfully accomplished, from moderately reforming the Cuban legal system to building and repairing roads and bridges.[30] And in a 1915 address titled "The Civil Obligation of the Army," a prominent reformer, Maj. Gen. Leonard Wood, pointed out that the army was capable of carrying out a number of tasks other than winning battles. These included medical tasks such as discovering the causes of typhoid and combating yellow fever in the tropics. They also included the administration of government after the conclusion of hostilities. Reflecting the army's confidence in its capability to conduct postwar governance, Wood noted that the army had established civil governments in Puerto Rico, Cuba, and the Philippines "with great success." In Cuba the army transferred to the Cuban people a "completely organized republic," in Puerto Rico the army transferred the island to the American government itself, and in the Philippines, the controversial and difficult nature of the army's handling of the 1899–1902 insurrection notwithstanding, the army had turned over to the American civil commission a "well organized government and a well-filled treasury."[31] While all these claims could be significantly challenged, Wood's comments revealed the sense of pride and confidence senior officers had had in the army's ability to conduct postconflict government functions.

Throughout the first decades of the twentieth century, the army continued to incorporate the Geneva and Hague Conventions into its training. War Department bulletins published the texts of the conventions at the outbreak of World War I. In a 1914 lecture to medical officers, Lt. Col. John Biddle Porter, a judge advocate, discussed not only the efforts throughout the nineteenth century to "codify the customs of war and to obtain for them a code of international recognition." He also noted the explicit connection between these rules and the army's own Lieber Code, the "first code of the laws of war which were ever published," noting that "the code adopted at The Hague Convention in 1907 . . . departs but little in principle from the code of 1863." He concluded his lecture by pointing out that all officers needed to become familiar with the laws of war, and to study them during peacetime, and not to wait until "a crisis arises and a thousand other duties call upon their time."[32] Many of these officers would put many of those conventions to use four years later in an occupation effort that would prove to be of profound and lasting impact.

The Rhineland Occupation and the Hunt Report

The Allies occupied a relatively small part of Germany following World War I. In accordance with the 1919 Rhineland agreement, troops from Belgium, Great Britain, France, and the United States eventually occupied an area covering twelve thousand square miles on the west bank of the Rhine with three bridgeheads opposite Cologne, Coblenz, and Mainz. It was not especially large in size or population, consisting of an area roughly the size of Belgium and containing seven million inhabitants (11 percent of the overall German population). The Americans occupied Rhineland territory between the Belgians and British to the north and the French to the south.[33] Despite this seemingly modest effort, the post–World War I occupation profoundly shaped the American army's conceptions of how military government would be conducted after World War II. The American role in the Great War, as it was then known, would be far overshadowed by its later, far vaster, and more consequential involvement in the later conflict. Nonetheless, that earlier involvement signified America's coming to age as a great power. The US Army came of age as well. At least in the mind of its leadership, it was now on par with the other world's great militaries.

The American occupiers took control of territory that had been run by the highly rationalized and autocratic German civil service system. The Rhineland civil government had been largely controlled by a Prussian political elite, and while American military government officers perhaps saw that elite rule as antidemocratic, they also believed that it comported with the means and ends of military government. As sociologist Morris Janowitz has shown, the interwar army's officer corps was especially infused with values that would predispose it toward such a system: his study revealed that 92 percent of the corps in the 1910–1920 period came from either the American upper class or upper middle class. The officer corps of the period was largely Anglo-Saxon, and most came from traditional mainline Protestantism, with a heavy concentration from conservative Episcopalianism, which stressed "authority, ceremony, and mission."[34] Especially in light of what many perceived as the anarchy and destructiveness of the Bolshevist movements in post–World War I Germany, American military officers viewed the order and control of the Rhineland civil service, and the corresponding acquiescence of the populations that it governed, as a system that conformed to their own values. As Maj. Gen. Henry T. Allen, the commander of the occupation troops in Germany noted, "regardless of the reasons that may be marshaled against such a form of government, it is obvious that its autocratic nature peculiarly qualified to adapt itself to the requirements of an occupying military force."[35] Capt. Truman Smith, a capable officer from America's patrician class who authored much of the so-called Hunt Report on the occupation, also viewed the order and seeming efficiency of the German civil service with admiration and respect. He noted that the civil officials were essentially "army officers without uniforms" and saw the seeming advantage in linking the military government with that system as soon as practicable.[36]

Overall the American experience in the Rhineland, while it had its problems, was relatively benign. The occupied territory had effective civil governments still functioning. The population did not resist, and it did not question the supreme authority of the military governorship established by the Americans. Indeed, for many American occupation troops, the experience was by no means unpleasant.[37] In contrast, the Belgians, British, and French all had a variety of difficulties in their occupied zones. Acts of terrorism occurred in the Belgian zone, such as the bombing of a train that killed ten soldiers. There was anarchy and looting in the Cologne area occupied by the British. There were riots and unrest caused by perceived humiliation because of the French use of black colonial soldiers. There was far less apparent animosity between the Americans and Germans. The United States, after all, had suffered far less than those other nations, and relations went from neutral to good fairly quickly. Compared to the trench warfare in France, the experience must have been nearly idyllic, with afternoons free for doughboys to explore such locales as the famous fortress of Ehrenbreitstein in Coblenz or to wander the countryside of the Rhine and Moselle river valleys. The troops were billeted in private homes with good effect. In September 1919 the prohibition against fraternization with German women was lifted, and German-American marriages soon followed.[38]

The army derived some practical lessons from its experiences during the Rhineland occupation. In 1920 the Fort Leavenworth School

Press published a manual titled *Military Government*. It was filled with rule-based prescriptions, defining military government as a "branch of international law, and noting further that its sanctions are the sanctions of that law." It specifically referred to the Hague Conventions that dealt with postwar occupation. It cited the continuous American practice of military government, from the Mexican War to the present, and provided examples of general orders related to military governance, especially General Orders No. 100, which was, according to the manual, the army's "Bible" in all matters dealing with occupations since the Civil War.

It also favorably commented upon the way German civil officials and the population overall conducted themselves. Contrasting the occupation of the Rhineland city of Treves with that of Vera Cruz during the Mexican War, it stated that Treves "was composed of a highly organized, educated, and disciplined people—a clean, modern, up-to-date city. [Vera Cruz] was composed of people with no organization and uneducated and undisciplined in every sense of the word." Furthermore, it noted that in Treves all civil officials had remained at their posts when the Americans began the occupation; in Vera Cruz none did. The manual also asserted that military government was a *military* responsibility that should be exercised by army officers and that it should not be made complicated or obscured by lawyers or excessive legalisms: "In searching for a good officer to make a military governor or chief of staff for civil affairs, do not select a man who travels with a large legal library. . . . Avoid the man who is continually seeking for precedents to bolster up his opinions, but select rather one endowed with initiative, zeal and vision, one who will more likely create than follow precedents." As the manual indicated, more was needed to perform postwar occupation than the simple application of a set of rules. Needed especially were practical solutions to accomplish military missions—in other words, military government led by military commanders and conducted by on-the-ground military forces. Despite the ominous sound of "military government," this actually led to a somewhat minimalist approach. Because the accomplishment of *military* missions was paramount, the greater civil administration required, the greater the drain on resources and personnel. Because the primary responsibility was on order and on the security of the occupying army itself, the appropriate form of military government essentially left laws in place and made as little change to civil and social life as possible: "Err on the side of too few rather than too many regulations."[39]

An even more important postwar occupation document was the so-called 1920 Hunt Report, named after Col. Irvin L. Hunt, who had been attached to the American occupation force as an adviser in civil matters and who was later appointed its officer in charge of civil affairs. Consistent with the confidence of the army at the time, the Hunt Report opened in vivid and melodramatic style, proudly asserting that the victorious American force of "a quarter of a million men of a new race from overseas began their march down the valley of the Moselle to the Rhine," advancing forward at war's end "in the closing scene of the greatest drama of history." The Hunt Report also noted quite explicitly the harmony between the American occupation force and local German government officials, pointing out that those officials "with few exceptions have cooperated to the full extent of their authorities in making the occupation bear as lightly upon the civil population as the exigencies of time would permit."[40] More important, the Hunt Report looked upon postwar occupation as a military problem, as something clearly within not only the authority but also the ability of the American army, even if occupation responsibilities were significant tasks separate from wartime efforts.[41]

In military terms, the Hunt Report "operationalized" postwar governance. Its analysis moved beyond considerations of abstract legal concepts and definitions and dealt with practical administrative concerns, principally (though not exclusively) using the experiences of the Rhineland occupation. Accordingly it made observations and recommendations that, while simple and straightforward, had considerable influence on prewar and wartime military government planning. Specifically the Hunt Report stated that there were two "fundamental principles which profoundly affected the whole course of military government [by the American forces]" in the Rhineland after World War I. First, the American occupation separated the overall tactical commander from the civil administrator of the occupied territory. The governor directly represented (and was directly reportable to) the commander in chief of the American Expeditionary Force (AEF) and was "entirely independent of Third Army headquarters at Coblenz," and that therefore "limited the authority of the Commanding General of the latter force." This caused an "awkward division of authority." The "legislative powers of military government" that were lodged in the Office of Civil Affairs at Advanced General Headquarters (GHQ) were separated from the army tactical commander's executive authority to maintain public order and safeguard American forces. While this divided government scheme may have resembled American separation-of-powers concepts, it was "wholly unsuited for military occupation." Essentially it violated the notion of unity of command, and had it not been mitigated by a "spirit in which the several headquarters subordinated personal matters" to the mission as a whole, it could have caused severe difficulties in military government administration.

Yet while the Hunt Report stressed unity of command, it also recommended the separation of occupational functions from more traditional military ones. The second principle the Hunt Report considered was the use of tactical units as units of military government. The report considered this a serious mistake that caused administrative and bureaucratic difficulties. Tactical units had other nonmilitary government functions to perform (among them to disarm the German army and to be prepared to go to war if Germany decided to break the armistice), and they lacked the specific training to link their staffs to the sophisticated German governmental system at the local levels, which remained virtually intact. Instead, given the very precise and hierarchical system of Rhineland governments at the levels of *Provinz* (province), *Regierungsbezirke* (government district), and *Kreise* (incorporated city or county), American military government should have readily conformed and linked to that working system rather than use tactical formations to attempt to control and monitor that government. Neither the French nor British "committed [the American] mistake, and modeled their military government from the outset along lines paralleling the civil system."[42] This apparently more sophisticated approach of the French and British was in keeping with their colonialist traditions. The British in particular had a long tradition of so-called indirect rule in the colonies, allowing control of huge expanses of terrain by relatively few administrative and military personnel.[43]

Along with these fundamental concerns, the Hunt Report noted that while the American occupation force had created a civil affairs "G-5" staff section at the theater-level headquarters during the occupation, it dissolved the section at the conclusion of military government. Subsequent senior leaders did not attempt to establish a civil affairs section as a permanent feature of a staff at any unit level, nor did they seek to implement any training for future civil administrations. No higher-level service school, such as the Army Command and General Staff College or the service war colleges, had devoted any courses to studying civil affairs and military government. This was "extremely unfortunate" according to the report because the history of the United States was filled with an "uninterrupted series of wars." Intrinsically bound up with the conduct of war was the conduct of *post*war operations, and despite numerous precedents, ranging from Mexico to the Rhineland, the lesson was "seemingly not learned."[44] This assertion of failure was testimony to the ongoing professionalizing efforts begun in the nineteenth century and pushed forward by Root, for it both indicated institutional self-awareness and displayed institutional self-criticism. Indeed, the very phrase "lessons learned" would later achieve a potent status in the army, a virtual requirement following both military exercises and operations.[45]

Additionally, the observations revealed a tension between the army's effort, on the one hand, to seek unity of command and to subordinate ends wholly to military requirements and, on the other, to ensure that it had the professional capability to perform functions that were beyond warfighting. As would be seen, the army's World War II solution would be to ensure military necessity was paramount, keep postwar occupation under army control, and keep military government at least initially unified. At the same time the army would create a cadre of experts, establish specialized doctrine and training, and, at the appropriate point during the occupation, divide the administration of military government between tactical units and units solely devoted to occupation administration.

The Hunt Report would become a highly influential document, and Colonel Hunt spent the interwar period seeking to ensure that the army was prepared for its next occupation. He submitted the report to the commanding general of the American armed forces in Germany with the request that it be forwarded to the War Department for publication to serve as a "basis for technical study of Military Government by the General Staff of our Army as well as for future historians."[46] Army War College student committees frequently relied on the Hunt Report in the interwar years.[47] Much of it eventually influenced *FM 27-5*, the principal doctrinal guide for military government during World War II.[48] During World War II, army officers referenced it in testimony before Congress when explaining the nature of military government training and policy.[49] Secretary of War Stimson, when planning how to respond to President Roosevelt's apparent discomfort about the military government program, relied on its conclusions. He called it "the finest document of its kind ever to come out of the Army."[50]

The Rhineland occupation, via the Hunt Report, in turn became the experience-based template for post–World War II occupations for unsurprising reasons. For the first time, the army had closely examined how it organized and implemented occupations. Previous commentators such as Birkhimer and Magoon had laid foundations, but their works were legalistic and more like learned treatises than manuals for action. The Hunt Report not only examined those legalistic issues, it also actually supplied a practical model. It discussed in great detail how units should be organized and how staffs should be arranged, and it broached the subject of educating officers in civil administration. In this sense, the Hunt Report anticipated the rationalized, doctrinal-based approach to American military thinking that would become prevalent during and after World War II.

Furthermore, even though the post–World War I occupation experience was atypical for the army, it was the most recent in time, and even more important, it followed in the wake of a total conflict between powerful nation-states, the sort of conflict that most fit the category of war that the army would prepare for in the future. It is therefore unsurprising that the Rhineland occupation and the report it generated were the basis for assumptions and expectations for the post–World War II occupiers. At least during the planning stages, they likewise assumed functioning civil structures, unquestioned authority of the military government, and a benign environment free of partisan guerrilla activity. And where assumptions and expectations met a reality that most conformed with them, for example in Austria and to a lesser degree in Germany, the occupations were, if not exactly smooth and problem-free, manageable. In Korea, where they did not, expectation and reality diverged, and the occupation proved extremely difficult.

Interservice Difference and Interagency Isolation

The Hunt Report dealt with the problem of military government following a conventional war (what is today sometimes referred to as a "high-intensity conflict"). As Max Boot has pointed out, the army did not develop anything resembling an antiguerrilla or counterinsurgency doctrine during the nineteenth or early twentieth centuries.[51] There was a clear distinction between war, in its standard sense as a lawful armed struggle between nations, and other conflicts, defined by Marine Corps doctrine as "small wars." Wars, not small wars, were the province of the army. Small wars were instead suited for the relatively small size and more limited capabilities of the marines and were important, no doubt, but did not involve the planning and conducting of major battles and campaigns. John Lejeune, the commandant of the Marine Corps throughout most of the 1920s, specifically noted that a Marine Corps expeditionary force, when "landed in a foreign country, is primarily intended to protect the lives and property of American citizens residing there during periods of disorder."[52] As a point of comparison, the largest number of marines brought together for battle prior to World War II was as part of the multimillion-man World War I AEF—and it was a force that amounted to a brigade of 8,500, less than a third of one army division. During the interwar period when the army had been reduced to 125,000 men, the Marine Corps only had 16,800.

The Marine Corps's *Small Wars Manual,* published in 1940 and reflecting decades of doctrinal development, underscored Lejeune's understanding of the marines' primary interwar mission. Small wars were low-level military actions and technically not considered "true" wars at all. They "var[ied] in degrees from simple demonstrative operations to military interventions in the fullest sense, *short of war*" (my emphasis).[53] The use of forces in such conflicts did not necessarily require a declaration of war or consultation with Congress since they often involved the protection of US lives and property overseas.[54] As the manual stated, small wars were considered "routine active foreign duty of the Marine Corps in which this manual is primarily interested."[55] Interestingly enough, within the Marine Corps itself, even the idea of fighting primarily small wars became challenged. During the interwar years, many prominent marines thought the emphasis should be on amphibious operations. The publication of the *Small Wars Manual* in 1940, an apparent victory for the small-wars adherents, actually came at the very time when the doctrine became seemingly irrelevant with the onset of World War II. The Marine Corps subsequently shifted its focus to organizing, equipping, and planning for amphibious operations, and the *Small Wars Manual* was largely forgotten until the early twenty-first century.[56]

The specific and circumscribed association of small wars with Marine Corps operations highlighted another important difference between the strategic cultures of the army and the Marine Corps. Both services, carefully delineating their particular areas of expertise, distinguished between the strategic imperatives involved in conducting small wars and major military operations. As the *Small Wars Manual* pointed out, "military strategy for small wars is more directly associated with the political strategy of the campaign than is the case in major operations."[57] In other words, there was a much less clearly defined division between matters of policy and matters purely military in small wars. In contrast, major wars were undertaken only as a last resort—only when other political options had been exhausted and when the need for military victory was paramount. Therefore, military requirements (and military necessity) were of primary importance.[58] Policy was subsumed by military requirements. Warfare required a totality of effort and a necessary subordination of political goals to military objectives. This same logic applied during the initial postconflict stage of a military occupation: because military ends trumped political ones, military necessity would likewise hold sway.

If there was interservice distinction between wars and small wars, with the army and Marine Corps going their respective ways, there was also a complete indifference outside the military itself to any of the army's lessons learned from postwar occupations. In fact, partly as a result of the post–World War I disillusionment, in the 1920s and throughout most of the 1930s the view toward things military in the United States varied from disinterest to contempt, as the United

States steadily moved toward isolationism. Concern about entangling alliances and military involvements in overseas adventures accompanied a widespread antimilitarism. Such concerns combined during the Republican 1920s with calls for fiscal austerity. The National Defense Act of 1920, for example, provided for a standing force of 280,000, approximately half of what the War Department had proposed, and even that remaining force was cut by over half in the next two years. Living conditions for officers and enlisted soldiers sometimes were at near-poverty levels. Basic requirements, such as fuel for vehicles, were often luxuries in many instances, making meaningful training nearly impossible.[59]

The reforms of Root and others, including their push for military professionalization, therefore occurred in an insular way. The military was no longer seen as part of progressive government but, to many, as an impediment to larger reform. During those interwar years, public administration came to mean *civil,* and decidedly not military, administration.[60] Despite the army's professionalizing efforts, some doubted whether in fact the military was a proper profession at all. Two prominent scholars in the 1930s consciously avoided calling the military so, given that the service soldiers were called to render—warfare—was one that was hoped they would never have to perform. Other scholars determined that the military was wholly state-controlled and therefore not somewhat autonomous and self-regulating like true professions of medicine, law, or education.[61]

The dismissal of the military as a proper profession was consistent with thinking in American politics and society during the interwar period. Up to and through the Great War, what Samuel Huntington called the "neo-Hamiltonian consensus"—a view that advocated strong central government and an ability to project American power throughout the world—led to a movement to reform and strengthen the military.[62] In the wake of the carnage of World War I, this largely vanished, replaced by an antimilitarism that ran across the political spectrum. Big-business Republicans of the period viewed the military as essentially outdated in the current world of global commerce. Many such Republicans had been instrumental in blocking US entry into the League of Nations following World War I.[63] This so-called "business pacifism" had its counterpart in "reform liberalism" that contained strands of both domestic Progressive–era thinking about social improvement and "liberal internationalism" that saw war as outmoded and barbaric. In the new order, nations would work together amicably and, via treaties such as the Kellogg-Briand Pact, would outlaw war altogether.[64]

This disdain for the military in American culture was visible in American government as well. President Wilson had stated that a soldier should have "nothing to do with the formulation of [American] policy. He is to support [that] policy whatever it is."[65] The State Department shared Wilson's view. Foreign Service officers saw warfare not on a continuum with other forms of policy but as an aberration in international relations. In large part they effectively shut out the military from policymaking throughout the 1920s and 1930s. And while military leaders voiced concerns about the lack of policy guidance from the State Department, they accepted the supposed sharp distinction between matters political and military. There was only occasional significant communications between the War Department and State and other important components of government, with intermittent attempts at coordination ending in failure. It was not until 1935 that the State Department agreed to participate in joint board deliberations for War Plan Orange, developed by the War Department for possible conflict with Japan, by naming a Far Eastern expert as a participant, and not until 1938 that State agreed to allow the military to be part of a high-level State-War-Navy liaison committee.[66]

The interwar years essentially fostered a highly isolated military culture.[67] Nonetheless, there was development within the army during the period. The Root reforms continued to take hold. The power of both the army chief of staff and the Army General Staff progressively expanded, and the independence and authority of the subordinate War Department bureaus declined.[68] World War I had only reinforced the need for an effective way of organizing and planning the nation's wars, and movement began toward a more robust staff system, a process that was finally completed with George C. Marshall's staff reorganization in the early 1940s.[69] And the army's continuing emphasis on professional education was most prominent at the Army War College, where planning committees developed methods and concepts for postwar governance that would prove to be of singular influence.

The Army War College Planning Committees

Historians have contended that military prewar planners were short-sighted and did not take into account international affairs. But research into the Rainbow war plans that were devised primarily at the Army War College has challenged that view.[70] The interwar period was actually a time of prolonged reflection for the army. Isolated from the rest of government well into the 1930s, the army was virtually the only US agency looking at potential major conflicts.[71] Unilaterally and in the absence of higher direction, army planners during the period began to formulate their own definitions of what US policies should be, as a way to establish guidelines for their own plans.[72] In particular, the Army War College was at the height of its influence.[73] Student officers at the college devised numerous plans for future conflict, including scenarios that foresaw the need for postwar occupation and the establishment of military governments. Brig. Gen. George S. Simonds, commandant of the War College during the early 1930s ensured a level of realism and sophistication in planning. He required, for instance, an approach that brought in ideas about coalition warfare, and he encouraged the students to think creatively about a whole range of issues normally not dealt with in typical military planning.[74]

In the interwar period at the War College, various committees examined questions that had arisen in the recent past and proposed recommendations. Furthermore, student committees devised, often in collaboration with the Army's War Plans Division, plans that specifically addressed future potential conflict. These plans, collectively dubbed Rainbow, posed scenarios in which the United States waged future war with various nations. For example, War Plan Green addressed potential instability in Mexico, Red addressed war with Great Britain, Orange with Japan, and Black with Germany. Colors combined to show the possibility of a coalition of threats. Red-Orange, for example, was a plan to deal with a British-Japanese alliance. Not all plans were developed or used as extensively as others. For example, the Green and Red plans were used to cover other threat scenarios that might be applicable in a variety of contexts and to provide training for the students.

Part of the planning included the occupation and military governance of defeated nations. Throughout the 1920s and 1930s, Army War College student committees studied postwar occupation and military governance issues no less than thirteen times.[75] Student planners frequently examined postwar governance, and the answers provided, while never made official for use at the Army War Plans Division, were fundamental to the eventual training, doctrine creation, and planning for military government in the postwar world. The committees formulated solutions to a variety of problems, with subsequent conferences involving both faculty and outside officers to review student work.[76] In the 1920s, issues of primary concern were procedural, focusing especially on whether or not a civil affairs organization should be made a permanent army staff fixture. Throughout the 1930s, as the emphasis moved to planning against potential enemies, student committees involved in the Rainbow effort shifted focus to the actual governance of conquered territories. A result of these various examinations was the creation, as an appendix to the 1933–1934 committee study, of a postwar occupation guide titled *Basic Manual for Military Government by U.S. Forces*, a document that would serve as a seminal text for later military government doctrine.[77]

Plans for Military Government Organization: The 1920s Committees

The chairman of the first student committee on postwar occupation in 1924 was Colonel Hunt himself, a student in that class, and he was influential over several years. For example, he lectured the 1933 class on principles of military government, stressing among other points the need for the army to have technical experts in what would become known as civil affairs. In that lecture, he emphasized the importance of the military commander's supreme authority during occupation. He also emphasized that even high-ranking civilian authorities had to be subordinate to the military commander of the occupied territory: "The military commander must, in every case, be the military governor. That carries all the way down. The assistant military secretaries . . . are merely the civil staff of the subordinate military governors."[78]

The first committee reports established a methodological approach that would be used repeatedly by different War College committees throughout the interwar period. Essentially, various American military occupations, from the Mexican War to the Rhineland occupation, were studied, and from them the student committees derived lessons learned and possible standard practices and procedures to be adopted. The 1924 committee noted that one problem in the occupation of the Philippines at the end of the Spanish-American War was "the injection of civilians" (meaning US civilian governmental officials) into military government. The power of civilian government officials during that occupation "crippled the efficient conduct of military operations." Furthermore, civil affairs were supervised and directed through an operating branch known as the Office of Military Secretary for Civil Affairs, greatly diminishing the military governor's power. Relying no doubt on Colonel Hunt's own knowledge and experience, the committee further studied the World War I occupation, noting issues raised in the Hunt Report. Specifically, US military and civil authority during World War I was divided between higher-level commands. Military commands were not coextensive with political subdivisions. Tactical units doubled as military government units. There was also no staff section for civil affairs—instead, an officer in charge of civil affairs was simply appointed in an ad hoc fashion.[79] The 1925 committee similarly indicated that the establishment of military government along tactical lines and the division of military and civil authority in the Rhineland caused the US occupation there to differ "radically" from the French, Belgian, and English approaches.[80] In any case, as the 1927 committee pointed out, there was a consensus that the improvisation that had occurred by the AEF during the Rhineland occupation was not good policy and that organizing an occupation in a planned systematic manner, as the European allies apparently did, required detailed peacetime study of the problem.[81]

Based on these experiences, the committees gave further analysis and recommendations. The 1924 committee that Hunt chaired produced a report that studied the advantages and disadvantages of creating a general staff section for civil affairs in occupied territory. Advantages included a centralized decision-making authority at the highest levels, presumably better able to integrate strategic decision making into civil affairs policy. Yet the disadvantages outweighed any potential advantages, primarily because of the staff structure itself. A "general" staff was precisely that—it provided general guidance and advice over a wide range of activities that were not specialized. A general staff covered a gamut of tasks and requirements, regardless of type or phase of operation, and did not provide sufficient specialized focus on occupation matters. A "civil affairs" general staff function, with a specific purpose of providing guidance on the administration of occupied territories, was precisely *too* technical. The general staff concept was still a fledgling notion for the US Army in the early twentieth century, and this new concept of a staff, after all, had been purposefully constructed to allow for a staff that handled broad, "general" functions, not highly specialized ones. The committee voted against a civil affairs (G-5) section but offered no ultimate solution to the problem of organizing for postwar occupation.[82]

The 1925 committee similarly examined an appropriate occupation command and staff organization at theater-of-operations level and below. It proposed five options: (1) a separate division of the general staff for civil affairs matters; (2) an additional technical or operating civil affairs staff section (akin to the provost marshal)—in other words a staff section but subordinate in priority to the General Staff; (3) a civil affairs staff section under an existing staff section (likely G-1); (4) a separate civil affairs section not under the staff scheme at all but reporting directly to the commanding general; and (5) the creation of a civil affairs agency or bureau directly under the War Department—in essence controlled by civilian and not military authority. That committee unanimously recommended option 2, the creation of an additional technical or operating section to administer civil affairs in an occupied territory. Such a staff section "would ensure harmony and preserve the principle of supervision and coordination under which all existing General Staff divisions and sections function." In so doing, the committee did not recommend the creation of a civil affairs section at the Army General Staff or War Department level; rather, the Army General Staff would enunciate "broad principles" that would be transmitted to the commander, who then, through his civil affairs technical staff expert, would execute policy.[83]

The 1927 committee enunciated some broad conclusions about the possibility of military government. Civil affairs agencies and methods would have to vary with respective conditions. Accordingly, it was not possible to formulate a complete plan for military government to be used in all cases. Additionally, the War Plans Division needed to develop preparatory measures prior to the departure of an expeditionary force. Also, a commander should have a separate, highly specialized staff section, with specifically qualified personnel. The army's War Plans Division should determine what the initial composition of such a civil affairs staff section should be.[84]

The 1927 committee also focused on military government's legal basis, noting that the War Department had codified the laws of war and military occupation, including the Hague Conventions, in chapter 8 of its Rules of Land Warfare field manual.[85] Two supplements to the committee report analyzed the issue in depth. The first supplement examined the applicability of the Hague Conventions to American law as well as the rights and responsibilities of military government under common law. The supplement provided a summary, which stated that such government was supreme and its authority absolute, subject "only to the law of nations, the Rules of Land Warfare, and such Hague Conventions or Geneva Regulations as the United States has by treaty adopted." Furthermore, absent express legislation otherwise, US constitutional law and other laws enacted by Congress were not binding upon military government, though the supplement did note that a separate treaty or armistice as well as rules, regulations, and orders issued by the president or secretary of war for the organized territory could limit the military governor's power.[86] The second legal supplement, written by Maj. Archibald King, a judge advocate, affirmed that the Hague Conventions were binding upon the US military in conquered territories and in countries not at war with the United States though occupied by American forces. While these points may seem obvious and even self-evident to contemporary understanding, the extensive supplements underscored the effort of the committee members to ground the planning for postwar occupation in applicable law. At the same time King sought to maximize the authority of military government within the boundaries of that law. This included not only the Hague Conventions but also an extensive list of US cases, which laid out the constitutional and common-law understanding as to when various forms of military authority could be imposed. Subsequent regulatory and policy documents on military government would bear this same legalistic tone, with recurring references especially to various provisions of the Hague Conventions' laws about governance in occupied territories.[87]

Plans for Implementing Occupations: The 1930s Committees and the Final Work Prior to World War II

Whereas in the 1920s the committees focused on organizational questions and remained somewhat theoretical, during the 1930s postwar occupation planning was integrated into the Rainbow planning scheme. Specifically, occupation plans were prepared to accompany War Plan Red, dealing with the military occupation of Canada during and after war with Great Britain, and War Plan Green, which called for the occupation of Mexico after war with that country. And while it was certainly not a main effort of the War College, General Simonds thought military government planning significant, commenting that it was a subject of "great importance to the higher commanders and staff" and further noting that the army had amassed a wealth of material on the subject.[88]

In the occupation plans for both Red and Green, there was significant consistency with both the Hunt Report and the more theoretical committee work in the 1920s. The Red occupation proposals grounded themselves in historical experience. In particular, the problems of the AEF in the Rhineland and the German army in Belgium were examined, and positive lessons were drawn from the American occupations in the Philippines and Cuba.[89] Additionally, the plenary authority of military government was expressed in legalistic terms. Citing the Supreme Court case *U.S. v. Wallace,* the 1931 Red committee report stated: "The power invested in the President and his military subordinate is large and extra-ordinary. The Supreme Court has ruled that the governing authority 'may do anything necessary to strengthen itself and weaken the enemy. There is no limit to the powers that may be expected in such cases save those which are found in the laws and usages of war.'"[90]

The Red occupation plans were also consistent with past analysis regarding the structure of military government. In particular, for the postwar Canadian occupation, the senior commander in theater would serve as the overall civil authority / military governor, a civil affairs staff would be assigned to perform the specialized duties of military government, and in a rare instance of interagency coordination, the proposed plan called for a State Department representative to advise the military commander. Drawing on the perceived positive experiences of the Cuban occupation, the Red plans also stressed that local government structures should be left in place as much as possible and that the local population should be given as much responsibility to govern as the situation permitted. Local laws, officials, and civil courts would continue, and civilian government officials would be used whenever possible. Finally, both plans provided that the form for military government law should be in the form of proclamations with supplementing regulations as required.[91]

The Green plans for the occupation of Mexico in the 1934 and 1937 committee reports contained proposals similar to those of Red. Green postwar occupation also saw use of Mexican government officials and the existing Mexican political structure. Civil affairs units would be territorially, and not tactically, established.[92] As in the Red plans, use of civilians in the military government was considered objectionable, not only because use of them would violate the principle of unity of command but also because such civilians were "liable to be political appointees, entirely unsuited for the work."[93] Additionally, there were two recommendations that added some further depth to occupation concepts. First, one Green proposal called for the adjutant general to keep a current roster of approximately five hundred reserve officers who possessed qualifications to administer a military government.[94] The second proposal proposed a "constabulary" force to assist in pacifying and maintaining order in the occupied country.[95]

As part of the 1933 Green plan, the student committee also created a manual that would serve as a prototype for possible future policy and doctrine regarding military government. Six sections and twelve appendices laid out the thinking that had been done on military government throughout the interwar period. The manual, while not formally adopted by the War Plans Division, nevertheless looked remarkably similar in substance to the major doctrinal statement on military government, *FM 27-5,* which would be published in 1940. As with much of the work done by the committees during the 1920s and 1930s, the manual was a legalistic document. It began with a definition of military government as "that form of Government which is established and maintained by a belligerent by force of arms over occupied territory of an enemy, and over the inhabitants therein." The applicable Hague Conventions formed a constant, binding thread throughout the manual's text on issues such as the duty of the occupant, taxation, oaths of allegiance, prohibitions against military service, destruction and seizure of enemy property, respect toward private property, and requisition and contribution. "War rebels," or what might be today called "insurgents," were discussed in legalistic terms as well, war rebels in fact being a phrase taken from the Lieber Code. The manual described these "rebels" as "persons within occupied territories, who rise in arms against the occupying forces or against authorities set up thereby." The manual briefly stated, "If captured, they may be punished by death." Regardless, none was to be punished "without a fair trial by competent tribunal," even if a swift execution, as in the case of those found to be war rebels, would almost certainly follow.[96]

Also consistent with the prior committees' work and the Hunt Report was the stress on the importance of exclusive military control of postwar occupation and the need for unity of command. Military government was to be exercised by the "Military Commander under the direction of the President" and was not a form of civil government with checks and balances. Personnel involved in occupation responsibilities, whether in executive or administrative roles, needed to be integrally bound to the military establishment. The manual called for a corps of officers for each expeditionary force that was "especially fitted by judgment, experience, and training" to conduct military government. The manual explicitly noted that while some civilians could be used in a "purely clerical capacity," all personnel with any significant responsibility "should be commissioned in the Army," with "no civilians whatever used on such duty until commissioned." Unity of command was also emphasized. There could not be division at the highest level between a "civil" governor who maintained the responsibility over the administration of the conquered territory and the highest-ranking military commander. The administrator and commander should be one and the same person, in order to follow the "essential military principle of unity of command."

The manual also provided an organizational scheme for military government. The commanding general at the theater level served as either the military governor or governor general (if there were more than one conquered theater or territory). While this ensured unity of command at the highest level, as figure 1.1 indicates, the division of labor then occurred immediately at the staff level. The standard "tactical" work fell within the realm of the normal general staff, whereas the newly created civil affairs staff section, on the same level as the general staff, oversaw the administration of occupation in two corresponding ways: first along functional, technical lines (e.g., fiscal, legal, or sanitation) and second through a channel of control to administrators of various territories and towns. The manual reflected the need, if not at the Army General Staff level at the War Department, then at least at the highest tactical and operational levels, for a separate civil affairs structure to oversee military government operations. Relatedly, and also reflecting the consistent thinking done by the committees, was the manual's emphasis on organizing the occupation along territorial lines. The military government organization was to parallel the existing civil governmental structures, such as villages, townships, provinces, and regions. While tactical units would rotate and continually move to new locations, military government organizations would remain constant and attached to political boundaries as much as possible. While this would be difficult during the early stages of the occupation, it was an ideal that the occupiers should strive to attain. Territorial organization was closely related to another principle of military government: wherever it could be done, local officials should perform the tasks of civil governance. Changes in existing government were to be as "few as practicable" and only after a sufficient study that indicated that such changes were warranted.

Finally, the manual listed four standard temporal phases for military government. There was typically armed resistance in the first phase, with tactical units performing military government functions and with civil affairs sections being linked to tactical units at the corps level and below to perform governance duties. The second phase was true military government: when American forces had broken armed resistance, military government was formally established, and tactical units were generally relieved of governance responsibilities. During this stage, mil-

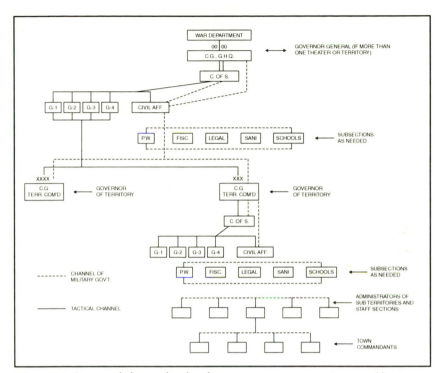

Figure 1.1. Proposed theater-level military government organization. (*Basic Manual for Military Government by U.S. Forces,* in G1, Report of Committee, No. 6, Subj.: Provost Marshal General's Plan, Military Government, file 1–1935–6 [Washington, DC: Army War College, 1934], US Army Heritage and Education Center, Army War College, Carlisle Barracks, PA [AHEC]).

itary government sought to mirror as much as possible existing political structures. During the third phase, the predominant responsibility of the supreme military commander was governing the occupied population and not performing tactical and operational tasks. The fourth and final stage transitioned from military to purely civil administration. Military forces also withdrew during this final stage, and control was handed back to the enemy's government or handed over to the US civil government or given to a newly formed state. Despite the reference to civil administration in the last phase, what was notable throughout any proposed phase was a lack of discussion about any ongoing coordination with, much less subordination to, any civilian agency. Except for a brief reference made to cooperating with the navy when joint operations were conducted, occupation was envisioned as a nearly exclusively army domain.[97]

Planning in Isolation

The committees' work during the interwar decades reveals that long before the United States was involved in World War II, the Army War College, the army's premier educational institution, had on numerous occasions studied contingencies and set up plans for possible occupations, however hypothetical such plans were. Further, the War College had published a manual that laid out many of the basic concepts for military government. And while none of the plans were formally adopted by the War Plans Division, the work done by the student committees was undoubtedly influential.[98] Contrary to statements by some military government officers during wartime and some scholars afterward, ideas about postwar occupation did not lie in the unread pages of the Hunt Report, "in storage for nearly two decades."[99] The principles had permeated the Army War College planning committees over the years, the organization most linked to the Army's War Plans Division.[100] Additionally, both General Simonds and General Craig, the War College commandants during the 1930s (Craig serving as army chief of staff from 1935 to 1939) maintained a tight connection between the two organizations, with each year several graduates of the War College being assigned to the War Plans Division and other key positions on the General Staff. Of the 127 Army War College graduates from 1934 to 1939, for example, over 50 percent had key staff positions, and by wartime that number had risen to more than 70 percent.[101] In the words of an official army historian, the student committees' work "was the fountain from which U.S. military government principles, organizations, procedures, and publications flowed in the period before World War II."[102]

As the United States became involved in World War II and began postwar planning, many of the committees' ideas were put into practice and reiterated and clarified many times. These included the primacy of the military in occupation, the unity of command in one military governor, the establishment of civil affairs as a separate staff section, the separation of tactical units from military government detachments, the linkage of military government to existing political entities, and the repeated insistence, whenever possible, to reempower local governmental officials and reestablish local governmental structures.

The planning was militarized, with no civilian input. It was a logical consequence of the army's working nearly alone (though there was some consultation with the navy and Marine Corps, whose student officers at the Army War College served on some of the committees).[103] This was also the consequence of the perceived hard separation between peace and war, accepted not only by the military but also especially by the State Department. A comment in a 1937 committee presentation by Maj. Francis G. Bonham is instructive: "There are no other agencies, in time of peace, that are concerned with war planning but the War and Navy Departments." He further noted that "nobody else will take the responsibility, or at least the initiative, and go ahead and do that in time of peace."[104] Bonham's comment underscored what would become one of the most important arguments the army made in asserting its primacy over postwar governance: planning for war necessarily required planning for postwar occupation. The military requirements for maintaining victory required the military to plan for and to set the conditions for the peace.

2

Military Government Doctrine, Training, and Organization, 1940–1941

An institution is as limited as an individual is in its capacity to process information, and its rationality is, as anthropologist Mary Douglas points out, just as inherently bounded. As there are limits to an individual's abilities to act as a purely rational choice-making agent who seeks to maximize interests based on a straightforward cost-benefit analysis, there are likewise limits to an institution's abilities to so analyze and calculate. Rather, both individual and institution are bounded by norms, societal contexts, and historical precedents.[1] And not only is the institution bounded by its norms, by its place in society, and by the past in what it collectively *knows*—it further is constrained in its ability to *act*. For it is not enough simply to have knowledge. Knowledge, in and of itself, is not power. Knowledge must be institutionally encoded in such a way that is meaningful to it and then distributed throughout the organization for practical effect. In military terms, knowledge must be "operationalized." It is imperative that knowledge be properly distributed in militaries, since they are, at once, the most intricate and vast, and the most diffuse and tightly knit, "perhaps the most organized of organizations."[2] In the American army, this has been done in a variety of forms such as orders, plans, and directives. But since the early to mid-twentieth century, in its most widespread form knowledge has been operationalized as doctrine.

As Samuel Huntington has pointed out, all bureaucratic organizations have some form of doctrine, but few if any civilian agencies go so far as military organizations do in making such doctrine "formal, self-conscious, and explicit"—and in the US Army especially so.[3] Doctrine is currently defined by the army as authoritative guidance that consists of "fundamental principles by which the military forces or elements thereof guide their action in support of national objectives."[4] Army doctrine is both backward- and forward-looking, not only an overt expression of what the institution collectively remembers from its usable past but also a statement about what the institution collectively affirms as having current practical value.

Doctrine developed rapidly in the interwar period. Before World War I, military thinkers often used private printing houses to publish their work, William Birkhimer's work being one example. Statements about the army accordingly tended to reflect simply an individual's opinion. After the Great War, a variety of factors prompted doctrinal advances, including technological change, interaction with other militaries, greater control and reach of the Army General Staff to manage overall army policy and procedure, and the federal government's own ability to resource and publish documents.[5] The doctrinal-based approach further connected with the efforts at larger-scale professionalizing, and it fit neatly into management concepts explored by the interwar army in which expertise and corporate knowledge were sought to replace individual brilliance. The codification and standardization of this practice focused, as might be expected, on common military operations, with officers such as Lt. Col. George C. Marshall, while serving as assistant commandant of the Infantry School, working to make doctrine clearer, more practical, and more relevant to the modern battlefield. It was during this period that the template for "basic" field manuals was determined: such manuals would "concentrate all applicable information pertaining to a certain area of instruction, training, or doctrine into . . . a 'package' format, or treatment."[6]

The doctrinal approach came with advantages and disadvantages. On the one hand, it allowed an officer to grasp the subject more readily. On the other, it tended to frame the issue in such a way that answers were rarely sought outside of the doctrinal "school solution." Military historian Jorg Müth has contrasted unfavorably the formalized, doctrine-based approach of interwar American military education with the more freewheeling, outside-the-box viewpoint of the German military of the same period, noting in his study how the American officer, viewed more as a manager and bureaucrat, avidly sought doctrinal, prepared solutions and models from which to proceed.[7] Doctrine, after all, was authoritative guidance that US Army leaders were required to be familiar with, and it served as a general guide as to how to employ military force. It was also meant to serve as a model or template for use in a variety of situations. As one field manual of the period states, "commanders of all grades must be familiar with tactical doctrine. Their tactical judgment should be developed and confirmed by applying the doctrine in the solution to all types of problems."[8]

The Creation of Occupation Doctrine: *Field Manual 27-5*, the Basis of American Military Government during and after World War II

The work done by the War College in the decades prior to World War II led to the creation of the primary doctrinal source for postwar occupation, *Field Manual (FM) 27-5*. It was be the source for planning, training, and implementation of all American military government following World War II.[9] The army G-1 staff had proposed the document's creation in 1939 to codify the work of the War College committees.[10] *FM 27-5* bore great similarities to that previous work, and in fact Maj. Archibald King, the judge advocate who had participated in military government planning done at the War College in the 1930s, largely wrote the document.[11] Its publication came with dissension within army ranks. The army's judge advocate general objected to its publication, contending that a field manual already existed—the 1934 *Rules of Land Warfare* (in 1940, published as *FM 27-10*)—and that, therefore, a separate doctrinal statement was superfluous.[12] The *Rules of Land Warfare* could trace its lineage to General Orders No. 100, the famous Lieber Code of 1863, which was essentially revised in the *Rules* in 1914, 1934, and 1940, taking into account many, though not all, of the international laws and agreements that had been promulgated since the Civil War.[13] Additionally, the *Rules of Land Warfare* included the provisions of the Hague Conventions about military occupation.[14] Yet there was an important reason justifying *FM 27-5*'s publication. *FM*

27-10 simply dealt with the question of the legality of military government and not its policy, organization, and possible implementation.
The G-1 proposal stated that the army needed a manual similar to the
War College's, which dealt with the administration of military government in occupied territory.[15] The argument prevailed: army chief of
staff Gen. George C. Marshall thereafter approved *FM 27-5,* and it was
published on July 30, 1940.

Some commentators have viewed *FM 27-5* as merely derivative.
The official history of the planning for and organization of US military
government, published in 1945 by the provost marshal, stated that *FM
27-5*'s policies and procedures were "premised almost entirely upon the
Rhineland experience" surveyed in the Hunt Report.[16] A more recent
assessment concluded that it was essentially a modern version of General Orders No. 100.[17] But *FM 27-5* was a prime example of army
doctrinal creation. It was more than simply a restatement of older principles. It was the culminating product of decades of army cultural practice and thinking that took concepts from Lieber, Birkhimer, Magoon,
the Hunt Report, and the War College committees and updated, clarified, and refined them to create a new, coherent idea of military government. In doing so, it not only served as a blueprint for the postwar
American occupations, but it also did what the most important military doctrine does: it bridged the military domain of operations and
organization and the civilian domain of grand strategy.[18]

At the outset, *FM 27-5* stated its practical purpose. Whereas *FM
27-10* dealt with the "legality of military government . . . [which] tells
what may legally be done," *FM 27-5* provided "what it is advisable
to do"[19]—in other words, what was achievable as a practical solution
within the legal mandates of *FM 27-10. FM 27-5* went on to define
military government in language virtually identical to that found in
the War College's *Basic Manual for Military Government by U.S. Forces*
of 1934 as well as *FM 27-10* and similar to that found in Birkhimer.
Military government was "that form of government which is established and maintained by a belligerent by force of arms over occupied
territory of the enemy and over the inhabitants thereof." In this definition the term *territory of the enemy* includes not only the territory of an
enemy nation but also domestic territory recovered by military occupation from rebels treated as belligerents.[20]

FM 27-5's greater emphasis on the authority of the presiding military commander represented a development and departure from its predecessors: "The exercise of military government is a command responsibility, and full legislative, executive, and judicial authority is vested in the commanding general of the theater of operations. By virtue of his position he is the military governor of the occupied territory and his supreme authority is limited only by the laws and customs of war."[21] This definition wove together concepts from prior documents to firmly link postwar occupation with explicit military rule. The War College's *Basic Manual* had associated military government with a military commander, as had *FM 27-10*, in saying that both government and commander are under the president's direction.[22] *FM 27-5* strengthened the military commander's power, stating that the commander's only restraints were the "laws and customs of war." It also connected the exercise of military government with "command responsibility," asserting that the commanding general in theater would be the "military governor." Additionally, in language similar to a provision in the Lieber Code as well as a recommendation from a 1933 War College committee on military government, *FM 27-5* vested "full legislative, executive, and judicial authority" in the commanding general as military governor.[23] This plenary authority would prove especially important in the postwar occupations precisely because it was concomitant to *military* command, as opposed to standard civilian authority. In contrast, for example, with the highly centralized decision making of the State Department, enormous discretionary power devolved to the on-the-ground military commander as a necessary function of wartime responsibilities. Charles Riddleberger, who served as the Central European State Department desk officer during World War II, noted the profound difference between the army's and the State Department's modes of decision making, the former being highly decentralized, with great deference given to the commander, and the former centralized and directed by the secretary or his subordinate in Washington. Commenting on the army's method, he stated that "it could be called the antithesis of diplomatic procedures."[24]

Furthermore, *FM 27-5* stated in paragraph 9a that the fundamental policy that governed the conduct of military government was military necessity:

The first consideration at all times is the prosecution of the war to a successful termination. So long as hostilities continue, the question must be asked, with reference to every intended act of the military government, whether it will forward that object or hinder its accomplishment. The administration of military government is subordinate to military necessities involving operations security, supply transportation or housing of our troops. If hostilities are suspended by an armistice or otherwise, all plans and dispositions must be made so that the troops may resume hostilities with the least inconvenience to themselves and to the operations of the military government, and above all, under conditions most conducive to a successful termination of the war.[25]

In paragraph 10a, it followed as a corollary from the "basic policy of military necessity" that the commanding general of the theater of operations must "have full control of military government therein."[26] In this full definition, the essential conditions of military government were set forth: the primacy of wartime objectives over longer-term "political" ones, the predominance of military necessity in all matters, and the total authority of the commander presiding over the military government. *FM 27-5*'s definition of military necessity came especially freighted with law and history, for "military necessity" was a term defined by Lieber and in its essence had been reproduced in the 1914, 1934, and 1940 *Rules of Land Warfare*.[27] Lieber had defined military necessity as "the necessity of those measures which are indispensable for securing the ends of the war, and which are lawful according to the law and usages of war." In his view, military necessity "admitted of all direct destruction . . . of *armed* enemies, and of other persons whose destruction is incidentally *unavoidable*. . . . [Generally] military necessity does not include any act of hostility which makes the return to peace unnecessarily difficult."[28]

Commentators have noted the relative ambiguity of Lieber's concept in its initial form given the uncertainty about military necessity's limits in extreme cases.[29] The 1914 and subsequent versions of the *Rules of Land Warfare*, relying on post-Lieber international law developments, largely reduced that ambiguity by adding two complementary principles of "humanity, prohibiting employment of any kind or degree of violence as is not actually necessary," and "chivalry, which denounces and forbids resort to dishonorable means, expedients, or conduct."[30] Both the 1914 and later versions of *Rules of Land Warfare* presumably added the humanity and chivalry principles to mitigate the concept of military necessity.[31] Although those principles were absent in *FM 27-5,* the immediately subsequent paragraph 9b stated that military government should be "just, humane, and as mild as practicable. . . . Those who administer it [should] be guided by the principles of justice, honor, and humanity."[32]

At the same time, the language of military necessity in *FM 27-5* departed somewhat from the more legally grounded terminology in the previous orders and manuals. Specifically *FM 27-5*'s definition oriented the "absolutist" quality of necessity toward occupation both during and *after* hostilities. Instead of the "destruction of armed enemies," military necessity in *FM 27-5* focused on the war's "successful termination" if conflict was still under way and presumably allowed the full sweep of the military governor's authority to accomplish this. If it was during a period of armistice, *FM 27-5*'s necessity language was slightly less clear. What paragraph 9a stated was that soldiers must have the "least inconvenience" afforded to them if fighting had to resume and under conditions "most conducive" to the war's successful ending.[33] This appeared to mean that, if required, military operations would trump other considerations—a variation, however unclearly presented, of standard military necessity.

In so doing, *FM 27-5* linked a refined, if not revised, idea of military necessity to military occupation. As earlier pointed out, military necessity had been defined only generally in the 1914 and 1934 *Rules of Land Warfare* and *not* defined in terms of occupation responsibilities. Nevertheless, in spite of the absence of the 1914 and 1934 "humanity" and "chivalry" principles, in no way could *FM 27-5*'s military necessity be read as meaning that those principles were invalid, given the subsequent language about "just and humane" government. Even without such "just and humane" language, *FM 27-5* could not be read in isolation—the explicit protections in the *Rules of Land Warfare* remained equally extant in army doctrine (and law) to guide the occupation. Rather, what the language of *FM 27-5* could be reasonably read as doing was tightening the linkage between occupation and expressly *military* responsibility. If the primary concern was military necessity, then logically a military commander should be responsible for governing *in order* to determine that necessity.

FM 27-5 also established a temporal framework for occupation. According to paragraph 33, military government "usually pass[es] through [three] successive phases." Though recognizing that not all occupation governance passed through all the phases, *FM 27-5* stated that generally an occupation would have a first phase while fighting was still occurring—a predominantly tactical phase in which little could be done to set up military government. During the second phase, organized, conventional resistance ceased, military government was formally organized, and the military governor issued more comprehensive ordinances. This phase was indeterminate: during it, peace had not formally been declared between the United States and the occupied country. In the third and last phase, as a result of some formal arrangement, such as an armistice, a peace treaty, or a formal surrender, or of even the complete destruction of the armed forces, "military necessity . . . operates with greatly diminished force, if at all," and "more and more of the operations [will be] taken over by the civil government until the latter assumes full control and the army becomes merely a garrison or is withdrawn."[34] Based upon a nation-state construct that conformed to American experiences, *FM 27-5*'s phasing contemplated a civil government that could be restored and a state that could reenter the international political order following a peace treaty. It thereby conformed to the American military government model that had been developed and implemented in the post–World War I Rhineland. In this model, postwar occupation was not a long-lasting or comprehensive societal project but a return, at least to some extent, to status quo ante.[35] Societal and political transformation occurred outside the scope of the objectives of military government.

The rationale behind the phasing—that of reestablishing the previous political system—paralleled that of the treatment of civil order and civilians in general. In keeping with the Hunt Report and the War College's *Basic Manual*, paragraph 10d of *FM 27-5* stated that

existing laws, customs, and institutions of the occupied country have been created by its people, and are presumably those

> best suited to them. They and the officers and employees of
> their government are familiar with them and any changes will
> impose additional burdens upon the military government.
> Therefore it follows from the basic policies of welfare of the
> governed . . . and economy of effort . . . that the national and
> state laws and local ordinances should be continued in force,
> the habits and customs of the people respected, and their gov-
> ernmental institutions continued in operation, except insofar
> as military necessity or other cogent reasons may require a dif-
> ferent course.[36]

Correspondingly, the same paragraph recommended, as much as military necessity permitted, to retain existing civil personnel, to keep in
place existing political units such as states, provinces, counties, departments, cities, and communes, and to conform units responsible for
military government to those divisions.[37] This understanding of civil
government was in keeping with the "contractual" premise of the Lieber
Code and the Hague Conventions. It went beyond both in elaborating
in detail the principle that civilians should be permitted to keep governmental structures as intact as possible. It was also obviously a product of a preideological era. One could challenge the assertion that the
"existing laws, customs, and institutions" of Hitler's Germany or Stalin's Soviet Union were "created by its people," much less "best suited
to them." Instead, this portion of *FM 27-5* recapitulated and expanded
upon the Hunt Report's reflections on post–World War I occupied Germany, which still possessed relatively nonauthoritarian political norms,
and which, in declaring defeat, had kept its internal governmental
structures somewhat intact and had suffered little damage to its infrastructure. It also continued the Hunt Report's endorsement of the British and French military governments' practice of aligning their civil
affairs units to existing political structures and boundaries.[38]

This underlying idea of early return to power—of restoring the
civil government as soon as possible, including using existing civil
political structures—would be a powerful concept in American World
War II occupation policy that would be in tension with competing
policies to ensure occupied territories' political systems were purged of
offensive ideologies. Admittedly, as doctrine, the principle was only a

guideline—"military necessity" was broad enough to encompass any number of reasons why laws should be overturned and why political structures would need to be altered. But if "military necessity" was the primary, overarching principle for such actions, then the purpose had to relate back to primarily military ends, ends that were presumably decided by the military commander. How military and civilian US leaders grappled with resolving when and how to return power to conquered (and liberated) territories proved to be one of the most important and complex issues from 1945 onward.

FM 27-5's 1943 Revision

Two reasons prompted a 1943 revision of *FM 27-5*. First, the navy's growing involvement in the occupation of Pacific islands led to greater joint cooperation between the services on civil affairs matters, and this further prompted a review of *FM 27-5* in order for it have usefulness and relevance to both services.[39] Second, there was significant criticism of the doctrine's actual content. Some of this criticism came from within military circles, arguing that the manual was actually too lenient, despite the rather sweeping authority that it gave to commanders. One lecturer at the School of Military Government stated that *FM 27-5* gave the impression "that the objective of promoting the welfare of the governed in occupied territory is almost as important as the objective of military necessity."[40] On the other hand, critics from the civilian community contended that the manual gave the military far too much authority and stated with "soldierly bluntness" the army's supreme authority over "almost the entire range of human activity."[41] There were also practical concerns with its "non-interference" policy in the light of the occupation of Sicily after the Allies invaded the island in July 1943. Strategic directives had required the abolishment of the Fascist Party, and yet at the same time administrators were directed to keep military government and purely political matters distinct. The tension between the two led to unease and confusion.[42]

A new version was published on December 22, 1943, this time as a joint army-navy manual (the navy's designation for the manual was *OpNav 50E-3*), an exceedingly rare occurrence of joint doctrine during the pre–Defense Department era.[43] The process was cumbersome, with revisions going back and forth and objections being made from army reviewers about proposed navy versions that the manual "should state and discuss principles and doctrines rather than prescribe rules"— likely a cultural misunderstanding about the manual's purpose due to the relative scarcity of naval doctrine in comparison to the army's.[44] Despite criticisms, most of the essentials of the earlier manual remained the same in the 1943 version, with differences of degree and emphasis. Largely because of the Sicilian occupation, where Fascist laws had to be abrogated, there was a provision that stated that laws "which discriminate on the basis of race, color, creed or political opinions should be annulled as the situation permits." Nonetheless, the clause "as the situation permits" meant that military necessity would still be the controlling principle, and the remainder of the section also provided military officials some flexibility in determining which laws to annul: "However, the practice of such customs or the observance of such traditions as do not outrage civilized concepts may be permitted."[45]

The opening definition of military government was slightly less absolute sounding: "The term 'military government' is used to describe the supreme authority exercised by an armed force over the lands, property, and the inhabitants of enemy territory."[46] But a later paragraph clearly reaffirmed the supremacy of the commander: "The exercise of civil affairs control is a command responsibility. In occupied territory the commander, by virtue of his position, has *supreme legislative, executive, and judicial authority, limited only by the laws and customs of war and by directives from higher authority.*"[47] What the document revealed was a sense of both greater ease and confidence in the military's postwar role, as well as a greater understanding of military government's strategic significance.[48] As a drafter pointed out, the new manual expanded the objectives of military government. Now included in those objectives were the "further[ance] of national policies" and the promotion of "military and political objectives in connection with future operations."[49]

The most significant revision involved the distinction between the terms "military government" and "civil affairs."[50] The 1940 manual defined the former term but not the latter, which it seems to have used interchangeably with "military government."[51] In the 1943 manual, the term "civil affairs" encompassed "military government." It became a more expansive term that provided authority beyond that of controlling conquered enemy territory. "Civil affairs control" in the 1943 manual specifically described the supervision of the activities of civilians by an armed force, "*by military government, or otherwise.*"[52] Under this conception, military authority could presumably cover the administration of territory conquered, liberated, or otherwise claimed by the Allied forces. A subsequent paragraph in the 1943 manual confirmed this:

> An armed force may exercise control over civilians to a lesser degree than under military government through grant of, or agreement with, the recognized government of the territory in which the force is located. . . . In such cases military necessity has not required the assumption of supreme authority by the armed forces, but limited control over civilians is exercised in accord with these grants or agreements and the territory is not considered "occupied." While this manual is primarily intended as a guide to military government, some of the principles set forth may be applied in these other situations as circumstances dictate.[53]

Reflecting the reality of 1943 when the Allies conducted military occupations in territories that were not the homelands of enemies, such as in North Africa, and in locations where the governments actually switched from adversary to ally, such as in Sicily and the Italian peninsula, the 1943 manual thus permitted a far wider range of circumstances in which military authority could be exercised.

FM 27-5's Practical Influence

In addition to its influence in shaping the army's institutional ideas about postwar occupation, *FM 27-5* had a more immediate practical influence. Specifically it provided guidance on how to train, to plan, and eventually to implement military government. Just as important, as army doctrine it provided the needed official sanction to launch into reality the most extensive postwar occupation program in American history. It did so in four ways.

First, it provided the official basis for establishing the first-ever School of Military Government, in Charlottesville, Virginia. In March 1942 the Army G-1, as the manual's proponent, permitted the provost marshal general to establish such a school. The basis of the permission was paragraph 7 of *FM 27-5*, which stated that "the necessary personnel, commissioned, warrant, and enlisted, will be selected and procured" in order to staff plans developed for possible postwar occupations.[54] Logically, therefore, a school to train such personnel was needed.

Second, *FM 27-5* became the intellectual cornerstone of the training of all the officers who attended the School of Military Government. As students were told upon arrival at the school, the "little pamphlet" would soon be their "bible."[55] Other biblical allusions to the document were made. As Earl Ziemke noted in his official history of the occupation of Germany, *FM 27-5* would eventually be regarded as the "New Testament" of military government (with *FM 27-10* being considered the "Old Testament").[56] In the students' classes, the document served as a primary organizing principle for analyzing classroom problems. For example, when dealing with military government scenarios in class exercises, students were to classify those facts that could be listed under categories found in *FM 27-5*, paragraph 13—areas ranging from public works and utilities to education, public welfare, and economics—and those facts that could not. After doing so, the students would then prepare staff estimates and mission statements.[57]

Third, the document was the basis for the formation of military government units that would administer postwar American occupation throughout the world. In determining how and where to assign graduates of the School of Military Government, army officials again used the manual. In September 1942 the adjutant general determined that civil affairs sections in theater headquarters would "consist of a sufficient number of officers for adequate attention to the work of the nine departments described in paragraph 13, *FM 27-5*."[58]

Finally, it served as a starting point and an organizing principle for analyzing the internal structures of all the countries where the army might have a postwar responsibility. Recognizing that there was a limit to what the relatively short manual could cover, early in the military government planning effort army planners realized that each poten-

tially occupied country needed to have studies detailing the areas that
FM 27-5, paragraph 13, had listed as relevant. Using *FM 27-5*'s categories, the end result was an immense, comprehensive project resulting in
hundreds of "civil affairs handbooks."[59] The introduction to one such
handbook (on the monetary and banking system of Austria) set forth
their purpose: "The preparation of Civil Affairs Handbooks is a part of
the effort to carry out these responsibilities as efficiently and humanely
as possible. The Handbooks do not deal with plans or policies (which
will depend upon changing and unpredictable developments). It should
be clearly understood that they do not imply any direct program of
action. They are rather ready reference source books containing the
basic factual information needed for planning and policy making."[60]
By May 1944 there were nineteen separate handbooks for Germany
alone, on issues ranging from agriculture (170 pages in length) to
money and banking (294 pages) to transportation (156 pages).[61] The
responsibility for the creation of the handbooks was the army's Civil
Affairs Division, created in 1943 as an expansion of the burgeoning
military government effort. That division outsourced the responsibilities for researching and writing these handbooks to a plethora of governmental agencies, departments, and other organizations. In so doing,
the effort helped to make that division the actual center of the US government for postwar matters.[62]

From Doctrine to Plans

By 1945 the army was communicating a consistent position on postwar occupation. Recognizing a continuous movement from *FM 27-5*'s
original concept, the army saw the need to bring about some ideological change in occupied territories that had been ruled by authoritarian
regimes. Nevertheless, the model that was set forth in various plans and
publications still bore significant resemblance to *FM 27-5*'s 1940 and
updated 1943 versions. As an example, in 1945 Col. E. H. Vernon, an
infantry officer assigned as an instructor to the army's Command and
General Staff College, reiterated the basic template for military government in the army's professional journal *Military Review.* Pointing out
that *FM 27-5* was a doctrinal statement "which usage has proven to be
sound," he noted that it was a "guide, but not a directive." He then elu-

cidated the fundamental concepts of US military government, essentially restating *FM 27-5*'s basic precepts. Military government existed by reason of military necessity and by right of military power; it acted through indigenous officials by necessity, given the limits of military manpower; existing laws and customs should be retained whenever possible; and military commanders should conform to political boundaries and subdivisions. Vernon discussed the two doctrinal forms of military government organization: operational, by which military government remained linked to tactical units, and territorial, by which military government units detached themselves from tactical commands and operated independently, associating themselves with local political structures, falling directly under the supervision of the overall military commander/governor, and bypassing the tactical chain of command. Noting the advantages and disadvantages of each, he stated that experience had shown that the solution was to start with a tactical approach and, as security and order prevailed, to shift to the territorial method. Vernon made no mention of major societal reorientation in his article, though he noted that some form of political change within reasonable boundaries was a likely requirement. It would be usually necessary to remove many political officials from office. At the same time, "so far as practicable, subordinate officials should be retained in their office" unless it was desirable to remove them because of their associations with such organizations as the Nazi Party, the Gestapo, or the Japanese Kempai Tai or Black Dragon Society. The issue was left open somewhat to particular requirements: there was recognition that some political reorientation would occur, though how deeply it would extend into governments and societies was up to the particular situation and the practicalities of implementation.[63]

Army planning in both the European and Pacific theaters reveals that *FM 27-5*'s doctrinal template was standard practice and policy in the last years of the war. In Europe, it was US-UK policy by the time of the Normandy invasion.[64] Approved as the "basic principles for combined [US-UK] Civil Affairs operations," the "Standard Policy and Procedure" (SPP) for occupation responsibilities in occupied territories had as its primary objective the assurance that "conditions exist among the civilian population which will not interfere with operations against the enemy, but will promote those operations."[65] The SPP had been written with *FM 27-5* as its model, and planners noted there was very little substantive difference between the two documents.[66] In the SPP, as in *FM 27-5,* military government, at least in its wartime conception, was entirely focused on the attainment of military objectives, which included the restoration of law and order and the stabilization of conditions, the maximum use of local resources, and "measures of assistance for the civil population as may be required by military necessity."[67] For the Korean occupation, much of the original planning was done by the Tenth Army G-5 staff, only shifting to the Twenty-Fourth Corps, a subordinate unit in Tenth Army, near the end of the war in August 1945. The Tenth Army's military government section relied on *FM 27-5* to construct the organization that would perform occupation tasks.[68] Reviewing *FM 27-5*'s various types of military government in the doctrine and looking at its own recent experience in Okinawa, the section determined that the organizational type employed in Korea would be initially the "combat type" of military government that linked military government units with tactical ones, as a precaution against possible Japanese resistance. Gradually it would shift to a "territorial" model as circumstances permitted.[69]

Sometimes criticized as inadequate, *FM 27-5* must rather be seen in retrospect as forcefully accomplishing its task. While it was a doctrinal, and not a strategic or political, document, it nonetheless structured the postwar occupation model in accordance with the army's institutional imperatives and with the army's intellectual understanding that had developed over nearly a century. Additionally, as official doctrine, *FM 27-5* bore the imprimatur and explicit endorsement of Chief of Staff Marshall, which provided interdepartmental justification for turning the military government concept into practical reality very early in America's involvement in the war. Likewise, as doctrine, it provided a coherent consensus view for the army to present to other departments and agencies. It served, in other words, as the army's "expert opinion" not only on military government administration itself but on important questions such as who would run the occupation, what the course of occupation would be, and what would be the relationship of the occupier to civilians. Debates would later rage about the military's place in the postwar world and about whether postwar military governments should have been the template. What is often overlooked is that this template was largely derived from *FM 27-5*. As a result, the document's influence would rival high-policy documents of great apparent influence. Occupation historian Earl Ziemke compared it to two such strategic level products, noting: "The officers who conducted the post–World War II occupation of Germany were brought up on *FM 27-5,* not on the Morgenthau Plan or even JCS [Joint Chiefs of Staff Directive] 1067."[70]

The Establishment of the School of Military Government and Its Curriculum

FM 27-5 served as the intellectual foundation of the army's conception of postwar occupation. Following its publication, the army's G-1 section, which was responsible for military government, needed to train and to educate on the principles in that manual.[71] Even before the United States entered the war, senior officials were determining how best to do this, though the ever-increasing list of administrative tasks across the General Staff was making it difficult to do so. Nonetheless, Brig. Gen. Wade Haislip, the G-1 chief, wrote a memorandum in December to General Marshall proposing the establishment of a military government school, relying upon a proposal by the army's provost marshal general, Maj. Gen. Allen Gullion.[72]

FM 27-5 had been prepared under Gullion's supervision while he had served as the army's top lawyer as its judge advocate general, a position he held before serving as the army's top policeman as its provost marshal general.[73] Gullion's experiences and background made him well suited to be in charge of military government planning. He was a West Point graduate who had served as a Third Corps judge advocate in World War I. He was best known as the prosecutor in the 1925 Billy Mitchell court-martial. He had also served on US delegations to two international conventions on the laws of war and had been the administrator of the National Recovery Act in Hawaii from 1933 to 1935. Made judge advocate general in 1937, Gullion was appointed to be provost marshal general in July 1941, for a short time actually holding *both* positions, until becoming solely provost marshal general in December of the same year.[74] He was also instrumental in executing a highly controversial facet of martial law in the continental United

States: he advocated and oversaw the exclusion of Japanese Americans from the Western Defense Zone in early 1942 on the grounds of military necessity.[75]

Gullion's energetic efforts to push forward a military government school and to bring a military government program into being would later bring him criticism from President Roosevelt himself. Interestingly, resistance to the idea came first within the army's ranks. While Gullion, Maj. Gen. Myron Cramer (Gullion's successor as judge advocate general), and the War Plans Division all agreed that the provost marshal should run the school, the G-3, in charge of the army's overall operations, did not concur, stating that the requirements were too vast and too dissimilar to military police matters.[76] In the back-and-forth exchanges between army staff sections, however, Gullion eventually carried the day. FM 27-5's concept of military government's totality, including its linkage to operational requirements, gave the G-3 a basis to push back against the idea of the provost marshal taking on the job. But Cramer, in siding with the provost marshal against the G-3, extensively cited the Hunt Report, quoting its assertion that there had been a "crying need for personnel trained in civil administration and possessing knowledge of the German nation." While recognizing and even to a certain extent agreeing with the G-3's opinion about the provost marshal running military government, Cramer pointed out that while there was some controversy as to which staff element should be responsible for military government, not only was Gullion willing to undertake it but he also had a "wide and varied experience, both civil and military."[77]

Gullion prevailed, and on February 9, 1942, he was directed to take "immediate action by order of the Secretary of War" and was charged with training officers for "future detail in connection with military government," which involved establishing a school.[78] After initially trying to establish the school at Fort McNair in Washington, DC, so as to use the Army War College's resources, Gullion brokered an arrangement to use facilities at the University of Virginia, three hours southwest of Washington in Charlottesville, Virginia. In March 1942 the War Department concurred with his plan.[79] Initially, the school was not to exceed one hundred officers per course and have a small staff with permanent staff not to exceed twelve officers and civilian instructors, twenty-five civilians, and one enlisted soldier.[80] The lecturers were a mix of officers, some of whom had practical experience, and civilian lecturers, some of whom were distinguished professors in their fields.

Two other influential figures helped to establish the school. The school's commandant, charged with its daily administration, was Brig. Gen. Cornelius Wickersham, in civilian life a prominent New York lawyer. Wickersham also had a military background, having served as a major in World War I and a reserve officer for twenty years. Like Gullion, he would be the subject of criticism during controversy about the school. Nonetheless, he served as the commandant until 1944, when he became the primary American military adviser for the European Advisory Commission.[81] Col. Jesse Miller would serve as the director of the Military Government Division within the Office of the Provost Marshal General when it was created in August 1942, and even beforehand he was instrumental in establishing what became a comprehensive military government training system.[82] Miller was a Kentucky lawyer who had served in the army as a judge advocate and as an aide to the provost marshal general from 1918 to 1919. He had also held a variety of federal governmental positions, serving as a special US representative for the Nicaraguan presidential elections, as an assistant solicitor for the Bureau of Internal Revenue, and as executive director of the National Labor Relations Board in the early 1930s.[83]

Miller, in a detailed memorandum to Gullion in January 1942, set forth a plan for the school's nature, scope, and personnel. Relying on the army's understanding of military government principles, he stated that the "ideal type" of military government school "integrates the local laws, institutions, customs, psychology, and economics of the occupied area and superimpose[s] military control with a minimum of change in the former and a maximum of control by the latter." The basic materials for such training would come from *FM 27-5,* the relevant international laws of occupation, and the records of the American occupations of Vera Cruz, the Philippines, and the Rhineland. On this foundation, more specialized and particular studies could follow, including intensive study of the culture, language, and political systems of the countries to be occupied and then practical application of relevant principles to school-generated problems.[84]

A review of class lectures and course notes from students confirms that faculty and administrators essentially adopted Miller's approach, albeit modified and refined over the course of the war. Lecturers referred to both *FM 27-5* and *FM 27-10*. In his class notes, Maj. Richard van Wagenen, who later worked in the Military Government Division, wrote that "*27-10* is binding and mandatory" and commented on *FM 27-5,* though noting one could not "use [a] field manual as [a] substitute for thinking." While students studied contemporary occupations, the American military's historical experiences were the standards by which postwar governance were to be judged.[85] In particular, students reviewed the Hunt Report carefully to glean lessons learned.[86] One lecturer, Professor Ralph H. Gabriel (who was also a professor of history at Yale), noted that only Britain had a comparable record of occupation experience: the United States and United Kingdom were the "two nations with the longest and most varied experiences with military government."[87] In another lecture, Lt. Col. Paul Andrews also stressed the distinctiveness of American military governments, a theme of anti-colonialism that comported with America's image of itself as a nation devoid of European imperialist ambitions: "American history also affords, to its honor, examples of the occupation of territory not for profit, not for restoration of a previous sovereign, not for annexation, [and] not to compel the signing of a treaty or the payment of reparations; occupations where the motive of benevolence was predominant." Andrews went on to cite Cuba, the Philippines, and Puerto Rico as examples of American military government working toward the goal of autonomy and self-reliance for these islands and, eventually for the Philippines, independence.[88]

This revealed a not-quite-resolved tension in the American understanding of military government. The actions of American officers in locales such as Cuba or the Philippines often promoted reforms that fostered "American" values and virtues. As Gabriel pointed out in a lecture, an American military governor or civil affairs officer "carries the culture of the United States and his life is governed by the values of that culture." But Gabriel said that this was a problem that the principles of military government sought to redress: "The existing laws, customs, and institutions of the occupied country have been created by its people and are presumably best suited to them." Gabriel went on to say, "That is a recognition of the fact of uniqueness in cultures."[89] Another lecture by Thomas Barber provided "four great axioms of civil affairs." The first and fourth of these axioms were related to the paramount importance of "military necessity." To "prevent the population [from] interfering with" and/or to "induce them to helping" the occupying force was the first axiom, and "the will of the commanding general is the law of the land" was the last. But the second and third axioms related to noninterference: "Military government supervises the existing government. It does not govern," and "The best government is the least government. . . . This is always true. . . . The existence of a military government is an almost intolerable burden on the people, and the presence of every member of that government is an insult to their pride."[90] Noninterference was related not only to American benevolence but to practicality and necessity: injuring a people's pride by excessive and interventionist government would only antagonize the population that the military was attempting to control.

The question perhaps hardest to answer was, when *did* a military governor intervene to impose a social, economic, or cultural change? Regardless of the nonideological premises of some of *FM 27-5*'s principles, the lecturers and students were by no means oblivious to the world around them. There were detailed lectures at the school, for instance, on the growth of Nazism and anti-Semitism in Germany and on Nazism's destructive influence on German culture.[91] One way to address the question was to separate military government "administration" from American "policy." Barber went so far as to compare military government with "plumbing"—providing basic services and keeping things running.[92] Higher, far-reaching strategic decisions that could affect the course of a nation's society or culture would have to come from a source that was presumably nonmilitary. As the school's official history stated, the army's role was to be "administrative, the precise pattern of which would be determined by high policies which the army itself was incompetent to prescribe, but which properly should be laid down by civilian agencies of the government."[93]

At the same time, and in keeping with the doctrinal premise of *FM 27-5*, it was essential that such civilian agencies not interfere with the military government "as long as military necessity prevailed." To quote from the school's official history, "research of the School's faculty and student body . . . revealed one fact with great clarity, i.e., that, in the early stages of any occupation and so long as any military necessity continued, complete and exclusive control of the area would have to be entrusted to the Army." But at what point did larger strategic imperatives, including, for example, the need to impose sweeping reform, override military necessity? There was no clear answer, and the strong belief by the army's military government planners that "every effort should be directed by the War Department toward insuring complete control by the Army" would cause controversy—and collision—with civilian governmental leaders as the war progressed.[94]

Expansion of the Military Government Program

The program for military government grew steadily over the course of the war. The War Department approved the School of Military Government in February 1942 to train one hundred officers per class, with each class operating on a four-month cycle to meet the curricular requirements. Deficiencies became quickly apparent after the course started in May of that year. Notably, class sizes were far too small (the first class only had forty-nine students). If one hundred students were trained per class, that meant a maximum of three hundred officers per year could be trained to perform military government duties. By any estimation of the possible postwar responsibilities the United States might have, such a number was grossly inadequate. The German occupation force had used thirty-five hundred military government personnel in Belgium alone in World War I and currently used seven thousand in Poland. Regardless of whether such models of military government were worthy of emulation, there would be a significant lack of American personnel for duties in nations far larger.[95] More officers—and more locations for training—would be needed.

To meet this need, Marshall approved in August 1942 an expansion in the number of students and faculty for the school, provided that they came from personnel of the Army Specialist Corps—which meant that once they had completed training, such officers would be returned to an inactive status without pay if there were no active-duty vacancies.[96] Specifically, Gullion was permitted to appoint twenty-five hundred candidates from the Specialist Reserve Section of the Officer

Reserve Corps (which replaced the Army Specialist Corps), provided that the rate of intake would not exceed three hundred a month and that those brought in for such duty were skilled in civil government functions such as public works and utilities, fiscal affairs and economics, public health, sanitation, public relations, law, or other fields relevant to military government.[97] The officers would serve, if activated, for the period of the war and for six months thereafter.[98]

With this greater pool of personnel approved, Gullion began actively recruiting for possible candidates from other governmental agencies. He therefore sent out a form letter to those who had been recommended for such duties. Gullion's letter reveals that he launched an energetic campaign:

Dear Sir:

The Provost Marshal General is creating a pool of highly skilled men, in a variety of technical and professional fields, for future use in military government of hostile areas ultimately to be occupied by American armed forces. In assembling these groups, the War Department is relying heavily upon nominations submitted by other governmental agencies having special interests in particular fields. Those selected will be appointed in the Officers' Reserve Corps and may be called to active duty for a period of four months for training after which they will be carried in an inactive status, without pay, permitting the continuance of their present civilian activities until their services are required.

Your name has been submitted as a person qualified for appointment on this roster. If you are interested in having further consideration given to it, please accomplish and return the inclosed questionnaire (in duplicate), with a small photograph, at your earliest convenience. If a further examination of your qualification results in your selection, an effort will be made to tender you a commission which will be commensurate with your ability and experience and at the same time fair to officers who have been commissioned for a relatively long time. A self-addressed envelope is inclosed for your use.

Selective service registrants classified IA or Class II are not eligible for this appointment. If you are ineligible or are not interested in this opportunity, a reply to that effect will be appreciated.[99]

The letter is revealing. Professionalism was a paramount requirement for a skill that was now thought of as firmly within the army's area of expertise, and by sending the letter the War Department was extending its reach into the interagency domain. As it turned out, Gullion's approach was successful, though it would ultimately anger civilian governmental officials, who felt it was overreaching.

Eventually the school requested to increase its capacity to 175 students per course and to decrease its length from four to three months, which was approved in September 1943.[100] But the Charlottesville school would still prove inadequate to meet the demands that Gullion had set. The solution was to partner with civilian universities throughout the country to create so-called civil affairs training schools. Miller worked to set up the concept at various civilian institutions—most of which, out of an apparent desire to assist in the war effort, were ready to cooperate.[101] The roster of institutions was impressive, including among the training locations Harvard, Yale, Stanford, the University of Chicago, and Northwestern. It neatly solved the resource dilemma, all the while presumably providing quality training for the future military government officials.[102] Under the civil affairs training school system, students being readied for military government in the European theater first received basic military training and general military government principles at the Provost Marshal General's School at Fort Custer, Michigan, for one month, then went to one of ten civilian institutions for more extensive training. Students with Asian assignments were sent to Charlottesville first, then to the respective civilian schools.

By mid-1943 the training structure for military government was essentially in place. In a July letter to Secretary of State Cordell Hull, Assistant Secretary of War Robert Patterson described what was then available for military government personnel. He listed four categories of training. First, officers in the grades from captain to colonel who would have top administrative functions were trained at the School of Military

Government at Charlottesville, where the curriculum included "theory and practice of military government, liaison with friendly civil governments, special conditions in certain foreign areas, and language study." Generally two-thirds of the class came from various arms and services; the remaining students were commissioned directly from civil life. They received four months of training (later reduced to three months and then reduced even further). Second, those with highly specialized technical or professional knowledge were recruited directly from civilian life and given training at one of the civil affairs training schools. They spent one month at the Provost Marshal General's School at Fort Custer, then three months at a civilian university. Instruction included the "theory and practice of military government, specialized training, and language training." Third, less-extensive training was provided for junior officers who were expected to be assigned as occupation military police or as junior civil affairs officers. They were given four weeks of training in military government at the Provost Marshal General's School. Finally, enlisted personnel identified to be utilized as occupational military police were trained for eight weeks at an enlisted course, also at the Provost Marshal General's School.[103]

This system varied over the course of the next three years, before finally being completely phased out in 1946. Nonetheless, the essential division of labor between the Charlottesville school and the civil affairs training schools endured throughout the war. Guillion had predicted that a total of 6,000 military government personnel would be needed for postwar occupation responsibilities throughout the world. The end result achieved was remarkably close: a total of 5,925 officers were trained in military government by the time occupation duties began in Japan—3,465 for Europe, 2,370 for the Far East, and 90 foreign officers.[104] As impressive as this mobilization of personnel was, the ultimate value of this corps of military government professionals would prove to be less certain. After the war ended, a survey of military government officers indicated that most thought the training was "generally adequate." But training and education deficiencies were noted—one prominent criticism being that the training was not particular enough and not focused on specific geographic areas—an ongoing criticism of an excessive reliance on a standardized, doctrinal approach.[105]

Establishing the Military Government Division and Military Government Units

The proper recruitment, training, and placement within military commands also required the establishment of an organization within the War Department that could interact with other departments and agencies, including civilian agencies, in the army's postwar occupation planning efforts. Therefore, the same August 1942 memorandum that permitted personnel expansion also established the Military Government Division within the Office of the Provost Marshal General, with Colonel Miller assigned as director.[106] The division was a direct suborganization under Provost Marshal Gullion, with a gradually expanding number of branches and responsibilities. (See figure 2.1, which shows the Military Government Division in relation to other Provost Marshal Office functions, and figure 2.2, which shows the Military Government Division within the Provost Marshal's Office.)

Miller subsequently worked to expand the division's reach and wrote to Gullion in October 1942 recommending that the Military Government Division "assume responsibility for the preparation, in collaboration with all competent agencies of the government, of a series of blueprints for the military occupation of the following areas, among others: Germany, Italy, Japan, France, Belgium, Holland, Denmark, Norway, Poland, and Czechoslovakia." Miller listed various agencies that needed to be coordinated with in order to accomplish the project, including the State Department, the Board of Economic Warfare, and the Office of Strategic Services. In collaboration with these organizations, the Military Government Division would assemble data for a "detailed plan, including personnel requirements, for the military government of each area," which could serve as a recommendation for the theater commander for use in the initial stages of the occupation.[107] This effort led to these civilian agencies assisting in creating the aforementioned civil affairs handbooks on a variety of *FM 27-5*-driven topics. At the same time, Miller and his division set forth recommendations on how to organize military government teams in theater commanders' commands.[108]

What emerged from these and other recommendations were the organizations that would administer civil affairs and military government at operational and tactical levels. These organizations' creation

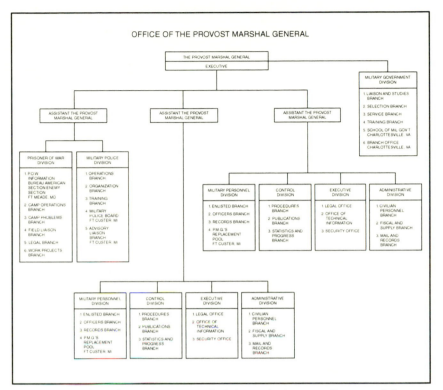

Figure 2.1. Office of the Provost Marshal General (showing all responsibilities, to include military government), 1943. (Office of the Provost Marshal General, Military Government Division, box 718, unclassified decimal file 1942–1946, RG 389, National Archives and Records Administration, College Park, MD [NARA].)

provided proof of the army's ability to produce internally the bureaucratic apparatus to support its doctrinal mission. At unit headquarters, civil affairs/military government staff sections were given either general staff or special staff status and authority. General staff sections were those that dealt with traditional, large-scale issues that spanned the breadth of a military operation—personnel, intelligence, operations, and logistics—and the officers on these staffs were usually those with considerable experience. Special staffs dealt with technical matters, and the officers usually had special skills, such as in law or medicine, but usually lacked the knowledge and breadth of military experience to operate at the general staff level.[109]

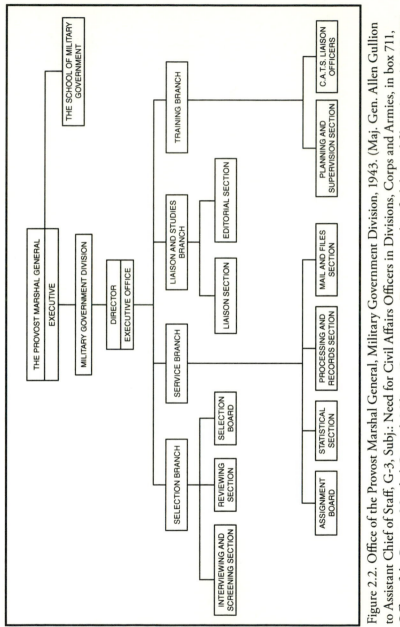

Figure 2.2. Office of the Provost Marshal General, Military Government Division, 1943. (Maj. Gen. Allen Gullion to Assistant Chief of Staff, G-3, Subj.: Need for Civil Affairs Officers in Divisions, Corps and Armies, in box 711, Office of the Provost Marshal General, Military Government Division, unclassified decimal file 1942–1946, RG 389, NARA.)

In the European theater, the civil affairs/military government staffs attained the more authoritative general staff stature, eventually were given "G" status, and became known as G-5 staff sections.[110] The creation of the staff office, at least in the European theater, as a general staff section indicated recognition of civil affairs' and military government's importance.[111] In a March 1944 report to Maj. Gen. John Hilldring, the director of the army's Civil Affairs Division, civil affairs officer Maj. John Boettiger noted how important civil affairs staff sections at the Supreme Headquarters, Allied Expeditionary Force (known as SHAEF), had become.[112] By V-E Day, the G-5 organization at SHAEF had grown into a large and complex organization, with eight subdivisions focused on military government administration and covering all the military government duties required in *FM 27-5*.[113] Likewise in the European theater, civil affairs/military government staff sections were set up below SHAEF, down to army group, army, corps, and division levels, and authorizations for such personnel were provided. In April 1944 the authorizations for European theater US armies, corps, and divisions were issued. While there was initial confusion and uncertainty about the use of such personnel, by V-E Day the army had created over two thousand authorizations for G-5 staff personnel in Europe.[114] In the Pacific, the formation of military government staffs varied widely, though more typically the civil affairs/military government teams existed as special staffs, reflecting the lesser importance of occupation governance during the island-hopping campaigns. The Tenth Army, for example, which was originally slated to serve as the force to provide military government for Korea, had a special staff section and had been involved in the occupation of Okinawa. But below that level, there were serious staff shortages for civil affairs: one of the Tenth Army's tactical units, the Twenty-Fourth Corps, would be given the mission of occupying Korea, a role for which it was unprepared.[115]

Whereas G-5 staff sections, general or special, interacted with other staff sections at unit headquarters, the civil affairs/military government detachments were needed to operate in the field and to interact directly with the populations of occupied territories. Detachments were specifically created to relieve combat units of civil responsibilities and to provide on-the-ground expertise in governance and civil administration. At the same time, the detachments remained, at least during combat operations, under the authority of local tactical commanders. Detachments could have varying responsibilities: while some performed purely administrative functions, many performed operational duties, accompanying divisions in combat and often serving as "spearheads"—moving ahead of the division headquarters and serving as its advance party.[116] Detachments could also vary in composition and number depending upon the communities where they were located. The civil affairs/military government detachment in an industrial city, for example, would have more men assigned to it, with a greater variety of civil skills than one in a small coastal fishing port. Regardless of location, detachments were often kept busier with day-to-day problems, such as getting local authorities to bury dead civilians after a town was taken or overseeing the clearance of rubble from the streets, than with the implementation of intricate governmental policies.[117]

Difficulties and Controversies

This rapid training, organizing, and allocating of personnel to civil affairs/military government structures showed clearly the power of the army to assemble organizational structures rapidly. Yet doing so was not without internal difficulty and controversy, much of it inherently related to the army's difficulty in linking military objectives to longer-term political goals. Because military operations had their own timetables, it was often difficult to predict when areas would fall under Allied control and to which units. Training was therefore not always properly coordinated and linked to the location. Nowhere was this truer than in the Far East, when the sudden surrender of Japan threw off all timetables and forced planners and organizers to scramble to put together sufficient assets to get to occupied locations. While much work had been done regarding the probable Japanese occupation, little had been done regarding Korea. There had been little to no formal study of Korean language or culture at the School of Military Government or one of the civil affairs training schools. Many of the units that eventually arrived in Korea had either been units that had performed civil affairs functions in the Philippines or that were originally assigned for duties in Japan.[118]

Additionally, not all such personnel in military government organizations, particularly in the detachments, received sufficient training and education to perform their tasks fully, partly because the end state that they were supposed to work toward was not clearly defined. There had been major efforts by army officials in the military government division to set up extensive training, both at the Military Government School and the various civil affairs training schools at prestigious American colleges and universities, and there were efforts, at least in the European theater, to ensure the curricula at such schools were aligned with current policies and procedures.[119] In accordance with *FM 27-5*, further specialized training was given in theater to ensure further understanding of the particular problems to be faced in the occupied territory.[120] A fundamental training problem, at least in the first two years, however, was that there was little information provided on policy goals: what were the civil affairs/military government personnel ultimately trying to achieve? This was due in large degree to the deliberately apolitical stance of the training and also due to the lack of clear policy direction provided beyond winning the war.[121]

There was also dispute as to whether the detachments should be assigned to commanders of combat units or in a separate chain of command under a civil affairs officer. Some senior civil affairs officials, including SHAEF G-5 Brig. Gen. Frank McSherry, contended that having such units fall under tactical commanders and not an overall civil affairs commander made each tactical commander in effect the military governor for the area in which he was operating and thus created a hodgepodge of policies and procedures that lacked uniformity and consistency.[122] The British civil affairs leadership in SHAEF disagreed. Responding to McSherry, UK senior civil affairs officer Maj. Gen. Roger Lumley indicated that integration into the tactical chain of command was politically the better option. In nations that the SHAEF forces expected to liberate, separation of civil affairs units, as McSherry and the American staffers preferred, suggested an intention to set up a longer-term military government in those countries. Lumley pointed out that doing so would rouse suspicions of America's allies, who contended that civil affairs should only be for what was strictly necessary for military operations and "not an invasion of national sovereignty." Of course, American military government doctrine and historical practice actually indicated a preference for early exit from occupied countries. And the McSherry-Lumley debate illustrated an internal tension between the American army's attempt to manifest organizational expertise and its desire to end occupation duties as swiftly as possible. What was agreed upon was a compromise, though in accordance with *FM 27-5*. The detachments remained under tactical commander control, at least during and shortly after combat operations. After victory was assured and the occupations had clearly moved beyond assuring enemy defeat, detachments were put directly under civil affairs command authority.[123]

The most fundamental dispute, however, was not within the army, or even within the US-UK coalition, but between the army and other US government agencies. The actions by Gullion and others were seen as farsighted and appropriate by senior army officials but also as aggrandizing and overreaching by prominent civilian leaders in the Roosevelt administration. Disputes took place throughout the war. The most serious occurred in late 1941 and throughout 1942, when high-ranking civilian officials significantly challenged the army's authority to administer postwar military government. In a series of interagency disputes, the army would prevail.

3

FDR, Interagency Conflict, and Military Government, 1941–1942

The army's rise to preeminence and ultimate predominance in matters such as postwar governance came with the nation's move to a wartime footing. According to Randolph Bourne, in a modern nation-state a total commitment to war links together societal activities with great speed, and the government is able to arbitrate and even determine matters of private enterprise as well as public opinion and societal attitudes in a much more total way. In such an environment, military solutions are often preferred and even presumed: "The inextricable union of militarism and the State is beautifully shown by those laws which emphasize interference with the Army and Navy as the most culpable of seditious crimes. . . . [The] Army and Navy . . . are the very arms of the State. . . . To paralyze them is to touch the State itself."[1] In such a context, military professionals have obvious advantages. If war is a matter of such existential importance, then arguments supporting the military's goals (which are presumably deferred to, given the military's expertise) have a far greater weight. But Bourne's points about a military's advantages can be overstated, and his general proposition about military dominance during wartime, while insightful, does not reveal any ironclad law of nation-states. Bourne, it might be said, shows a *tendency* toward militarization, not an inevitable *outcome*. A military's success in making such arguments should not be assumed as necessarily given, especially in matters not directly related to actual combat operations. Military decisions need to be contextualized in the political environment where they occur. In the early 1940s, just before and during

America's first year in the war, such decisions emerged from a turbulent political scene that included domestic uncertainty, a particular presidential managerial style, and competition with other federal agencies.

The War Cabinet, Uncertain Policymaking, and the Pitfalls in Building Consensus

Indeed, federal government civilians contested the army's assertion of predominance in postwar governance throughout World War II. As a result, clashes occurred at the highest levels of the Roosevelt administration, clashes exacerbated by frictions in FDR's cabinet that predated America's entry into the war. In 1940 Roosevelt had been reelected for an unprecedented third term of office. As a way to build consensus, both for his reelection and to prepare for the war that he saw on the horizon, he assembled a team within his cabinet and on the various boards and agencies that had been established during the New Deal era of the 1930s. The team included progressive New Dealers such as Secretary of the Interior Harold Ickes, the self-styled "curmudgeon" who had championed some of FDR's more controversial social programs, and Vice President Henry Wallace, who was admired as a visionary and common-man crusader by some and derided as a naive dreamer and communist fellow traveler by others.[2] But FDR did not confine his political choices to progressives for his third administration. One choice included the archconservative, free-market-oriented Jesse Jones of Texas as his secretary of commerce. Most important for the war effort, he also chose two Republicans who had bucked their party's isolationist stance, Henry Stimson and Frank Knox, to serve as his secretaries of war and navy, in no small part to ensure that military preparedness did not become a partisan political issue.[3]

In so doing, he helped form a national consensus by creating a team of rivals that could unify the parties and the nation on big goals such as winning the war that he was sure would come. At the same time, within the team itself, the conflicting personalities and viewpoints often caused an actual breakdown of consensus on smaller issues. Some contend that Roosevelt's desire to dominate events may have led him to create such deliberately competing interests. Others have argued that he was simply an incompetent administrator. Historian Robert

Dallek takes the former position and contends that FDR became "a court of last resort on major issues" who therefore purposefully and skillfully kept control in his own hands.[4] Dean Acheson thought differently, calling such a claim "nonsense," and noted a certain inability of FDR to control subordinates, asserting that he was "tone deaf to the subtler nuances of civil governmental organization."[5] Secretary of War Stimson was frequently exasperated with Roosevelt's management and leadership style. He commented on having to endure "all the typical difficulties of a discussion in a Roosevelt Cabinet" and complained of the president's apparently exclusive remedy of more meetings rather than decisive leadership and of his habit of not delegating and "want[ing] to do it all himself."[6] FDR himself often seemed to let the logic of events determine policy choices rather than relying on close, detailed planning to do so.[7] Sometimes there was no decision at all, and events would sometimes be decided essentially by default.

Particularly when it came to postwar planning, FDR seemed not to decide or seemed to defer, for what he perceived as sound, practical reasons. After all, in the first months of the war, whether the United States and the Allies would actually prevail against the Axis powers was still an open question. Even then his administration was flooded with plans, proposals, and ideas on how to organize, lead, and reconstruct the postwar world.[8] Roosevelt could well have perceived that he had to tread carefully when dealing with postwar matters. He had assembled a fractious coalition within his own administration to create a political consensus to win the war, and he did not want to lose it over efforts to win the peace. According to biographer James MacGregor Burns, FDR was haunted by Woodrow Wilson's political defeat and the League of Nations debacle after the First World War. He moved, especially during the first years of America's involvement, with "almost fanatical cautiousness on postwar organization."[9] He might allow committees to be formed and experts in one department or another to do some quiet, general planning, but any movement to detailed planning, especially when the outcome was not certain, could detract from the war effort.

The electorate was also uncertain about what America's postwar role should be. Two 1943 reports revealed the ambiguous feelings of Americans. A March 1943 intelligence study concluded that while most agreed that the isolationism of the 1930s was an "outmoded formula," nonetheless they were "far from happy about the alternative of international cooperation." Most Americans (63 percent) agreed with the idea of the United States participating in a world organization of nations. Additionally, 77 percent believed that the United States should "completely disarm its enemies." But a far lower percentage (49 percent) held that America should "change people's way of thinking in the enemy countries" by taking charge of education and other significant postwar societal reconstruction efforts. Importantly, the study also noted that even the positive responses did not "suggest the timorousness with which they [the American public] approach the task of building a secure peace, the reservations they hold, or the tentativeness of their new opinions." The study noted a public that "nervously shies away from concrete plans for bringing a more secure world into being." It further concluded that the public was "appalled at the complexity of the problems involved in world reconstruction."[10] A second survey, done in later 1943, provided similar concerns for FDR. Summarizing its findings in a note to presidential adviser Harry Hopkins, economist adviser Isador Lubin stressed the greater importance that the American public gave to domestic, as opposed to international affairs.[11] While 73 percent expressed "considerable" interest in domestic affairs, 46 percent expressed only an "average" interest in foreign affairs. According to the survey, "people are almost twice as much interested in domestic affairs as international affairs. . . . Two-thirds of the people think we should not give postwar aid to foreign countries if to do so would lower the standard of living in the United States."[12]

Government officials were also concerned. World War II had brought an unprecedented investment by the federal government in the nation's industry. The Defense Plant Corporation, the US government's investment agency, owned hundreds of plants that produced aircraft, communication equipment, and machine tools, and the government's investment in industrial plants and equipment was twenty-six times greater than that of AT&T's. Unsurprisingly, shifting to a postwar economy concerned many in the government, who feared a retriggering of a depression. A 1943 study by the War Department's Ordnance Office indicated that current interest in dealing with postwar problems that were "global in scope" could cause the government to "fail to see clearly what is under our nose. . . . Many domestic problems are casting their shadows ahead." The study focused on the readjustment of the national industrial economy from a wartime to peacetime basis. As it noted, "with the disappearance of the common interest in winning the war, the basic conflict among [business and industry] for maximum participation in the profit (but not in the loss) resulting from the operating of industry, will re-assert itself."[13] If the government was not careful and did not create policies that would sensibly terminate war contracts, liquidate factories, properly inventory equipment, and transfer industry to a peacetime footing, then chaos and economic disaster could result.

A 1943 presidentially approved report by the National Resources Planning Board, another FDR-created executive agency, further highlighted concerns about home-front prosperity following the war. The board prepared the report, in the president's words, to assist Congress in "development and consideration of appropriate legislation to achieve normal employment, to give assurance for all our people against common economic hazards, and to provide for the development of our National resources." The report stated: "We look to and plan for . . . the fullest possible development of the human personality, in relation to the common good, in a framework of freedoms and rights, of justice, liberty, equality, and the consent of the governed." In idealistic language, it asserted that the war America was waging was "not a war for revenge and conquest, for more lands, and more people; but for a peaceful and fraternal world in which the vast machinery of technology, of organization, and of production may be made to serve as the effective instruments of human ideals of liberty and justice."[14] But idealism had to be tempered by pragmatism. The most vital problem would be the "maintenance of full employment and avoidance of a prolonged depression following a short-lived post-war boom." The report pointed out that for there to be international order, there had to be national prosperity. Plans were offered for the development of the economy, for actions by state and local governments, and for the demobilization of the huge American armed services as well as the demobilization of war plants. At the same time, the problems abroad still had to be addressed in order to "make victory secure." All the tasks associated with ensuring such victory—disarming Axis forces, repatriating prisoners and displaced persons, rehabilitating devastated areas—required the United States to

"gear its agriculture and industry to the tasks involved." While not
precisely clear what this effort would look like, it would be "on a scale
unknown heretofore."[15] This remained a daunting challenge. What
should be done and which agency should lead the effort in postwar
matters, including postwar governance of territories following the war,
were open questions.

Yet there *was* certainty and clarity regarding one issue: winning
the war. And as might be expected, during the war all things military were of paramount importance. FDR's wartime ties to the military were strong, and he was comfortable in his role as commander in
chief. Secretary of State Cordell Hull recounted how Roosevelt "loved
the military side of events" and how he preferred to be called commander in chief rather than president during the war years.[16] Army
Chief of Staff George Marshall and Chief of Naval Operations Ernest
King reported directly to him, and FDR made Adm. William Leahy
his White House chief of staff. At the same time, his relationship with
his military chiefs regarding strategic issues was complex. While ultimate authority remained in civilian hands throughout the war, the
Joint Chiefs of Staff became especially powerful, and the War Department emerged as the most influential organization within the executive branch.[17] Admittedly, on some issues of strategy Roosevelt would
decide against his military subordinates, such as when he overruled
Marshall's call for a cross-channel attack in 1942 or 1943. Yet on many
other matters that were predominantly military in nature, FDR was
deferential, and military necessity could trump all other matters. John
J. McCloy, who had served as assistant secretary of war during World
War II, later observed: "The President's consultations with his uniformed officers—unlike those of his distinguished colleague in victory,
Mr. Churchill—rarely resulted in the imposition of his views on the
military but rather in his acceptance, almost without question, of the
views of the military."[18]

In particular, Secretary of War Henry Stimson was, in historian
Michael Beschloss's words, a figure with whom Roosevelt dared not
play too many games. His knowledge, experience, and key standing in
the coalition cabinet made him a powerful ally as well as adversary.[19]
Often overshadowed historically by Chief of Staff Marshall, Stimson
was as influential as Marshall in the army's development of postwar

occupation planning.[20] A paragon of the American WASP establishment and spiritual father of the Cold War "Wise Men," Stimson, a Yale and Harvard Law graduate, was a distinguished Wall Street attorney and had been secretary of war under Taft and secretary of state under Hoover. He had also been a colonel of artillery during the First World War (and would thereafter always be called "the Colonel"). Many of Stimson's most important experiences were shaped by his military service. He wrote in his diaries that his "best lesson in democracy had been in the 77th Division"—the American unit in which he had served during the war.[21] He had even had considerable firsthand experience in a form of American colonialism that strongly resembled military government, having served as governor-general of the Philippines in the 1920s.[22] While there, Stimson had introduced an American paternalism that resembled European colonialism: he was an opponent of granting Filipino independence in the near future, determining that the country was not suitably advanced at that time. Nonetheless, he was willing to let local Filipino authorities conduct the day-to-day administration largely by themselves, essentially leaving laws and customs intact.[23]

Stimson was also an internationalist who had broken from the isolationist wing of his party. As a lawyer, he was appreciative of the rules of international law and the prerogatives that came with sovereignty. He noted in a 1939 article, for example, that international law required that the United States treat the elected Republican government of Spain, not Franco's Nationalists, as the lawful government and therefore entitled to receive assistance from the United States: "Until the insurrection has progressed so far and successfully that a state of belligerency is recognized by the outside nations, no rules of neutrality apply."[24] Whatever the political status of the Spanish Republic, whose socialist government likely did not appeal to Stimson, the norms of international law were clear and had to be followed. Stimson was further a strong proponent of military government's necessity in conquered or liberated territories. To him, it was a "great and proper function," and the American tradition of military government a long and honorable one.[25] In the postwar memoir that he authored with McGeorge Bundy, he wrote that "World War II demonstrated with unprecedented clarity the close interconnection between military and civilian affairs; nowhere was this connection more evident than in military government. . . . It was a natural and inevitable result of military operations in any area where there was not already a fully effective friendly government."[26]

As for the president himself, Stimson believed that the president thought the idea of military government was "strange" and even "abhorrent."[27] Yet what Roosevelt really thought of military government—as a vestige of Old World imperialism, as a required and appropriate postwar process, or as an obstruction to needed societal transformations—would never actually be clear to the War Department or, for that matter, to other members of FDR's wartime team. That lack of understanding about Roosevelt's intentions helped to create disputes and tensions between those on opposite sides of the political spectrum—between the New Dealers who remained in FDR's post-1940 administration, and the newly on-board Republicans such as Stimson.

While most of the New Deal's impetus had been spent by the late 1930s, it still had powerful voices in the higher political circles.[28] Two in particular were at the center of early postwar planning controversies. One was Henry Wallace, who represented such an important part of the diverse FDR coalition that Roosevelt made him his 1940 vice-presidential pick. As a champion of civil rights, he was years ahead of his contemporaries, and as a true believer in building a better world, he was a strong proponent of what would become the United Nations. At the same time, many also viewed Wallace with deep suspicion. He had only become a Democrat in 1936 and was distrusted by members of his new party as a not-quite-convincing Republican apostate. When Roosevelt elevated him from agriculture secretary to vice-presidential nominee, booing broke out in the convention hall. Some Democrats and Republicans alike thought of him as a "doe-eyed mystic," the living manifestation of the "hopelessly utopian, market-manipulating, bureaucracy-breeding New Deal."[29] To many he appeared bumbling, ineffectual, and disorganized. He could make statements misinformed, misleading, or both, as when, in a speech at the Commodore Hotel in New York City in May 1942, he said that Russia "was changed from an illiterate to a literate nation within one generation and, in the process, Russia's appreciation of freedom was enormously enhanced."[30] Stimson, who thought little of Wallace's managerial abilities, in particular held him in distrust and disdain. As one example, the war secretary recorded in his diaries the first meeting of the then Economic Defense Board (the future Board of Economic Warfare), which Wallace chaired. Stimson scornfully noted that Wallace kept everyone waiting by being initially absent, having "forgotten his own date which he had fixed himself."[31] Wallace would serve as chairman of the Board of Economic Warfare, an organization presumably with major responsibility for postwar planning, and in its short history many of the cracks and fissures of the FDR coalition would reveal themselves.

A second New Deal figure of importance was Harold L. Ickes, secretary of the interior. Another New Deal progressive, he was, like Wallace, a civil rights champion and tireless promoter of Roosevelt's Four Freedoms, and he was not afraid to confront the War Department over matters he regarded as morally significant. He once brought to Stimson's attention allegations of discrimination against five hundred members of the Abraham Lincoln Brigade, the famous outfit of American volunteers that had fought for the Spanish Republicans. If true, Ickes contended, "they are so shocking, particularly in an army that is fighting for the Four Freedoms, that the army itself ought to be the first, on its own initiative, to clear the record."[32] Ickes was especially suspicious of military plans and designs and echoed Henry Wallace's view that what was needed was a "people's peace . . . founded upon certain elementary principles," that came with a "list of rights—to think, speak, print freely, equal education, etc." What Europe and the world did not need was a return to realpolitik after the war, so "power-statesmen [can] . . . return to their pleasant little game of international penny-ante."[33] His experience with American military government in Hawaii following Pearl Harbor only confirmed his suspicions that military men would grab power and then refuse to give it up. Believing his authority as secretary of the interior had been circumvented there, he fulminated that "without protest" the territorial governor of Hawaii, Joseph Poindexter, had "abdicated" his responsibilities to the military and had allowed the army to establish a military governor of Hawaii, "an office not recognized by our Constitution, and an office that was brought into being for the first time since we became a nation."[34] Ickes also had a very real interest in postwar occupation responsibilities. The Interior Department had actual authority and responsibility over the governance of American territories such as Guam and the Philippines, and he argued that because of Interior's "unique experience with primitive people," it should "participate actively in the administration of any islands in the Pacific which may be occupied and governed by the United States."[35] He actively campaigned for a prominent role in postwar planning and wanted to lead a group to discuss postwar planning for the Far East.[36]

Wallace and Ickes, then, were both representatives of the New Deal and progressive side of FDR's war cabinet. They, along with others, would also play key roles in controversies that had civil-military implications, such as the fate of the Board of Economic Warfare, the army's establishment of the School of Military Government, the imposition of martial law in Hawaii, and the exclusion of Japanese Americans from the Western Defense Zone. Yet what is evident in the aforementioned civil-military controversies was that the civilian New Dealers lost in every case. Wallace, in his role as chairman of the Board of Economic Warfare, did not succeed in promoting or implementing his postwar visions. Ickes and others also failed in stopping the army's School of Military Government. Ickes, as an unafraid and unabashed skeptic of notions of military necessity in wartime, was also generally unsuccessful in disputes with the army over martial law in Hawaii. So were other civilian members of FDR's cabinet over the Japanese-American exclusion policy that was ultimately upheld by the Supreme Court, itself relying on military necessity in justifying the policy. As the latter three controversies revealed, the army's internal culture, including its patterns of organizational control as well as its years of prior thinking and planning of postwar occupations, gave it major institutional advantages. These advantages, given FDR's predisposition to favor military choices, resulted in the army not only prevailing in these issues but also ultimately becoming the predominant agency in postwar governance planning.

The Board of Economic Warfare and Interagency Dispute

The federal government experienced unprecedented growth during FDR's presidency. Most noteworthy was Roosevelt's creation of myriad new federal agencies to deal with the unprecedented economic and military challenges. As sociologist Carl Grafton notes, the creation of a plethora of new agencies is predicated upon sudden, discontinuous socioeconomic and/or technological shifts. However, the very process of attempting to understand the major change, which Grafton calls "conceptualization," can cause agencies to reorganize or even to self-destruct as they attempt to grapple with the problem.[37] In the Depression 1930s, FDR established eight executive agencies to implement New Deal programs. In the early phase of World War II, he created an unprecedented eighteen new agencies. During his administration, agencies at the federal level grew by a total of 29 percent— even higher than other expansive administrations. (The Kennedy and Johnson administrations increased the federal bureaucracy by 23 percent, and the Nixon administration grew it by 18 percent.)[38] The result of all this was serious and intense interagency rivalry.[39] As James Stever has pointed out, these newly created agencies created intense feuds over jurisdictions and domains. Far from creating an all-encompassing federal bureaucracy during the FDR administration, something of the opposite resulted: the supposed centripetal movement toward total control was nowhere near as powerful as were the centrifugal tendencies caused by the politically charged and competitive interagency environment.[40]

By executive order, FDR directed the establishment of offices, committees, and boards to as a way to manage America's involvement in the global conflict. Many FDR-created agencies focused on wartime economic activity, including the lending or leasing of defense items to nations resisting the Axis, the control of commercial exports to protect American materiel, the procurement abroad of strategic materials, and in the field of postwar activity, the relief and reconstruction of liberated areas and the planning for economic reorganization in defeated Axis countries. The Office of Lend-Lease Administration was the most famous example. Established in 1940 to provide critical defense materiel to countries fighting the Axis while America was still officially neutral, it was under the personal direction of one of FDR's closest advisers, Harry Hopkins.[41]

While wartime goals were somewhat clear, when it came to postwar economic reconstruction and rehabilitation of countries either liberated or conquered, FDR's goals were enigmatic. Roosevelt did appear concerned about moving too fast with postwar schemes and about alienating the electorate and his own coalition-style administration. At the same time, there was another large section of the FDR constituency, that New Dealers such as Wallace and Ickes represented, that positively *did* see the need to plan and pursue an activist postwar agenda. As early as 1941, there were disputes as to who should ultimately run overall postwar economic planning within his administration. The secretaries of interior, treasury, and state all thought that their organizations should play large roles, though only the Interior Department could credibly claim occupation authority over US territory (primarily the Philippines) and only Treasury could assert primacy over financial matters. Shortly before and during the North African campaign, the State Department in particular looked to be a candidate for the postwar leadership role. Yet FDR had significantly reduced that department's influence, especially in the early war years.[42] As Secretary of State Cordell Hull noted, after Pearl Harbor he did not sit in on meetings that involved military matters, and FDR did not take him to the conferences in Casablanca, Cairo, or Tehran—he had to learn what actually happened at those meetings from sources other than the president.[43]

On July 30, 1941, FDR established the Economic Defense Board under the chairmanship of Vice President Wallace (renamed the Board of Economic Warfare after Pearl Harbor). Its wartime functions were somewhat limited—the Office of Lend-Lease, for example, covered much of the economic activity in Europe. However, as defined in the board's founding executive order, its functions and duties included "advis[ing] the President on the relationship of economic defense . . . measures to post-war economic reconstruction and on the steps to be taken to protect the trade position of the United States and to expedite the establishment of sound, peace-time international economic relationships."[44] Chairman Wallace sought to make the board an agency that advanced postwar ideas about global industrialization and higher living standards. He intended to use the organization as a platform to promote his own vision of the New Deal abroad, in order to develop systems to create international economic cooperation, and then to combat worldwide illiteracy, poverty, and imperialism. But there were significant problems from the outset. There were the bureaucratic difficulties of establishing a complex organization made up of other governmental agencies, many of them long-standing and each with its own agenda, staff, and budget. Furthermore, the president's views of the postwar world were not clear to Wallace, and while the board had major authority, including the authority to deal directly with foreign governments, FDR kept a hold over the board's fiscal spending.[45]

Wallace especially fought the State Department over prerogatives. He angrily pointed out that the department's difficulties with the board were "mostly jurisdictional ones without any reference to principles."[46] He was determined to have unilateral authority to act with foreign governments, informing State but not necessarily obtaining State's permission to do so.[47] But when he attempted to get exports under the board, he had to get FDR to sign an executive order to transfer State's export authority to him and only after great resistance.[48] While Wallace was successful in getting this much greater responsibility, it brought a need for board reorganization and expansion of powers that took months to complete. And though it did become a functioning bureaucracy with twenty-five hundred people and three divisions, making it such took considerable start-up time: the board did not meet at all for the first four months of 1942.[49]

If Wallace's relationship with State was uneasy, with Secretary Jones of Commerce it simmered with mutual contempt.[50] Not only was conservative, big-business Jones miles apart ideologically from Wallace, but he also was chairman of the Reconstruction Finance Corporation, a Hoover-era organization that FDR had kept in existence. The corporation represented another side of the New Deal, one that promoted competition, expansion, and economic development. It provided government loans to businesses, and Jones's parsimonious views about government dollars soon clashed with Wallace's expansive ideas of using government monies to increase industrial production and enact social transformation.[51]

Jones likely would have been happy for Wallace to fail. Matters came to a head when Wallace got the president to sign an executive order in April 1942 granting Wallace's board broad authority, which included permitting the board to represent American interests to foreign countries, an apparent encroachment upon State Department authority. The order also transferred from Jones's corporation to Wallace's board the power to buy materials for production overseas. To inflame matters further, Wallace obtained the order without consulting State or Commerce, though apparently leading Roosevelt to believe that he had. Hull was infuriated. For his part, FDR felt that Wallace had duped him, and his relationship with the vice president went permanently off course.[52] Shortly afterward, another showdown with Jones hastened the end of Wallace's grandiose postwar plans and sealed his board's doom. The conflict erupted when Wallace made public allegations about Jones's supposedly derelict handling of the Reconstruction Finance Corporation, a huge political mistake since Jones was very close to the president. The fighting and bickering went on, with Wallace generally getting the worse of it, until finally Roosevelt intervened. In July 1943 he abolished Wallace's organization outright, placing its functions within a new executive agency, the Office of Economic Warfare (later the Foreign Economic Administration) under Leo Crowley, a businessman and a fiscal conservative close to Jones.[53] Crowley was not one to attempt to impose a New Deal vision on the postwar world: he lacked both the desire and the interagency influence to accomplish Wallace's goal. Indeed, Crowley would have difficulties in dealing with the army even in modest ways regarding occupation policy. Near the end of the war, for example, Crowley dispatched a Foreign Economic Administration economist to London to discuss German occupation policy. He was given a cold reception by planners, and there is little evidence that Crowley's organization had significant influence on postwar governance planning during wartime, though it was eventually included on the relatively short-lived Informal Policy Committee on Germany.[54] It ended up partnering with and subordinating itself to the army, and it was not capable of conceiving or planning a postwar world beyond matters of providing economic aid and logistics—essential tasks to be sure but a far cry from the conceptions of Wallace, whose lack of managerial and political skills helped to destroy his own organization. New Deal visions for postwar reconstruction, at least under Wallace's direction, were dashed.

The failure of the Board of Economic Warfare did not end postwar planning efforts by civilians in FDR's administration, as efforts in North Africa revealed (to be discussed in detail in the next chapter). There were other civilian organizations that were involved in postwar matters, though none had the opportunity as the board did to leverage civilian influence. For example, the Office of Foreign Relief and Reconstruction Operations under the direction of Gov. Herbert Lehman of New York was intended to coordinate and direct relief efforts in liberated countries, but since its authority was not established by formal executive order, disputes broke out between it and other agencies, and it ended up being folded, like the board, into the Foreign Economic Administration.[55] Roosevelt also established the State Department's Office of Foreign Economic Cooperation in July 1943 as the agency to coordinate American policy in liberated areas, and as part of its charter it was supposed to pay "major attention to the relations of civilian agencies with the Army."[56] The office was an attempt to regain some responsibilities to State, but in the end its existence only increased the interagency warfare: the Office of Foreign Economic Cooperation tended to side with Lend-Lease against the Board of Economic Warfare (before it folded) and the Office of Foreign Relief and Reconstruction Operations. Soon the Office of Foreign Economic Cooperation too was folded into Crowley's organization.[57]

This brief account of the Board of Economic Warfare and the other civilian agencies created to plan and execute postwar responsibilities illustrates the centrifugal tendencies of such ad hoc civilian organizations. The infighting, the dueling over prerogatives, and the lack of internal coherence, as opposed to the more unified direction of the army, were not lost on commentators of the period. In an article written in September 1942, economist and journalist Eliot Janeway wrote about what he called the "consequence of Washington's aimless and over advertised whirl." He placed the blame for the chaos squarely on the failure of "the inhibited civilian agencies to check or balance anything." Of course, civilians were failing to check or balance the military, and Janeway begrudgingly gave the military its due: "The truth is that the Army and Navy have been the only groups in Washington pressing for more power. Instead of being checked by the counterpull of the civilians, they have run headlong into a vacuum."[58] Janeway was writing about the virtual takeover of key economic positions by military men, but his comments could be applied with only slight modification to postwar planning efforts as well. What Janeway noted was the failure of anyone taking over as a "chief of staff" of all the civil-

ian agencies, which, properly managed, would direct the wartime economic effort. The army and navy, while "far from free of incompetence,
bureaucracy, and a fantastic amount of self-defeating paperwork," had
bureaucratic advantages: "they are disciplined, unified military organizations with a concentration of power at the top . . . [and] able to dominate . . . civilian committee colleagues."[59]

The School of Military Government Controversy

Yet another controversy, this time involving the School of Military
Government, would threaten the army's role in postwar governance.[60]
By the summer of 1942, high-ranking officials and FDR himself
became suspicious of the army's military government training. Noting
that his wife, Eleanor, had apparently expressed some concerns about
the school and perhaps fearing it was a conservative training ground,
the president inquired about it in a memorandum to Undersecretary
of War Robert Patterson.[61] As an indication of how little high-ranking
officials knew, Patterson reported to FDR on July 20 that while some
work had been done in the War Department, "very little attention" had
been paid to the training of personnel, even though the School of Military Government was in operation and midway through its first class.[62]

By August 1942, suspicions among the FDR administration about
the school had heightened. Rumors that it was either a reactionary
hotbed or filled with incompetents (or both) had gotten to the point
where the president demanded further investigation. Roosevelt called
for another meeting with Patterson, and he also sent a memorandum
to General Marshall stating that he wanted specifically "a breakdown,
and possibly the names of those who are taking the Charlottesville
course, and why they were selected."[63] As the memorandum indicated,
what raised Roosevelt's suspicions had as much to do with who was
in the school as what was taught there. Was it a magnet for anti–New
Deal politicos who wanted to influence America's postwar goals? Even
if FDR was concerned with braking the perceived utopianism of Wallace, he needed to placate his still powerful New Deal/progressive front.
The last thing he wanted was the perception that Old World imperialist
and colonialist attitudes would shape American postwar policy. For his
part, Marshall sent back a detailed study that same month, as well as a

student roster. Clearly intending to assuage FDR's concerns, he pointed out that the navy had a similar, though much smaller, school under way at Columbia (perhaps a subtle way to get the naval-oriented Roosevelt's favor). He also linked the army school's rationale for existence to the army's doctrine on the subject, *FM 27-5,* providing FDR a copy for him to read and quoting its text as a justification for the training in several places. Marshall also cited in particular paragraph 7, which prescribed qualifications and backgrounds of those required for key positions in military government.[64]

Additionally, Marshall included a report from the army inspector general (IG) that validated the school. The report stated that the school was developing officers to be efficient managers, and it sought to dispel notions that it was training them to be statesmen: the personnel being trained were to handle purely military matters of administration, leaving policy questions to those outside the War Department. The report also repeatedly stressed the practicality of the school—its emphasis on training engineers, sanitation officials, and the like—and noted that while the first class had spent excessive time on "international law and political philosophy, which are not essential to subordinate officials," that apparent overemphasis had been remedied. Perhaps most important for FDR, the report indicated that only 8 of the 51 personnel in the current class had any political background. Finally, it made four recommendations: that the school be retained under army control, that it be expanded to take in 150 rather than the 100 students now authorized, that the additional 50 come from the Army Specialist Corps, and that they be returned to their civilian jobs upon completion of the course and called up when needed.[65]

Meanwhile, John McCloy, the assistant secretary of war, also examined the issue.[66] Harry Hopkins had asked McCloy informally to look into the school, and McCloy wrote back to him that "somebody has been seeing things. The School is simply a necessary component of military education." McCloy also tried to normalize the school by noting that in World War I there was similar training. (This was actually erroneous—one of the Hunt Report's points was that such a school had been badly needed.) McCloy also referred to some of the faculty, including Paul Andrews, dean of the Syracuse Law School, and Hardy Dillard of the University of Virginia Law School faculty, and he mentioned that Colonel Jesse Miller, the Military Government Division director, was a friend of Isador Lubin, an economist adviser to FDR. He further pointed out that almost all the students had been selected by commanding officers, and none had been selected based on political affiliation.[67]

In his response to Hopkins, McCloy also structured the notion of postwar occupation in a way that reflected the army's classic understanding: "In the present war we will be apt to have all types of jurisdiction—martial law, as we now have in Hawaii; military government, such as you would have in an occupied zone; and liaison work in communities in which we merely support the civilian administration." His comment revealed how extensive the army's involvement in areas outside of the battlefield had become. While the idea of "communities" where the military would "support the civilian administration" was undefined, such involvement was presumably appropriate if military necessity required the army to have jurisdiction. On the other hand, both "martial law" and "military government" were doctrinally defined and practices with apparent legal standing. Military government was to be considered reasonable and de rigueur in the current context. It was a logical, codified, and appropriate practice for the army to prepare for, and the army had done exactly that by promulgating it in doctrine and by establishing training for it. McCloy contended that the attacks on the school were by "chronic under-the-bed lookers who had visions of grand rehabilitation schemes after the war, in which they themselves might play no mean part. . . . [Such persons] suddenly became alarmed when they heard of this School without realizing that it was not only the normal but the necessary function of military government."[68]

McCloy convinced Hopkins, who wrote back to him: "I have heard all about the school that I want to hear for the present. I am sure it is all right."[69] Yet this did not end the matter. FDR did not respond to Marshall in September or October, and it was in October that Provost Marshall Gullion's energy and ambition, discussed in the previous chapter, triggered an eruption in the cabinet. As Gullion had gotten the military government program under way, he had sent notifications to various agencies within and outside the government, requesting liaisons with agencies, and seeking assistance and recruiting personnel as possible students for the school.[70] Initially Ickes seemed to go along with this and designated Undersecretary Abe Fortas to maintain liaison with Gullion in connection with the program. On September 30, 1942, Ickes wrote to Stimson that the administration of territories and insular US possessions were under his department's jurisdiction, which provided Interior with much experience in the matter, hinting at his own department's prerogatives in such matters.[71]

What apparently set Ickes off occurred in October, when Miller asked Fortas for the names of engineers, economists, lawyers, and other civilians who might be qualified to serve as advisers to military governors.[72] Ickes recorded in his diaries that he met with FDR in early October and that he told the president that the army was training "proconsuls" at the school in Charlottesville. He also noted that a reason he wanted to establish his department in occupation planning was to start a civilian training program of its own "and thus crowd the Army out." Most interesting in Ickes's account was FDR's response. Roosevelt knew all about the school and indicated that he was going to do something about it: "[Roosevelt] does not think that Army men are the people who should have civil administration entrusted to them." But Ickes was also concerned that FDR would put off deciding the issue until it was too late to change course.[73]

The controversy came to a climax in two cabinet meetings in late October and early November 1942. And while FDR did not allow minutes to be taken at his cabinet meetings, the recollections in the diaries of Stimson and Ickes and the postcabinet notes of Attorney General Francis Biddle provide valuable insights. At the meeting, according to Ickes, FDR chastised Stimson for the school, with Ickes remarking that it looked like "militaristic imperialism" and that it should be stopped. Around the same time, Roosevelt sent an admonishing note to Stimson on the school stating that the "whole matter is something which should have been taken up with me in the first instance. The governing of occupied territories may be of many kinds but in most instances it is a civilian task and requires absolutely first-class men and not second-string men."[74]

Ickes thought that Stimson seemed surprised about the school, though Ickes believed that the secretary of war surely knew that it was in operation. Ickes further remarked that the school was in his mind "one of the most dangerous indications that has come to my notice. . . . We ought to be getting ready to administer for the interval necessary to reestablish governments after the war. But the administration ought to be by civilians, although it would be necessary to have troops at hand to keep the peace."[75] Biddle's notes of the meeting mirrored Ickes's, though with an interesting addition. Afterward he met with Vice President Wallace, suggesting to him that a study be made of turning the training over entirely to civilian colleges such as Harvard and Columbia and apparently avoiding any charge that the army was training a pool of modern-day proconsuls, with Wallace responding favorably.[76]

The notion of the army being the "lead" in postwar occupation duties, at the very least in conducting the training for such duties, would thus seem to have been in jeopardy at this point. The president was skeptical, and the vice president and two prominent cabinet members, Ickes and Biddle, opposed the concept. There was speculation that even Secretary of Navy Frank Knox thought that civilian governors should run postwar occupations.[77] In reality, however, the case against military government was not as strong as its proponents would have liked. Stimson viewed the affair as a "foolish rumpus" and saw it less as a civil-military crisis and more of a power play by other departments that were "greatly piqued" at the army for "setting up something that would encroach on their prerogatives." He blamed the matter on what he called the New Deal "cherubs" and noted that Assistant Secretary of State Dean Acheson accepted the school.[78] Perhaps most important, FDR's own view was more nuanced. Regardless of what FDR told Ickes in a private meeting, what he had objected to publicly was not the idea of the school but that some of the faculty and students there were perhaps not up to the task. This was corroborated in Biddle's account: "There was a good deal of discussion about the problem of the administration after the war of reconquered territory. The general consensus of opinion was that the school at Virginia was not very good and that the problem should be approached on the basis of the military starting with the control and then turning it over to the civilians."[79] The distinction was important. FDR was siding seemingly with his New Dealers by attacking the school, but he left a way out, presumably, to Stimson: fix the school, and all might be well.

Ickes and others such as Wallace were, however, determined to stop the school and to gain some control over what they expected to be extensive postwar governance in conquered and/or liberated territory. Yet the arguments they provided were far from convincing. The substance of much of the arguments consisted either of ad hominem attacks about the quality of personnel at the school, which could be rebutted, and irrelevant to the central issue, or were vaguely sinister-sounding attacks on "militarist imperialism." Two of the more comprehensive civilian arguments against the school and military primacy in postwar occupation—one a report by key Roosevelt aide Jonathan Daniels and the other a counterproposal on a civilian-run training system by Saul Padover, an Ickes assistant (later a distinguished historian and political theorist)—were revealing in their arguments' weaknesses.

Daniels's report was essentially aimed at FDR's concern that the school might be a breeding ground for imperialists or at least opponents to FDR, and Daniels framed the issue in a way to appear that the president did have something to worry about. He reported that 53 percent from the school's first class at least had some previous government experience and that the school was somewhat hostile to the Roosevelt administration.[80] Daniels's evidence of this hostility, however, was scarce, and what did exist often amounted to little more than character slurs. He admitted that it was not "strictly true" that "no friends of the Roosevelt Administration need apply." But he speculated all the same, basing his finding on conjecture and selective anecdotal evidence: "My impression is that while many of the officers are not on record as to their political and social views, more of them would probably be politically sympathetic with Major George Norwood, a wealthy anti–New Dealer . . . from South Carolina, than with . . . New Dealer . . . Major Lewis Hyman Weinstein, from Boston." He wrote that Gullion seemed defensive, calling himself a "Kentucky Democrat" and a "New Dealer enough to run the NRA [National Recovery Administration] in Hawaii." Daniels characterized Cornelius Wickersham as a "sincere, ineffectual-appearing man, whose eyes blink in a nervous tic," and noted that Miller, "while intelligent and highly regarded by many, is vigorously disliked by some important elements in Labor because of his opposition to the creation of the NLRB [National Labor Relations Board]." Yet that was as far as his survey of the school's administration went: he admitted that apart from Wickersham and Miller, he had not interacted with other members of the faculty.[81]

The central issue for Daniels was "the place and meaning of the School and the Provost Marshal General's Division of Military Government in America's plans for successful war and sensible peace." Daniels conceded that the military was needed to run the "truly military phase." But he noted that, in the army's view, this might be lengthy and would even include things such as supervising education. Daniels also pointed out that, if the same personnel were used when the transition to civilian control occurred, then "a military attitude toward people and problems might be carried over into civilian control." His solution was to turn the process over to the State Department and appoint a New Dealer to run it, "someone aware of the democratic process and devoted to the welfare of people under it. In this connection, while he may not have foreign experience, I think of such a man as David Lilienthal of TVA [Tennessee Valley Authority]."[82]

Whether Daniels's recommendations had traction is debatable. It is true that in June 1943, FDR directed Cordell Hull to establish the Office of Foreign Economic Coordination under the State Department's direction, an agency whose responsibility it was to serve as "one central point in Washington for the coordination of interrelated activities of the several U.S. agencies operating abroad."[83] But the organization's charter, especially vis-à-vis the military, was unclear. Even after its setup, it was not certain whether War or State had ultimate responsibility for postwar planning. And after the office's establishment, the army continued to plan for its postwar occupation duties, to train military government officials, and to set up an even more powerful and influential section, the Civil Affairs Division, which would dominate much of the postwar governance planning process. This suggests that Roosevelt was playing both sides (or simply allowing events to unfold without much overarching guidance) in directing the Office of Foreign Economic Cooperation to be stood up though it would soon fall by the wayside and, as previously mentioned, be absorbed into another federal agency and in letting the army continue to conduct training and planning. No doubt FDR wanted to avoid comparisons of postwar occupation to the New Deal, and taking Daniels's suggestion of putting the TVA director in charge of it would almost certainly have had that effect. Additionally, Daniels likely did not understand the military government model as the army understood it, which sought precisely to "maximize" the independence of the occupied territories as much as possible in order to ensure the least interference with military efforts.

In fact, the real concern about the military government model should not have been the imposition of a kind of jackbooted militarism similar to Hitler's *Gauleiters* but the acquiescence to local control by the American military authorities.

Padover's memorandum to Ickes, sent in January 1943, was a more aware and penetrating document than Daniels's report, and Ickes, who adopted Padover's arguments, forwarded the document to FDR for consideration. In his memorandum, Padover admitted that the army has a "plan and a purpose. The Army's plan is to train administrators for the post-war world and thereby to control it." In so doing, the army will "monopolize all of the training and research facilities of the country by a process of total absorption. In other words, the present plan is to put the men skilled in social science, public law, administration, scientific management, etc., into uniform." While this is exaggerated (Stimson and his War Department would certainly contend that a notion that the army sought to "control" the postwar world was ludicrous), Padover got the essentials correct. The army *did* have a plan, *was* moving forward on it, and *was* actively recruiting to put in uniform a large manpower pool from all the areas he mentioned.[84]

Padover's solution to civilianize the postwar planning and training process involved the creation of a "Center of Administrative Studies" that would be "interdepartmental—most important of the agencies are the Department of the Interior, the State Department, and the Board of Economic Warfare." As proposed, the agencies would set up a planning board for "training and research, to draw up administrative plans and work out policy." The establishment of the center was phase one. Phase two involved setting up a research agency "for the study of what the British call 'colonial problems,' but which we prefer to call problems of non-industrial groups and areas." Phase three involved organizing contact with major scholars, universities, and learned bodies in the United States.[85]

In retrospect, given the increasing call for interagency cooperation in postconflict reconstruction, some of Padover's ideas seem remarkably ahead of their time. But Padover's proposal had serious flaws. His justification for a civilian agency was that by "tradition, training, background, and outlook, the army is not equipped for long-term administration of foreign areas." This was institutionally myopic. One could argue that if any agency had studied and had experience in administration of foreign areas, it was the US military, and the army especially, which had done it many times in its history around the world. Furthermore, the army was already far ahead of any governmental agency in developing doctrine and setting up training. In contrast, for Padover's scheme to work, an entire postwar administration apparatus would have to be interdepartmentally established to even begin to get to some level of institutional expertise—a "Center for Administrative Studies" followed by a "research agency."

What civilian agencies lacked was precisely what the army had— in strategist Michele Flournoy's words, a "training culture."[86] With the advent of professional military schooling in the late nineteenth and early twentieth centuries, additional training and education were virtually mandatory for military officers to rise to higher levels, and occupation and military government were topics extensively covered at the Army War College in the 1920s and 1930s. Padover's call for such a cross-cutting center pointed out the lack of expertise and the corresponding lack of an institutionalized training culture at intermediate and advanced levels in other executive branch departments. (As an example, George Kennan was on the verge of resigning from the State Department in 1928 to pursue more formal education. Only the intervention of his former teacher at the Foreign Service School that allowed him education abroad prevented him from doing so.[87]) What Padover was attempting to do was to create training in the absence of such a culture and without the requisite doctrine, organizational knowledge, and experience to effectuate the training. Additionally, what made his proposal perhaps most problematic was a neocolonialist approach: Padover even made mention of it in his proposal by referencing so-called British colonial problems.

In contrast to the above arguments, Stimson had major advantages in the interagency controversy. The army had a historical and intellectual foundation for postwar occupation. It had a formulated doctrine, historical examples, and a staff working hard on military government issues. Stimson did not have to propose new structures or make unsettling proposals about New Deal–like postwar orders. He could forcefully lay out the case for both the school and the army's overall management of postwar occupation duties rooted in the army's institutional conceptions of military government and postwar occupation responsibilities. Accordingly, after the October cabinet meeting, Stimson prepared a lengthy written rebuttal to Ickes's charges. While he did not send it, the document reflected the essence of the arguments that he would make to FDR in favor of the school and the army's conception of postwar occupation. In the document, he discussed the October cabinet meeting in which he understood FDR to "feel that the idea of the Army's School of Military Government . . . was a good one, if confined to a proper scope, but to have misgivings about the caliber of its faculty." He separated Roosevelt's concerns from other cabinet members, who sensed in it the "germ of imperialism."

Stimson used the argument most likely to appeal to Roosevelt as a war president. Because civilians might commit acts of sabotage and other perfidy, "military necessity, therefore, demands that the army be in complete control," at least immediately after conflict. To Stimson, the issue was self-evident: "No one, I believe, would quarrel with the view that, so long as military necessity exists, it is the army and no other agency which must hold the reins of government." He asked rhetorically, "When does military necessity come to an end?" Here he relied on the American army's tradition and experience. "No rule of thumb," he asserted, could answer this. He cited two examples: during the Civil War and in the Philippines after the Spanish-American War, "we paid a heavy price for concluding prematurely that [the need for military government] had disappeared. The treacherous nature of our present enemies will make a correct determination of this question more important than it has ever been in the past." He then went on to point out that it was eminently reasonable that occupation duties would last in places throughout the world at least as long as the fourteen-month Rhineland occupation.[88]

Stimson quoted from the Hunt Report and noted that it became the basis for "a Field Manual on Military Government (*FM 27-5*)." He also addressed concerns about "militarist" occupations. He stated that the most ideal form of military government was one "that preserves to the fullest extent consistent with military necessity, the local institutions and customs of an occupied area." While this preservation was a central aspect of occupation, military necessity still demanded that a specifically *military* government be established and be prepared to

supervise all aspects of public administration. Those who would execute those policies were the officers being trained at the school. They
would not be military governors but rather "the administrative assistants to Military Governors. Nor [will they be] civilians. They [will be]
all officers of the Army of the United States." Likewise these officers
would be administrators, executing policy from agencies presumably
outside the War Department. Stimson also forcefully, and in sharp
contrast to the civilian agency arguments, linked postwar occupation
with the actual winning of the war. Wartime and postwar strategy
were conflated. It was not, so to speak, "in winning the war, we must
not lose the peace," a formulation sometimes heard regarding nation-
building strategies, but rather "in winning the peace, we must not lose
the war." As an argument, it therefore both addressed FDR's concerns
and preserved the army's prerogatives.[89]

As noted, Stimson did not send the letter, though the ideas in it
framed his thinking and his arguments at a follow-up cabinet meeting.[90] There Stimson attempted to show "how ridiculous was the proposition that we were trying to train Army officers for proconsular
duties." According to Stimson's account, Roosevelt himself looked to
derail his efforts, "constantly interrupting" him with "discursive stories," but Stimson said he kept going, and he concluded that he thought
he "finally got it across."[91] Yet according to Ickes, FDR stated "in clear
language" that "while the army might have to take over temporarily, it
should be the purpose to turn the civilian government back to civilians,
even native ones, as soon as possible."[92]

While Ickes's account seems to indicate that Roosevelt favored the
interior secretary's understanding, again what FDR said was ambivalent. After all, FDR's assertion that the military ultimately turn over to
civilians the occupation responsibilities was not a point of contention
for Stimson. The more fundamental question was *who* was going to
control the overall process for postwar planning. There would be significant dueling between agencies and departments for the next several
months. FDR would personally criticize Gullion for "lacking elasticity
of mind"—an enigmatic reference to a document by Gullion regarding
the need of military government, and Ickes would continue to attack
the school.[93] The school would get bad publicity, ironically, as being
an agent of Wallace-driven utopianism ("globaloney" as one opinion

writer termed it) and would actually go to ground for a short period in the spring and summer of 1943.[94] FDR also said throughout much of 1943 that the State Department should have significant postwar responsibility by putting the Office of Foreign Economic Cooperation under it, though that organization's charter was itself ambiguous.[95] But it was also during 1943 that the army stood up the army's Civil Affairs Division without any apparent objection, and it was during this year that the School of Military Government both increased its student body and also branched out to prestigious colleges to establish its civil affairs training schools. And on November 10, 1943, in a letter to Stimson, Roosevelt directed that the army undertake the planning necessary to ship and distribute relief supplies in occupied areas, subsequently clarified to its being responsible for the first six months after liberation from the Axis forces.[96] Stimson clearly felt vindicated, as he stated in his memoirs: "So clearly did the Army prove itself to be the proper agency for such work that more than two years after the end of the war, long after the military importance of the overseas theaters had been superseded by the dominance of economic and political problems, the War Department was still carrying on the administration of the American occupation in defeated countries."[97] If this is not what many of the New Dealers wanted, then they had not made their arguments well, and they may have missed a chance at a more collaborative interagency relationship by overstating claims about "militarism" and "imperialism"—notions that the historical record could disabuse. Such claims only alienated someone such as Stimson, who considered them affronts. Furthermore, any hint of utopian schemes was not what FDR wanted in his role as "Dr. Win-the-War": he was instead comfortable with goals that could be explicitly linked to wartime success.

Martial Law in Hawaii, the Western Defense Zone, and the Japanese-American Exclusion Policy

The army showed its widespread and lasting power in the Hawaiian Territory, where it operated a military government, and in the continental United States, especially in what was called the Western Defense Zone in the western United States, where it exercised control bordering on martial law, and where it significantly shaped and influenced the Japanese-American exclusion policy. In key confrontations over martial law or exclusion policies, both of which involved control over civilian populations in *American* territory, the War Department's views prevailed.

The direct, unexpected attack on Pearl Harbor, which was within American territory, sent shock waves through the populace. It was the catalyst for the imposition of martial law in Hawaii. Furthermore, racial prejudice was a powerful factor in the Japanese-American exclusion policy. Accordingly it has been suggested that the War Department simply acted in accordance with popular beliefs, when it successfully advocated for the removal of Japanese Americans from restricted areas.[98] But outrage and prejudice alone are insufficient explanations. Rather, whether in Hawaii or the western United States, the War Department utilized "military necessity" arguments as rationales for its actions when dealing with civilians. As interpreted in international law, military necessity has traditionally been applied within the context of determining appropriate military actions against foreign enemies or while occupying foreign countries, and not traditionally associated with actions involving one's own military force or actions against one's own population.[99] Yet military necessity was invoked when justifying martial law in Hawaii, an American territory, and when justifying Japanese-American exclusion policies (and other policies) in the Western Defense Zone of the continental United States. Even though not used with legal precision, the seeming ease with which it was invoked in those contexts underscored the prevalence and influence of military imperatives within American government and society at the time. Military necessity was argued consistently and successfully within a framework of law and regulation: it was seen not as a departure but as an extension of existing laws. Perhaps even more important, a widespread army presence largely set the conditions by which the laws would be subsequently defined. Prior planning, the establishment of headquarters, and the employment of military officials—all these low-level and mid-level actions gave an immense advantage to the army in creating the conditions for what military necessity actually meant.

The army had previously drawn up plans for military government of the Hawaiian Islands during the Rainbow plans of the 1930s, and there were already two hundred thousand military personnel assigned there by 1940 (increasing to five hundred thousand during the war). Throughout 1941, calls increased for expansive authorities to be granted to the state's executive and to the US military in the event of Japanese attack. In September 1941, the Hawaiian legislature enacted laws that would grant the governor extensive authority in the case of war, a position endorsed by the commanding general of the Hawaiian Department, Lt. Gen. Walter Short. Following the attack on Pearl Harbor, Gov. William Poindexter sent a message to FDR in which he acceded to martial law and military government, and Roosevelt wrote back that the governor's action "in suspending the writ of habeas corpus and placing the territory of Hawaii under martial law [in accordance with] USC Title 48, section 532, has my approval," explicitly referencing the legislative underpinning of the imposition of military rule.[100]

Martial law swiftly became prevalent everywhere in Hawaii. Sweeping powers were granted to the commanding general as military governor. The police station in Honolulu housed army military police and navy shore patrol personnel, and military law enforcement organizations became the most significant police forces on the islands. Beginning on December 8, 1941, state courts no longer had criminal jurisdiction, and military tribunals were established to try civilians. The press was duly censored, wages frozen, and blackouts and curfews mandated. The army's authority was so pervasive that the commanding general threatened to court-martial two federal judges if they entertained habeas corpus petitions in their courts; to avert a constitutional crisis, the solicitor general of the United States had to directly intervene. Most significantly, on October 16, 1942, FDR designated Hawaii "a military area" pursuant to Executive Order (EO) 9066, granting to military authorities great power to exclude residents under penalty of law from areas on the islands (and in the continental United States as well) that it deemed militarily sensitive or vital. Hawaii had been transformed into a huge military camp, if not an outright fortress.[101]

Cabinet members argued heatedly with the War Department over Hawaii. Attorney General Francis Biddle voiced complaints about the high-handedness of the army's rule. Secretary of Interior Ickes fumed that civilians had abdicated authority in Hawaii and that the term "military governor" was "not recognized by our Constitution." He angrily protested that there was no basis or excuse to set up a military governor on American soil: "That form of government has hitherto been reserved for conquered territory." While recognizing the tragedy of Pearl Harbor, he believed such governorship completely unnecessary and argued to eliminate it altogether.[102] But neither was persuasive enough to carry the day. The arguments for military necessity were reaffirmed throughout the war, typified by the one made by Lt. Gen. Delos C. Emmons, then military governor, who wrote to Assistant Secretary John McCloy regarding a dispute with Attorney General Francis Biddle over the relinquishment of civil authority in Hawaii. Finding Biddle's proposals inadequate, Emmons asserted, "My responsibility as Commanding General and Military Governor requires me to defend the Hawaiian Islands at all costs, and as the prelude to such an eventuality, to organize the military and civil population to co-operate in that defense." The army's authority only gradually diminished over the course of the war and finally ended in October 1944, the same month that FDR restored the writ of habeas corpus by proclamation.[103] The precept that the authority of the military commander in wartime, even in American territory, must remain paramount was held long after any significant threat to Hawaii had passed.

Placing Hawaii under military government was perhaps not that surprising. It had been directly attacked, it was a vulnerable American outpost in the Pacific Ocean, and it was not at that point one of the fifty states. In the Western Defense Zone of the continental United States, while the power to impose absolute martial law was lacking, the authority given to its commander, Lt. Gen. John DeWitt, was nearly as great.[104] Relying on presidential executive orders and a common-law understanding of military authority, DeWitt published a series of proclamations throughout 1942. Public Proclamation No. 3 (March 24, 1942) established a curfew for Japanese Americans along with all alien Japanese, Germans, and Italians. Public Proclamation No. 7 (June 8, 1942) excluded Japanese Americans from Military Area No. 1 (which encompassed the western coastal areas of the continental United States as well as a considerable distance inland). These proclamations were followed by orders that gave precise instructions on times, locations, and methods of exclusion.[105] For all these actions, army officials in the Western Defense Zone and in Washington relied on their understanding of the law and the requirements imposed by military necessity. For example, an opinion from the Western Defense Zone staff judge advocate on December 15, 1941, quoted extensively from US common-law cases in setting forth the case for military authority in emergency situations. As the opinion concluded, military authority could require actions even if outright martial law was not imposed: "When the exigencies of the situation require, the commanding general may, in time of war, use every means necessary to accomplish his military mission, including the summary taking of privately owned property. This authority exists irrespective of any declaration of martial law."[106]

Most infamously, the previously referenced Executive Order 9066 led to the forced removal of Japanese Americans from their homes on the West Coast to inland camps. As historians have pointed out, the exclusion policy essentially became a source of dispute between those in the Roosevelt administration who opposed it, including Attorney General Francis Biddle, and those in the War Department who sought the exclusion, primarily Stimson and McCloy, as well as very influential mid-level actors such as DeWitt. Irrational racial fears, white resentment toward the relative success of the small Japanese-American community, and a lack of understanding of the nonassimilated aspects of Japanese-American communities explosively combined with the fear that swept the western United States not only following the attack on Pearl Harbor but also during the successive Japanese conquests of Singapore, Malaysia, and the Philippines. All these apprehensions essentially coalesced around the conditions imposed by military necessity. In his memoirs, Francis Biddle argues that FDR was predisposed to issue EO 9066 even without DeWitt's specific impetus, and it has been argued that FDR's own attitude to the exclusion policy was one of indifference if not callous disregard and that therefore the military's role in the exclusion policy should not be overstated.[107] But Roosevelt's actions were provided an ostensibly impartial basis by the War Department. And while racial prejudice and nativist fears, prevalent during the interwar years, were fanned into flame following Pearl Harbor and the stunning Japanese victories in the Far East, they do not themselves adequately explain the long-term success, if it can be called that, of the exclusion policy. Rather, that success must be primarily attributed to the military's power in ensuring the success of the exclusion policy, shown in its ability to intertwine the concept of military necessity into the fabric of constitutional law, legislation, and judicial opinion, to employ the War Department bureaucracy, and to cause the other parts of the federal government to accede to its will.

As stated in the War Department's own comprehensive final report on the evacuation, EO 9066 was "predicated upon a series of intermediate decisions, each of which formed a progressive development of the final decision."[108] One of the most important was the establishment of the Western Defense Zone within the continental United States. Creating that organization provided DeWitt, as its commanding general, power to "crystallize a program of forthright action to deal with subversive elements of the population."[109] The framework for ultimate exclusion was set forth in the memorandum of February 14, 1942, that DeWitt forwarded to Stimson. The document argued that Japanese Americans were in close proximity to vital defense industries, and "possible and probable enemy activities" such as naval attacks on shipping and coastal cities, air raids, and sabotage were likely to occur, no doubt aided by those Japanese Americans. Based upon this presumed danger, DeWitt recommended with implacable certainty to the secretary of war that Stimson obtain from the president the authority to designate military areas from which he could specifically exclude "all Japanese, all alien enemies, and all other persons suspected for any reason by the administering military authorities of being actual or potential saboteurs, espionage agents, or fifth columnists."[110] Though DeWitt used the words "Japanese" and "Japanese-Americans" somewhat interchangeably, to eliminate any confusion elsewhere in the document he specifically referenced "Japanese-American citizens" as persons to be excluded. The authority contemplated was consistent with the requirements of military necessity: not only actual but *potential* "fifth columnists" (not a legal term), among others, were to be affected and even those, regardless of Japanese ancestry, suspected "for any reason"—reasons the army itself would no doubt supply.

DeWitt also clearly indicated that as commanding general he would need to be responsible for the evacuation to, and the administration and supply of, all the internment locations and that all phases should be coordinated by the provost marshal of the army. And once EO 9066 was promulgated, DeWitt in short order established a civil affairs division as an addition to his general staff, specifically noting that "the requirements, ramification and the complex interdependent aspects of the [evacuation] program demanded the centralization of [the civil affairs division], under the Commanding General, of full responsibility for the conduct and supervision of the Commanding General's direction in the civil control field." Under it, he established the Western Civil Control Administration, offices of which were established in each major Japanese-American population center. Eventually, in carrying out the evacuation, the civil affairs division comprised 45 officers, 12 enlisted personnel, and 260 civilians in the Fourth Army Headquarters and 1,660 in the field.[111]

Assistant Secretary of War John McCloy deferred to DeWitt's judgment regarding the Japanese-American exclusion as simply a question of military necessity.[112] Attorney General Biddle and members of the Justice Department (including FBI director J. Edgar Hoover) argued that the Japanese-American exclusion policy was unwarranted.[113] But Biddle's own account revealed a somewhat hapless Department of Justice outmaneuvered by the army. Biddle had assigned one of his lawyers to coordinate with DeWitt and the California state leadership to ensure especially that both were presented with the more moderate Justice Department view on possible exclusion. According to Biddle, however, that Justice official construed his assignment to "patriotically follow the military" and did essentially that, dashing any chance at modifying the army position at ground level. Meanwhile in Washington, Stimson and McCloy advocated to the White House the merits of Japanese-American exclusion even before DeWitt's memorandum had reached the War Department. By the time Biddle attempted to stop the policy, it was too late. The president had said that exclusion was a question of "military judgment," and Biddle himself acquiesced.[114]

The president promulgated EO 9066 five days after DeWitt's report was sent to Stimson. It was a prime example of military necessity becoming legalized and bureaucratized within the mainstream of American governmental policy. The first paragraph of the order legally anchored the underlying premise of the policy by referencing specific legislation—statutes passed by Congress in 1918 and subsequently amended in 1940 and 1941 to protect against espionage and sabotage. The president's inherent authority as commander in chief was invoked in the next paragraph; he thereby directed the secretary of war and his military commanders to determine which military areas from which "any and all persons may be excluded." He further authorized the secretary and military commanders to "take such other steps as he or the appropriate Military Commander may deem advisable to enforce compliance" with any required restrictions. Finally, the president further directed other executive departments to assist the secretary and the commanders to carry out the executive order. Roosevelt granted sweeping power to the military—all without once mentioning the ultimate target of the exclusion policy, the Japanese Americans who resided on the West Coast.[115]

The two most prominent Supreme Court cases dealing with the exclusion policy, *Hirabayashi v. United States* and *Korematsu v. United States,* both upheld the army's position. *Korematsu* in particular relied on poorly based facts and assumptions about the possibility of a Japanese-American fifth column in the western United States, the key document relied upon being the *Final Report: Japanese Evacuation from the West Coast, 1942* provided by DeWitt to Marshall and Stimson.[116] The document listed a series of alleged incidents that were largely based on innuendo and insinuation or that were downright false— examples included claims of hidden caches of contraband being found in the Western Zone, along with ominous assertions that critical airfields, utility stations, and military bases were "flanked" by Japanese-American communities. These strained efforts to tie Japanese Americans to an actual threat were bolstered by the proximity of apparent attacks by Japan, from a presumed submarine attack near Santa Barbara to a bombing in Oregon by a submarine-based plane.[117]

But these far-from-overwhelming examples were structured in terms that the Supreme Court found persuasive. In *Hirabayashi,* Chief Justice Harlan Fiske Stone wrote that "constitutional government, in time of war, is not so powerless and does not compel so hard a choice if those charged with the responsibility of our national defense have reasonable ground for believing the threat is real."[118] Similarly, in *Korematsu* the court deferred to the military, stating it was "charged with the primary responsibility of defending our shores."[119] In the same way that EO 9066 relied exclusively on claims of military necessity, and never once mentioning Japanese Americans, Justice Hugo Black stated:

> To cast this case into outlines of racial prejudice, without reference to the real military dangers which were presented, merely confuses the issue. Korematsu was not excluded from the Military Area because of his race. He was excluded because the properly constituted military authorities feared an invasion of the West Coast and felt constrained to take proper security measures because they decided that the military urgency of the situation demanded that all citizens of Japanese ancestry be segregated from the West Coast temporarily, and finally, because Congress, reposing its trust in this time of war in our military leaders—as inevitably it must—determined that they should have the power to do this.[120]

Chief Justice Stone likewise in *Hirabayashi* wrote that "distinctions between citizens solely because of their ancestry are, by their very nature odious to a free people whose institutions are founded upon the doctrine of equality."[121] Nonetheless, Stone went even further in postulating the case for military authority in wartime: "The war power of the national government . . . embraces every phase of the national defense, including the protection of war materials and the members of the armed forces from injury and from the dangers which attend the rise, prosecution, and progress of war."[122]

The Hawaii martial law and the Western Defense Zone exclusion controversies revealed not only the Roosevelt administration's seeming deference to the military on such matters, but they also showed how the army used arguments for military necessity in ways that maximized the army's influence and interests by referring to terms and conditions that were established by a subordinate army command. In large bureaucratic organizations, as the span of control widens the particular ability to grasp the intricacies of a problem falls to those with subject-matter expertise. And in twentieth-century American organizational culture, specific professional opinion became the means by which expert opinion was sought. For the issues in Hawaii and the Western Defense Zone, military professional expertise was relied upon to shape and define what became seen as, fundamentally, a military problem.[123] In wartime, the army, as the subject-matter expert, was the best judge of what would constitute possible invasion or sabotage in Hawaii and the Western Defense Zone. The army was able to thwart other actors and agencies and therefore prevailed in the interagency dispute.

Lacking the same internal coherence, hierarchies of control, and historical precedents, neither cabinet departments (such as Justice, Interior, or State) nor the ad hoc FDR war committees (such as the Board of Economic Warfare) provided a coherent and meaningful counterweight to the War Department in wartime interagency conflicts. As inefficient and wasteful as that department could be, it was training personnel, producing plans, and refining doctrine for postwar goals and utilizing military-necessity arguments to further its wartime objectives in a way that competing civilian organizations could not match.

4

North Africa and the Establishment of the Civil Affairs Division, 1943

Relatively little planning for postconflict administration was done for the North Africa campaign, begun in November 1942 with Operation Torch, the invasion of French Morocco and Algeria.[1] No doubt some of this was due to poor planning assumptions that included the expectation that the French in the occupied areas would warmly welcome the Allies as liberators, thus making the question of military occupation irrelevant.[2] But the situation was further confused by Roosevelt's uncertainty as to who should take the lead in occupation responsibilities. French North Africa, with its Vichy government, only added to the complexity. Robert Murphy, Eisenhower's political adviser in North Africa, noted in his memoirs that Roosevelt could never firmly decide whether French North Africa was to be occupied or liberated.[3]

In North Africa there was also confusion and significant frustration. Marshall noted Eisenhower's "disgust with . . . seventeen civilian agencies roaming around areas in Africa, causing him more trouble than the Germans."[4] Eisenhower was consumed with civil affairs matters, claiming it took a majority of his time—more than even the conduct of combat operations.[5] In a secret cable to Marshall on November 30, 1942, he wrote, "Sometimes I think I live ten years each week, of which at least nine are absorbed in political and economic matters." He went on to say that the sooner he was rid of such matters "outside the military in scope," the happier he would be.[6] At the same time, he did not want to cede control or authority to anyone outside the military. In a cable sent to Marshall just a few days earlier, Eisenhower pointed out that no one was more anxious than he or his deputy, Maj. Gen. Mark Clark, to "rid ourselves completely of all problems other than purely military." But the brutal truth was that because civil affairs matters so greatly influenced the military situation, there was no choice. Because of this direct impact on military operations, Eisenhower therefore argued that the State Department representative on his staff, Robert Murphy, not be independently accountable to State. Instead, "single headed responsibility" for all aspects of the operation, including those dealing with civil and political matters, had to remain with the theater commander.[7]

To Stimson, interagency wrangling for power in what he thought was a military domain was a source of consternation. Despite his best efforts in the School of Military Government dispute, Stimson had not yet convinced the president that the army should have occupation primacy. Stimson noted that Roosevelt "distrusted the army as an agency for the temporary handling of civilian matters."[8] Instead, Roosevelt continually seemed to prefer civilians, whom Stimson wrote dismissively of as the "whole crew of agencies which have been squabbling with each other in their haste to get into North Africa."[9] The purportedly haphazard arrangement of government agencies, often without clear charters or mandates, seemed to verify Stimson's point about the need for unified control under the overall authority of the military.

At least in the initial stages of the operation, Roosevelt had granted authority over all the liberated territories of North Africa to a number of boards and agencies seemingly under the Department of State. The Office of Foreign Territories, among its other duties, was responsible for the implementation of US economic and social programs in North Africa. The Interdepartmental Advisory Committee was established to assist the Office of Foreign Territories and was made up of representatives of the Departments of State, Treasury, Agriculture, Lend-Lease, the Board of Economic Warfare, and others (the War Department being initially omitted). Its mission was to serve as a clearinghouse for civil affairs. There was also the Office of Foreign Relief and Rehabilitation Operations, which was intended to provide for the essential necessities for the peoples of the occupied territories. Last, there was the Committee on Combined Boards, a board that had both US and UK representatives and that served as an inter-Allied clearinghouse for civil affairs questions.[10]

These agencies had overlapping functions and responsibilities. The Interdepartmental Advisory Committee was intended to be a collaborative agency that would receive civil affairs–related questions in the theater and either send them to the appropriate US agency for resolution, if the question was US-specific, or to the Committee on Combined Boards, which would then attempt to best resolve the issue. Yet the Interdepartmental Advisory Committee was not successful as a coordinating agency. Not only was War Department membership lacking, but the committee also lacked specific terms of reference and had a vaguely defined authority.[11] Instead Eisenhower decided to go directly to the Committee on Combined Boards as his conduit for all civil affairs questions, leaving the other agency out. The committee, which had been set up based upon a recommendation from the US-UK Combined Chiefs of Staff, was decidedly military in its orientation, and the secretariat for both organizations was the same. Eisenhower could send a civil affairs question to that unified secretariat, an organization more oriented toward the military requirements of the problem and also presumably less likely to get entangled in the more problematic political questions—and therefore less likely to get caught in the competition of various agencies on the Interdepartmental Advisory Committee.[12]

Brig. Gen. Lucius Clay, the assistant chief of staff for materiel in the Services of Supply command, recommended that all government agencies funnel through the conduit of the Combined Chiefs of Staff and the Committee on Combined Boards.[13] By December 1942, this was the army's preferred communication route. Later that month, having Assistant Secretary of War John McCloy assigned to the Committee on Combined Boards for the duration as the War Department representative further improved the army's ability to maintain some semblance of military control over the burgeoning North Africa occupation questions.[14] Yet while there may have been some success in the Committee on Combined Boards as a coordinating body, its utility was limited. Marshall noted its ad hoc nature: "[It] exists with the acquiescence of the Combined Chiefs of Staff. . . . It has no charter. It has no staff. The secretariat is furnished by the [Combined Chiefs of Staff]."[15] In large part because of these organizational limitations, the Committee on Combined Board's success would not extend beyond North Africa.[16]

Regardless of the army's moderate success in using the Committee on Combined Boards as a way to control civil affairs questions, the prospects for complete military primacy in civil affairs in North Africa looked uncertain throughout much of 1943. FDR still sent mixed signals over authorities. On March 19, for example, he wrote a letter to Herbert Lehman, director of the Office of Foreign Relief and Rehabilitation Operations, authorizing him to "plan, coordinate, and arrange for the administration of the Government's activities for the relief of war in areas liberated from Axis control through the provision of food, fuel, clothing, and other basic necessities." Yet the president also gave at least an ostensible primacy to the military by stating that Lehman's organization would be "subject to the approval of the US military commander as long as military occupation continues."[17] Relying on FDR's March letter giving him authority to plan and organize civilian relief efforts, Lehman himself issued a statement on May 8 that indicated that he had broad postwar authority. In the statement, Lehman asserted that after the first ninety days following cessation of hostilities, all plans, information, and requirements for supplies would be entirely accomplished by his organization. FDR's letter also stated that his organization's field officers in North Africa would be directly under Lehman's authority and not the army's.[18]

Seeing this bureaucratic ambiguity and confusion, Stimson realized his department's comparative advantage. He responded directly to Lehman in June, reiterating the standard military position: the theater commander, as military governor, had complete responsibility for all matters regarding supply, distribution, and transportation for relief until a civilian government was established or until the commander was relieved of duties by the president. Lehman, who was actually quite amenable to military interests and willing to work with the army, somewhat relented but offered a further proposal. In it he proposed that his organization would be responsible for relief requirements for both the purely military and subsequent civilian periods of civil administration, separating these requirements from purely military ones. In response, the army continued to resist: no separation of relief requirements from military supplies. The War Department wanted to have one overall supply effort that was an integral part of all the procurement and distribution plans. Separating civilian relief from the overall military supply scheme would delink the two efforts and potentially lead to confusion. The mission could not be compromised.[19]

Lehman lost the argument to the War Department. And while it may seem in retrospect that, given Lehman's close relationship with the army, a compromise more amenable to him might have been brokered, by this time senior officials in the War Department were in no mood for any compromise of authority. By mid-1943 alternative civilian agencies such as Lehman's were at a significant disadvantage. His field teams were, compared to what the army could muster, small. Furthermore, even under Lehman's own proposal, the administrative and logistical mechanisms to distribute relief would largely have to be provided by the army, which was hardly interested in turning over authorities to an ad hoc agency. And last, Lehman's organization had limited reach: its charter lacked the authority to do much more without direction from the president himself.[20]

Another presidential plan for coordination of postconflict governance efforts took place in June 1943, in what appears to have been a last-ditch effort to bring together into a meaningful and coherent relationship all the civilian agencies that Eisenhower had complained were swarming over North Africa. The plan, developed at Roosevelt's behest by his Bureau of the Budget, sought to create "one central point for the coordination of interrelated activities of the several U.S. agencies operating abroad." The effort would be under the leadership of the State Department, and a committee would be established consisting of State, War, Treasury, Navy, the Board of Economic Warfare, the Office of Lend-Lease Administration, and the Office of Foreign Relief and Rehabilitation Operations. In each liberated area there would be appointed an "area director" who would "provide overall direction and coordination to the economic activities of civilian agencies in their respective areas," though that area director would be subject to the military commander's orders.[21]

In a cover letter to Secretary of State Cordell Hull, FDR went into additional detail: "Civilian agencies must be adequately prepared to assist our military forces in performing those services and activities which they are expert. We must harness together military and civilian efforts." The president then listed respective agencies—the Office of Foreign Relief and Rehabilitation Operations, the Office of Lend-Lease

Administration, the Board of Economic Warfare, and the Department of Treasury—and explained their particular roles. It was the most comprehensive attempt to unify civilian and military efforts in postconflict operations so far, and, at least on its face, the plan had merit. It did not seek to override the military's primacy, it expressly indicated that the role of the civilian agencies was to assist the commander, and it subordinated the area director to him. It gave the overall coordinating responsibility for the many agencies to the State Department, recognizing that longer-ranging foreign policy would be the overarching concern. It further attempted to delineate the specific requirements for each agency. The Office of Foreign Relief and Rehabilitation Operations, for instance, was to be "responsible for the relief and rehabilitation of victims of war in certain liberated areas." The Board of Economic Warfare was to be responsible for "foreign procurement, the development of strategic and critical materials . . . and other prescribed economic warfare measures." Treasury's role was to fix exchange rates and "assist on monetary, currency control, and general fiscal matters." FDR told Hull: "I shall rely on you to unify our foreign economic activities to the end that coherent and consistent policies and programs result. The Department of State should provide the necessary coordination, here and in the field, of our economic operations with respect to liberated areas."[22]

What resulted was the Office of Foreign Economic Coordination under the direction of Assistant Secretary of State Dean Acheson. The organization was intended to settle jurisdictional disputes between the agencies, both among the civilians and between the civilians and the military. It was to be a central point in Washington at the State Department for the coordination of interrelated activities of the several US agencies operating abroad. Furthermore, in each liberated area it was to be a central point of leadership and coordination similar to that in Washington. By being a kind of clearinghouse, it would allow for the participation of all relevant agencies and, at the same time, not remove the responsibility or authority of each agency for carrying out its own functions.

Yet as set forth, the bureaucratic difficulties of trying to be both a central point while allowing agencies responsibility and authority became apparent, and once again the effort ended in failure.[23] As FDR biographer Kenneth Davis notes, "as was generally true of Roosevelt's administrative arrangements . . . responsibilities were not accompanied by a commensurate assignment of authority or power."[24] Lehman argued that the plan left civilian agencies with responsibilities but took away the authority to ensure the responsibilities were carried out. The army, while acceding to the overall concept, would not alter its military planning to fit plans for other civilian agencies, reiterating that at least initially the first occupation phase must be completely run by the military.[25] In particular, the aforementioned idea of area directors was problematic: such representatives needed to work through the theater commander and not have direct access to Washington. Treasury, on the other hand, objected, countering that such direct access was required.[26] This took place concurrently with *other* interagency disputes, including the long-running (and previously discussed) dispute within the Board of Economic Warfare. So once again, FDR decided to overhaul the process. Acheson's organization was absorbed (along with the Board of Economic Warfare, Lend-Lease, and Lehman's organization) into the Foreign Economic Administration under the direction of conservative, big-business advocate Leo Crowley in September 1943. But it never gained the authority or stature that had been envisioned for it. The bureaucratic momentum had moved in the army's direction, and Crowley was not going to overcome it. Yet another civilian interagency attempt resulted in falling far short of what was intended.

Establishing the Civil Affairs Division

By the end of 1942, the army had established a School of Military Government and a Military Government Division, with both organizations remaining under the control of the Provost Marshal General Division. That division continued to do a variety of planning, much of it theoretical, and the school continued to produce military government officers throughout 1943. The school expanded its training program that year by creating the civil affairs training schools at numerous universities across the United States. Yet neither school nor division was at a high enough level in the War Department organization to have major impact on the course of strategic thinking. As figure 4.1 shows, following the 1942 reorganization of the army staff, the Provost Marshal

General Division itself was a subagency of the Services of Supply. Any action from either the Military Government Division or the school had to work its way through three layers of higher authority to have access to the chief of staff.

Stimson believed that he needed a military government planning and policymaking organization powerful enough to assert military viewpoints, provide clear control and direction, and shape and fashion policy in a way to ensure military interests were protected. The scope of occupation matters in North Africa showed that the army's current organizational methods were inadequate. Prior experience and planning had not contemplated the scale and complexity of occupation requirements. The War College committees of the 1920s and 1930, for example, only briefly discussed centralized War Department planning. Instead, virtually all of the committees' attention had been on actions taken by theater commanders.[27] Furthermore, though army doctrine, expressed in *FM 27-5*, stated that the G-1 remained responsible for military government matters, after the 1942 War Department reorganization the G-1 staff was reduced dramatically from seventy-three officers to thirteen and from one hundred civilians to twenty.[28] It was therefore clear that the G-1 could not take on such a responsibility. As for the Military Government Division (itself within the Provost Marshal General's Office), its primary mission was the training of military government officers for future occupations, and though it had a limited role in long-range planning, it could not handle day-to-day planning for North African civil administration.[29] Additionally, it was too far down the War Department hierarchy to have meaningful influence at the strategic policymaking level.[30]

However frustrated Stimson may have been in persuading FDR of the need for military control over postconflict governance responsibilities, he did have the ability to establish an organization *within* the War Department. In so doing, he could create an organization that could have much greater influence than anything in the past, especially because the president himself had greatly strengthened the War Department's status and authority. In March 1942 the president, through Executive Order 9062, had already permitted the most sweeping reorganization of the War Department since Elihu Root had established the General Staff in 1903. Not only did the order allow for

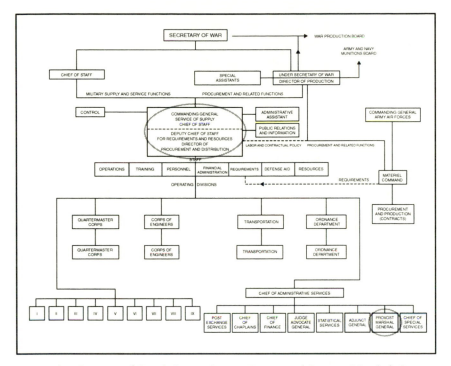

Figure 4.1. Services of Supply/Army Service Forces and Provost Marshal General. (Otto L. Nelson, *National Security and the General Staff* [Washington, DC: Infantry Journal Press, 1946], 383.) In terms of closer command-and-control proximity, the relative position of the provost marshal general and the commanding general of the Army Service Forces would later improve in a reorganization completed in 1944, though well after the Civil Affairs Division had already been established. Ibid., 432–33.

Stimson and Marshall to unify command and control in a much more powerful way, it also allowed an unprecedented direct line between the War Department and the president. On matters of "strategy, tactics, and operations," the president in his commander-in-chief role made explicit his ability and authority to consult directly with the chief of staff himself. Accordingly, staff sections directly under the chief of staff could have a far greater ability to shape national policy than in any previous time in American history.[31]

As the war progressed, the army continued to assert its interests more forcefully, especially whenever military operations intersected with longer-range foreign affairs. The Joint War Plans Committee, for example, was established in early 1943 to advise the Joint Chiefs on political considerations when doing strategic planning.[32] During that same time, the Joint Strategic Survey Committee was set up to formulate grand strategy—the first time that a military planning group had moved deeply into a realm considered primarily related to foreign policy and political decision making. Its charter stated that military authorities should "share with diplomatic and economic authorities the responsibility for shaping the national policy in peace as well as war."[33] Additionally, as part of the burgeoning departmental bureaucracy that came with the responsibility of managing a worldwide conflict, the War Department began to create high-level staff sections distinct from the General Staff that had functions that did not fit neatly within traditional domains.[34] Doing so allowed for more direct control from senior War Department leaders, which became especially important since so many of these new staff sections required interaction with civilian counterparts.[35]

All these organizational developments made it clear that it was not enough for high-ranking officials such as Stimson only to make arguments to the president about the military's need to have primacy in postconflict governance. Bureaucratic methods and organizational controls were also critical in gaining success. In the Roosevelt administration, a competent and cohesive army agency had to represent the army's view of the military's primacy in occupation matters at the point of planning and implementation. Throughout late 1942 and early 1943, officials in the War Department urged the creation of just that. A key meeting in early February 1943 attended by Lucius Clay, then assistant chief of staff for materiel, revealed the scope of the army's current concerns. Clay went to discuss civil affairs policy with key civilian leaders in civil affairs matters and key administration officials such as Herbert Lehman and Milo Perkins, chief of FDR's Bureau of the Budget. For Clay, the meeting illustrated the problem of what he called "idealistic" civilian agencies that sought to "improv[e] conditions throughout the world." Moreover, Clay was concerned that apparently little thought had been given to the army's role in an occupied zone, especially in the initial phases of the operation.[36] More telling were the disagreement and friction in the meeting. Lehman, frustrated with the lack of direction from the administration, wanted one overall agency in Washington to set a clear direction. According to Clay, however, many, including Assistant Secretary of State Acheson, did not agree. Rather, Acheson defended the current arrangement that gave the State Department a putative overall authority. For Clay, "the War Department [needed] to formulate a definite War Department policy as to its own relationship to civil affairs in occupied countries at the earliest possible date so that its views may be presented before a policy which may be contrary thereto has been established."[37]

A series of conferences between Stimson, Marshall, and Lt. Gen. John Hull, a senior official in the Operations Division, resulted in the creation of the Civil Affairs Division.[38] Officially Stimson directed its creation by order, and the organization went into existence on March 1, 1943.[39] Both Marshall and Stimson each believed that he was responsible for the organization, and both played key roles in its establishment. Marshall asserted that he established the division "to take charge of civil matters" and as a way to relieve him and others of the various diplomatic and political burdens of civil affairs.[40] Stimson also stated that he established the division, noting in his diaries that he created it "to carry on the absolutely essential work which is necessary to be done on behalf of Eisenhower, the military commander, in regards to civil affairs."[41] The secretary went on to say that he had "quietly" set up the division in spite of the president's preference for civilian control of postwar governance of occupied territories.[42]

Stimson had not acquiesced to FDR's predisposition to put a non-military agency in charge. Instead he had worked within his own department as a way to create a strategic-level organization that would favorably represent the army in the interagency domain. Stimson's diary comments clearly reveal how he connected occupation responsibilities with the necessities of military operations: "These civil affairs stem directly from the military occupation. They affect its safety and its interest." Noting that the president "obstinately refuses to see it yet," Stimson pointed out that the requirements and responsibilities of occupation would give rise to "far-reaching problems." Interestingly and consistently, he emphasized those problems were not primarily political problems but military ones that required military solutions: matters of civil affairs "will inevitably give rise to far-reaching problems which in part at least must be handled by the military commander and . . . the War Department."[43]

In early February, Stimson directed John McCloy to establish the Civil Affairs Division.[44] It was a logical and astute choice. Both Stimson and Marshall appreciated the assistant secretary's adroitness in problem solving and in maneuvering through Washington. McCloy had already worked skillfully in representing the army's interests in the interagency disputes over the School of Military Government, the Japanese-American exclusion policy, and the question of martial law in Hawaii. On the school issue, McCloy had successfully moved key FDR aide Harry Hopkins onto the army's side.[45] On the Japanese-American exclusion policy, he had successfully, if controversially, carried the army's position in arguments with the Justice Department.[46] And on the Hawaii martial law matter, he gradually gave back authority to civilians but at a pace amenable to military leadership.[47] Even Harold Ickes, while going so far as to wonder whether McCloy had fascist leanings, liked him personally and got along with him.[48] He also had on-the-ground knowledge of current civil affairs problems. In early January 1943 Marshall had personally requested that McCloy go on a mission to assess the North African situation (though Stimson demurred, saying that he was much too valuable and was needed at home, convincing FDR to send McCloy only on a short trip in early February).[49] While there, McCloy soon noted the rampant confusion in civil administration. Whereas the British had "competent people," the United States had confused monetary and fiscal policies, scrambled communication setups, and too many departments established without clear direction. After talking to General Clark, McCloy reflected that he had never realized "how closely we sailed to a military occupation that we were not prepared to deal with."[50]

Along with such a prominent War Department civilian, the Civil Affairs Division needed a military director who would administer the division and who would have as significant, if not an equal level of influence as McCloy's. Marshall had discussed with Hull who should run the division, initially favoring a civilian, Boykin Wright, a high-powered official who, according to Lt. Gen. Brehon Somervell, the head of the Services of Supply, was "of Cabinet stature."[51] Perhaps because McCloy had a nearly cabinet-level role, Marshall instead chose a professional military officer whom he knew personally and who had a reputation as a solid administrator, Maj. Gen. John H. Hilldring. He proved to be a wise choice. An infantry officer who had been awarded the Distinguished Service Cross for heroism in the 1918 Meuse-Argonne offensive, Hilldring later served under Marshall at the Infantry School at Fort Benning when Marshall had been assistant commandant there. He had experience in wide-ranging areas: he had served in the Philippines in the late 1920s and had also commanded Civilian Conservation Corps districts in the late 1930s. Hilldring was also currently the army G-1 and already had apparent if not actual responsibility over military government matters. Additionally, he had recently gained Marshall's respect. General MacArthur had slated him to take command of a division in New Guinea, but before he left the United States in mid-1942, Hilldring suffered a heart attack and instead was about to be involuntarily retired for medical reasons. Awaiting the decision, he wrote to Marshall, pointing out that being retired due to risk of death from work-related stress should not be an impediment to his continued service when so many men were risking their lives in combat.[52] This impressed Marshall, and he kept him on active service. Instead of a combat command, Hilldring got the job as the Civil Affairs Division's director, and he remained in the position for the duration of the war.[53]

Organization and Purpose of the Civil Affairs Division

The hierarchical position of the Civil Affairs Division within the War Department's organization was essential to its success in representing its interests within the army and also in intergovernmental and inter-Allied domains. Hilldring stated that, in his opinion, what was most important in the division's establishment was its standing in the War Department vis-à-vis other staff organizations. He doubted whether he could have coordinated the various civil affairs activities without the direct authority to speak for either the chief of staff or the secretary, something only possible if the division were high enough in the department. This point was reaffirmed by the division's executive officer, who stated that its most vital feature as a staff section was its direct access to either Marshall or Stimson.[54] Figure 4.2, displaying the overall War Department structure in early 1944, shows both the division's position in the department hierarchy—essentially one remove from the chief of staff (the deputy chief generally concerned with department administration and not policymaking) and two from the secretary and with an informal supervisory line to the assistant secretary. Not only was the division as near to the chief and secretary as the Army General Staff (Operations and G-1 thru G-4), it was comparatively much closer than the Military Government Division, not displayed on the chart at all. That division was a subsection of the Provost Marshal General, which (as figure 4.1 illustrates) was itself a subordinate of the Services of Supply (renamed the Army Service Forces) staff function.

Furthermore, the Civil Affairs Division had a charter drafted by the Operations and Plans Division and signed by Stimson. The division was to "inform and advise the Secretary of War in regard to all matters . . . other than those of a strictly military nature, in areas occupied as a result of military operations." The charter also linked the division to the Operations and Plans Division, the most important in the War Department, by requiring communications to theater commanders to be coordinated first with the Operations and Plans Division in order to ensure integration of civil affairs planning with purely military requirements. Equally important, the Civil Affairs Division was the primary coordinating agency for the army in dealing with civilian agencies "exercising functions in any theater in which [the Division] may be engaged."[55] It became the War Department organization that represented War Department interests in postconflict occupation matters at all interagency meetings.

By March 1943 the Civil Affairs Division's structure was essentially in place and most of its personnel provided. As shown in figure 4.3, it was organized by functions, remaining so until the end of the war, when it was reorganized by geographic areas. The division's director reported to the chief of staff and advised the secretary. Its deputy handled special projects, and its executive officer transmitted the director's decisions and coordinated the various branch activities. The branches were military government (changed later simply to "government," in part to sound less forbiddingly martial), civilian relief, economics (later merged into the economics and relief branch), and personnel and training. Whereas actual training of future military government personnel continued to remain with the Military Government Division under the provost marshal, the division's personnel and training branch assumed long-range requirements for training and procurement. Because it was

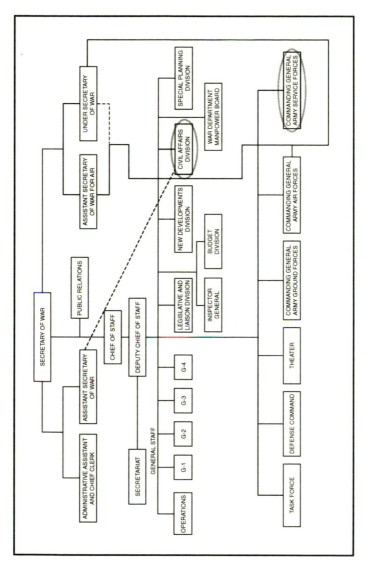

Figure 4.2. War Department hierarchy showing the position of Civil Affairs Division. (Otto L. Nelson Jr., *National Security and the General Staff* [Washington, DC: Infantry Journal Press, 1946], 469 [with the dashed line from the Civil Affairs Division to the assistant secretary of war a modification by the present author].)

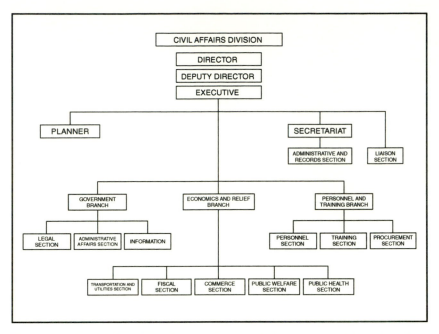

Figure 4.3. Civil Affairs Division organizational chart, approved by order of the secretary of war on December 10, 1943. (Records of the US Joint Chiefs of Staff, box 18, central decimal file, 1942–1945, RG 218, NARA.)

responsible for long-range planning as well, in August 1943 a planner position was created exclusively devoted to charting the division's course for six months and more in advance.[56]

The Civil Affairs Division's functions and duties included formulating policy and preparing plans for civil affairs in occupied territories; coordinating such matters with other agencies; preparing directives, proclamations, and other documents for civil affairs administration in occupied areas; preparing surrender terms; supervising the setting up of machinery for the control of enemy countries; and preparing and supervising training programs.[57] Within the US military structure, it quickly gained preeminence as the organization that planned for occupation responsibilities and represented the army's interests in postwar matters outside the War Department. Inside the army, as its charter stated, it formed a close link with the Operations and Plans Division, which always had a working member on the Civil Affairs Division to ensure that there was integration. It established a connection with the

Army Service Forces because of the Military Government Division's placement within the latter's organization and because the Army Service Forces had War Department responsibility for the handling of all fiscal and economic issues. Indeed, in postwar matters, it even predominated over that other organization. When Eisenhower queried which organization, the Army Service Forces or the Civil Affairs Division, he should look to for fiscal advice on nonmilitary matters, Hilldring successfully argued that because so many such issues were interwoven with civil administration concerns (such as foreign exchange rates, currency control, and taxation), the Civil Affairs Division had to be given direct responsibility to solve those problems.[58]

As a special staff section in the Pentagon, it had no command authority over any civil affairs/military government staff officers assigned to various units, nor did it possess such authority over military government detachments. Nonetheless, the division was in the so-called technical chain of both. It could use its relationship, which was based on the particular expertise required for civil affairs issues, to provide policy guidance and direction to civil affairs/military government staffs (dubbed G-5s) at unit headquarters and civil affairs/military government detachments in the field. Hilldring frequently corresponded with military government officials directly on a number of issues, providing information and policy guidance. Regarding the planning military government in Germany, for example, Hilldring's advice and counsel was sought by the G-5 of the Supreme Headquarters, Allied Expeditionary Force (SHAEF), Brig. Gen. Frank McSherry, on a number of key issues, from the details regarding the activation and administration of the US component of the Allied Control Council (the organization that would jointly preside over Germany's occupation) to ensuring that SHAEF public announcements on military government to the German populace were aligned with larger policy interests.[59]

As another example, the correspondence Hilldring conducted with Brig. Gen. Lester Flory, who would play a key role in the Austrian occupation as the US commander in Vienna, further revealed the depth and breadth of his involvement as the army's technical supervisor in civil affairs matters. In a February 1945 letter, Hilldring had provided his views about the possibility of the future Allied Control Council administering joint government throughout all of Austria. Apparently disagreeing with Flory, Hilldring stressed that zonal commanders should at least initially retain their full authority, noting further that it would be inappropriate for the European Advisory Commission, an international Allied body, to attempt to alter "the conventional channels of command by an intergovernmental agreement." To do so meant changing the fundamental command structure of military government at the outset of the occupation.[60] In that same letter, Hilldring also responded to a previously asked administrative question, and his response revealed the boundaries of control that the army's military government bureaucratic structure placed on occupation matters. Previously asked by Flory whom a military government financial specialist should look to for guidance, Hilldring was clear: the specialist was not to look either to the "U.S. Treasury or to any other civilian agency of our government for approval of a directive on financial policy." Instead the information should flow through military command channels. During the period of wartime operations in Austria, it would flow up to the Supreme Allied Commander, Mediterranean, to the Combined Chiefs of Staff, and during the occupation period, it should go from the Commanding General, European Theater of Operations of the US Army, to the Joint Chiefs.[61] In a subsequent March 1945 letter, Flory thanked Hilldring for sending to him the latest working drafts on Austrian occupation matters. Doing so enabled him and his staff to keep abreast of the latest thinking at the highest levels of policymaking.[62]

In joint army-navy relations, the Civil Affairs Division was likewise successful in establishing itself as the military's primary organization for handling civil affairs concerns. In April 1943, the Joint Chiefs concurred on three fundamental points: (1) civil affairs were the "responsibility for the Theater Commander in his role as Military Governor until he was relieved of his responsibilities by the Commander-in-Chief"; (2) just as that commander was the commander in chief's representative in the field, the War Department was the commander in chief's executive representative in Washington; and (3) the Civil Affairs Division was the appropriate War Department agency to "plan and coordinate the handling of civil affairs in nearly all of the occupied territories."[63] Wherever the navy had interest in civil administration (such as the occupation of certain islands in the Pacific), the navy was represented on the Civil Affairs Division as well.[64]

The Civil Affairs Division and the Interagency and Inter-Allied Process

With McCloy providing nearly cabinet-level stature that the army needed, the Civil Affairs Division also expanded its influence beyond the military departments and established itself as a predominant force in the interagency process. By April 1943, division members were regularly meeting with State, Treasury, and the numerous other FDR-created agencies. The division prepared plans and policy statements, often at a theater commander's request, and then coordinated these plans with the appropriate agencies. After getting general agreement, the division then forwarded these plans to the appropriate commander, who used them to formulate his own detailed military government plans.[65] It also began to assert a steadily growing control over civil administration in North Africa. Division officials provided guidance to civilians in the Board of Economic Warfare, the Office of Foreign Relief and Rehabilitation Operations, and the other agencies. Later in May, McCloy told Hilldring to start working on Italian armistice conditions, suggesting that he obtain information from the School of Military Government and noting that the school had previously worked on the armistice as a school practical problem.[66]

The Civil Affairs Division also directed the Military Government Division to serve as the War Department's gatekeeper for information requests related to nonmilitary concerns in countries that might possibly be occupied.[67] The civilian Office of Strategic Services, after being requested for information in June, attempted to take over the researching of such information entirely and thereby to supplant the other civilian agencies. Instead, at the behest of Civil Affairs Division senior leadership, an editorial committee was created that contained the various organizations, including the Military Government Division, the Office of Strategic Services, and civilian agencies. The chairman of the committee was a Civil Affairs Division official, and, under the division's direction, the committee became responsible for the preparation of civil affairs handbooks as well as other studies. By the end of 1943, the State Department itself had membership in this committee, essentially confirming the division's oversight role for the production of information for potentially occupied areas.[68]

The Civil Affairs Division further played an important intergovernmental role on the State-War-Navy Coordinating Committee. This committee was largely the result of efforts by Secretary of War Stimson and Assistant Secretary McCloy, and as its name indicated, it consisted of representatives of the State, War, and Navy Departments, with War Department Civil Affairs Division personnel serving in important subcommittees. Its chairmanship, at least in its early phase, has historically been identified with McCloy, with Hilldring serving as his military adviser—a designation that, while inaccurate, nevertheless correctly reveals McCloy's dominating role.[69] The committee became deeply involved in the most important aspects of postwar governance policy and was especially influential in establishing occupation policy for Japan and Korea. Considered a forerunner to the National Security Council, its purpose was to "coordinat[e] the views of the three departments in matters of inter-departmental interest."[70]

Due to its limited membership, it excluded all other cabinet departments as well as all other agencies and committees set up during the Roosevelt presidency that War Department officials such as Stimson had found so problematic and annoying in the past. This exclusion created intense interagency conflict between those in the committee and those left out. In April 1945, pressure, particularly from the Treasury Department, forced the creation of the Informal Policy Committee on Germany, which for a brief period worked with the State-War-Navy Coordinating Committee on postwar German matters, though not with any measure of success: the Informal Policy Committee folded by the end of August of the same year.[71]

Agency conflict resurfaced in June 1946 when the Department of Commerce asserted that any notion of equality between State and War and other agencies on the committee was a sham and that the State Department did not guide postwar policy regarding Germany, apparently having ceded all its authority to the military. What therefore was needed, according to Commerce officials, was an independent agency in which Commerce, as well as Justice, Agriculture, and other departments and agencies, would be represented. While the idea was rejected, there was much truth in Commerce officials' allegations that, at least in the first year of the postwar occupations, the committee was militarily dominated and militarily focused.[72] Called a "ratification of the

War Department's de facto supremacy in foreign affairs," the committee's recommendations on matters connected to military operations—essentially *all* significant matters discussed—were required to go the Joint Chiefs for approval.[73] The framework for determining policy matters in committees oriented around military interests. When a question was "primarily military in character" and policies were prepared by "non-military persons of the Government" (e.g., the State Department), military policies would govern. If there was a question that was political, it would govern, unless the policy itself would "serve to defeat a military objective."[74]

Ultimately the Civil Affairs Division moved beyond the interagency sphere and into the Allied coalition and represented War Department interests in the combined US-UK domain. The Combined Chiefs of Staff had already been set up in January 1942, consisting of the British and American Joint Chiefs. Strategic imperatives had compelled the two nations to form multiple combined boards under the military chiefs of the two nations. For civil affairs matters, the initial proposal in late 1943 was to continue to use the Committee on Combined Boards as the organization, but the American Joint Chiefs completely rejected the idea: that committee, as Marshall had pointed out, was a derivative organization without formal standing. Furthermore, while its secretariat was linked with the Combined Chiefs, its membership was predominantly civilian, and the organization needed to be a military one.[75] This seemed unnecessary to the British, far more used to combined military and civilian efforts that conducted integrated strategic thinking, a necessity that came with presiding over a worldwide empire. But the Americans counterproposed with the Combined Civil Affairs Committee. Its function was to recommend to the Combined Chiefs general policies for occupied areas and areas to be occupied and to be responsible for civil affairs planning. Most important, its charter asserted ultimate military control over the entirety of the process: "The decision as to when and to what extent civilian departments and agencies will assist the military in the administration of civil affairs will be determined by the [Combined Chiefs of Staff], upon the recommendation of the military commander in the area. Generally, responsibility for the handling of civil affairs should be relinquished by the military as quickly as this can be accomplished without interference with the military purposes of the operation."[76] This clearly reflected the American view, and specifically the American army's view, of postwar occupation responsibilities.

The establishment of the Combined Civil Affairs Committee was not met without British resistance. The UK chiefs recognized that there was a need for better coordination, given the problems in North Africa for the past several months, but they were reluctant to defer to the Combined Committee, no doubt fearing that this meant further loss of control by London. Other UK-based organizations, in particular, the Administration of Territories (Europe), which presumably had responsibility for advanced occupation planning in Europe, would undoubtedly lose influence in determining postwar occupation policy.[77] The American response, however, had an irresistible logic, even over British objections. Because the Combined Chiefs existed, it needed a similar combined committee on a matter as important (and, so far, mishandled) as civil affairs for occupied areas. Furthermore, as McCloy effectively argued, it needed to be colocated with the Combined Chiefs of Staff in Washington.[78] It was also, as McCloy noted, politically necessary. McCloy asserted that Anglophobia was prevalent in the United States and Americans needed to be shown that the war was not simply a "European" one among the nations of empire that had postwar colonialist ambitions.[79]

The Combined Civil Affairs Committee was ultimately established in Washington, with McCloy indeed serving as its chairman. The Americans on the Combined Committee wanted the military and civilian domains separated as much as possible, openly asserting the apparent difference between American and British viewpoints. Marshall at a Joint Chiefs of Staff meeting in the spring of 1943 commented that in the Middle East, the British had a committee "dominated by civilians which, to a large extent, exercise control over the military concerning their relations with the civil population."[80] Stimson at the same meeting noted that the British believed that "almost immediately after an occupation takes place, the foreign office will be called upon to take action." Stimson was actually incorrect: the British government had decided that the War Office would have primary responsibility for at least the initial postcombat phase of the occupation period. Furthermore, the Colonial Office, the long-established

civilian agency that typically dealt with governance of overseas territories, and not the Foreign Office, which had much more in common
with the US Department of State, would act in an advisory capacity during the first phase.[81] Despite this error, Stimson's point did
highlight a fundamental difference between the American and British strategic cultures: the British had agencies, systems, and processes
in the civilian sphere long accustomed to overseas governance, which
the British War Office could rely and build upon. No comparable
organizations existed in the US government: postwar governance had
been developed, trained, and organized for almost entirely within the
US Army.

As the Combined Civil Affairs Committee proceeded, the American position—to large degree a manifestation of *FM 27-5* doctrine—
became evident. The Americans sought a unified military government
largely free of civilian interference and control. Their major concern
was to ensure that military requirements were met in order to achieve
overwhelming victory. Regarding the future occupations of Sicily and
Italy, Stimson remarked that "we want to have purely military and
non-political government so long as we have any connection with it."[82]
He also noted a difference between the United States and United Kingdom over Italian surrender terms: whereas the US position was "unconditional surrender," Stimson was concerned that the United Kingdom
might go "on a different line and . . . recognize some Italian government as the authorized one, instead of imposing a military government
of the conqueror on it."[83]

Throughout the remainder of the war, the Civil Affairs Division's
interagency and inter-Allied influence in the Combined Civil Affairs
Committee and elsewhere continued to grow. As serious planning for
the invasion of northwestern Europe commenced in 1944, the division
drew up the basic policy guidance for all postwar operations in Belgium, the Netherlands, Luxembourg, and Norway.[84] It then drafted
the guidance and submitted it via the Combined Civil Affairs Committee to the Combined Chiefs for review and ultimate approval. The
division also played a crucial role in the extremely complex and difficult
determinations of policy for liberated France.[85] And as further proof
of the army's dominance in civil affairs matters, in the interim period
between final approval of the negotiated agreement and what would be

called the de facto French authority, Eisenhower relied upon the field civil affairs handbook that had been issued shortly after D-Day, which made him, absent further guidance, the interim supreme authority in France.[86]

The division also profoundly influenced the formation of, and the subsequent actions taken by, the European Advisory Commission, which was established in January 1944 in London, and with representatives from the United Kingdom, the United States, the Soviet Union, and eventually the French provisional government. Its American representative was John Winant, the US ambassador to Great Britain. According to Winant, the British government insisted that the commission deal with larger political questions, and as Lucius Clay recounted, the British already had zonal boundaries for Germany created before the commission actually met.[87] The US position (shared by the Soviets) was that the commission should have a much narrower focus, dealing nearly exclusively with the surrender and related issues of Germany and Austria.

US military officials also wanted to limit the European Advisory Commission's encroachment into what was considered exclusive military domains.[88] The War Department agreed to the commission's establishment, and agreed to send military representatives, largely from the Civil Affairs Division, but only on the condition that the body "keep strictly within the letter and spirit of its directive and in so doing be particular to avoid problems relating to the conduct of military operations, and concerning civil affairs of liberated or enemy territories incident to such operations prior to the end of hostilities."[89] The representatives sent from the War Department included, as Winant's military adviser, Brig. Gen. Cornelius Wickersham, who had served as commandant of the Military Government School, and members of the Civil Affairs Division, who would serve as the US military's representatives on the Working Security Committee of the European Advisory Commission. Many of the Civil Affairs Division representatives were actually lawyers in uniform who were used to adversarial roles in negotiation. As Philip Mosely, one of Winant's political advisers noted, they "seemed to regard the jurisdiction and prestige of the military service as they might regard the interests of a client."[90]

In an attempt to get out from under US dominance, the British wanted the commission to have wide-ranging jurisdiction over postwar occupation matters. The US view, as represented by McCloy and Civil Affairs Division officials, was to restrict it to the absolute terms as set forth in its commission—which amounted to surrender terms and a limited number of occupation control functions. The American Joint Chiefs in particular did not want the commission to leverage civilian control over civil administration during the immediate postconflict period.[91] Instead, Civil Affairs Division officials insisted that the Combined Civil Affairs Committee be the means to resolve occupation questions, going so far as to refuse to provide to the commission a military adviser until the British relented. The British did, and the Combined Civil Affairs Committee retained the authority.[92]

The European Advisory Commission's work on such matters as zonal boundaries and surrender terms was by no means insignificant. But it was nearly powerless as an autonomous entity. Winant, after first going through the Working Security Committee, which included Civil Affairs Division representatives, then had to send any commission recommendations to Washington for approval.[93] The War Department's approval, along with that of the Joint Chiefs of Staff, was of even greater importance than State's in Washington, and Winant had to confer directly with McCloy, who was essential in getting final clearance on proposed commission directives.[94] The commission's limitations were likewise revealed in February 1945, when Wickersham corresponded with Eisenhower's G-5, General McSherry, on the need for Eisenhower's coalition command, SHAEF, to provide detailed directives regarding the occupation of Germany in order to begin planning. Wickersham commented that although the commission had prepared thirty-six directives, only sixteen had actually been approved by the Joint Chiefs, and even these approved directives were being carefully scrutinized to ensure their conformity with another Joint Chiefs document, the so-called Joint Chiefs of Staff Directive 1067 (JCS 1067), which would serve as the army's primary directive for the first years of Germany's occupation. Only after such directives were approved by the Joint Chiefs could Wickersham forward them to Eisenhower's command in Europe.[95]

The European Advisory Commission's autonomy was further frustrated by its Working Security Committee's own authority and composition. That committee lacked a formal charter, and it also lacked any mechanism for unifying the disparate viewpoints of the agencies involved. As a result, any member of the subcommittee had essentially veto power, a power that Civil Affairs Division representatives used to its fullest.[96] In his memoirs, Kennan, who served as Winant's political adviser, was particularly scathing when recounting the Civil Affairs Division's intransigence, noting that the "main source of the trouble was, quite clearly, the Civil Affairs Division of the War Department, which refused initially even to take part in any interdepartmental discussion looking to the instruction of the American representative on the EAC, and which later, having grudgingly consented to take part, did so in a manner so lacking in both candor and enthusiasm as to give the impression of sabotage."[97]

The Civil Affairs Division representatives essentially dominated the US position at the committee by establishing that virtually *all* the questions on the table, especially regarding the postwar occupation of Germany, were military matters and therefore largely beyond the province of the committee to decide.[98] Much of the thinking about zonal boundaries and authorities had already been developed at military operational levels among the Combined Chiefs of Staff, which was planning the invasion of northwestern Europe. To the Civil Affairs Division on the European Advisory Commission, therefore, any further discussions usurped military primacy.[99] On nearly all major issues, the US military's position either prevailed or was only modified after intense labor and very often after much contention. Civil Affairs Division representatives did vigorously push, at one point, for having the American zone switched to the northwestern part of Germany, which was contrary to the Combined Chiefs' design. This was done because of Roosevelt's initial insistence on having the American zone in the north, in part to ensure American access to Baltic ports and also because of fear of potential collapse of the postwar French government and subsequent revolution in that country, leaving American forces in southern Germany exposed. But Secretary of War Stimson, Assistant Secretary of War McCloy, and Secretary of State Edward Stettinius all agreed that FDR's rationales did not merit making the change, and the president ultimately acquiesced to the originally set zonal boundaries.[100]

War Department Primacy

As the above reveals, the formation of the Civil Affairs Division was central to the continuously expanding authority and ultimate predominance of the army, not only in US government interagency but also in inter-Allied postconflict occupation planning. Near the end of 1943, FDR himself finally relented and granted the army greater authority. In his memoirs, Stimson noted two actions by FDR in November 1943. He pointed out that on November 10, FDR wrote a letter that declared that the War Department "must assume the responsibility for civilian relief in all liberated areas during the first six months after their liberation." Clearly then, the army had won the immediate postconflict job. Second, and nearly as important, he asserted "that all arrangements for civil administration and dealings with the French people must initially be purely military." Given that France was the most important nation that the Anglo-American forces would liberate, this was a clear signal of "how far the President had moved."[101] In his diary, Stimson recollected that in a meeting with McCloy, Hilldring, Clay, and others he said that "this directive of the President was a final recognition of the proper function of the army in those matters and that it was up to us to go ahead and carry it out."[102]

Why did FDR finally, and seemingly begrudgingly, defer to military advice regarding postwar occupation primacy? Part of the reason for his delay in doing so was probably because of his distrust of military government, as well as his concern that imposition of military rule, especially on "liberated" territories, would look decidedly suspicious if not hypocritical from a nation that espoused the Four Freedoms, democracy, and anticolonialism. Throughout 1943 it seemed that more than once Roosevelt sought a way to reconcile a postwar occupation policy that could meet military requirements yet yield to civilian prerogatives. But those efforts failed, largely because of two institutional reasons. First, it failed because of an organizational system, perhaps due to FDR's management style, that sent one civilian agency after another into North Africa without clear lines of jurisdiction between them. Second, and correspondingly, it failed because the army had developed an effective organizational system that represented its interests and that ultimately successfully promoted its interests in interagency and inter-

Allied forums. In the interagency scramble, the army's organizational advantages proved decisive. The Civil Affairs Division was to be the army's and the Joint Chiefs' executive agency for civil affairs. McCloy, who oversaw the division's direction, in turn became the chairman of the Combined Committee on Civil Affairs and played a crucial role in the State-War-Navy Coordinating Committee. The division also helped to limit the power of the European Advisory Commission. In the Civil Affairs Division, the army found a powerful internal body to represent its views on postwar occupation matters, views that, expressed through the division, were relatively clear, consistent, and unified.

This unity of vision came at a strategic price. The relentless focus on military objectives at the expense of longer political goals and the militarized form of government that army doctrine espoused meant that occupation planning was, by its very nature, limited, backward focused, and often unhelpful to the military governors who would be responsible for executing postwar governance. Over and over, whether in Germany, Austria, or Korea, the military leaders in charge would complain that much of what they had to do had to be improvised. They had little guidance beyond what were the basic strictures of a military-style governance, a governance, that, in the end, was meant to be temporary and focused on sustaining military victory. The stage was therefore set for a complex series of events to unfold in the occupied territories, especially in Germany, Austria, and Korea, in the first postwar years before the geopolitical imperatives of the Cold War emerged with greater clarity. Paradoxically, in the first years of occupation, the short-term militarized focus of the occupations led to outcomes in those nations that were profound and long-lasting.

5

Planning and Implementing Military Government in Germany, 1943–1946

The origin of the Cold War is often presented as a series of grand strategic moves in the form of policy decisions followed by actions that revealed either subtle or dramatic shifts in superpower behavior. There is utility in such a presentation as historical shorthand for highly complex events. However, if not recognized as only partially explanatory, such presentations are historical examples of the intentional fallacy of attributing events solely or predominantly to high policy. The postwar American occupation of Germany, in contrast, points out how often significant actions were driven from mid or lower military levels.

Germany was crucial to both superpowers, and its integration into an international order favorable to either the United States or the Soviet Union was of vital strategic importance.[1] Yet US efforts, especially during the first critical year of the American occupation, were largely formulated by military planners and were driven by military objectives, not long-range policy. These efforts were directed and implemented by military leaders, particularly by Lt. Gen. (later Gen.) Lucius D. Clay. Most revealing were the interactions by Clay and other US Army leaders with Soviet leaders and the Communist Party in Germany, the quick reempowerment of German officials in the US zones, and the less than vigorous enforcement of denazification. All were examples of military imperatives shaping larger policy outcomes, sometimes in conflict with the strategic thinking of high-ranking American civilian officials.

Initial Strategic Considerations

The European Advisory Commission completed the Tripartite Agreement on Control Machinery in Germany in November 1944. The Yalta Conference in February of the following year subsequently established three zones of occupation for the Americans, British, and Soviets (the French gaining one later), with the Allied nations pledging themselves to general goals of denazification, reparations, and the control of German industry. After the war ended, the victorious powers determined at the Potsdam Conference of July–August 1945 that Germany would fall under an Allied Control Council that would determine joint occupation policy, that Germany would be disarmed and denazified, and that the German political structure to some extent would be decentralized.[2] But these too were general principles only. The details were to be worked out by the occupiers in their own respective zones.

Within the larger geopolitical context of the Yalta and Potsdam Conferences' decisions, America's long-range postwar goals for Germany were vague. While FDR wanted to make sure Germany was permanently defeated and never again a threat, he apparently did not want a long-standing American military presence in Europe. Anything beyond that was unclear—how long he wanted forces there or the nature and size of their presence. The president wrote in early 1944 that he did not want the United States to have the "post-war burden" of reconstituting many of the liberated nations. For Roosevelt, the "principal object" was to "take part in eliminating Germany as a possible and even probable cause of a third World War."[3] Within the State Department, there was likewise uncertainty. There was some indication that State officials recognized only the army could administer the occupation, even though the State Department wanted ultimate policy control.[4] But officials in the State Department shared Roosevelt's hesitation and also indicated a reluctance to take, in the words of the Central European Division's James W. Riddleberger, a "long-range view." According to Riddleberger, longer-range planning was virtually impossible until the Allies had "entered a considerable portion of Germany and kn[e]w the conditions . . . existent there."[5] FDR's and State's uncertainty notwithstanding, there were those within the US government who felt that the only way to defeat Germany permanently was to reorient its society radically. The most famous was Henry Morgenthau, who advocated a thorough social and political reorganization of German life, to include deindustrialization, and who asserted that the path to peace led through farm and pasture.[6] The War Department held a much more moderate position, aligned with the doctrine promulgated in *FM 27-5* and the army's own history. For War Department planners, reform should occur in a tempered and gradual way, German officials should be restored to power as soon as possible, and the army as a whole should not engage in major societal reorganizing.

Yet even had there been more definitive policy planning, it would have been predicated upon assumptions and understandings throughout the US government about both German and Soviet behavior that were either confused or downright mistaken. Up until mid-1944, it was assumed by many US strategists, based upon apparently credible intelligence, that there would be a sudden, overwhelming internal collapse of Germany similar to what occurred in 1918, which would allow for a shift of resources and personnel to the Pacific theater in order to invade Japan in 1946. It was further assumed that the structure of German government would remain relatively intact at the national through local levels, again similar to what occurred at the end of World War I. An occupation would thereby facilitate a return to power by appropriate German civil authorities with relative ease.[7]

Such assumptions, while perhaps understandable, were flawed and had to be revised as the war dragged on into the late fall of 1944 and the winter of 1945. Support for the Third Reich within Germany did erode badly, and the populace was filled with a sense of imminent doom. But sudden collapse did not occur, not necessarily because of a population held in thrall by Nazi ideology but because of ruthless repression of doubters and dissenters and because of (often accurate) stories told to the people about the atrocities of the Soviet armies in the east. Nazism, far from unifying the German Reich, had atomized it and had therefore prevented any full-fledged national sense of defiance.[8] German forces resisted bitterly, in a chaotic, disconnected way, even after the fall of Berlin and combatted the Allies with a ferocity that was as stunning as it was pointless. The disintegration of the Reich as a result broke down the overall governmental system. Hitler may have had his Götterdämmerung in his Berlin bunker, but the Reich ended in an ignominious whimper outside the small northern German town of Flensburg, with its leadership vainly seeking cease-fire terms but with no country to govern at all.[9]

Furthermore, there was an assumption, more widely held by US military leaders than by civilian policymakers, that the relationship with the Soviet Union would not deteriorate to the point of hostility that would result in the four-and-half-decade Cold War. Outside the military, there was far greater skepticism about the Soviet Union's intentions, notably from the State Department, especially men such as Averell Harriman, the ambassador to Moscow, and George Kennan, author of the famous containment formulation. And in retrospect, the assumption of post-war amity appears to have been an example of confusing a temporary wartime alliance with a longer-term peacetime one, when there was no longer a threat of a mutual enemy. The assumption was consistently held nonetheless, especially within military circles. For instance, the SHAEF Civil Affairs Division prepared a paper titled "Comments on Political Guides for Areas of Probable Occupation" in January 1944. It specifically noted that all relevant political guides assumed that military government in the American, British, and Soviet zones would be "tripartite from the time of entry"—that is, there would not be exclusion but cooperation among the Allies in all the zones and not the West/East dichotomy that would ultimately develop.[10]

Such incorrect assumptions helped to contribute to a decided clash of perceptions about Germany and the Soviet Union between high-ranking American civilian officials and on-the-ground American military leaders and to differing opinions about occupation issues. Despite the view of key US civilian officials that the Soviet Union was a threat that had to be contained, US-Soviet relations in the occupied zone were relatively friendly during much of the occupation's first year. And despite the reticence and even resistance by American civilian leaders, German officials were returned to power relatively quickly in the American zone, and US-led denazification efforts ended fairly soon.

US Military Planning

US Army occupation planning unsurprisingly focused on military, not political, objectives. There has been some dispute among historians whether leaders such as Eisenhower were so purely militarily focused.[11] Yet the argument that Eisenhower was more politically oriented and sought to achieve longer-ranging political goals in military operations is belied by his own assertions in his wartime memoirs. In *Crusade in Europe,* he noted that while politics and military activities were "never completely separable," he nonetheless stated that "military plans . . . should be devised with the single aim of speeding victory." On the decision not to capture Berlin, he declared, "It was politically and psychologically important as the symbol of remaining German power. . . . I decided, however, that it was not the most desirable objective for the forces of the Western allies."[12] While one might conclude this was postwar circumspection on Eisenhower's part, it was consistent with his wartime actions and statements. Eisenhower's wartime diaries were almost totally devoid of political discussions, except for brief references to the Free French government and even then in relation to ensuring the French Resistance supported his military goals.[13] In reviewing his wartime correspondence, it is evident that he was by no means blind to intricate political issues. A June 1943 letter to his brother Milton about the complex civil-military dilemma during the campaign in Tunisia, a neutral nation with fascist leanings, makes this clear.[14] But as Stephen Ambrose points out, while on occasion Eisenhower did subordinate military requirements to politics, he typically made his decisions "solely on military grounds as he saw them." His task was to defeat the Wehrmacht forces arrayed against him as soon as possible.[15] Such military primacy was likewise made clear in wartime correspondence between Marshall and him. Writing to Eisenhower near the end of the European campaign, Marshall requested Eisenhower's comments on a British proposal to capture Prague by combined US-UK forces, noting the British Chiefs of Staff thought there would be "remarkable political advantages" in doing so. Eisenhower responded: "I shall *not* attempt any move I deem militarily unwise merely to gain a political prize unless I receive specific orders from the Combined Chiefs of Staff."[16]

Eisenhower's wartime view carried over into the occupation itself. As the military governor (primarily in name, with the day-to-day functions being performed by Lucius Clay) during the first months of the occupation, he believed that American military government in Germany was to perform military functions and not to immerse itself deeply into political matters. In a letter to President Truman in October 1945, Eisenhower noted that civil government was "entirely separate" from the army's occupational duties and those duties would continue no longer than absolutely necessary. Clearly, duties lay elsewhere: "The true function of the Army in this region is to provide for the United States that reserve of force and power that can insure within our zone the prompt enforcement of all law and regulations prescribed."[17] In other words, the army needed as quickly as possible to turn over purely political responsibilities to authorities capable of administering them and at the same time retain military forces to perform occupational duties that were much more within the scope of traditional military functions—the establishment or, as necessary, the reestablishment of order and discipline.

Such apoliticism was not confined to Eisenhower. It was, as Ambrose points out, a "deeply ingrained principle" in him and the army officers of his generation.[18] US military planning for the initial stages of the occupation was correspondingly apolitical and almost entirely done within military channels. Beginning in early 1943, army planners at the Civil Affairs Division and at what later became the Supreme Headquarters Allied Expeditionary Force (SHAEF) began to formulate a series of plans for the eventual occupation of Germany. Ostensibly the State Department still had general supervision over postwar policy, allowing the army only to administer postwar occupation duties. But neither the State Department nor any other nonmilitary organization had the size, ability, or authority to direct the course of the occupations toward nonmilitary goals. Commenting upon a proposed policy of the US and UK governments to replace civilian agencies with military personnel during the Germany's occupation, SHAEF civil affairs planners noted in early 1944 that "no such agency is available at present, or likely to be so for some time after operations begin."[19] In contrast, the army had, in establishing the Civil Affairs Division and subsequently asserting the division's authority in various agencies, committees, and commissions, ensured that the army's viewpoints were expressed and, more often than not, complied with by civilian organizations. The army also had access to, and had an ability to gather, huge troves of information on potentially occupied territories. Finally, it also had an ability to integrate with ongoing military operations and to transition seamlessly to postconflict occupation responsibilities in a presumably coherent and ordered way.

Accordingly, the first occupation plan so devised, named Operation Rankin, was conceived entirely as a military operation. Premised on a World War I–type collapse of the Third Reich, it called for the speedy occupation of a barrier zone along Germany's western frontier and for the quick stationing of forces in key strategic locations in order to secure control over the country and to disarm the Wehrmacht. It was an occupation plan in the most literal sense: the Allied forces would control spaces and critical access ways, particularly routes that led back into Germany, with the expectation that hundreds of thousands of German soldiers stranded in occupied territories would try to return. The location of occupation forces in Germany would be determined by the tactical location of the Allied troops as they entered the physical territory of the Reich. Since the Normandy landings, British troops had been positioned north, American troops south. By military logic, the British and American axes of advances into Germany thus followed this initial scheme of maneuver. While FDR would seek to reverse the occupation zones as the war ended, wanting the Americans to occupy the northwest and the British the south, Rankin's premise held: the zonal occupation in the west was ultimately determined upon the disposition of forces, not political considerations, as the Western Allies entered into the conquered territory.[20] Rankin was, in large part, deliberately planned as a "limited occupation," since beyond the disarmament goal little was known about what to do next. Even though the planners were undoubtedly aware of the enormous political ramifications of the plans they were formulating, they were reminded to avoid delving into policy questions and not to commit the American government to a particular political agenda that had yet to be determined. In the words of an official history of the occupation planning, General Eisenhower's influence was "exerted constantly in the direction of avoiding the political implications." He gave strict instructions throughout the planning process that the occupation should focus on military, and not political, issues.[21]

Rankin would be obsolete by D-Day on June 6, 1944, and was replaced by Talisman, which attempted a more in-depth examination of postwar issues. In the words of one senior military planner: "We cannot wait for policy to be laid down by the United Nations. It is essential that we should prepare now, as a matter of urgency, papers on all these problems."[22] Planners therefore drew up special studies on a range of issues from imposition of sanctions to disarmament and the establishment of martial law. Yet Talisman still envisioned occupation around military ends: it called for disarmament and a lodgment in the Reich to seal off enemy forces. It also focused primarily on the occupation's early stages, with limited interaction between the occupying forces and the German people.[23]

Eclipse was the last and most comprehensive SHAEF occupation plan, promulgated in November 1944. The plan was intended to provide interim guidance to the Allied forces prior to a turnover to the Allied Control Council. It accordingly revealed a more political awareness than its predecessors. In the text of Eclipse was recognition that the overthrow of the Nazi government within Germany was "at present remote." It further acknowledged that there would likely be no unconditional surrender until the enemy had suffered a "further major defeat such as would enable the Allied forces to penetrate deeply into the Reich."[24] Yet despite the more astute political analysis, Eclipse said little about long-range plans for Germany other than that German forces would be disarmed and demobilized, law and order would be established, and Allied forces would be properly distributed throughout the country.[25] Furthermore, Eclipse fundamentally relied upon the army's military government doctrinal model as the approach to execute postwar governance. The plan's objectives in Germany were, first and foremost, "disarmament and control of German forces . . . thereby preventing a renewal of hostilities" as well as the enforcement of relevant surrender terms, establishment of law and order, redistribution of Allied forces into respective occupation zones, and prisoner-of-war evacuation. Assistance could be provided to Allied agencies and indigenous governments of liberated countries as long as such activities did not "interfere with the military object[ives]."[26]

The Eclipse plan was to be accomplished in two phases. During the first phase—"really the consummation of OVERLORD"—Allied forces would seize strategic areas deep within Germany. In the second phase, deployed forces in Germany would establish "firm control . . . [and] carry out the disarmament and disposal of enemy forces . . . and

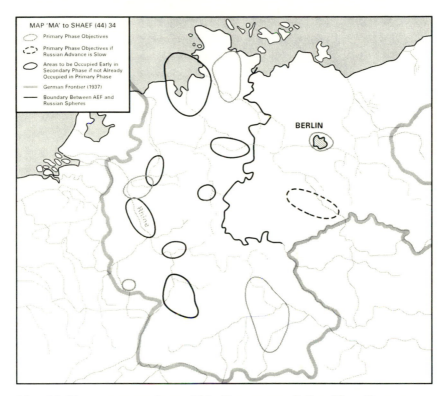

Map 5.1. Troop concentrations within Germany per Eclipse Plan. (Supreme Headquarters, Allied Expeditionary Force, *Operation "ECLIPSE": Appreciation and Outline Plan,* November 10, 1944, map MA to SHAEF [44], 34.)

. . . [adjust] . . . dispositions of national forces to coincide ultimately with the national zones of occupation." As map 5.1 illustrates, Eclipse planned for a set of military objectives first to be captured within the German land mass: such objectives were essential for reasons of security, not governance. The initial premise set forth in Rankin about US and British occupation zones corresponding to troop dispositions still held.[27] There was also a boundary decided upon between the Western Allies and the Soviets, but while that line had been agreed upon by the summer of 1944, it was simply an educated guess at where the respective fighting forces would be when the fighting stopped.[28]

The partitioning of Germany into Western and Soviet zones of occupation was not even considered a political matter. When the

US-UK Combined Chiefs of Staff discussed the zonal distribution, they did so in a way that entirely reflected military objectives. In the so-called Octagon Conference held by the Combined Chiefs in the fall of 1944, the Chiefs stated, "The following subdivision of that part of Germany not allocated to the Soviet Government . . . is acceptable from a military point of view." The acceptable American zone had US forces occupying Germany east of the Rhine, south of Coblenz, with a northern border between Hessen and Nassau, and west of the Soviet allocated zone. It also included the city and port of Bremen and Bremerhaven in the northern part of Germany. This zone was established "for disarmament, policing and preservation of order" as well as for its utility for staging areas, implicitly referencing future combat operations against Japan.[29]

At the broad conceptual level of Rankin, Talisman, and Eclipse, there was little specified notion of the longer-range and more political aspects of occupation. It was hardly surprising, therefore, at the more specific level of implementation, that postwar occupation was formulated in terms of army doctrine, organization, training, and practice on military government. As an example, SHAEF planners fashioned mock directives from higher headquarters as a way to frame their own planning assumptions. One, drafted as if sent from the Combined Chiefs of Staff, stated that the occupation would be firmly under military control: "Except by the express direction of the Combined Chiefs of Staff, there will be no Political Agency or Political Representative of either the United States or British government taking part in the Administration." That mock directive further noted that the occupation would have an initial military phase, during which Eisenhower, as presumed military governor, would have full authority to take all administrative or other measures necessary for the conduct of operations. But the end point of that phase was not clearly stated. Only when the military situation allowed would civilian authority enter the scene. And such authority would assume control as the military governor decided. He would likewise decide when civil relief agencies such as the United Nations Relief and Rehabilitation Administration and the Red Cross would be permitted to function, and in all instances all actions would conform to the requirements of military necessity.[30]

The planners also worked to ensure a close linkage between tactical forces and military government and civil affairs units. They determined that it would be necessary from the outset to integrate closely the civil affairs units with the tactical chains of command during operations and movements toward and into Germany and that, at least in the initial phases of the occupation, there would be a tactically oriented form of military government. SHAEF planners would also prepare at their levels policy directives that lower-level echelon G-5s would provide to the military government and civil affairs units. Furthermore, the SHAEF planners established a school in Great Britain at Shrivenham, in large part to ensure a better integration of civil affairs personnel with combat units.[31]

Additionally, SHAEF planners developed a so-called Standard Policy and Procedure (SPP) that contained underlying principles to inform civil affairs planning. As draft notes reveal, the planners explicitly drew upon *FM 27-5* in order to ensure that any principles that they adopted were in general alignment with the doctrinal principles in the army manual. The SPP noted that *FM 27-5* provided for two basic types of military government organization—tactical and territorial. The SPP also affirmed that initially the tactical model would be adopted, though it also noted that it would be necessary to provide a territorial type of organization for an orderly transition to Allied Control Council authority at a future point. It also discussed a variety of issues, such as the handling of displaced persons, occupational military police, and the disposal of government records and archives, referring throughout to *FM 27-5*'s guidance in dealing with such matters.[32] In further drafts and comments, it was clear that the planners understood the need to comply with international law requirements. At the same time, the absolute primacy of military authority was continually stressed, as was the focus of the occupation on purely military objectives. Brig. Gen. Frank McSherry, who was the SHAEF G-5, commented upon the proposed SPPs, and stated that under international law a supreme commander was responsible for the maintenance of law and order, the well-being of the civilian population, and the restoration of conditions to normal, insofar as the military situation permits. He also noted that "military necessity is the first question to be considered; it is still the duty of the Commander under International Law to govern the country which he has occupied as well as possible subject to

military exigencies."[33] Comments about the SPP did note the requirement for aligning military objectives with longer-range political goals.
One draft titled "Allied Military Government in Occupied Territory"
pointed out that an objective of military government was "to promote
political objectives of the Allied government" as well as "military objectives of their combat forces." But even within that particular draft, ultimately the "objectives of a military government [were] primarily to aid
in the successful prosecution of the war."[34]

The Handbook Controversy, the Morgenthau Plan, and JCS 1067

Throughout 1944, civil affairs planners in the SHAEF German country unit worked on a guide for military government in Germany that
would provide concrete guidance for the occupiers. At the end of that
year the SHAEF planners produced the *Handbook for Military Government in Germany*.[35] Promulgated in December 1944 by order of Eisenhower, though available in draft beforehand, it relied on past thinking
about occupation. It only referenced *FM 27-5* once and even then to
point out that if any provision in that manual conflicted with the handbook, the latter would control. Nonetheless, the document elaborated
upon *FM 27-5*'s doctrinal principles without significantly departing
from them. Conditions of military necessity were "in every instance
overriding." The supreme commander would possess full legislative,
executive, and judicial authority. The conduct of military government
would at least initially be conducted based upon the tactical disposition of units, using military government detachments and G-5 special
staff personnel—the organizational structures that had been developed
by the Military Government Division during the early years of the war.
Furthermore, military government would align itself with the German regional governmental system and would eventually, after fighting was over, conform to German administrative borders. The method
of control would be by "indirect rule," with military government units
"controlling the German administrative system . . . not operating it
themselves." Specifically the German civil service apparatus, as it had
been in World War I, would be employed where possible.[36]

The one major departure from the standard "hands-off" approach in military government doctrine (though not that far off from *FM 27-5*'s 1943 version) dealt with denazification. The handbook was clear: the Nazi Party was to be destroyed and Nazis purged from the police and government and positions of influence. Yet there was still leeway given: an exception was provided, somewhat vaguely, that if the "administrative machinery of certain dismissed organizations" was required to fulfill necessary functions, such as relief, health, or sanitation, then that "machinery" could be retained. The vagaries of the provision, if read in light of the affirmation of the absolute power of the supreme commander, thus seemed to tip the balance toward allowing more flexibility in denazification, though the absolutist denazification language could also be used to argue against such a view.[37]

President Roosevelt read a draft of the handbook after Secretary of Treasury Henry Morgenthau, a strong proponent of severe terms for German surrender, returned from Europe with a copy. Apparently, even given FDR's deference to military matters, it was not punitive enough for him. Writing to Secretary Stimson in August 1944, Roosevelt complained about the handbook, calling it "pretty bad." He demanded to know who wrote it and how it came into being, noting that it gave him the impression that Germany was to be treated no differently than liberated countries such as the Netherlands or Belgium. FDR in particular noted comments in it such as "Your main and immediate task, to accomplish your mission, is to get things running, to pick up the pieces, to restore as quickly as possible the official functioning of the German civil government in the area for which [you] are are responsible. . . . The first concern of military government will be to see that the machine works and works efficiently." Elsewhere the handbook stated that "all existing German regulations and ordinances relating to . . . production, supply or distribution will remain in force until specifically amended or abrogated." FDR further commented to Stimson that he saw the handbook as too gentle and friendly, with too much of a "helping hand" approach: "I see no reason for starting a WPA [Works Progress Administration], PWA [Public Works Administration], or a CCC [Civilian Conservation Corps] for Germany when we go in with our Army of Occupation," a reference to the various New Deal agencies Roosevelt had created during the Depression.[38] In reality, such a massive social welfare effort was *not* what the US Army contemplated. What the handbook pointed to was restoring Germans to power quickly, in accordance with military government doctrine and organizational practice, with as little interference and oversight from the army as could be allowed.

The handbook caused great protest within FDR's cabinet. Even prior to its publication, a cabinet committee consisting of the secretaries of state, treasury, and war had proposed to the president a far more severe approach than the "mild" occupation envisioned by SHAEF. The committee's proposal included Germany's demilitarization and the total political destruction of Nazism. It also, most controversially, called for keeping the standard of living of the German population at subsistence levels and for reconverting the "German economic capacity in such manner that it will be so dependent on imports and exports that Germany cannot by its own devices reconvert to war production."[39] Secretary of Treasury Henry Morgenthau went even further. In the so-called Morgenthau Plan, he called for keeping Germany at subsistence levels as well as in a state of nearly permanent deindustrialization and pastoralization.[40] Morgenthau explained his proposal in some detail in his book *Germany Is Our Problem*. He stressed that the occupation of Germany by Allied troops, and especially by Americans, would take years: "Germany's road to peace leads to the farm. . . . If the German people are to make the best use of their soil, they are going to have to substitute the work of human hands for machinery for years to come."[41] Yet paradoxically, and perhaps astutely, Morgenthau argued against putting too many American troops in Germany. He urged that there should be no "line officers or combat troops" as part of the American military government, contending that they would grow too soft and sympathize with the Germans. He noted that after World War I, American soldiers were "homesick and bored and without very much to do" and were "subjected to a barrage of German propaganda." To Morgenthau, the "whole purpose of an army of occupation is to enforce unpalatable terms," something that American soldiers, to Morgenthau's estimation, were not very good at doing.[42]

Often criticized for the crude reductionism of his approach, Morgenthau was to a certain degree perceptive about the wisdom of a US Army–led occupation, at least for the purposes of meeting his plan's goals. For it was not simply, or even primarily, that American soldiers were too soft to enforce a harsh, societally radical peace. It was that doing so was not within the register of US Army historical outlook, doctrine, organization, or training. Such a harsh occupation required intense and overwhelming purpose, a disregard for a society's laws and government structures, and a massive and long-term commitment— none of which the army was prepared to do in Germany. The army's institutional direction ran counter to everything Morgenthau sought. His proposal rested on a contradiction. Such a transformative project required a massive infusion of resources, but the only organization capable of performing what was required, the US Army, was the very organization Morgenthau thought was not fully capable of doing what was required.

Stimson certainly did not object to the destruction of Nazism and even the restructuring of German political life to some degree, as both the Morgenthau Plan and the cabinet committee plan had recommended. But he fulminated against the plan to deindustrialize Germany. Stimson was utterly opposed to the idea in either plan, saying that to hold Germany to subsistence levels would not prevent but rather create the conditions for future war. He added that he could not conceive of such a plan being possible and effective and instead saw "enormous evils" as a result of it being implemented.[43] Doing so would have a potential twofold effect that Stimson, both an internationalist and a veteran of the Great War, thought could be disastrous. Implementing the Morgenthau Plan would deprive not only the Germans but key Allies access to one of the most industrious regions on earth—German recovery was needed for postwar European recovery overall. Furthermore, and more linked to a strictly military rationale, its implementation might overshadow the horrors of Nazism and create conditions for a Versailles Treaty–like resentment in the defeated nation and thereby cause a resurgence of German militarism.[44]

The Morgenthau Plan was never imposed. Rather, what emerged was something far less draconian, in part influenced by Stimson's thoughts and FDR's own vacillations and uncertainties. The document that became the major statement of American postwar occupation policy, Joint Chiefs of Staff Directive 1067 (JCS 1067, its full title being "Regarding the Military Government of Germany in the Period Immediately Following the Cessation of Organized Resistance"), was something less harsh than what the treasury secretary wanted. But it was not merely a deliberately conceived compromise between the rigors of Morgenthau's concept of occupation and the perceived softness of the army's, as is sometimes believed. JCS 1067 developed concurrently with the controversies over the SHAEF handbook and the Morgenthau Plan, and its fundamental substance did not change from first draft to final approval. As such documents typically are, the directive was a bureaucratic, iterative document that went through eight versions between the initial draft in September 1944 and the first postwar promulgation, published on May 11, 1945 (other versions would follow).[45] JCS 1067 was also, as its title indicated, a military document—it was, after all, not from the State Department or even the president but from the Joint Chiefs of Staff.[46] And while it is not precisely clear who drafted its versions, according to occupation historian Earl Ziemke it was largely the work of the army's Civil Affairs Division.[47] There is other evidence that it was authorized, if not drafted, by the State-War-Navy Coordinating Committee.[48] John McCloy proffered in a later interview that *he* specifically was given the job of drafting the document.[49] This very uncertainty is consistent with such a bureaucratized product. And this lack of clarity indicated the very lack of any high-level unitary strategic design about the long-range policy goals of the United States regarding Germany. JCS 1067 focused on short-term goals that provided the on-the-ground commander/military governor sufficient flexibility to perform the mission on hand.[50] SHAEF planners themselves indicated that they interpreted JCS 1067 as an interim, short-term military directive meant to be replaced at some point with a long-term, more political document.[51]

JCS 1067 contained its share of weighty pronouncements. Germany was to be treated as a "defeated enemy nation," and it needed to be "brought home to the Germans that Germany's ruthless warfare and the fanatical Nazi resistance have destroyed the German economy and made chaos and suffering inevitable," language that could be read as foreshadowing a Morgenthau Plan–like occupation. But such language was in large part rhetorical. According to McCloy, JCS 1067 deliberately deflected the Morgenthau Plan's more punitive measures. The document contained a series of clauses that permitted the on-the-ground military governor freedom to maneuver, as McCloy pointed out, noting throughout the document such language as "except in case of emergency." McCloy took at least partial credit for this ameliorating language and contended that JCS 1067 was designed to mitigate the more vindictive and retributive character of both State and Treasury plans.[52] And while McCloy exaggerated the softening tone of JCS 1067, a prominent example of such was the provision that allowed the military governor to take action to "prevent disease and such disorder as might endanger or impede military occupation."[53] Such "disease and disorder/unrest" clauses remained constant in the various versions, and Lucius Clay, de facto military governor of the US zone in Germany from 1945 to 1947, fully exploited them as he saw fit.[54]

The overall language of JCS 1067 was sufficiently broad that Clay did not find JCS 1067 particularly restrictive.[55] He did feel that certain pronouncements made at the Potsdam Conference about Germany's international restoration and its need for economic viability alleviated some concerns about the document's implementation.[56] But even before Potsdam, he did not appear especially concerned about it being excessively burdensome. As he wrote to McCloy in June 1945 shortly after arriving in Germany, "like all general directives, JCS 1067 can be interpreted many ways. My own interpretation is that it requires what is manifestly necessary, a realistic and firm attitude toward Germany. It does not, as I see it, prevent the holding out always of a ray of hope to the German people."[57] As 1945 concluded, he did not see the need for it to be substantially rewritten, stating to John Hilldring that it was workable as it was. He did not propose a new version until September 1946, following Secretary of State James Byrnes's major statement on US policy toward Germany, the first significant one after the war, and even then Clay noted that the updated version should be "short and concise . . . conveying general principles."[58]

Where the authority of the military governor in JCS 1067 was apparently most delimited was in a denazification policy that did not allow flexibility in returning Nazi Party members to civil authority. Here it appeared that the requirements to denazify held sway, though, as would be seen, the practicalities of using a military government structure to conduct such a vast social experiment showed the limits of such pronouncements. And still, another consistent provision throughout all versions was the supreme authority of the military governor, who was "by virtue of [his] position, clothed with supreme legislative, executive and judicial authority in the areas occupied by forces under [his] command. This authority will be broadly construed and includes authority to take all measures deemed by [the military governor] necessary, appropriate and desirable in relation to military exigencies and the objectives of a firm military government."[59] Additionally, constant throughout the JCS 1067 versions was the assertion that Germany's rehabilitation was in "preparation for an eventual reconstruction of German political life on a democratic basis." However, any such goal was subordinate to the primary one, which related back to the original and underlying purpose of the occupation—to prevent Germany from reemerging as a military threat: "The principal Allied objective is to prevent Germany from ever again becoming a threat to the peace of the world."[60]

Despite SHAEF planners' beliefs about JCS 1067's temporary nature, its supposed interim guidance was the most explicit the American occupiers would receive from any source during the first two years of the occupation. In fact, the published papers of the wartime Yalta and Quebec Conferences never revealed any longer-range policy beyond ensuring Germany's permanent military defeat. The Yalta Communiqué, released to the press on February 11, 1945, stated that the requisite steps for Germany's occupation were "disarmament, demilitarization, and dismemberment," but it did not discuss the establishment of a permanent German democracy. And in the agreed-upon "Principles to Govern the Treatment of Germany in the Initial Control Period" adopted by the Allies at the Potsdam Conference in August 1945, democracy was portrayed much more as a future project: "The purposes of the occupation of Germany by which the Control Council shall be guided are . . . to prepare for the eventual reconstruction of German political life on a democratic basis and for eventual peaceful cooperation in international life by Germany." Whatever discussions there were related to democratization were linked explicitly with more pragmatic ones, such as ensuring that German militarism was destroyed and that government authority was decentralized in order to prevent the reemergence of Germany as a major military power. The Potsdam Principles were explicit on this point, stating that while local self-government was to be restored throughout Germany on democratic principles, such restoration would only occur in accordance with requirements for "military security and the purposes of military occupation."[61] Apart from these generic principles, guidance for the American occupation during the critical initial years of postwar governance was formulated largely by the US Army, the same organization that subsequently implemented it.

Lucius Clay and American Military Government in Germany

While Eisenhower served as the first military governor of the US zone in Germany until November 1945, followed by Gen. Joseph T. McNarney until 1947, the real wielding of power and authority in the American zone was by Lt. Gen. Lucius Clay, deputy military governor from 1945 to 1947 (and military governor from 1947 to 1949).[62] He was not the initial choice. In September 1944, the cabinet committee had recommended the appointment of an American high commissioner (as opposed to a military governor) for Germany. Although not explicit, its recommendation seemed to recommend a high-ranking civilian, an "official of high political ability and considerable prestige who can speak with authority for the Government in all matters where a common policy must be worked out with the U.K. and the U.S.S.R."[63] But there were no takers for the assignment. Clay later remarked that he did not believe anyone would have volunteered, given the job's breadth, complexity, and the possibility of its failure.[64] FDR himself initially wanted the job to go to John McCloy. But after Roosevelt, in mock fashion, held up his hand in a Hitler salute and said to McCloy in 1944, "*Heil,* Commissar for Deutschland," McCloy rebuffed the president, pointing out that the war was not yet over. While there would be a time when a civilian high commissioner would be needed, that time was not during the war or even after surrender. Instead he analogized Germany to a natural calamity—a "Mississippi River disaster." It was a job for a military man, who could handle all the distress and questions of food and supply: "This is a job for a soldier at this stage, who can move with other soldiers."[65] After FDR remarked that he knew of no one in the army able to do this, McCloy responded that he knew Lucius Clay, "a sort of right hand man for General [Brehon] Sommerville [the commander of the Army Service Forces]—really running to a large degree Somerville's office over there."[66] In another example of his deference to War Department decisions, FDR apparently did not dispute McCloy's recommendation, allegedly remarking that he was too tired to argue about it.[67]

Clay was an army engineer who had worked on a series of complex logistical problems throughout the war. He also came from a political background: his father had been a prominent Georgia senator, and he had even been a page in Congress.[68] He possessed high intelligence, organizational ability, and an intensity and a work ethic that many found intimidating and even frightening. He had also been involved in civil affairs disputes, especially during the North Africa campaign. He had desperately wanted a combat command during the war, saying he would have "given his eyeteeth to have commanded a division."[69] But his work in the Washington bureaucracy proved invaluable to Sommerville, Marshall, and others, and it provided excellent training for his role as military governor. Interagency dealings made him particularly aware of the back-and-forth of Washington politics, and Clay recognized the absence of clear high-level direction and strategy, as evidenced by his correspondence to McCloy in June 1945, in which he requested that a "small group having the requisite authority" steer American policy.[70]

By no means a military martinet, Clay was rather sophisticated in civil-military affairs. At the same time, he possessed a determination to move things in the direction that he personally thought profitable. He sometimes ran afoul of political leadership, particularly with officials at the State Department, some of whom felt that Clay ran matters in Germany too free of higher Washington influence. Clay on more than one occasion, while strenuously objecting that he had no intention of doing anything but execute State Department orders, protested for more control and authority, as when he wrote to Hilldring urging that the State Department in Washington either directly deal with him or the War Department and not via State functionaries on the ground in Germany.[71] Over the course of the occupation, his sometimes less than temperate disregard for State prerogatives became evident. A State Department representative once recommended, for example, the postponement of licensing of German newspapers in early 1946. Rather than listen to the reasons for the proposal, Clay vehemently objected: "If you send a message to the Department of State with your recommendation, I shall resign." Even though Clay eventually did what the recommendations advised, he implemented them largely on his own terms.[72]

Prior to Clay's arrival, American military government officials began entering the Reich as early as December 1944, eventually to occupy the US zone shown in map 5.2. They relied on the explicit authority of Proclamation No. 1, issued by Eisenhower, who for an interim period served as supreme military authority over all the areas occupied by the Western Allies. The proclamation reiterated the underlying principle of military government, asserting that "supreme legislative, judicial and executive authority and powers within the occupied territory are vested in . . . [the] Supreme Commander of the Allied Forces and as Military Governor." Furthermore, all Germans were to "obey immediately and without question" all the enactments and orders of the military government, and resistance to the Allied forces would be "ruthlessly stamped out." The proclamation stated that all officials charged with the duties of remaining at their posts would do so until further orders were issued, including all those at "public undertakings and utilities" and "all other persons engaged in essential work."[73]

The years of planning and organizing had some positive results, and there was a measure of purpose and organization that reflected a detailed level of postwar planning unprecedented in the history of war.[74] American military government officials began the occupation with a wealth of information on all conceivable issues and problems: how to set up military courts, how to establish curfews, how to compel the surrender of firearms, and even how to use carrier pigeons to transmit messages, to name just a few. A somewhat idealized version of American military government appeared in an army periodical, *Army Talks,* in February 1945. Indicating that rule was by "military government—pure and simple," the article discussed how a particular military government detachment in a town (its name was censored) conducted activities. The unit studied and analyzed "thousands of documents—maps, blueprints, photographs, charts, rosters, books and secret reports." The first order of business was the installation of the *Bürgermeister* (mayor): "A handful of Military Government men isn't intended to accomplish its mission without making full use of local support and assistance."[75]

Map 5.2. Allied occupation zones in Germany. (Office of Military Government, US, *Monthly Report of Military Governor, US Zone, no. 1, Intelligence and Confidential Annexes,* August 20, 1945, AHEC.)

A report on the work of Military Government Detachment F-213 in Munich from May 1945 to January 1946 similarly set forth occupation objectives. Composed of twenty-four officers and forty-eight enlisted men, the unit spent a year prior to its occupation duties preparing for its mission, poring over maps and air photos and studying all aspects of the location of its assignment. The unit members knew Munich "better than their own towns." Upon arrival, the detachment went to work: its commander appointed an *Oberbürgermeister* (the equivalent of a lord mayor or mayor of a major city), established law and order, got utilities working, and empowered those on the so-called white list—that is, those officials who were determined not to be Nazis—to act as temporary mayor and heads of municipal departments.[76]

Still the very vastness of the project of the occupation sometimes seemed overwhelming in spite of all the preceding planning efforts. The scope of urban destruction could be at times staggering: one observer called Germany a "country without cities."[77] Many cities were nearly empty due to populations having fled fighting or bombing; many relatively undamaged cities, in turn, teemed with tens of thousands of displaced persons who had gone to them for food and shelter. And as military government units attempted to restore order from the incredible chaos, the roads were clogged with innumerable German families trying to return to their hometowns.[78] Expectedly, any early successes at restarting basic requirements were elusive: surveys conducted of military government teams in getting industry, commerce, mining, and agriculture restarted and providing for basic nutrition indicated that they were less than successful.[79] The latter was the fundamental problem: how to prevent a highly advanced society from starving. According to an American military government official in Leipzig, "the first and foremost [problem was] *food* for a thoroughly dislocated industrial population."[80]

The overall situation, one of seeming chaos and collapse, looked quite unlike the placid Rhineland occupation following the previous world war. And yet the attitude of the German people in the American zone was typically often reported as calm, at worst apathetic, and at best constructive and supportive, with few overt acts of resistance and with relatively easy living provided for the occupiers themselves. A June 1945 intelligence report indicated that "the Germans look at the Allied Forces with fairly understanding eyes," noting that it was not a novelty for the Germans to have large numbers of troops billeted throughout the country. The same report noted that hooligan and Nazi resistance activities were "infinitesimal."[81] A soldier describing his living conditions in Bremerhaven (which, though even in the British zone, was under American control) pointed out "table settings, with sparkling white linen and heavy silver" and that his bathroom was "a marvel of gleaming tile and polished brass. . . . We seem to have found our way to wonderland." He was also struck by the "utter lack of energy and the absence of hostility in the men. None of them had shown the slightest resistance, none had any thought of escape."[82] Saul Padover, who wrote an alternative proposal to the American Military Government School in 1941, later served as an intelligence officer in the European theater. After entering Germany, he noted the apparent prestige of the Americans, viewed as "powerful conquerors." He also became aware quickly that when walking the streets of Aachen, one "hears the sound of hammering. People are repairing lightly damaged houses. They seem to be cheerful."[83] Elsewhere, such as in parts of the Ruhr Valley, the Germans were noted to be as apathetic and self-absorbed as they were docile and compliant. The dire predictions of SS-led "Werewolves" turned out to be, with just a few exceptions, false.[84]

Clay wrote to Hilldring in July 1945 that political activity was dormant: "German masses seem totally unpolitical, apathetic and primarily concerned with everyday problems of food, clothing, and shelter. . . . There is no evidence of an attempt to organize a Nazi underground."[85] Even after the cold and brutal first occupation winter of 1945–1946, intelligence reports indicated that the population in the US zone was outwardly placid—the Germans apparently expressed their greatest concerns about local military government detachments withdrawing too quickly, since many still placed relatively little faith in German administrations.[86] What the American occupiers noted was a "monotonous repetition of the usual complaints" that centered on the theme that the occupation authorities did not show enough interest in the immediate reconstruction of Germany.[87]

It was apparent to the American occupiers that Nazism had been defeated not only on the battlefield but also as an ideology, and Germans had no desire to return to it. A number of historians have pointed out Germany's willingness to be occupied in the Western zones as a key, perhaps *the* key, reason for the occupation's seeming success—a willingness that corresponded quite well with the American military government's own pragmatic orientation. According to Richard Merritt, the Germans chose democracy and the West because few alternatives were available. The Allies would not permit a return to Nazism, and Germans had little interest anyway in returning to a disastrous and disgraced past.[88] As Jan Werner Müller points out, the whole point of Nazi supremacism was that it had to be proven in deed even more than in word, and militarily Nazism had been utterly crushed. Müller contends that there was a certain reluctance by the Germans to embrace subsequently a free and unconstrained democracy—after all, the will of the unchecked masses had seemingly led to the public's embrace of and submission to Hitler. Democracy would be, in light of the recent totalitarian experiment, modest, chastened, and pragmatic. Military government under a Western democratic system that restored power and that modestly denazified did not seem such an affront in such an environment.[89] Clay especially was a pragmatist in his dealings with the Germans, and his political efforts toward reempowerment were, fundamentally, a practical solution to the problem of a military occupation that could not sustain itself over a lengthy period.[90]

In one major respect, then, the Second World War's occupation in the American zone did resemble the First's—not in the level of destruction or in the postwar ideological framework but in the relative compliance of the Germans themselves and in their apparent desire not to engage in an extensive guerrilla uprising. Accordingly, Clay was able to act according to doctrine and separate military government from tactical command rapidly. In his estimation, military government did "not belong in one of five staff divisions at theater headquarters."[91] He achieved such separation faster than was accomplished in Austria, a nation far less damaged. During the summer of 1945, command and control of military government flowed through the tactical commanders of the Eastern and Western Districts in the American zone. But by September 1945, Clay had created directors and offices of military government directly linked to the respective *Laender* (German states) that the American forces occupied and in accordance with the territorial model of military government. By October the G-5 civil affairs staff sections detached from tactical district commanders and fell under the *Laender* military governments.[92] From January 1, 1946, onward the directors of the offices of military government in Bavaria, Württemberg-Baden, and Greater Hesse each became completely independent of the district tactical commanders and reported to General McNarney (though de facto to Clay). The directors themselves were in turn responsible for all activities related to military government in their districts, which included coordinating with and gradually ceding authority to German civilian police and all other German agencies.[93]

American Military Government and the Soviets

Throughout 1945 and 1946, American military government was moving in a direction not necessarily consistent with what American civilian policymakers wanted. In particular, there were differences between the views of civilian leaders in Washington and military leaders in Germany, especially Clay, regarding the Soviet Union. When Harry S. Truman assumed the presidency following Roosevelt's death in April 1945, he did not initially intend to reverse FDR's cooperative strategy with the Soviets.[94] At the same time, he relied more on counselors than his predecessor had, and many of them held suspicious or skeptical views of the Soviet Union.[95] In May 1945, Director of the Office of Strategic Services William J. Donovan sent a memorandum to the new president titled "Problems and Objectives of United States Policy," which focused almost exclusively on the Soviets. According to Donovan, the Soviet Union put "little store by proposals of compromise or by international agreements." Donovan spoke of the Soviet Union as a possible "menace more formidable to the United States than any yet known." He also focused on the importance of Germany in the future of US-Soviet relations. The "German problem" was at the center of any possible conflict. Donovan was forthright: a Russia "that dominates Germany will dominate Europe." Furthermore, the Soviet Union would "almost certainly fight to prevent the Western domination of Germany." Rather than seeing any hope in the four powers resolving issues peaceably, Donovan saw the only alternatives to war as permanent partition between Western and Soviet spheres of influence or a totally neutralized Germany "balanced between the Eastern and Western blocs but aligned with neither."[96]

There was some initial sympathy toward the Soviets, who had designs on postwar Germany. They had undeniably suffered far greater than the Western Allies had. They also, justifiably to them, viewed Germany's occupation as a tremendous opportunity. The Reich had been laid waste and thereby was available both for materiel exploitation and as a platform for communist expansion into Western Europe. Soviet leaders contemplated huge reparations, including the wholesale removal of large industrial factories. Furthermore, social reorientation for the Soviet-controlled zone was consistent with communist ideology. As Stalin had pointed out, whoever occupied a territory also imposed upon it his own social system.[97] Relations at the strategic level broke down significantly by early 1946. Truman himself placed the "point of departure" of his view toward the Soviets in early January of that year. He was particularly disturbed by the continuing Soviet retention of troops in Iran, believing that it was without justification and that it paralleled Russian aggression in the Baltic States and Poland.[98] As he stated in that same correspondence, "I'm tired [of] babying the Soviets."[99] That same month, Secretary of State Byrnes gave the first public expression of the administration's new policy toward the Soviet Union in a speech to the Overseas Press Club in New York. Though not mentioning the Soviet Union by name, Byrnes stated that while the United States welcomed the Soviet Union as part of a postwar international order, America would not abide with aggression or threats of force contrary to the purposes and principles of the United Nations Charter—a clear reference to the Iranian situation.[100]

But within the American army, relations with the Soviets were slower to cool. Averell Harriman pointed out that neither Marshall nor Eisenhower was quick to see coming conflict with the Soviet Union. He also said that both tried their best to get along with Stalin. Marshall himself did not change his views conclusively until after the Moscow Conference in 1947. As for Eisenhower, he was, according to Harriman, convinced that Stalin "kept his military commitments," specifically referring to the massive Operation Bagration in the summer of 1944 while the Western Allies struggled to break out of the Normandy hedgerows.[101] While one might write this off as partisanship on the part of Harriman, who was early on alarmed at apparent Soviet intentions, Eisenhower's relationship with Marshal Georgy Zhukov was good during and shortly after the war: the record is replete with statements of warmth between the two men.[102]

Clay likewise viewed the Soviet Union in a not unfriendly light. It is true that in his memoir of military government, *Decision in Germany,* he portrayed the Soviet Union as an aggressor nation only temporarily held in check. According to his memoir, at the time of Potsdam the Soviet Union seemed to be willing to accept four-power control but only grudgingly, attributing this reluctance, at least in part, to American military strength in 1945. The Soviet Union's policy of "world domination" had only temporarily been in "moth balls" because of the war and "clearly formed the basis of [its] day-to-day planning."[103] But this was Clay's view in 1950, only after the United States was well in the midst of the Cold War. The record shows that he did not begin his occupation duties as a doctrinaire anticommunist. Initially Clay saw the Soviets as allies and did not pay attention to their revolutionary ideology.[104] In fact, in 1945 and 1946, Clay was far more sympathetic to the Soviets than anticommunists such as Secretary of Navy James Forrestal and George Kennan, the author of the containment policy, whom Clay once deridingly dismissed as "all theory." Kennan would later remark on "being taken severely to task in a private meeting with Gen. Lucius Clay in 1945 for what the general then viewed as the excessively anti-Soviet attitudes of the State Department. The military, I was given to understand, would have known far better than the diplomats how to create a collaborative relationship with the Russians."[105] Clay was, in his own words, "appalled" by Kennan's famous 1946 Moscow cable that outlined the containment strategy, and he upbraided Kennan for his apparent anti-Soviet prejudice when the two met in Berlin in the spring of 1946.[106] He profoundly disagreed with Kennan's conclusion about Soviet conduct and thought that his influence on American foreign policy was "pernicious."[107]

Nonetheless, Clay's seemingly relaxed attitude toward the Soviets during the early phase of the occupation did not give an advantage either to the Soviet Union or to communism in the Western zones. The German Communist Party (KPD) never gained any significant foothold in them. This failure has led to various speculations among scholars about deliberate suppression of more politically "radical" movements. Richard Merritt contends that the US mission was to limit the spread of socialism in the Western zones.[108] Rebecca Boehling argues that the Americans essentially short-circuited grassroots democracy (especially far-left efforts), and the emergence of the Cold War caused a purge of any leftist inclinations. According to this view, actions by the United States not only suppressed the KPD, but they also prevented any possibility for true participatory democracy.[109] But these contentions are belied by Clay's actions. For example, he protested the establishment of Radio Liberty in Munich in August 1946, arguing that it would not be in the spirit of four-power harmony.[110] He also refused to provide assistance to either conservative or moderate parties during the crucial elections in heavily communist Berlin.[111] An examination of political suppression by the American occupiers reveals that the only party suppressed outright in their zone was the monarchist far-right Bavarian Home and King Party, which sought to break away from Germany altogether.[112] On the other hand, throughout the years of the occupation, the KPD was allowed at least officially to campaign rather freely in the US zone. Arrests of KPD leaders were made there from time to time but often because of the violation of clear restrictions. Moreover, any punishments for such violations were often revoked, or incidents were ignored altogether, perhaps in fear of turning the KPD members into martyrs.[113]

Overall, the historical record shows little evidence of an active, consistent, or aggressive anticommunist campaign in the US zone during the critical opening years, from 1945 until at least early 1947. And a principal reason for this was that in the first year and a half of the occupation, political ideology was far less important than the pragmatic requirements of military government. It was this very lack of ideology that characterized the American military government's moves in 1945 and 1946—primarily the disengagement of military government from German civil government and the reempowerment of that government, at least on a localized level, as soon as possible. Clay's federalist approach toward reenergizing German government on a step-by-step basis was the method by which that was accomplished.

Return to Power through Federalism

American military government returned power to Germans in the US zone relatively quickly. In just over a year, Germans there were electing their own officials at the local, provincial, and state levels and essentially running their own political affairs. This was consistent with the goal of a demilitarized Germany: empowered local governments would provide a brake and an impediment to the centralizing forces that allowed for the concentration of military power under the Reich's banner. And it was consistent with the fundamental military government principle of letting locals govern themselves. The ancillary result was the marginalization of communist influence in the American zone, though this was not deliberately sought. Nonideological military goals, in other words, led to an outcome—decentralized, relatively autonomous German government—that was to the detriment of a particular political ideology.

JCS 1067 (and later the postwar Potsdam Agreement) stressed decentralization as an essential step for Germany's rehabilitation and its "preparation for an eventual reconstruction of German political life on a democratic basis." But this democratic goal was subordinate to the goal of ensuring that Germany remained defeated: "Ultimately, the principal allied objective is to prevent Germany from ever again becoming a threat to the peace of the world."[114] In one particular area, the American document emphasized the importance of decentralization even more emphatically than Potsdam did. When discussing the formation of political parties, the Potsdam Agreement stated that "all democratic political parties with rights of assembly and of public discussion shall be allowed and encouraged throughout Germany."[115] However, JCS 1067 placed strict controls on the formation of political parties and aligned those controls with the authority of the military governor: "No political activities of any kind shall be countenanced unless authorized by you [the US military governor]. You will assure that your military government does not become committed to any political group."[116] According to JCS 1067, nonideological military prerogatives were supreme.

Clay implemented his own vision of decentralization, though in a manner that many, including civilian advisers and even German officials, thought was too soon, too fast.[117] Indeed, the historical record indicates that Clay did so on his own authority with little to no imposed (or requested) guidance. In a letter he wrote to Lt. Gen. O. P. Nichols, who after the war replaced John Hilldring as the director of the War Department's Civil Affairs Division, he set forth his interpretation of

US policy, which saw a decentralized German government that would empower states with "substantial responsibility for self-government." He did note that the federal government needed requisite powers for economic unity but at the same time he saw the need for greater local political autonomy, seeing Germany as a potential "confederation or federal type of government."[118] Clay therefore believed that the US occupiers were going to have to, in his words, "build from the bottom up" by empowering through elections local governments at the smallest possible level first, only afterward allowing elections at succeeding higher levels.[119] Clay was candid to McCloy about the twofold purpose of his approach: "If the Germans are to learn democratic methods, I think the best way is to start them off quickly at the lower levels. Besides, this will help us reduce substantially the personnel required for military government."[120] He did not believe that a long occupation was sustainable by the army, which was then in the process of massive demobilization and which was neither trained nor equipped to perform such a task.

Prior to elections taking place, Clay strove to create autonomy for the appointed German governments in the US zone. In the fall of 1945, he directed that relationships be established between the three US-appointed *Laender* governments of Bavaria, Hesse, and Württemberg-Baden and the corresponding American military government directorates at their levels, giving the appointed officials near parity. All instructions passed from Clay to his military government directors in those *Laender,* who in turn communicated with US-appointed minister-presidents to implement them.[121] He also established the so-called *Laenderrat* (Council of Minister-Presidents), comprised of representatives from the three US-zone German states. The *Laenderrat* served as a council of the American-appointed minister-presidents in the US zone that had the power to recommend, if not promulgate, legislation that the US military government would enact.[122] It rapidly became a powerful body within the US zone, so much in fact that many in Bavaria, the most independent-minded *Land* (state), felt that the *Laenderrat* had *too* much authority and operated too much as an autonomous government.[123]

Clay also pushed for Germans to elect their own officials in accordance with the federalist objective. In August 1945, he ordered that the administration of the US zone "should be directed toward the decentralization of the political structure and the development of local responsibility."[124] By the spring of 1946, American military government contact was to be only with *Land* governmental structures, with nearly complete reliance on the Germans themselves to conduct governmental functions at local levels: *Gemeinde* (village or town with a population less than fifty thousand), *Stadtkreise* (incorporated city), and *Landkreise* (county).[125] Political parties were allowed to form at the local level only below the *Laender,* and they could not merge beyond that level or form blocs because such blocs were "contrary to traditional American concepts of political activity and vigorous political life in a democratic sense."[126] Throughout the fall of 1945, Clay began withdrawal of military government detachments from rural areas where the first elections were to be held: the military government's stated policy was "not to govern the German people but to control and supervise them in governing themselves."[127]

In September 1945, detailed instructions were provided to Germans to prepare codes for all local governmental units below the *Land* level, specifying their structure and powers. The codes had to contain provisions regarding popularly elected councils "with substantial powers" located in each *Gemeinde, Stadtkreise,* and *Landkreise.* Other requirements included "at least a majority vote of the council" required for the passage of any legislation. To prevent *Land* governments from dictating local governmental codes, the American military government provided for the "freedom for all communities either to adopt a standard charter drawn up by *Land* authorities or to draft charters containing variations of their own devising." The regional military government officer had authority to review the codes, and only after he approved the codes would local elections be held.[128] Clay further directed that all *Gemeiden* elections were to take place by the end of January 1946. In October, he directed that Germans prepare their own election codes to set the stage for local government voting, with an essential restriction imposed: active Nazi Party members and any who had joined the Nazi Party prior to May 1, 1937, were excluded, as well as sympathizers and collaborators.[129]

The US military government's actions in setting up voting in one particular *Land,* Bavaria, provides an example of how decentralizing political reform took place and how the KPD in particular became politically marginalized there. In compliance with policy, the US regional military government in Bavaria allowed for the formation of political parties in late August 1945 but only at the level of *Landkreis* and *Stadtkreis* and subject to ultimate approval of the American military government. Parties were expressly forbidden at the *Land* level, and party mergers were not encouraged.[130] A fuller explanation of requirements came in October 1945. At that point, the *Land* military government directorate allowed for the formation of political parties upon written application, signed by at least twenty-five sponsors. When the directorate approved the application, a party could engage in political activity at the local level only. Sponsors and members had to be German citizens and to have been Bavarian residents for one year. Party agents, speakers, and other members outside the US zone could speak at party meetings, but first they had to obtain approval from the military government. Solicitation or acceptance of funds, loans, or contributions from persons who were not party members was forbidden.[131]

It was from this "bottom-up" arrangement that political parties emerged. The conservative Christian Social Union (CSU) arose (the Bavarian version of the Christian Democratic Party [CDU] and a descendant of the Bavarian People's Party [BVP]).[132] The Weimar Republic's moderate/liberal Social Democratic Party (SPD) returned, as did the KPD and other relatively minor parties such as the Free Democratic Party (FDP). Yet all these parties were localized. They could only operate in small political venues and could only debate mainstream issues, such as who should have the right to vote.[133] These restrictions, imposed pursuant to federalist principles, proved to impede the KPD structurally in Bavaria, where there was little grassroots support, especially in the villages and countryside. In order to strengthen its political power, leaders of the KPD sought to merge with the SPD at various levels. For example, in the summer of 1946, US military intelligence reported that three KPD-SPD "unification committees" had been set up in Bavaria without military government permission.[134] And American military government officials had viewed with suspicion the merging of the KPD and the SPD into the Socialist Unity Party (SED) that occurred in the Soviet zone in early 1946 as part of a "broad pattern of events occurring in all eastern and central European countries, and in all European countries where there is an active Communist movement."[135] Nonetheless, despite these concerns, the overall response by the Americans to the purported political crisis was relatively mild. Clay, for example, did not prevent SED leaders from seeking political followers in the US zones, did not arrest Communist Party members, and never suppressed the KPD.[136]

A more forceful response was not required precisely because the KPD was doing very poorly in garnering political support at the local levels. Elections began as early as January 1946, barely eight months after V-E Day, at the *Gemeinde* level.[137] According to US intelligence reports, local influences, such as village priests and ministers, apparently played major roles in helping sway the outcome. As one report put it, "the conservative, highly religious Bavarian peasantry reject[ed] any political influence which [was] at variance with the dogma of its faith."[138] The voting turnout vastly exceeded expectations. As was expected, the CSU received a large majority, nearly nine hundred thousand votes, and the SPD received slightly over one-third that amount. The KPD found next to no sympathy or support among the Bavarian villagers, netting a mere forty-six thousand votes.[139] After these initial election results, the KPD leader in Bavaria, Bruno Goldhammer, contended that the elections lacked political legitimacy because they were localized.[140] The Bavarian *Kreise* elections occurred in April and May of the same year. In June, elections were held for constitutional assemblies in the US zone *Laender*. Although the KPD did better in urban areas, the local system effectively prevented outsiders from providing significant assistance. For example, the KPD obtained 3.6 percent of the vote in the *Landkreis* elections in April and 6.7 percent in the *Stadtkreis* in May. Political localization still was mandatory, however, and without external support the KDP never gained significant traction even in urban areas to garner major electoral gains.

Following a steady pattern of elections without incident throughout the US zone, by the summer of 1946 Germans were electing *Land* assemblies, with the primary responsibility for the elections resting upon the German *Land* and local government officials themselves. Military government officials were explicitly told to maintain a hands-off policy toward the elections, other than to ensure their honesty and orderliness.[141] The results were nonetheless highly favorable to the Americans. In the *Gemeinde* elections, for example, 87 percent of the eligible population voted, and 76 percent of the military government appointees remained in office.[142] By December 1946, when the elections for the Bavarian state parliament were held, federalism had become deeply entrenched in Bavarian political life. The results were fairly predictable. Known parties or their descendants, such as the SPD and CSU/CDU, dominated the results. Various splinter parties across the political spectrum continued to exist but never were sufficient in numbers to become a force in national politics. The KPD, unable to form beyond local levels or to connect with the Soviet-zone party, could not muster sufficient strength or support. In fact, as a result of a provision in the recently drafted Bavarian Constitution (by the Bavarians themselves), the KPD was barred from holding any seats whatsoever in the Bavarian parliament because it failed to obtain 10 percent of the votes in any one electoral district.[143]

Bavaria provides the clearest example of bottom-up, decentralizing politics shaping the outcome of elections. The same pattern was repeated, to a lesser extent, in the other US-occupied *Laender*. By the time the Western occupiers relinquished military governmental authority to what became the Federal Republic of Germany, the federalist system was largely in effect. Restrictions on parties merging beyond local levels, as well as the pattern of bottom-up elections, structured the ultimate outcome that favored the conservative-to-moderate/liberal CSU and SPD parties. The CSU, with its northern sister party the CDU, became the dominant force in German politics. The Basic Law, adopted in 1949, placed significant checks and balances on the central government's power. West Germany had become, in effect, a federalist democracy.

Some critics of the American occupation argue that true grassroots movements never had the ability to flourish. Arthur Kahn, who served in military government during the period, points out that, especially in Bavaria, democratic processes were short-circuited because urban population centers were where embryonic political parties were generally formed, and the bottom-up approach prevented sufficient gestation in the cities and subsequent dissemination to the towns and countryside.[144] And it does appear that efforts to embed democratic concepts by the American military government were sparse. Harold Zink, one of the first to write about the military government efforts in Germany, noted that American efforts were overly focused on the process and "machinery" of government and not enough on the substance of democracy. Too much emphasis, according to Zink, was placed on "the holding of elections, [and] the framing of constitutions and laws" and too little on the more painstaking and longer-term tasks of "filling public offices with able Germans who could be expected to fight for a democratic cause during critical periods of attack in the future, and educating the Germans as to the meaning of representative democracy."[145] But a return to democracy was a long-range goal essentially outside the scope of what Clay and the American military government sought. To do so envisioned a long-lasting occupation that was, in Clay's eyes, fundamentally unworkable. The emphasis on such mechanics, of process over substance, however, allowed Clay to move along a federalist path and to return power to Germans as rapidly as possible, and in so doing he attained goals that were militarily focused.

Denazification

In accordance with JCS 1067 and the Potsdam Agreement, denazification primarily focused on the trial and removal or nonemployment of Nazi Party members, along with other goals such as the purging of Nazism from textbooks and the removal of Nazi propaganda from cities and towns. It was an incredibly vast and complex legal procedure. Indeed, the American denazification effort circa 1945–1946 is an example of a policy at odds with the army's own military government imperatives. It called for immense effort but was constantly restrained by the lack of internal resources. It was criticized as being bureaucratic and insufficiently transformative, though it is difficult to see how a more socially transformative approach could have been accomplished given the assets provided. After much criticism, efforts were made to enact laws that called for a more sweeping purge of Nazis. But this more severe policy was short lived, and ultimately denazification was turned over to the Germans themselves. Barely a year into the occupation, Germans largely ran denazification in the American zone, and undoubtedly former Nazis returned to positions of authority. On the other hand, Germany was politically denazified: Nazism was discredited and was never again seized upon as a political possibility. This seemingly paradoxical result had little to do with overarching US policy and far more to do with the convergence of the American military government imperative to return power to local control with the German populace's own sense that Nazism was thoroughly discredited. Individual justice was undoubtedly inappropriately served in many cases. But the engineered-from-above social revolution that Morgenthau and others sought proved unnecessary.

Before V-E Day, US denazification policy required that Germans appointed to public office down to the *Bürgermeister* level after January 30, 1933 (the date Hitler became chancellor), be removed from public office.[146] A more nuanced policy followed the surrender. Only those high-level government workers who had joined the party before May 1, 1937, the date when the Nazi Party opened its membership to the masses, were to be removed. Additionally, the new policy placed former Nazis into "active" and "nominal" categories, requiring the removal or debarment from civil office of active Nazis who had held government positions in the Reich; those who participated in or authorized crimes, racial persecutions, or discrimination; those who professed belief in Nazism or a similar racial/militarist creed; or those who voluntarily gave moral, material, or political assistance of any kind to the Nazi Party.[147] Such a sweeping definition entailed extensive background checks and vetting.

To gather the requisite information, military government officials issued a lengthy and complex questionnaire called a *Fragebogen* to virtually every able-bodied adult in the US zone. Germans had to truthfully answer questions about their private lives, employment, membership, and military service, with an understanding that lying or misrepresentation carried criminal penalties.[148] The process often took weeks, with only a small number of military government personnel available for the task. In Bavaria, for example, no more than three hundred US military government personnel at any one time investigated nearly eight hundred thousand adults from the spring of 1945 to mid-1946.[149] A military government unit would typically distribute a *Fragebogen* to each city or town employee when he reported for work, as well as to any Germans who held positions of influence in industry. When returned, the assigned denazification officer screened the document, gave it a first evaluation, and then sent it to various counterintelligence and military police units and offices, where those officials in turn checked it against Nazi rolls, police records, and lists prepared by US intelligence officers.[150]

Denazification soon ran into serious problems with both Germans and the American occupiers. The populace quickly became disenchanted, with some at least initially believing the denazification process was actually *in*adequate. Early intelligence indicated that leading German citizens were dissatisfied with the American efforts because Nazis were still in power and still doing business "in comfortable positions now as ever."[151] Intelligence reports in the fall showed a significant hardening in Germans attitudes, though now in a different way. More and more Germans were sympathetic to those they felt were arbitrarily dismissed from public service and to those arrested. Meanwhile, many US military government officials found that the policy was deeply problematic. By August, military government officials reported a shortage of competent German replacements to positions of public office. They felt they needed a more flexible, case-by-case approach to determine employment or not.[152] There was also a glaring lack of resources to vet Germans in accordance with the *Fragebogen* scheme. Clay reported to Hilldring that he could not denazify the US zone as thoroughly as directed even if he had ten thousand military government officials to do the job.[153] Concurrently, demobilization was draining away manpower. By August, 7 percent of military government personnel in Bavaria were eligible to be inactivated. By the next month, following V-J Day, that had risen to 25 percent, and with the Japanese surrender the public clamor to bring the troops home dramatically increased.[154]

The military government imperative of reempowering locals and the US policy of thorough denazification collided during the summer and early fall of 1945, most notably in Bavaria, where the US-designated Bavarian minister-president, Friedrich Schaeffer, had been appointing ministers with Nazi ties. Over a third of the Bavarian Ministry of Interior—twelve of thirty-one officials—had Nazi associations, so the entire ministry had to be reorganized.[155] The apparent lack of concern by American occupiers for denazification made its way into the American press, and scandal erupted. Comparing unfavorably the Soviet and American denazification policies, the editors of the opinion journal *The New Republic* launched a scathing broadside, noting the contrast between the Soviet and American occupations and pointing out that "the Russians are squarely tackling the problem of rejuvenating democracy in Germany by encouraging anti-Fascist democratic forces." Criticizing the supposed "non-political" American military government, the editors went so far as to say that the US occupation was "discouraging democracy" by giving power to discredited extremist politicians.[156]

The scandal and related public relations debacles, such as Gen. George S. Patton Jr. comparing Nazis to Democrats and Republicans, helped to create Military Government Law Number Eight, promulgated on September 26, 1945. It set forth new denazification policy in the US zone, and it marked an apparent resurgence of denazification's intent and mission.[157] The military government proclaimed: "Military Government in the U.S. Zone was again reminded that the United States entered this war as the foe of Nazism, and that victory will not be complete until every active adherent of the Nazi Party is eliminated from positions of responsibility, and that no compromise may be made with Nazism." The new law prohibited employment of *any* Nazi Party members (regardless of when they joined) in any sort of managerial employment, public or private. Former Nazis could only work in "ordinary labor." The new law also mandated that any business wishing to stay open would have to certify that it employed no Nazi Party members. To make sure it was enforced, it charged the various military government special branches with making spot checks within the various districts, cities, and towns.[158]

US military government officials swiftly took control of thousands of business properties, and business owners who were determined to be Nazis were dismissed.[159] As might be expected, the new law caused dismay among the population. In one town, for example, the detachment reported that the population was confused as to "just what sort of work a Nazi is allowed to do under the heading of ordinary labor." Small businesses would close one day, reopen the following day, and then close again. There appeared to be a fear (whether genuine or self-serving) that former Nazis who had otherwise been accounted for, if not rehabilitated, would now become outcasts and go underground and thereby create greater havoc.[160]

Almost as soon as the law was put into effect, therefore, the American military government made modifications to it. A directive issued in November 1945 provided employers and employees subject to removal or punishment the right to appeal before either American or German local review boards. In the same month, Clay directed a denazification policy board to recommend solutions, including allowing Germans to manage denazification themselves as much as possible.[161] The board's findings, released in January 1946, identified weaknesses under the new law: denazification produced arbitrary results, it failed to reach all the active Nazis, it was not integrated into other military government programs, it did not have a long-range focus, and it did not have significant German participation.[162]

The pendulum therefore swung back toward German control and autonomy. In March 1946, General Clay, along with the US zone minister-presidents, signed the Law for Liberation from National Socialism and Militarism, which turned over to the German people the power to dispose of denazification cases.[163] American involvement in implementing denazification subsequently diminished. Military government officials were instructed not to influence in any way the decisions of the tribunals. As of June 1946, US screening operations on all persons virtually ceased except for certain key official members of certain ministries. The extreme "hands-off" policy of the new law was emphatically emphasized: "It cannot be overemphasized that [US military government] higher Headquarters has indicated that it will tolerate absolutely no interference by Military Government with German officials charged with carrying out the Law for Liberation from National Socialism and Militarism."[164]

With the new German-run law in place, it soon became clear that former Nazis were being reempowered, and the protestations of Clay himself had little effect stopping it. Relatively simple cases took weeks of effort for a German prosecutor to even gather relevant evidence.[165] Witnesses failed to appear before the hearings. For those who made it to hearings, the tribunals often exonerated or drastically reduced penalties of offenders. The overall numbers announced an even more damning conclusion: even though tens of thousands of cases were brought forward under the new law, the great majority were simply terminated, most never even going to a hearing.[166] Clay's angry protests to the assembled *Landerrat* in November 1946 included a threat: "Unless there is real and rapid improvement, I can only assume that German administration is unwilling to accept this responsibility."[167] Yet despite a last American military government spurt of action, the momentum of German-run denazification continued. Around the time of Clay's address, the amnesty of thousands of minor Nazi members had already been granted, and thousands more would follow by the close of 1946. By mid-1947, the application of the Law for Liberation from National Socialism and Militarism was in its last stage, with 90 percent of those who had registered under the law having had their status legally determined.[168]

Given the controversy denazification had already caused, it might seem strange to hand off a policy to the Germans and not expect it be subverted. But to conclude that the American occupiers deliberately sought to reempower Nazis by allowing the Germans to run denazification does not make sense. The very unsystematic nature of denazification policies imposed by the US military government shows such a claim has little credibility. American military government officials themselves had deep reservations about using former Nazis, even though they felt sometimes that they had no choice. As one put it, "Why should we now employ and use as our allies the same person whom we only a short time ago were attacking as blood-stained criminals?"[169] The argument that handing denazification off to Germans was an orchestrated attempt to establish an anticommunist bulwark similarly makes little chronological sense. Relations with the Soviet Union, at least from the American military government's perspective, were still relatively good up through early 1946, when the Law of Liberation from National Socialism and Militarism was promulgated. It was in the following year, with the announcement of the Marshall Plan, the publication of Kennan's containment strategy, and the first Berlin crisis, that significant Cold War realignment began. To argue that the diminishment of denazification was a result of Cold War efforts to build up Germany as a bulwark against perceived Soviet intentions is therefore to reverse the historical sequence of events. Denazification began in the US zone as a scaled-down military government program, when the relations between senior American and Soviet military leaders were tolerable if not good. It ratcheted up in the fall of 1945 largely after public protests in the United States but reverted a few months later with a new law that permitted Germans to run the process.

The more compelling reason why the Germans took over was because the occupation's imperatives dictated a return to control to them—early return to locals was fundamental to military government because military government was not designed for long-term, complex, societally transforming goals. Furthermore, while the Germans permitted former Nazis back into positions of authority, they had no interest in pursuing Nazism as a political agenda, and the essential wartime goal—ensuring Nazism and militarism never reappeared—was never challenged. The reempowerment of local German government, begun shortly after the surrender with the appointment of government officials and the establishment of the *Laenderrat,* was further complemented by successful elections held throughout the US zones at the local level. Nowhere was there evident any resurrection of political Nazism. Concomitantly, the already overstrained American military government was further pressed to reduce its force structure. All led to the solution of allowing the Germans to denazify themselves. Central to the Morgenthau-style theories about the occupation was the idea that German militarism and authoritarianism were so endemic that leaders who had served under the Nazi regime were, by definition, unacceptable and any Germans under their sway would revert to old ways. But this was proven wrong: the massive social experiment that denazification called for never occurred and, in the end, was unnecessary.

The US occupation of Germany in 1945 and 1946 reveals the need to focus on institutional and bureaucratic process as much as on high-level-policy decision making. One of the historical ironies about the occupation is that it is often considered (along with Japan's) the most successful occupation conducted in modern history.[170] But much of it was improvised at lower levels—often quite ably, particularly by Lucius Clay and his subordinates. This improvisation was the result of a gap between strategy at policymaking levels and execution at military/ operational levels during the occupation, inherent in the military/political divide that characterized American strategy during World War II. George Kennan, with whom Clay disagreed so strongly, pointed this out lecturing at Grinnell College in 1950, noting that the United

States "has no traditional concepts of military strategy or of the place of military power in the structure of our national life."[171] Kennan was correct: there was no methodology, no system, in place at the time and, perhaps more important, no *mindset* that provided for a postwar governance model that could have promulgated US long-range policy in Germany. It is one thing to assert the need for long-range goals. It is another to conceive what those goals are, and it is even more difficult to do so when planning has entirely acquiesced to immediate, short-term goals. Logically and inevitably, a military postwar-governance model executed those goals. Therefore to attribute the occupation's success to a triumph of US policymaking would be erroneous. Its success can be attributable to a number of factors. Doctrine, training, and personnel were roughly suited to the tasks at hand—not precisely so but enough. The work of Clay and subordinate military government officials should not be discounted. Clay himself possessed penetrating intelligence, tremendous drive, and political skills gained from years of experience in Washington. In particular, his push to return power to German local control proved fortuitous. Additionally, two crucial factors were beyond the control of the occupiers themselves—the territory occupied and the people therein. The postwar resemblance to the World War I Rhineland occupation was serendipitous: it was the German population's own *willingness* to be occupied that was perhaps of greatest importance.

Twenty-Sixth Infantry Regiment soldiers drill in the Rhineland in January 1919. The army's experience in the post–World War I occupation proved deeply influential in its later planning for post–World War II military government. (US Army Signal Corps; National Archives)

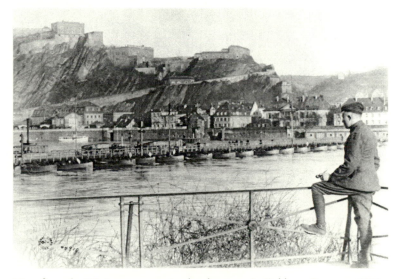

View from the US Army occupation headquarters in Coblenz, Germany, 1919. The placid and beautiful surroundings, along with a relatively nonresistant populace, helped make post–World War I occupation duties by the Americans less challenging than those of other nations. (US Army Signal Corps; National Archives)

President Roosevelt signs the declaration of war against Japan. Roosevelt's managerial style led to uncertainties among his subordinates as to his postwar occupation plans. (National Archives)

Army Chief of Staff Gen. George C. Marshall and Secretary of War Henry L. Stimson. Often overshadowed by Marshall, who focused primarily on wartime operations, Stimson dealt with most of the controversies associated with postwar occupation planning. (National Archives)

Vice President Henry Wallace, perhaps the most progressive member of FDR's administration. His attempts to lead the postwar effort as head of the Board of Economic Warfare ended in failure. (Acme; National Archives)

Secretary of the Interior Harold L. Ickes. A self-styled curmudgeon and veteran New Dealer, Ickes opposed many of the army's attempts to head the postwar occupation effort. (Harris and Ewing; National Archives)

John J. McCloy. As assistant secretary of war, McCloy proved to be a highly capable bureaucrat who successfully represented the War Department's positions in a number of military government controversies. (National Archives)

Maj. Gen. John Hilldring. Hilldring led the War Department's Civil Affairs Division, one of the most influential governmental organizations involved in postwar occupation planning. (National Archives)

Evacuees of Japanese ancestry await buses for their next stop to eventual internment at a camp in Lone Pine, California, April 1, 1942. The US Army was instrumental in ensuring Japanese Americans were evacuated and interned, citing "military necessity." (National Archives)

US infantrymen move through the ruins of Stockheim, Germany, February 1945. The immensity of the German defeat and the accompanying physical destruction were overwhelming. At the same time, largely because the defeat was so total, Nazism was repudiated by the German populace, and postwar resistance was negligible. (US Army Signal Corps; National Archives)

A seminar and general lecture at the School of Military Government in Charlottesville, Virginia, 1943. Controversy over the school was instigated by Harold Ickes, but Stimson and McCloy were able to preserve it. (US Army Signal Corps; National Archives)

Lucius D. Clay, then a lieutenant general. Clay was the de facto military governor of the US zone in Germany from 1945 to 1947. His intensity and work ethic were matched by high intelligence and generally astute political judgment. (National Archives)

American editors and publishers at a luncheon with Clay in Berlin in 1946. Controversies in the press about the slow pace of denazification helped prompt a more robust American effort, but within a few months after that resurgent attempt, the Germans were largely conducting the program themselves. (US Army Signal Corps; National Archives)

Munich residents cast ballots in summer 1946 local elections. Over protest within the US government, Clay pushed for early elections in the US zone, as both a way to show democracy in action and to return power to locals as soon as possible. (US Army Signal Corps; National Archives)

A US military government noncommissioned officer gives instructions to a German soldier, June 21, 1945. German soldiers functioning as messengers and even guards highlighted the need to use locals for common administrative functions during the occupation. (US Army Signal Corps; National Archives)

American GIs in Bremen raise money to buy newspaper ads to protest the slow-down in their redeployment and release from active service in 1945. Senior army leaders faced enormous pressure to demobilize millions of troops in the midst of the postwar occupations. (US Army Signal Corps; National Archives)

Gen. Mark Clark reviews UK troops in Vienna. Although later seen as a doctrinaire anticommunist, Clark generally got along better with his Soviet counterparts than with the British in the first phase of the Austrian occupation. (US Army Signal Corps; National Archives)

Two views of the relatively placid Austrian occupation. American troops take a tour of the Vienna woods, and a solitary GI quietly reads a book outside a command post. (US Army Signal Corps; National Archives)

Austrian governmental officials participate in a V-E anniversary ceremony, May 8, 1946. In the center is Karl Renner, who became president of the Austrian Provisional Government (to his right is Chancellor Leopold Figl). Clark's support of Renner, despite Renner's leftist leanings, helped create the conditions for an eventually unified and neutralized Austria. (US Army Signal Corps; National Archives)

A Korean shows an American military government noncommissioned officer the rice-sifting process. US military government officials were almost totally ignorant of the culture and customs of the Korean people. (US Army Signal Corps; National Archives)

Lt. Gen. John Hodge in front of the US military government headquarters, Seoul, Korea, November 1945. Hodge's straightforward virtues as a combat commander proved of little avail in postwar Korea's political maelstrom. (US Army Signal Corps; National Archives)

Hodge in a meeting with two Korean political leaders, Syngman Rhee (far right, facing toward the camera) and Kim Ku (far left, back toward the camera). Rhee especially proved adept at orchestrating political events that positioned him and his party in close alliance with the United States. (US Army Signal Corps; National Archives)

6

Planning and Implementing Military Government in Austria, 1943–1946

Austria was by no means as important as Germany was to the United States or Soviet Union geopolitically, and therefore neither nation was as concerned about Austria falling into its respective sphere of influence. Accordingly less studied than the more famous occupations of Germany, Japan, or even Korea, the American occupation in Austria nonetheless proved highly important for that country's future. In particular, Gen. Mark Clark's insistence on recognizing the provisional government of Karl Renner was essential to Austria's eventual disengagement from the Cold War. Power was returned to the Austrian people relatively soon, and the establishment of a unified Austrian government proved effective in preventing partition of the country. All the Allied powers left the country in 1955, and Austria became a neutralized state.

Given that Austria was the only divided nation that would ultimately be both unified and democratic during the Cold War, the Allied occupation of Austria, with the US military government playing a catalyzing role, was perhaps the most successful of all. One reason for this success was that postwar Austria most resembled what American military government doctrine asserted was the standard "template" for occupations: a relatively placid population and a local provisional government that was allowed to come to power quickly and that thereby took over the majority of governmental functions. In enabling the provisional government, the American occupiers focused on short-range military objectives and goals. In doing so, they, perhaps ironically, contributed to the seeming long-term success of the occupation.

Initial Strategic Considerations

The basis for the Allied occupation of Austria was found in the 1943 Moscow Declaration. Located in a longer document between statements about the future of Italy and Nazi atrocities, the declaration on Austria's postwar future was short and somewhat ambiguous. Austria's occupation would differ significantly from Germany's. Austria would be treated not as a conquered country but as a liberated one—the declaration asserted that Austria was the first free country to fall victim to Hitler's aggression. Nonetheless, Austria still had a responsibility for its participation on the Nazi side, and as a result, somewhat cryptically, the declaration stated that "in the final settlement, account will inevitably be taken of her own contribution to her liberation." On the one hand, because it had been unlawfully annexed, Austria was to be separated from Germany, made into a viable and independent state, and economically rehabilitated and restored. On the other, it was to be occupied by Allied militaries, power would be restored to it as the Allies determined, and denazification would take place as it had in Germany.[1]

The European Advisory Commission was tasked to prepare initial plans for postwar Austria, though its purview was even more limited than it had been when planning Germany's postwar future. Unlike for Germany, the commission was not empowered to draft a formal surrender document.[2] The commission began organized planning in early 1944 in London, and it eventually determined that, as in Germany, the Allies would occupy Austria using a zonal occupation structure. Each respective nation would occupy a demarcated area with an overarching control-council machinery that would set forth policies that each respective zone commander would implement. As to where the zones of occupation would be, and which nation would control them, planners primarily relied upon the logic of troop movements into Central Europe, and they accordingly demarcated zones where they believed nations' armies would move into Austria. Specifically they marked the region bordering Bavaria as the future US zone.

But while this zonal organization was militarily predictable, it was not necessarily ideal. If decentralization was an objective in Germany, the opposite was the case in Austria: a centralized state was needed for the country to regain a sense of sovereignty. In Germany, where the need to break up the aggressive German militarist state was seen as paramount, zonal division seemed logical. In Austria, on the other hand, the goal was to reinvigorate a state that had been swallowed up by Hitler's Reich. Austria's absorption into Germany had dissolved the Austrian governmental system entirely. The nation no longer existed, and the Nazi government had reconfigured the local governmental structure as well, leaving only seven provinces that received orders from Berlin. And contrary to the common wisdom that communist states naturally wanted unitary governments, the Soviet Union's interests in Austria were better served by a decentralized regime. By taking eastern Austria and placing it under Soviet control, the Soviets could extend their buffer zone beyond Czechoslovakia.[3]

Beyond these discussions of zonal boundaries, there was little in-depth planning done by the United States at the civilian high-policy level. This was partially because there was no government-in-exile to work with to establish a plan of restoration. But it was also due to the lack of direction and the hesitation by FDR and American military leadership to become significantly invested in the Austrian occupation. Both the president and the Joint Chiefs were reluctant to undertake a US occupation of Austria at all or even to participate in a possible control-council structure, largely because they feared that doing so might conflict with military objectives.[4] Throughout much of 1944, FDR had been adamant about having the United States occupy northwestern Germany, primarily so US forces could readily redeploy to the Pacific for the expected invasion of Japan. Additionally, there was concern, particularly among the Joint Chiefs, that having a US zone in Austria was a British-led maneuver to entangle America in traditional great-power rivalries in the Balkans—and to enmesh them in the sort of long-term political struggles that American military leaders sought to avoid.[5] Only after a yearlong struggle with the president and the Joint Chiefs did Amb. John Winant, the American representative at the commission, finally get an agreement by the United States to take a zone. But this was only if conditions demanded by the Joint Chiefs were met. These were primarily over troop strengths but also involved US access to Vienna. Even more important, these demands included allowing the United States to control the Bremen and Bremerhaven enclave in northwestern Germany in order to enable American troops to be shipped to the Pacific.[6]

Gen. Mark Clark, who was to serve as the American high commissioner from 1945 to 1947, was particularly emphatic about the lack of detailed postwar guidance provided to him by civilian superiors. Clark came into the job admittedly not up to date on the larger issues regarding either the German or Austrian occupation, hardly surprising for a general who had just fought his way up the Italian Peninsula. But he was nonetheless shocked about the uncertainty in US policy during the war and lamented it: "Never did I know in particular what the objective of my country was except to win the war or what their thinking would be on a subject of that kind." Clark noted that while given the objective to "fight war, defeat the enemy, and so forth," he did not know what the larger policy questions were.[7] Following the war, he found it just as difficult to find a voice of authority in Washington, with neither the War nor State Departments able or willing to make decisions. Furthermore, Austria was entangled with Germany, causing additional complications. As Clark noted, the US military government was involved "in a multiple show. And in a multiple show there is no boss."[8] He contrasted how British military leaders seemed to be aware of larger political purposes. The British commanders, at least down to the army and army group levels, knew "exactly what their government was thinking" in order for them to have a "unified position." And he especially compared American confusion with Soviet certitude. Clark reflected that the "Russians knew exactly what they wanted." Relatedly, he pointed out how the zonal divisions were carelessly chosen. Reflecting back especially on the food shortages during the occupation's early years, he noted that whereas the Soviets "carved Austria up . . . in such a manner that they got the grain basket where all the food [was] produced," the United States was "perfectly happy to get the ski area, and the [c]hamois hunting and the fishing and things of that kind."[9]

While Clark is sometimes viewed as a self-serving man, and the above reflections no doubt can be read in that light, his views are in fact borne out by the historical record, which indeed shows little in the way of definitive strategic civilian policy toward Austria. And his views of Soviet determination are verified by the contemporary views of others. In a letter from future Austrian political adviser John Erhardt to Gen. Joseph T. McNarney, then commander of US Mediterranean forces (from which came the US occupying forces), Erhardt relied on an April 1945 article in *Pravda* in discussing what was thought to be Soviet views on Austria. According to Erhardt, these views were "guided largely by a desire to prevent Austria from being used by a Central European or Western European structure in opposition to Soviet aims." The Soviets, in Erhardt's words, felt that "Austria should be a bulwark of the East against the West."[10]

The uncertainty and confusion manifested by American policy-makers, and also by American military planners who would set up the operational plans for the occupation, revealed that in a very real way, both military and civilian leaders were caught in circumstances aided and abetted by the army's own institutional thinking and the acquiescence of civilian leadership to this thinking. The insistence on military necessity, which meant subordinating longer-term goals to the immediate goals of military victory, turned out to be something of a zero-sum game. Emphasizing the military goals by its very nature diminished the ability to enact longer-term political ones. As a result, US military leaders and planners wanted more definitive guidance and bemoaned that the other Allies appeared to move with greater purpose. Unfortunately the planning agency that had been established to provide such long-range planning, the European Advisory Commission, lacked vision and initiative. Its solution for Austria simply reiterated that national zonal division would conform to troop movements into the country. This lack was in large part because American strategists, especially the Joint Chiefs, did not want the commission dictating so-called military objectives. And there was no other coordinating body outside the War Department with the particular ability of the Civil Affairs Division to organize and implement either postwar governance policy or administration. The American military planners at the operational level in Europe would therefore have to improvise and come up with much policy on their own.

US Military Planning

Specific US military planning for the Austrian occupation began in 1944. The Civil Affairs Division provided overall direction and oversight, while primary direction in the European theater came from the G-5 at SHAEF under Eisenhower. Other guidance also came from a G-5 group in the US Army headquarters in Italy and from a military government team established to determine requirements specifically for Vienna. Planners were aware that progress was likely to be slow. There were many unanswered questions, among them the extent of Soviet participation in Allied military government. Another complicating factor was the fundamental distinction between the hostility and post-hostility phases of the Austrian occupation and the European Advisory Commission's responsibility for Austrian occupation policy, which was limited to providing policy guidance only *after* the fighting stopped. Military planners were aware that the distinction could lead to disconnection and therefore came up with interim political plans to bridge the war/postwar divide.[11]

The pronouncements of the Moscow Declaration provided a minimal basis upon which to proceed with the Austrian occupation. As to what exactly the machinery of military government would look like the planners could only speculate. The occupation design was premised on the complete defeat of Germany. With this occurring, Austria's people could be, according to the Moscow Declaration's term, "liberated" from Nazi domination along with Austria's institutions, and Austria's government, economy, and society could all be disentangled from Germany. Denazification would also occur, with Nazi racial laws repealed, Nazi political activity suspended, and Nazi public officials removed.[12]

That Austria needed unification, and not decentralization, was grasped by the planners. At least in the spring of 1944, what was contemplated was a fully integrated and joint military government, in which American, Soviet, and British participation was full and equal at a national headquarters and with such a governmental structure running downward into the local level as well, with each *Gau* (province) being headed by some combination of Allied officers. The type of military government that eventually *did* occur—that of zonal division along national lines—was seen as problematic by the planners, who saw that such

division could form an "effective barrier towards the complete unification of all seven *Gaue,* which is the primary purpose of the establishment of a Military Government separate from that of Germany."[13]

Beyond this, however, it was difficult to do anything more specific.
As of late summer 1944, SHAEF still had no clear direction in regard to
Austria occupation plans, though there was some thought to occupying
Austria with four divisions from the Allied command in the Mediterranean if Germany suddenly collapsed.[14] In late fall 1944, some proposed
proclamations were drafted by British planners and forwarded to the
Combined Civil Affairs Committee for approval. The documents were
similar to those drafted for the German occupation. Draft Proclamation No. 1 discussed destroying German militarism and overthrowing
Nazi rule. It vested supreme legislative, judicial, and executive authority in the supreme commander of the Allied forces, and the Austrians
were to obey all military government orders "immediately and without
question." It further directed that all officials except those dismissed
or suspended would remain in their posts.[15] Regardless of the progress, difficulties in coordinating these efforts slowed down planning. As
1944 ended, no American high commissioner had yet been designated,
and a deployment plan for occupation forces had yet to be developed.[16]

What higher purpose that did exist in the US wartime planning
for Austria largely reflected the army's doctrinal precepts on military
government. In more generalized terms, American military government officials ultimately relied on their own knowledge and experience. As Austrian occupation historian James Carafano points out,
"they relied on what they knew: the *habits* of military operations."
American military planners relied upon "their warrior traditions, experiences, assumptions, preconceptions, organization, training, doctrine,
and routine practices."[17] A specific example can be seen in an exchange
between Brig. Gen. Lester Flory, who would be the American commander in Vienna, and Maj. Gen. John Hilldring of the Civil Affairs
Division. Even though planners initially contemplated a military government structure unified among the Allies even at the local level as
a way to foster quicker centralization, Hilldring disagreed with Flory
over this method of establishing military governance. While Hilldring
shared Flory's view that in Austria the centralization of authority in an
Allied Control Council was an appropriate objective, he did not believe

it could be achieved initially. Instead, military government would need to proceed under the total authority of the military commanders of the respective occupied zones, who would operate relatively independently of each other. To permit the control machinery to deal with all problems outright was to Hilldring an "unfortunate attempt to jump directly into the last phase of operations."[18] Rather, what was preferable was a model that allowed the military commanders to reempower the civilian authorities of the zones that they were in and have a "new national administration and government bubble up from the roots as a creature of the Austrian people themselves." Implied in Hilldring's rejoinder to Flory was that the ultimate political end state could not interfere with the immediate military objectives at hand. Ironically, as would be seen, the transitional phase that Hilldring thought necessary was not: the Allies were presented with a ready-made Austrian provisional government early—and Clark pressed for its approval.

Major strategic level finally came in February 1945 with the European Advisory Commission proposal to divide the country into three zones of occupation and with Vienna as a jointly occupied city. The Joint Chiefs approved, and their approval of the zonal structure clearly illustrated the American strategic mindset. The zonal area given to the Americans was contiguous to Bavaria, which allowed US forces in Austria easy passage into Germany, especially since any such troops might eventually have to move farther north to the US-controlled enclave in Bremen in order to be transported to the Pacific. With this zone secured, the Joint Chiefs were satisfied that the occupation was militarily feasible and in accordance with wartime objectives.[19]

The April 1945 *Handbook for Military Government in Austria,* published by Allied Force Headquarters, further illustrated how those military objectives framed the occupation's goals. Based on policy provided by the Combined Chiefs of Staff and intended for use by either US or UK military government officers in the field, it was the most comprehensive operational document on the Austrian occupation. It intended to serve as a bridge to eventual postwar governance. In doing so, it reflected the conference's ambiguities about Austria, noting that Austria had been exhausted by years of war, was demoralized, and was to be treated in a more friendly way than Germany. Still, the occupation need to be firm and just and was to eradicate Nazi influence by "root and branch." In the interim period while awaiting the higher policy guidance, the concept of military necessity prevailed: "Considerations of military necessity or practicability are in every instance over-riding and will be treated accordingly in the application of this handbook." Accordingly, the authority of the local military commander was to be absolute. There would be "strict, complete, and immediate obedience" exacted for all orders given, and all functions would be subordinated to the military aim of victory. The "first duty" was "assistance in the prosecution of the war by enabling the high command to reduce garrison troops for tactical use elsewhere and to provide from the resources of the country whatever materials are available to assist in the prosecution of the war." If there needed to be economic development in Austria, "military requirements must come first."[20]

Much of the document followed precepts set forth in *FM 27-5*. The handbook provided for the standard tactical command model for the initial occupation period, until such time that a separate military government structure could run parallel to local governmental structures. While acknowledging that there would be no functioning government to turn over control to, military government would have to operate as much as possible through indigenous organizations and to "initiat[e], supervis[e], and control executive work carried out by Austrians at the levels of *Reichsgaue* (the governmental administrative subdivisions created by the Third Reich) and below." Notwithstanding the planners' initial hesitation about zonal decentralization, there was no essential difference between the German and Austrian models of strict zonal division—a more nuanced appreciation of the peculiarities of the Austrian occupation did not substantially alter the occupation template. The extant *Gaue* were to be the highest level of functioning Austrian governmental administration, and the occupation would be operated on a zonal basis, with the respective Allied forces enforcing military control exclusively in their zones. The emphasis would be on working through Austrians, and the military government official's success would depend "in great part upon the degree of co-operation he elicits form the local population." Civil officials not removed from their posts would be ordered to remain and to continue to work. This would be governance, as much as possible, by indirect rule.[21]

Denazification was likewise ultimately governed by the exigencies of military operations. The handbook did apparently distinguish between Austria and Germany in that it specifically referred not only for the need to eliminate Nazism but also "pan-Germanism," noting that the latter was more of a "state of mind" than any particular organization. The only way to eliminate such pan-Germanism was to pull Austria definitively from Germany's orbit. Seeking to eliminate active Nazis and Austrian antidemocrats from politics, the handbook acknowledged that nearly all administrative officials had been, at least nominally, members of the Nazi Party. It would be impossible to intern them all: "This would cause the breakdown of all technical services, such as transportation or utilities." Therefore, key Nazi leaders would be removed, whereas those in subordinate positions who were Nazi Party members could be employed pending further investigation.[22]

The final arrangement for the Austria occupation was decided in July 1945, two months after Germany's surrender. The control machinery was remarkably like Germany's. Austria was governed by a four-party Allied Control Council, with each occupying power exercising supreme command of occupation forces in its zone, and with an inter-Allied governing authority (called the *Kommandatura*) jointly governing Vienna. The Allied Control Council was composed of commissioners, all of whom were military commanders (although technically this was not required), who would meet once every ten days.

But there were unresolved issues that included the complete separation of Austria from Germany, the establishment of a central Austrian administrative machine, and eventually the movement toward a freely elected Austrian government. These difficult tasks would have to be achieved through a partition structure (which had become fourfold because France now had an occupation zone) of wartime allies that would likely have competing if not contradictory postwar goals. Even more problematic was the authority of the Allied Control Council vis-à-vis the respective occupational zones themselves. The agreement indicated that "supreme authority . . . will be exercised jointly, in respect of matters affecting Austria *as a whole* by the Military Commissioners." At the same time, the commissioners would exercise supreme authority as commanders in chief of the forces of occupation furnished by their government. And while the agreement did say that the respective zonal authority was "subject" to joint authority, that authority only extended to matters that affected Austria "as a whole."[23] This ambiguity allowed for the possibility that the four Allied commissioners would jointly rule Austria, yet if a particular policy proved contradictory to an occupying nation's postwar goals, that nation's military commander could either attempt to prevent the policy from going into effect or, if unsuccessful, simply not implement it in his zone. The stage, therefore, was seemingly set for an outcome that could quite possibly run contradictory to the expressed overarching policy of an ultimately unified Austria.

Clark's postwar directive that he sent to the US military commanders was quite consistent with the wartime directives and the April 1945 handbook. Just as the wartime directives asserted, the postwar objectives were primarily related to the accomplishment of the strict enforcement of the Berlin Declaration, which included the elimination of Nazism and militarism, the separation of Austria from Germany, and eventual self-governance. The standard practices of military government applied, including the establishment of courts and local administrative governing bodies composed of "reliable Austrians." The emphasis on an early return to Austrian sovereignty was prevalent throughout the document. The commanders were directed to permit political activity and organization by democratic groups "at the earliest possible moment" and, "to the maximum extent possible," to "use Austrian authorities and agencies."[24] As stated in a later military government instruction, military government activities were guided by the principle of giving maximum responsibility to Austrian governmental agencies, with the military government providing general supervision and advice to such agencies, and a preference for local laws and ordinances issued by responsible Austrian authorities over military government legislation sent directly from US officials.[25]

American Military Government in Austria

Allied armies had made their way into Austria by the spring of 1945, with Soviet forces advancing westward into Vienna and surrounding areas (units from the Second and Third Soviet Fronts), the Americans moving southward from Bavaria (units from the Twelfth Army Group), a Franco-American army force coming eastward (units from the Sixth

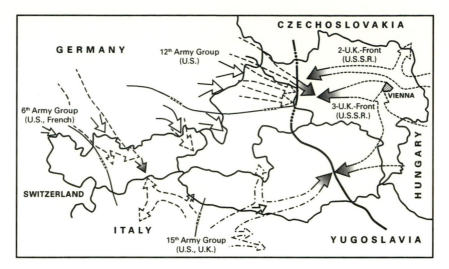

Map 6.1. Allied routes of penetration into Austria. (Headquarters, United States Forces, Austria, *A Review of Military Government,* January 1, 1947, charts, AHEC.)

Army Group), and American-British forces approaching northward from Italy (units from the Fifteenth Army Group). The unit advances largely conformed to planners' expectations as to where Allied forces would enter into the country. Accordingly, zonal occupations conformed to the Allied troop placements in Austria (see maps 6.1 and 6.2). The Wehrmacht resisted until the very end: there was savage fighting everywhere, including between US forces and the remnants of SS detachments. Progress was also disrupted by a quarter of a million surrendering German troops, hundreds of thousands of displaced persons, and spontaneous celebrations throughout the Allied ranks. Business and industry were at a total standstill as the forces moved into Austria proper. All communication services were cut off, rail lines put out of operation, road transport severely restricted, courts and schools closed, and water supplies contaminated in several cities.[26]

The man who would serve as the US high commissioner was a high-ranking field commander, the aforementioned Gen. Mark Clark. Clark had held key positions throughout the war, serving initially as Eisenhower's deputy in the North African campaign, where he also conducted a noteworthy secret mission by submarine to win over

AUSTRIA: ZONES OF OCCUPATION

American
British
French
Soviet
International

CZECHOSLOVAKIA

GERMANY

LOWER AUSTRIA

UPPER AUSTRIA

SOVIET ZONE VIENNA

U. S. ZONE

Salzburg

BURGENLAND

VOR-ARLBERG

FRENCH ZONE

TIROL

SALZBURG

STEIERMARK

BRITISH ZONE

HUNGARY

SWITZERLAND

KÄRNTEN

ITALY

YUGOSLAVIA

Map 6.2. Austrian zones of occupation. (Headquarters, United States Forces, Austria, *A Review of Military Government*, January 1, 1947, charts, AHEC.)

French forces to the Allied side. He subsequently commanded the US Fifth Army in Italy and later the Fifteenth Army Group (a US/UK command) there, leading forces that fought up the Italian Peninsula in a series of bloody engagements. His command had sometimes been controversial, especially during the Battle of Monte Cassino, when his handling of the Thirty-Sixth "Texas" Division led to a postwar congressional inquiry. While his battlefield tactics were sometimes questioned and his combat record was viewed with skepticism by some, Clark was nonetheless highly regarded by both Marshall and Eisenhower as an excellent organizer, and he was by all accounts highly intelligent and forthright, even to the point of abrasiveness. Having served as a key member of a coalition staff and later commander of a coalition force, he also had wide experience in international matters. Furthermore, he had dealt extensively with civil affairs in North Africa and Italy, and he had integrated military government units and G-5 staffs into his commands.[27]

Despite his experience in political-civil matters, Clark neither sought nor expected the job as US high commissioner. He had speculated that he might be sent to the Pacific theater after the surrender of German forces near the Italian-Austrian frontier. He later said that his appointment to the position came as a "complete shock," noting further that he had no idea where the US troops that would occupy Austria would come from or what arrangements had been made with the Soviet Union in particular.[28] Although lacking preparation, Clark was a quick study. His adept handling of many of the more complex issues and, prominently, his efforts in preventing Austrians in the US zone from starving and in offering to provide food to others outside the US zone won him general support from the Austrians themselves. He was so popular in the American zone, particularly in Salzburg, that he was cheered by local Austrians when he moved about the city.[29] He was also criticized for being somewhat impatient, but the trait may actually have served him well, given that he pushed hard for early recognition by the Allies of the leader of the Austrian provisional government, Karl Renner.[30]

History has portrayed Clark as staunchly anticommunist, a stance that only intensified as the Cold War proceeded. But during the initial, critical stage of the Austrian occupation, Clark's relationship with the Soviet Union was far more nuanced than his later views would lead one to believe.[31] He would later write that he began dealing with the Soviets "confident that I would be able to get along with them even though others failed."[32] Though he never built up the deep friendship with his counterpart in the Soviet zone, Marshal Ivan Konev, that existed between Eisenhower and Zhukov, his relations during 1945 and early-to-mid 1946 did not indicate anti-Soviet sentiment.[33] Clark had been concerned about Soviet influence in Austria during the early months of the occupation, as evidenced by his concerns expressed to Renner regarding the presence of Communist Party members in Renner's cabinet.[34] At the same time, he was willing to accept them, given Renner's reassurances. Furthermore, his desk diary entries reveal a consistent pattern of amicable relations with the Soviet officials in Austria during the period. Occasionally he even sided with the Soviets against other occupiers in the so-called Western bloc. He did so when he agreed with the Soviets and disagreed with the British over the supervision of the November 1945 Austrian elections, when the British wanted a much closer supervision than the United States or Soviet Union thought was necessary.[35] In that same month, Clark sent a message to Eisenhower in which he noted the positive results of conversations with Konev, who was much concerned about the negative treatment that Soviet policies were receiving in the American press. Clark went on to ask Eisenhower whether it would be a good idea if his Public Relations Bureau collected favorable articles on Soviet-American relations and had them sent to him.[36] And in a message of April 6, 1946, to the Joint Chiefs, Clark noted that he had recently had dinner with Konev and that the evening was "most pleasant and extreme friendship prevailed," going on to say that he actually detected a "pronounced improvement in [Konev's and his staff's] attitude."[37]

In fact, Clark and the other Allied commanders began the Austrian occupation, according to an official account, in a spirit of harmony, unanimity, and seeking "concrete accomplishment." While the early meetings were not always as smooth as the official accounts relate, there were quite often solid agreements. Even when there were not, Clark not only continued to get along with Konev but also acknowledged that the Soviet general often seemed powerless to act because he was apparently unable to take action without instructions from Moscow.[38] Clark termed his early dealings as a form of "appeasement," noting, "We gave in often."[39] Furthermore, not all of the obstruction—sometimes not even the most significant obstruction—came from the Soviets. Perhaps the most important initial impediment to the Allied Control Council came from the British high commissioner, Gen. Richard McCreery, who refused to have any formal meeting of the council until there was a resolution of a food issue that the British government thought the Soviets were not pursuing. Clark recommended to the War Department that it was appropriate to pressure McCreery to go ahead with the council meeting.[40] Throughout 1945 and much of 1946 it appeared as if many of the serious differences of opinion were resolved, culminating in the Control Agreement signed on June 28, 1946. This served as the primary directive for the remainder of the occupation. In it, the Allies agreed on fundamental principles, in particular that after a competent and independent Austrian government was established, all four powers would gradually withdraw their respective forces.[41]

Nonetheless, friction pointed to larger problems with the four-power occupation. The Soviets, as Konev had noted to Clark, were suspicious of the Western Allies forming a bloc. They were in a considerably different position in Austria than in other Central European countries. Allied Control Councils in Rumania, Bulgaria, and Hungary were totally Soviet-dominated because there were no Western occupation forces. Accustomed to dominating such commissions, the Soviets often felt outnumbered in Austria and in an inferior bargaining position.[42] Additionally, the problems of interzonal division exacerbated economic separation. While all the Allied powers wanted some circulation of trade, the Soviets were particularly fearful of completely opening their zone to the free flow of commerce until the question as to what could be taken as reparation from Austrian industries was resolved.[43]

As for how Soviet military government itself was conducted, Allied opinions on it varied. On the one hand, the lack of Soviet military government organizational structure was apparent. Though there were political commissars, there was nothing remotely comparable to a G-5 in the Soviet command structure, and certainly there was no command-and-control system as sophisticated as the American military government apparatus, with its numerous specialists carefully monitoring Austrian government officials at all levels. As one American official noted during his visit to Vienna, the Soviets made little attempt to control or supervise the local governments. On the other hand, another US official noted that Soviet control seemed firm and effective and that the commandants of various districts seemed hardworking, able, and efficient.[44]

Regardless of whether the Soviet officials were competent and hardworking, there was simply no way, given the lack of command-and-control structures, that the Soviet military command could monitor and supervise the Austrians or the occupying forces too closely. There was also little doubt that the Austrian people did not view the Soviet occupation as benign. US military government officials heard numerous stories of rape and other mistreatment: one US official was apparently told by a retired Austrian general that his invalid sixty-four-year-old wife had been raped four times by Soviet soldiers.[45] Such criminality and mistreatment occurred in the US-occupied territory and throughout the Western zones, to be sure, though far less often.[46] Overall the perception was that the Soviet soldiers existed barely above a state of barbarism. Wellington Samouche, the deputy US commander in Vienna, wrote how Soviet soldiers pillaged homes where they (for example) destroyed beautiful, luxurious decor and drank themselves into stupors with dozens of vodka toasts.[47] Americans and Austrian accounts alike referenced perceived savage and backward "Asiatic" soldiers given to brawling, drunkenness, and squalor. Particularly in Vienna—where the Viennese could see differences from one zone to the other—the Soviet troops were viewed as loutish cultural inferiors incapable of understanding the sophisticated, refined city that they had conquered.[48]

The contrast to the Americans, at least in their relative benignity and in their decidedly greater ability to provide material necessities, was pronounced, and US occupying forces and US occupation policy benefited enormously from it. When the Americans first arrived in their zone of occupation in late May 1945, the situation was by all accounts chaotic, with over 750,000 displaced persons, 200,000 refugees, and schools and courts closed down. But by the end of June, the situation had dramatically improved. The essential problem in Austria was a basic human need: food. After the breakup of the Austro-Hungarian Empire after World War I, Austria had never been agriculturally self-sufficient, and during the occupation hunger and potential mass starvation became a major problem. Accordingly, the efforts of the American military government hinged on the basic problem of raising the population's caloric intake. Most Austrians in the US zone were grateful to receive American-provided foodstuffs, and by early August the intake of Austrians in the American zone had gone from seven hundred to thirteen hundred calories per day.[49] The Austrians noted that initial postwar food relief was provided primarily from American warehouses and not confined to the US zone only. The very abundance of the American occupiers and their apparent ability to provide Austrians with the basic necessities of life provided the United States a significant comparative advantage.[50]

Though the US zone was not primarily agricultural but mountainous, the Austrians in the zone were nonetheless ultimately able to receive the daily ration of 1,550 calories daily as prescribed by the Allied Control Council, as long as the Americans controlled the food distribution. In the French zone, the 1,550-calorie ration could only be maintained until March 1946, and in the Soviet zone the ration varied throughout the early occupation years from around 800 to 1,200 calories a day. In fact, when the United Nations Relief and Rehabilitation Agency began to distribute food per Allied Control Council direction throughout all of Austria, the rate in the US zone actually *decreased* to 1,200 calories per day.[51] The agency, which provided relief nationwide, lacked the logistical capability to sustain the caloric intake as well as the sweeping power of the military governor, who could assert military necessity as a justification to prevent "disease and unrest," similar to what Clay had done with JCS 1067 in Germany. This apparent ability by the Americans to provide basic sustenance may have accounted for the general level of confidence Austrians had—or at least as perceived by the American occupiers themselves—in the ability of the United States to help them. Even in the first months of the occupation when hunger was apparently rampant, Clark believed that Austrians were confident that the Americans could materially improve their situation.[52]

Both the reality and perception of American abundance seemed to pay off in helping maintain a remarkably placid occupation. Nazi insurgency was nonexistent; the Austrians were even less inclined than the Germans to revisit the fascist experiment. And though some Austrians felt either the "sting of American arrogance or the shallowness of U.S. consumer democracy," the cultural superiority many Austrians felt over the Americans worked as a rationalizing mechanism. In a series of interviews of some sixty Salzburg citizens who lived through the occupation, few interviewees questioned the right of the Americans and other occupiers to take control of their affairs, though many provided comments that clearly showed that they viewed Austrian culture as superior to that of the conquerors.[53]

Clark had disdainfully noted that while the Soviets got Vienna and the industrial hub of Austria, the United States got the picture-book provinces. But the American occupiers received the benefits of occupying what for the most part was a compliant population in some of the most beautiful surroundings in all of Europe. Despite the effort in getting basic governmental functions established and occasional acts of sabotage, Americans quite often appeared to be enjoying themselves. Col. Clifton Lisle, who commanded military government detachments in the vicinity in the spring and summer of 1945, remarked on the "clearly enchanted locale, despite the chaos and destruction," and noted that alpine Austria was "truly a magic place," with "unbelievably beautiful" mountains.[54] Even more revealing were the comments of Donald and Florentine Whitnah, who both served in military government positions in Salzburg. They pointed out that by the summer of 1945, a limited version of the annual Salzburg Festival was held, with a concert by the Mozarteum Orchestra provided first for Americans and later for the Austrians. By September of that year, Donald Whitnah wrote home: "Here we are in Salzburg situated in nifty, modern, well heated apartment houses . . . with the snow-capped Bavarian Alps on three sides. . . . We have civilian help for our kitchen, cleaning of rooms and clothes."[55] The conditions in Austria were so favorable to the American occupiers that by the end of August 1945, Clark wrote to Eisenhower stating that he was "in wholehearted agreement" with a plan that would allow groups of enlisted men to travel "under their own supervision to points of their own choosing within our area." He began sending out groups of ten, and each group was free to choose its own itinerary and allowed to be provided its own transportation, gasoline, rations, and camping equipment. Clark's only restriction was to avoid entry into the Soviet zone.[56] By January 1946, Clark felt sufficiently comfortable enough to survey married officers, noncommissioned officers, and civilians in the occupation force as to whether they wanted their spouses and children to come to Austria to live with them in exchange for an additional year of occupation service. The results of the survey were strongly positive. As a result, a number of dependents came to the country, and they were housed in existing buildings without additional requisitioning.[57]

The relative placidity of the occupation facilitated the transition to the territorial model of military government, as envisioned in *FM 27-5*. As the occupation progressed, Hilldring expressed to Clark the preference, in accordance with doctrine, for a separation of military government from tactical personnel as soon as practicable. According to Hilldring, "such clear separation [would] facilitate transition to civilian control without confusion at whatever time may later be designated."[58] By April 1946, US military government had completely transitioned to the territorial model, separating the military government headquarters and detachments from the tactical units in the zone with little to no difficulty. The commanding general of the Forty-Second Infantry Division was the actual commander of all forces in the US zone that contained Salzburg and Upper Austria. However, one level below his level military government authority separated and ran to the chief military government officer and then to the respective commanders of military government detachments, which were separate from all other tactical organizations or staffs. Tactical commanders still had responsibility for disarming and demobilizing German armed forces and handling prisoners of war but were directed to deal with Austrian civilian authorities only through military government channels except in emergencies. [59]

Mark Clark and the Recognition of the Renner Government

During the Austrian occupation, it was commonly acknowledged that the central impediment to Austrian recovery and autonomy was the "abnormal position in which Austria was put in by Allied occupation and diplomacy."[60] The occupational structure directly interfered with the ability of Austria to gain any economic momentum. Military government structures impeded centralization of Austrian central government, which in turn caused problems in the free flow of internal and external trade. As stated in Joint Chiefs of Staff Directive 1369/2, as soon as Nazi governmental influences had been eliminated from public offices, a governing body should be established that would allow for the "nationwide administrative and judicial machinery as may be required to facilitate the uniform execution of its policy throughout Austria."[61] The dilemma was in large part created by the mechanisms of military government and reinforced by a hardening division, especially between the Soviets and the Western Allies. While to some degree the United States benefited from the perception of Americans as saviors and Soviets as savages and while the benign environment in the US zone made American occupation relatively easy, such perceptions also helped to harden zonal boundaries. The Allied governmental system needed some mechanism to arrest what appeared to be the centrifugal pull of the zones to separation.

The key was a unifying political figure. But Austria's political past was complicated. Having once been part of the sprawling and multilingual Hapsburg Empire, a last vestige of the Holy Roman Empire itself, after World War I the country was a rump state. It had resisted

Nazi absorption in the 1930s but via corporatist, antidemocratic governments that, while anti-Nazi, were not viewed by the Allies as viable models for the future. Rather, the alternative came from the moderate Left. And while it would go too far to call his arrival a deus ex machina, the US military government greatly benefited from the emergence of socialist politician Karl Renner. Living in relative obscurity in Lower Austria following the *Anschluss,* he had been chancellor from 1918 to 1920 and was the last president of the Austrian parliament. He was also a man of the Left who had had personal contacts with both Vladimir Lenin and Leon Trotsky.

Even prior to the arrival of Western troops, Renner had stepped forward and claimed authority to lead a provisional government. In April 1945, as the Soviets swept into eastern Austria and Vienna, he presented his credentials to Marshal Fyodor Tolbukhin, whose armies had conquered Vienna, and he ingratiated himself with the Soviet commander by stating that "the special trust of the Austrian working class in the Soviet Republic has become boundless." He thereby offered a provisional government that would freely allow communists in his cabinet.[62] The Soviets, in a move that they would later regret, cautiously took up Renner's offer and accepted him and his cabinet as able to speak for Austria within the Soviet zone. Renner himself appointed three communists to his cabinet, including Karl Honner as minister of the interior, a position that oversaw the incipient Austrian police force.[63]

Many Western Allies viewed Renner with skepticism, if not outright suspicion. The quick Soviet acceptance of his government, his clear socialist affiliations, and his appointment of communists to his cabinet gave Western leaders pause. But Renner was a capable and shrewd politician, and his cabinet appointments and his statements praising the Soviet Union were all calibrated to get the acceptance of that key member of the victorious alliance early, prior even to surrender, while wartime goals were still overriding. His next, equally critical task was to get the West, especially the United States, to extend, if not outright recognize, his provisional government throughout Austria. But this was by no means assured. The United Kingdom especially seemed opposed. At an Allied Control Council meeting on September 11, 1945, the British representative strongly objected to extending Renner's government throughout the country, wary of his apparent communist sympathies.[64]

Renner, however, was supported by Clark, which was particularly noteworthy given Clark's later hardline anticommunist reputation. Ironically, a lack of high-level policy worked to Clark's favor. After all, there was no long-range American plan for Austria and therefore not much to be suspicious of, other than vague fears of Soviet hegemony in a relatively placid Austrian occupation. Throughout September, Clark and Renner had multiple exchanges on Renner's plans for Austria and his commitment to a Western-style system of government. The Austrian politician met with Clark and personally assured him of his anticommunist credentials. In turn, Clark sent a long message to the Joint Chiefs that set out the case for supporting Renner's provisional government as a way to return an effective Austrian government to power quickly. For Clark there was agreement among the Allied powers in establishing an Austrian central administrative machine, except for the "possible exception" of the British. He further added that the other Allies and the Austrian people considered such administrative machinery an urgent necessity. He then provided several reasons to support Renner's position. Interestingly, he proposed support precisely because Renner's government was made up of members of the Socialist Party, the Communist Party, and the Austrian People's Party, which were the three democratic political groups in Austria. This cross-representation effectively legitimized Renner's government. It commanded the Austrian population's confidence and sympathy "to as great an extent as a non-elected group can," and it would be acceptable to foreign public opinion. Furthermore, Renner's coalition consisted of "patriotic and able men" who were also "free of Nazi taint." It had unity in its ranks, its legislative record was so far good, it had held conferences in each province to solicit input, and it had a suggested date, November 25, to hold nationwide elections.[65]

The dialogue between the two men was steady and constant. Renner drafted a series of questions to which he also prepared answers, which were then forwarded to Clark. In the questions and answers provided, Renner plainly set forth the case for an Austrian provisional government, with the eventual goal of an autonomous and independent state. When asked whether the system of zonal occupation was adversely affecting Austrian life, Renner noted that while the four "world-powers" were preoccupied with larger affairs and perhaps lacked sufficient time and attention to deal with Austria's, the damage suffered by occupation was "enormous and not amendable anymore." Goods and services could not be moved readily; raw materials had to be exported in order to buy bread to prevent starvation. And in response to any claim that the Renner government might be too acquiescent to the Soviet Union, Renner noted that "three of the four powers have seemingly decided not to lend us an ear. . . . If perhaps, they think to have reason to complain about one-sided leanings of our Government, they alone are to be blamed." Furthermore, Renner stressed that any fears about a communist takeover, given that, for example, Communist Party member Karl Honner was minister of the interior were misplaced. Renner said that Honner was trustworthy and that, at any rate, the communists were not favored by the Austrian people. Establishing a provisional government would provide the administrative machinery for an early election, which would "clear the political solution" and ensure that the rightward-leaning Austrian People's Party and Renner's Socialist Party would "remain the only two big parties as heretofore."[66]

Arguments were made against Renner, particular by the United Kingdom. He and the provisional government were "unduly susceptible" to Soviet influence. The British had been skeptical of Renner's apparent leftist tendencies very early on, and UK officials particularly found acceptance of Renner both "irresponsible" and acquiescent in the face of an imminent Soviet-communist threat.[67] The British continued to resist extension of Renner's government throughout September. In a September 30 note to the Joint Chiefs, Clark noted that the UK representatives strongly pushed for a de novo government rather than the existing Renner-led coalition and to have all new laws of such a government sent to the Allied Control Council for approval. The British proposed a much tighter supervision over any possible government, to include placing a Scotland Yard officer in charge of the Austrian police.[68]

However Renner's own credibility and responsiveness impressed Clark, and Clark was unwavering in his support: "The Renner regime in its composition and on its record is probably satisfactory from all standpoints. . . . It is my considered opinion that the United States should agree to extension of the authority of the Renner government throughout Austria providing we can satisfy ourselves that the present police set up will permit free elections to be held."[69] Clark had separate pragmatic reasons as well: he was keen on reducing the occupation forces in Austria as much as possible. In November, Clark wrote to the Joint Chiefs requesting a steady drawdown from the current strength of 31,000 to 16,000 by July 1, 1946, though wanting to ensure this occurred as part of an overall multilateral reduction. The plan called for only 5,000 soldiers from each of the Allies to be in Vienna by November 1946 and by then for only 12,500 American, 18,500 French, 20,000 British, and 28,000 Soviet soldiers to be in the entire country. And although he would later complain about the relative ineffectiveness of the United Nations Relief and Rehabilitation Agency, Clark nonetheless advocated progressively turning over relief efforts to the agency, corresponding with a steady relinquishment in the Allied Control Council's authority.[70]

Clark was indeed concerned about the presence of communists in Renner's cabinet, but that presence was not deal-breaking. In a conversation he had with Renner on September 28, he noted Honner's presence in the cabinet, and he was concerned that Honner might have undue influence over the Vienna police chiefs. Renner replied that he would keep Honner. Removing him would anger the Soviets and would be cause for agitation and troublemaking from the Austrian communists. He told Clark that most of the Vienna chiefs were indeed communists, because the Soviets had appointed them after they conquered the city. Nonetheless, he assured Clark that any elections would be open and free, that the election machinery would bypass Honner completely, and that the voting monitors would be 90 percent members of the Austrian People's Party and the Socialist Party.[71] These assertions apparently satisfied Clark, and even though there was continued resistance, including from the Truman administration, the Allied Control Council ultimately granted Renner's government authority to extend its authority throughout Austria on October 20.

Sometimes overlooked, Clark's advocacy and support was highly important, if not crucial, throughout the process. As Clark said, he felt Renner "needed . . . to lean on an objective friend like the United States."[72] And Renner accepted constraints on his government that

Clark himself had indicated were necessary: he continued to acknowledge that the Allied Control Council held supreme authority and reserved to itself certain governmental functions. Furthermore, the Allied Control Council granted extension of Renner's provisional government to all of Austria, not outright recognition of his government, which he obviously would have much preferred. And in agreeing to all this, Renner noted that he strongly felt the political tug-of-war, not between the Americans and the Soviets but between the Americans and the British. Indeed, he believed that the "political" maneuverings of the British were the cause of more friction with the Soviets than those of the United States, which more often seemed concerned about both meeting other military-related objectives and in genuinely seeking some rapprochement with the Soviets.

After the Allied Control Council granted Renner extension of the government over all Austria, he was not above attempting to push his authority beyond what the Control Council deemed appropriate, and he tried to pass laws without seeking its permission. He made unsuccessful arguments, for example, that the Control Council did not possess a superveto over standard, nonpolitical legislation.[73] But this did not cause serious friction: Clark noted throughout November that Control Council relations, especially with the Soviets, remained good.[74] Furthermore, Renner was generally compliant with the council's demands, and, most important, he kept his side of the agreement and organized the governmental machinery that would oversee elections at the end of November. These elections would install a popularly elected government throughout all of Austria.

The extension of Renner's authority set the conditions for the successful November 1945 elections, a new Allied Control Council agreement in 1946, and ultimately a successful outcome of the Austrian occupation.[75] Renner's government in essence centralized the country's politics. Since his government cut across zonal divisions, political elections could do the same, and a unified Austrian political system and government could emerge. The elections, held on November 25, were for representatives to the *Landtage* (the provincial legislatures) and the Nationalrat (the elected lower house of Austrian parliament). They were the first since 1930 and had heavy registration and turnout. The outcome fully satisfied the United States, though the Soviets were bitterly disappointed.[76] The voters elected 85 Austrian People's Party members, 76 Socialists, and only 4 Communists to the Nationalrat, and 213 Austrian People's Party members, 179 Socialists, and only 15 Communists to the *Landtage*.[77] The following month, the parliament was organized, and Leopold Figl of the Austrian People's Party was elected chancellor, with Renner elected as president. In January the members of the Allied Control Council unanimously recommended to their respective governments that the Figl government be recognized as the legitimate government of Austria.[78] In June 1946 a new Control Council agreement effectively turned over most of its authority to the Figl government and crucially stated that unanimous disapproval was required by the Control Council before any law passed by the parliament could be nullified.[79]

Also by June, Secretary of State James Byrnes proposed a draft treaty to the Council of Foreign Ministers in Paris that recognized the independence of Austria and provided for the withdrawal of occupying troops, with the British and French going along but with the Soviets submitting a counterproposal that stated further denazification and other actions were required.[80] And there would be difficult negotiations as the Cold War continued into the 1950s. Both the Americans and Soviets at varying times expressed reluctance about granting total independence and about the complete withdrawal of occupying forces. In the 1950s, for example, Secretary of State John Foster Dulles was reluctant to grant Austria neutral status absent a sufficient Austrian force capable of resisting a Soviet invasion and defeating a communist coup d'état.[81]

But in large part because the Soviet Union did not dominate it, Austria lacked strategic value to Moscow. Thus, unsurprisingly, the eventual grant of Austrian neutrality originated in Moscow.[82] It would be a mistake to say that the May 1955 Austrian Treaty was not part of a larger Cold War geopolitical struggle. Indeed, the Warsaw Pact Treaty had been signed the day before the Austrian one, and Moscow's decision to go along with neutrality may have even been part of a last-ditch effort to stop Austria's outright absorption into a Western alliance.[83] But these machinations took place in light of the fact that Austria had a functioning, pro-Western government in place that had authority over all of the country, not simply the Western zones. Furthermore, it would be very difficult to attempt to undo what the Soviet Union had explicitly permitted in 1945. Austria's occupation therefore ended in 1955 with a peaceful withdrawal of all occupying forces, and the nation became, no doubt happily to the Austrians themselves, relatively uninvolved in the remainder of the Cold War. Accordingly, it is hard to quarrel with the assessment of political scientist David Edelstein, who judged the Western Allies' occupation of Austria a success and the Soviet occupation a failure. The Soviet-controlled portion of Vienna, after all, was the only city mentioned in Winston Churchill's famous Iron Curtain speech that actually shifted back out of the Soviet orbit during the Cold War.[84] The Austrian capital never became a flashpoint of Cold War crisis like Berlin.

The underlying success of the occupation should be traced back to the occupation's beginnings, when military objectives still predominated and when the Cold War's ideological division had not yet occurred. From the outset, the structure of the occupation was militarily focused. The United States resisted any plan that did not defer to military objectives. And the four-power zonal configuration, in which each Allied power held supreme authority in its respective zone, largely conformed to where the military units of the respective powers were positioned at the conclusion of combat operations. This construction shaped the subsequent dynamics of Allied Control Council dealings. While militarily practical, the zonal solution seemed set to cause political failure. Yet the occupation, from a US perspective, nonetheless succeeded. Why was this so, in light of a configuration that should have led to the partitions that divided Germany until 1989 and Korea to the present day? First, from a US perspective, the Austrian occupation, of any conducted after World War II, most resembled that described in the Hunt Report and most resembled the army's doctrinal understanding, as set forth in *FM 27-5*. In the report and doctrine, the American military government presumed a relatively placid population with whom the US occupiers had good relations and presumed a return to normalcy, particularly in governmental structures, as early as possible. Both of these conditions were met in Austria. The Americans conducted an occupation that, while not free of rancor and criminality, was remarkably benign. Despite no doubt hard work, accounts of American occupiers showed they found the occupation as enjoyable an experience as could be imagined. Furthermore, the Americans were able to provide basic life support to Austrians more ably than other occupiers. For an occupation, this considerably reduced the natural tension and mistrust that often come in such environments. Additionally, despite the disdain Austrians had for their Soviet occupiers, US-Soviet relations during the early period were fairly good.

The conditions were primed, therefore, for the most critical factor, which emerged from the Austrians themselves. Karl Renner stepped forward with a provisional government ready to govern all of Austria, which also satisfied the US military government doctrinal premise of early governmental return. Renner and that government were palatable, at least initially, to the Soviets, who mistakenly thought they could use Renner to gain political advantage in Austria. He shrewdly maneuvered the Soviets into granting his provisional government control over the Soviet zone, which then meant the only impediment to achieving central government was with the Western powers. Ironically, the militarized and relatively apolitical stance of the Americans in the early occupation period proved beneficial. Prior to the ideological hardening of the Cold War, there was a certain political breathing space in the 1945–1946 period that allowed for compromise, negotiation, and even a relatively amicable relationship with the Soviets. More than once it was the British, the more "politically minded" of the Western powers, who blocked or attempted to block Austrian governmental unification. And Mark Clark, in particular, deserves credit for his adept understanding of the situation in 1945. Regardless of his later strong anticommunism, Clark correctly judged that Renner could be trusted and that the Americans could deal with the Soviets during the early period in order to set up centralized Austrian governmental machinery. It would therefore be a mistake simply to say that the US military government doctrinal model set conditions for ultimate US success in Austria. Instead, it is more correct to say that the model fit well with the conditions in Austria's particular environment and that the American leadership in Austria was astute enough not to hamper the development of incipient Austrian self-governance. In other circumstances—in a liberated country with conditions much more complex—US military government would fare much differently, as in the occupation of Korea.

7

Planning and Implementing Military Government in Korea, 1943–1946

Some historians have viewed the 1945–1950 period in Korea as a time of superpower strategic miscalculation at the expense of the desires and needs of the Korean people themselves. Bruce Cumings, for example, notes the confrontational Truman administration, which sanctioned the establishment of boundaries between American and Soviet spheres of influence and, as required, the use of military force.[1] Yet, as at least the example of Austria shows, Cold War confrontation did not inevitably lead to war or to permanent partition in occupied territories. While the attitudes or supposed interests of the superpowers are often studied to determine how and why Korea became the Cold War's first "hot" battleground, less examined is American military government during the initial phase of occupation and how it influenced the outcome that ultimately resulted in war and permanent partition. The US Army's military government in Germany and Austria helped produce positive outcomes. But the American occupation of Korea clearly showed the limitations of the army's occupation methods when confronted with a situation and environment both more complex and more alien than what the army experienced in those European countries.

The Korean occupation further revealed the lack of unity between the long-term political goal that the American government presumably espoused, however vaguely—an independent Korean state—and the military instrument meant to further that goal, which was mili-

tary government in accordance with American army doctrinal principles and organization. The military governorship of Korea was meant
to be short-lived, though as Cumings points out, even by December
1945, when the United States and the Soviet Union first discussed a
long-range plan for trusteeship of the country, the occupation already
had taken on a momentum that could not be reversed. But Cumings
is inaccurate when he asserts that "American planners in Washington
thought of military occupation as an extension of political policy and
infantry troops as the agents of policy implementation."[2] Rather, the
army's occupation was an extension of a *militarized* policy that generally subordinated longer-range political goals to military objectives.
Beyond a vague notion of Korean independence, there was little in the
way of long-term political objectives. Instead, the prevalence of militarized thinking during wartime in turn left the occupation of Korea
barely planned at all. Since Korea's military value during the war was
of little consequence, American planners largely ignored the details of
its occupation, and when the army began to administer it, it fell back
upon its military government model to provide the guide and template
for the occupation's first, crucial phase.

Initial Strategic Considerations

Japan had occupied Korea, a country with a millennium of autonomy
and independence, since 1905 and had annexed it outright in 1910.[3]
The Allied powers therefore considered the peninsular nation already
to have been occupied and under the oppressive yoke of the enemy. At
the Cairo Conference of 1943, Roosevelt, Churchill, and Chiang Kai-
shek declared that "mindful of the enslavement of Korea," they were
determined that "in due course, Korea shall become free and independent."[4] The Potsdam Proclamation of July 1945, which stated the
terms of Japan's surrender, reaffirmed the Allies' apparent commitment
to a free and autonomous Korea.[5] But such terms and conditions were
vague and provided little guidance. Not much thought was given to
what the Cairo Conference's phrase "in due course" actually meant.
FDR's indifference and nonchalance toward the phrase was not only a
product of his background and temperament but also an example of his
confidence that the United States would work out a solution, whatever

the ambiguities were.[6] "In due course" very possibly meant to the president some period of guardianship under a trusteeship concept, such as what the United States offered to the Philippines in its 1934 Independence Act. At Yalta in 1945, FDR apparently stated to Stalin that what he had in mind for Korea was a trusteeship in which representatives of the Soviet Union, the United States, and China would preside. Roosevelt speculated that it might be "twenty or thirty years" before Koreans were fully capable of self-governance, with Stalin apparently responding that the shorter the trusteeship, the better.[7]

Unsurprisingly, many Koreans translated "in due course" quite differently. Some translated it as "immediately," as in a period of weeks if not days. Prominent Korean politicians established the Western-oriented, anti-Soviet Provisional Government of the Republic of Korea in Chungking under the leadership of Syngman Rhee and Kim Ku (the latter having unsuccessfully requested that the United States outfit a Korean army to liberate the country in August 1944), with the expectation of early independence.[8]

Unlike for the European occupations, the United States did not plan for postwar Korean governance with any other nation. Neither the British nor the French had made any contribution to the possible invasion and occupation of Japan and Korea, nor did either country have any significant interests in the latter country. The Soviet Union, on the other hand, definitely had strategic interests in Korea: the two countries actually shared a very short border, and the peninsula's importance predated the Russian Revolution.[9] But the Soviet Union was not part of either the Cairo Statement or its reaffirmation at Potsdam because it was not yet at war with Japan. The Soviets were therefore excluded from any initial discussion and planning, though Roosevelt and Stalin clearly expected, as part of the Soviet Union's eventual declaration of war on Japan, some Soviet role in postwar Korea.[10]

But while the Soviet Union was linked to Korea by history and geography, the United States was not. Beyond the anticolonial, anti-imperialist sentiments of the Four Freedoms, Americans had only the vaguest notion of a way ahead for Korean independence. And the only clear postwar goal for the United States in Korea was that the Japanese military be effectively disarmed and demobilized. Accordingly, the pattern of military government, as exercised in Germany and Austria, repeated itself. Indicative of the lack of other alternatives was a May 1943 conversation between Assistant Secretary of State Adolf Berle and Clarence E. Gauss, the ambassador to China. Discussing the prospects of Korean independence with the ambassador, Berle noted that while the United States envisaged an independent Korea, the matter of recognition of the Provisional Government of the Republic of Korea should "rest in abeyance."[11] In May of the following year, in discussion with Secretary of State Hull, Ambassador Gauss referred to a conversation he had had with the minister of foreign affairs of the Korean provisional government, Tjo So-Wang. Referring to the possibility of recognizing the provisional government, Gauss noted that he had seen no official comment on what the Cairo Conference's phrase "in due course" meant. He personally believed that it meant that a "military phase of expelling Japanese from Korea . . . [would be] followed by preparation for civil government and in due course independence," though with no clear dates or milestones.[12]

A State Department paper produced for the Yalta Conference revealed how vague postwar Korea appeared to American diplomats. The document envisioned a postwar occupation of Korea by a military government. There would then be some form of administration or trusteeship that would be established under the authority of an international organization. Because the United States and Great Britain had been part of the Cairo Declaration's promise of establishing a free and independent Korea and because China and the Soviet Union were "contiguous to Korea and . . . had a traditional interest in Korean affairs," the four Allied powers would be prominent members of that organization. The paper discouraged unilateral military occupation. To do so would have "serious political repercussions," in that China and the Soviet Union might each be resentful if any other country predominated. Instead, it proposed a joint, though not zonal, partitioned administration.[13] In a mixture of vaguely articulated and at times naive assertions, the paper stated that the Koreans would implicitly trust the United States to administer the occupation of Korea because of America's anticolonial policies, presumably failing to recognize that it was President Theodore Roosevelt who brokered the 1905 Russo-Japanese peace accord that provided for Japan's occupation and annexation of Korea.[14] It assumed that there would be an organization capable of administering the trusteeship between the period of military government and Korean independence, though there was no such organization yet in existence, and there was little discussion of how long this trusteeship would be. Last, and most important, it presumed that the Koreans themselves would be willing to accept this arrangement in its entirety, though the paper did not address why citizens of a country with a thousand years of autonomous governance would do so.[15]

Beyond such speculative work, neither the State Department nor the War Department developed significant, detailed plans. There was little attention paid to questions of postwar Korean governance from 1943 to 1945. Unsurprisingly, Japan was the focus, and most planners thought the war would last into 1946 and even longer.[16] Instead, American planning for the occupation of Korea operated within a set of premises and assumptions that oriented the country's postwar governance around military objectives. In fairness, War Department planners, primarily in the Civil Affairs Division, recognized the absence of long-range postwar Korea strategy. The ability to bring about permanent political change was limited. The only thing that could therefore be done in the immediate postwar period was to advance, in collaboration with the Soviets, the reestablishment of normal political and economic relationships. However, this could only be done "on a military level." Any consequential change to postwar Korea could only occur after a centralized military administration and, following that, some period of trusteeship that was even less defined.[17] Within this construct, planners assumed that the United States would come to occupy at least a significant portion of the country.[18] Furthermore, the Joint Chiefs of Staff, per the Civil Affairs Division's recommendation, decided that the army would initially be responsible for the occupation of Korea and that planning for the occupation would be integrated into military planning for the defeat of Japan. Korea's only value to the United States, therefore, was its link to wartime strategies toward the Japanese.[19] Primarily, Korea held hundreds of thousands of Japanese troops and could be used as a possible site for bombing and submarine attacks following the American invasion of the islands. (The presence of Japanese troops in Korea and Manchuria was, in fact, the principal reason that the Joint Chiefs of Staff sought the Soviet Union's entry into the war.)[20] With these basic planning assumptions, the State-War-Navy Coordinating Committee decided that the standard military government model would be followed. Noting that there was no "agreed United States view as to the character of administration of civil affairs in Korea," it therefore recommended a bizonal US-Soviet administration by American and Soviet military commanders and a joint military administration akin to the Allied control councils in the European occupations.[21]

US Military Planning

Unlike in Germany and Austria, where the Allies had at least established some mechanism for "control machinery," there was no multinational governance plan in place for Korea. Instead, the primary military plan for its occupation was only part of the larger (and US-exclusive) one that dealt with Japan's occupation in case of sudden surrender, code-named "Blacklist." Even Blacklist had been created pending the issue of presumably more detailed Joint Chiefs of Staff directives and was meant only to serve as a general guide in the planning and preparation by subordinate commanders and units upon the termination of armed conflict. And as might be expected for a military plan, Blacklist framed the occupation entirely within military purposes, stating that the goals for US forces were to "occupy Japan proper and Korea, establish control of armed forces and the civil population, and impose thereon those prescribed terms of surrender requiring immediate military action."[22]

Blacklist asserted a series of planning assumptions, some of which were applicable to Korea. It stated that 270,000 Japanese troops needed to be disarmed in Korea and that the surrender of Japanese forces outside Japan proper might have to be "imposed by force." It went on to say that offensive action might need to be taken if the Japanese high command in Korea failed to follow the surrender of major forces in Japan itself. The plan listed the "reasonable probability" of post-surrender resistance of considerable magnitude, and there was great concern in the plan that in a "sudden surrender" scenario (in which the government surrendered in Tokyo, but forces in the field did not necessarily comply), military and civil resistance might be expected. Throughout

Blacklist this possibility framed the occupation as a military operation against possible enemy forces. The "primary initial missions" for the occupation forces were the "disarmament of Japanese Armed Forces and establishment of control of communications." US forces would need to be dispatched in strength to major strategic centers "against local opposition if offered." They would also need to be prepared to "immobilize enemy armed forces, and initiate operations against any recalcitrant elements in the two countries." Furthermore, reflecting its exclusively military goals, Blacklist referred to an initial occupation phase only. Once Japan was disarmed and there was assurance there would be no widespread resistance, the task of the occupying forces would be to prepare for the establishment of postwar governments in both Japan and Korea only "as subsequently directed." The instruments of surrender were not yet known, though it was assumed that the Japanese emperor would acknowledge total defeat, the commander in chief of US Army Forces Pacific would assume "supreme legislative, executive, and judicial power" over both Korea and Japan, and civil officials would remain at their posts and continue to perform their duties until told otherwise.[23]

The Blacklist plan mentioned Korea in a peripheral way and as little more than an adjunct to Japan. It did state that the occupation would likely be confined to major Korean population centers. But that condition aside, apart from the assumptions that discussed the comparative Japanese troop strengths in Japan and Korea, there was no specific plan for Korea's occupation. There was not, for example, even a separate annex for Korea. "Japan and Korea" were terms seen paired together throughout the document, with the same basic concepts, tasks, and missions for both countries.[24] As for the army units designated to occupy Korea, initially the Tenth Army and subsequently only a subordinate unit within it, the Twenty-Fourth Corps, were chosen to do so exclusively because of their location on Okinawa and thus their relative proximity to the Korean peninsula (see map 7.1).[25] The one major planning assumption about Korea was optimistic, though perhaps without much foundation, given a population that probably yearned for speedy independence: Blacklist assumed that "some degree of cooperation" could possibly be expected from the Korean populace.[26]

The Japanese surrender documents also indicated that little thought

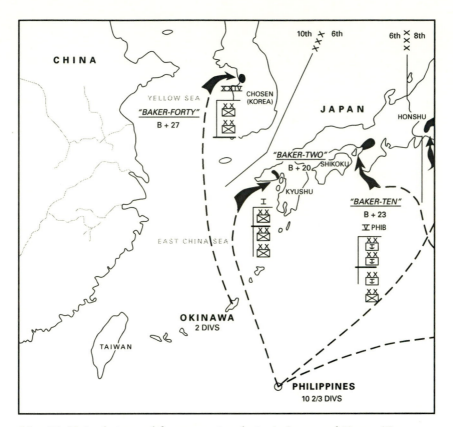

Map 7.1. Units designated for occupation duties in Japan and Korea. (General Headquarters, US Army Forces, Pacific, Basic Outline Plan for Blacklist, August 8, 1945, annex 3A, AHEC.)

had been given to postwar Korea. The initial postsurrender policy for Japan, which Gen. Douglas MacArthur endorsed and President Harry S. Truman approved, did not refer to Korea at all.[27] MacArthur mentioned the country in his first general order only in relation to the Japanese surrender provisions: senior Japanese commanders and all military forces in Korea north of "38 degrees North latitude" would surrender to the "Commander-in-Chief of Soviet Forces in the Far East," and south of the thirty-eighth degree they would surrender to the "Commander-in-Chief, U.S. Army Forces, Pacific," these commanders being the authorized Allied powers' representatives.[28] When MacArthur subsequently issued a military government proclamation to the Korean people on September 7, 1945, he stated that US forces would occupy Korea south of the thirty-eighth parallel and that all powers of government would be, "for the present," exercised under his authority. The proclamation restated, for the most part, standard US military government doctrine. Until further orders, all "governmental, public, and honorary functionaries and employees" would continue to perform their "usual functions and duties." All would obey military government orders "promptly" and any acts of resistance would be "punished severely." English would be the official language of government, and in any event of "ambiguity or diversity of interpretation or definition" between English, Japanese, or Korean, "the English text shall prevail."[29]

But while standard for a US military government document in that it reflected *FM 27-5* doctrine, the proclamation was not well calibrated to meet the particular circumstances of the Korean occupation, as the Americans soon discovered. It contained the vague "for the present" language like that of the Cairo Conference, creating another level of uncertainty for the Korean people as to when self-governance would come. It also made clear that the US would tolerate no dissent or disagreement with military government authority, and the proclamation made little attempt to mitigate any Korean fears that their Japanese masters were only to be replaced by Americans. Most critically, it restated the standard principle of military government that civil administration would remain in place, at least until "further orders" were given. But the reality was that Japanese officials had conducted much of the civil administration for decades, and the Koreans who cooperated with them were considered collaborators. As events unfolded, not only did many Japanese civil officials initially remain in place because of the order, but later, to the dismay and outrage of Koreans, an even greater public relations fiasco occurred when those same Japanese civil servants were *promoted* by the Japanese government, an action that the US military government in Japan had to nullify quickly.[30]

Finally, in October 1945, approximately a month and a half after American occupation forces had been on the ground, the State-War-Navy Coordinating Committee published the primary strategic-level document for the conduct of the occupation, sending it to MacArthur on October 17, 1945. Designated as the "basic initial directive" for the administration of civil affairs in US-occupied Korea, it indicated that the American military forces were vested with the "conventional powers of a military occupant of enemy territory." It stated that the "ultimate objective" was to foster conditions to bring about a free and independent Korea. It thereby set forth a plan that began with a joint period of US-Soviet civil administration, followed by trusteeship of the Allied powers and eventual Korean independence. It did call for the removal of Japanese administrators, though it did allow, if security factors permitted, the use of Japanese civil servants (and Korean civil servant collaborators) if needed for their unique technical qualifications. It also stated that the American administration of the Korean occupation was "principally" intended to ensure compliance by the Japanese with surrender policy, to bring about the political and administrative separation of Korea from Japan, to foster the establishment of local self-government, and thereby to restore a free and independent nation.[31]

Indeed, the document revealed the inherent, unresolved conflict between the long-range goal (Korean independence), the political way this would be accomplished (military government that would transition to some form of trusteeship), and the means that at least initially would begin the process (the staff and subordinate tactical units of a US Army corps). The very notion of a lengthy process that contemplated a period of trusteeship conflicted quite obviously with the standard doctrinal model of American military government—primarily in that such a model sought to return power to local governmental functions as soon as possible. The situation was further complicated because the enemy Japanese administrators had been the very officials conducting those functions. The potential for major trouble was recognized by on-the-ground US leaders. The acting political adviser in Korea, William Langdon, wrote to the secretary of state on November 20, 1945, noting that he was unable to "fit trusteeship to actual conditions" and that the United States should stop pursuing it altogether, pointing out further that military government had come as both a surprise and disappointment to the Korean people, who expected true and complete liberation.[32]

The Dividing of Korea along the Thirty-Eighth Parallel

Complicating the goal of independence and autonomy was yet another standard mechanism of military government—partition by zonal division. According to sociologist Robert Schaeffer, the partition of countries was a fairly widespread phenomenon following World War II.[33] But no political agreement at any wartime conference ever mandated the division of Korea. Nothing highlights the militarized American strategic viewpoint toward Korea more clearly than the decision to divide the country at the thirty-eighth parallel. That the rationale for the partition was for years cloaked in secrecy only added to the mystery about the decision, as foreign policy scholars and historians puzzled over why it was done.[34] The decision to divide looked so momentous that many observers assumed that it was decided by the Allied powers at Yalta. Only as the Yalta documents became declassified did it become apparent that Korea was barely mentioned at the conference, and never during the conference was there discussion of division.[35]

As map 7.2 indicates, the thirty-eighth parallel paid no respect to political boundaries, cutting through the two Korean provinces of Kyonggi-do and Kangwon-do. Its division provided little long-range strategic benefit to the United States: most of the heavy industry was in the region north of the thirty-eighth parallel, including the hydroelectric plants that provided power to Seoul, the nation's capital and largest city. As William Stueck points out, the thirty-eighth parallel line also followed no physical features: it passed through streams, rivers, roads, highways, and rail lines with total arbitrariness. But Stueck's conclusion that "the thirty-eighth parallel was a line drawn on a map, nothing more," while having compelling and simple force, fails to convey that there was an overriding military purpose for the decision.[36] A straightforward latitudinal dividing line had specifically military advantages: if the main purpose was to demarcate surrender lines, a parallel provided a line on the map that field commanders with maps could ascertain with relative ease, whereas a more political boundary required greater understanding of local geography.[37] Furthermore, the possibility of combat was not entirely far-fetched either. There was evidence of at least some resistance on the Korean peninsula by Japanese forces as late as mid-August.[38] Therefore, a clear military border between the US and the Soviet forces could simplify the operational zones of responsibility.

Correspondence between Edwin Pauley, the American representative to the Allied Reparations Committee and a close confidant of and adviser to President Truman, and the president and the secretary

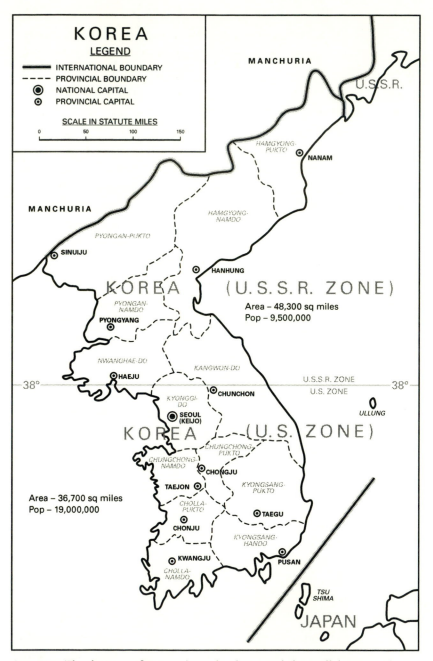

Map 7.2. The division of Korea along the thirty-eighth parallel. (General Headquarters, Supreme Commander, Allied Powers, *Summation of Non-Military Activities in Japan and Korea,* September 1945, on file at AHEC.)

of state underscored how depoliticized the division was. In it, Pauley strongly contended that American forces should occupy as much of the industrial areas of Korea as they possibly could.[39] But there is no evidence such a view was considered: as noted, the actual division left the majority of Korean heavy industry in the north. Senior US leaders affirmed the military rationale for choosing the thirty-eighth parallel as the dividing line. Secretary of State James Byrnes indicated that the division was "for purposes of military operations."[40] In a letter from Byrnes's successor, George Marshall, to Soviet foreign minister Vyacheslav Molotov in 1947, Marshall commented upon the demarcation, calling it "arbitrarily assigned for this [military] purpose."[41] John Hilldring, formerly chief of the Civil Affairs Division and later assistant secretary of state for occupied affairs, said that it was little more than "than a military expedient between two friendly powers. The line of demarcation was intended to be temporary and only to fix responsibility between the U.S. and the U.S.S.R. for carrying out the Japanese surrender."[42]

Senior US military officials had paid little attention to the initial determination of zonal boundaries in the European theater. The decisions to divide up Germany and Austria, for example, were driven almost entirely by British planners, and only when specific military objectives were involved were American senior military leaders particularly attentive. In the Far East, however, the British were not involved in occupation planning, and no multinational body such as the European Advisory Commission worked out surrender terms or multipartite control machinery. Instead, the planning for the occupation of Japan was almost entirely done by the United States and in particular by the Civil Affairs Division and the War Department–dominated State-War-Navy Coordinating Committee.

In the case of the Korean partition, the decision was made almost immediately after the Soviets had declared war on Japan in early August 1945. Two relatively junior staff officers, Maj. Dean Rusk, a future secretary of state, and Maj. Charles Bonesteel, a future four-star general, did the work. Rusk recounted that he and Bonesteel worked in great haste and under great pressure to pick the American zone. While it did seem important for them to ensure that the capital, Seoul, was in the US zone, they also knew that "the U.S. Army opposed an extensive area of occupation," given the rather threadbare occupation force the army would subsequently utilize. Because they could not find a "convenient dividing line," they simply noted the thirty-eighth parallel and "decided to recommend that."[43]

The State-War-Navy Coordinating Committee approved the division, which would be expected given that it likewise saw any potential occupation from the vantage point of military expedience. And it was presented to the State Department, at least according to the chief of the State Department's Far Eastern Affairs Office, as a fait accompli.[44] No one apparently was aware that in 1896, Gen. Yamagata Aritomo, one of the founders of the modern Japanese army, actually proposed to officials of the Russian Empire to divide Korea along the same parallel (the Russians refused the offer), though Rusk stated that had he known of it, they would have chosen another demarcation line precisely in order to avoid any political overtones to their decision.[45] In 1945 the Soviets readily accepted the division at the thirty-eighth parallel—Stalin had no reason to provoke the Americans by encroaching southward. Furthermore, the aforementioned division along the old sphere-of-influence line was possibly advantageous to the Soviet dictator. By playing along he might get a chance at a potentially bigger prize—an occupation zone in the Japanese archipelago itself.[46]

The partition of Korea along the thirty-eighth parallel was not created by American cold warriors as a way to keep the Soviets out or by clever Soviet negotiators as a way to trap half the nation in communist totalitarianism. It was a deeply militarized decision made to meet military objectives. The political end of trusteeship to be followed by independence, vague as it was, provided no framework or context for the decision itself, which was arbitrary and supposedly temporary. Of course, it would not be temporary but a decision that caused turmoil for the remainder of the American occupation and that in significant ways determined the fate of modern Korea. Lt. Gen. John Hodge, the senior US commander in Korea, recognized this when he noted that "no aspect of military government can escape the effects of an arbitrary division of Korea into two zones of occupation" that occurred north and south of the parallel.[47]

Absent all of this were the desires of the Korean people themselves. Unlike Austria, which was a rump state of the old Austro-Hungarian

Empire, or Germany, which until 1870 had been a multiplicity of states, duchies, and principalities, Korea had been not only an independent nation but also a united one for centuries. A zonal split wounded the collective consciousness of Koreans as much, if not more, than occupation itself. If anything bespoke the blatant apoliticism of the partition, it was this lack of historical awareness by the planners. And in making the division, the signal was clearly sent, albeit accidentally, that the old Soviet sphere of influence might well be back in effect and that the Korean people were, once again, at the mercy of powerful geopolitical forces far greater than themselves.

John Hodge and American Military Government in Korea

Had the Tenth Army, as originally planned, been given the Korean occupation mission, the US military commander would likely have been Gen. Joseph "Vinegar Joe" Stilwell, who had advised Generalissimo Chiang Kai-shek during the difficult campaigns in China. Stilwell was shrewd, acerbic, and blunt, and there is some indication that the generalissimo personally objected to Stilwell getting command over any American occupation forces. At least Stilwell had had extensive dealings with foreign leaders. With seemingly no thought given for experience or personality, the subordinate Twenty-Fourth Corps and its commander, Lieutenant General Hodge, were given the job instead. Hodge was described as tough, no-nonsense, and honest to the core. He had a reputation as an excellent combat commander and was even labeled as the "Patton of the Pacific."[48] He was a tactically skilled leader with extensive combat experience, having fought in the Meuse-Argonne in World War I as an infantry officer and in World War II as assistant division commander of the Twenty-Fifth Infantry Division at Guadalcanal, as commander of the Americal Division in the Bougainville Campaign, and as temporary commander of the Forty-Third Division in combat on New Georgia.[49] Rising to command the Twenty-Fourth Corps at Okinawa, both he and the unit were battle-tested. Nonetheless, Hodge lacked the civil-political experience for the occupation. In an unfortunate irony, the Korean occupation was the most difficult of any such mission carried out by US troops after the Second World War, and the man primarily responsible for it had the least civil-military experience of any senior leader involved in occupation duties. Unlike Lucius Clay, who had spent the war years in Washington, Hodge had no in-depth experience dealing with interagency problems or with politicians. Unlike Mark Clark, he never had to deal with leading coalition forces into battle. And while Hodge had some experience with military government in Okinawa, it could not compare with Clay's bird's-eye view in the War Department or Clark's experiences in North Africa and Italy. In retrospect, there seemed to be little rationale as to why he was selected other than that he commanded the Twenty-Fourth Corps, which, in accordance with Blacklist's operational requirements, was the closest unit to Korea in the Pacific.[50]

Historians have tended to treat Hodge rather harshly, seeing him as narrow-minded, reactionary, oblivious to the nuances of Korean culture, and excessively and even obsessively anticommunist. Stueck asserts that Hodge proved "abysmally insensitive to Korean desires for immediate liberation."[51] He was also, in the words of Allan Millett, "personal, confrontational, and impatient."[52] Bruce Cumings calls him a "classic nationalist and containment" figure and more generously but still critically notes his "courageous but ill-considered decisiveness."[53] Such criticism can obscure Hodge's insightfulness, despite his lack of experience. On more than one occasion, Hodge sent out correspondence to his unit commanders about his concerns that US personnel should not treat Koreans as a conquered people and that there needed to be better efforts to understand them, to respect their customs, and to learn elementary parts of their language in order to increase communication.[54] Hodge was also politically more aware than might be expected given his reputation. Shortly after arriving, he wrote that the situation in Korea was a "powder keg ready to explode." He further realized that his military government was woefully unprepared for the task: the Twenty-Fourth Corps was "small in strength and short of competent staff," and the military government was having "little overall effect."[55] He saw that the thirty-eighth parallel had become in reality a closed border and that negotiations needed to be started at once with the Soviets on all sorts of problems that crossed the two zones.[56] Hodge also believed that such problems could not be solved using military government as structured. In a message that ultimately went to the Joint Chiefs of Staff, he wrote that efforts at the military level to bring a joint US-Soviet collaboration between the occupation governments would likely not succeed. The issues between the nations were too fundamental: before any decision could be made, high-level negotiations between Washington and Moscow would be needed.[57] To Hodge, the situation in Korea during the first year of occupation was "impossible of peaceful correction . . . unless immediate action on an international level is forthcoming to establish an overall provisional government which will be fully supported by the occupation forces under common policy." Hodge was aware that recognition of a provisional government was a way to break through to a solution that could pull the country into the direction of unity under one central government, something that had occurred in Austria with the recognition of the Renner government. However, he also noted that the longer the division between the US and Soviet zones remained in effect, the more the separate interim governments would harden, making unity ultimately impossible.[58]

Yet despite some admirable traits and more insight than he has perhaps been given credit for, history's judgment that he was the wrong man for the job appears justified. He was needlessly and excessively abrasive in his dealings with Koreans. More important, Hodge simply acted too much in accordance with standard military government doctrine and his own personal inclinations, lacking the sense of nuance and context that, for example, Clay and Clark seemed to possess. Much of this was done simply because no alternative existed. Hodge, for example, had no choice but to administer the occupation through tactical units at first and thereby provide a heavy-handed military governance style in a nation that had already been occupied for decades, since only a handful of military government teams were part of the initial occupation force. Nonetheless, he lacked judgment and sensitivity that could have smoothed the harsher edges of military government policy. As an example, in one of his very first public actions, a press conference following the Japanese surrender, in September 1945, Hodge announced that Gen. Nobuyuki Abe, the governor-general, who had once served as premier of Japan, would be "retained temporarily as head of the government." Hodge further stated that Japanese officials would subsequently be replaced by Americans as soon as possible and *only afterward* by Koreans.[59] In contrast, in a similar situation, Soviet colonel-general Ivan Chistaikov quickly replaced Japanese officials with Koreans, though many of them had returned from indoctrination in the Soviet Union.[60] A man of personal integrity, Hodge also had a sense of self-righteousness and an inherently reactionary streak that on the one hand led him to believe that Koreans were incapable of self-governance and on the other to side with conservative Korean landowners and businessmen who were strongly associated with their former Japanese overlords, all of which made him intensely unpopular with much of the populace.[61]

Hodge's unit, the Twenty-Fourth Corps, which included the Seventh, Fortieth, and Ninety-Sixth Infantry Divisions (the Sixth Infantry Division later replacing the Ninety-Sixth), support units, an antiaircraft unit, and a bomber wing, began arriving in early September 1945. What he had in combat capability, he sorely lacked in military government and civil affairs expertise. Hodge soon realized he did not need heavy weapons and bombers and sought to convert one combat unit to military police. Accompanying the tactical formations were a total of three military government teams that would begin occupation duties in the Seoul-Inchon area. Only gradually over the weeks and months more military government teams arrived. Unlike in Germany or Austria, there was not a more gradual transition from combat to posthostilities. And without a transition, the occupation lurched ahead of the doctrinal model. Instead of moving forward into posthostilities with military government units at the ready and accompanying detailed plans (it is notable, for example, that there was no handbook available to the occupiers comparable to one for Germany and Austria), the occupation operated somewhat in a vacuum during the first critical weeks. For over a month outside of Seoul and its environs, military government was run entirely by tactical units that were unfamiliar with what was required. When a unit showed up in Kwangju, for example, the officers did not know what their assignments in the locale would be and knew nothing of the local administrative structures.[62]

An article in *Time* magazine on October 8, 1945, noted that the American military government in Korea was staffed with officers who are "combat officers and not proconsuls. They are short-handed. . . .

Men already punchy from combat (and anxious to go home) are driving themselves 15 hours a day and more, trying to get a country of 25 million people rolling again. Before it is done, the job will take experts."[63] Even the military government personnel who did eventually arrive were not trained for the Korean mission. Much training, including culture and language training, was provided for the Japanese and German occupations. Little to no training was Korea-specific.[64] Furthermore, the sudden surrender of Japan had thrown off training timetables, and what instruction that was provided was hurried and necessarily incomplete. One officer who served as one of the provincial military governors noted in a personal account that he had attended the School for Government of Occupied Areas at Carlisle Barracks, Pennsylvania (a school that replaced the original School of Military Government in Charlottesville, Virginia), where over a thousand graduates had taken a crash program in a last-minute attempt to meet military government requirements.[65]

The lack of training and knowledge about Korea was extremely unfortunate, for while Koreans were at the very least ambivalent about American military forces occupying their country, evidence suggests that they could have accepted American military government as a practical, short-term measure if effectively conducted. Public opinion surveys in September and October 1945 revealed concerns among the Korean people, in order of precedence: (1) retention of Japanese officials as advisers to the military government, (2) return of the provisional government in Chungking, China, (3) establishment of price controls, (4) the absence of military government officials in outlying areas, (5) conditions in northern Korea, (6) distrust of interpreters working for the military government, and (7) distribution of farm lands. Notably missing on the list was a desire to have the Americans end military government forthwith, and in fact one of their priorities (number 4) was concerned with the *absence* of an adequate number of military government personnel to administer effectively in the countryside.[66]

The Korean populace's relative tolerance therefore made the seeming disregard of their primary concern, the retention of Japanese officials, so revealing of the disconnection between the imperatives of military government doctrine and the realities of the Korean occupation. As noted, the military government's initial approach upon entering Korea was to work with the existing civil structure—standard military government doctrine and practice—which meant keeping Japanese officials in power.[67] Protests soon broke out. The retention of Japanese officials required major public relations damage control. Ultimately the complete elimination of all Japanese officials from government was required, though this did not completely occur until the spring of 1946.[68] That in turn led to a series of problems. As a military government agricultural report stated, confusion reigned when Japanese agricultural administrators, technicians, and policemen left, and "the entire government service to agriculture had to be reorganized, staffed, trained, and directed," a process that consumed months of time.[69] Prior to the establishment of a more robust Korean provisional government, the only solution was for the Twenty-Fourth Corps to assert direct control and governance over the Korean people south of the thirty-eighth parallel, which it was in no way adequately manned or trained to do, since its primary purpose had been to demobilize and disarm the Japanese.

Throughout the fall of 1945, more military government units came onto the peninsula. By January 1946, the demobilization and disarmament of the Japanese forces were largely completed. At this point a new organization was established, the United States Military Government in Korea (USAMGIK). Therefore, though still inadequate in numbers and training, the standard "territorial" approach to military government came into being, shifting entirely from tactical to military government units. Accordingly USAMGIK's first general order directed that control of military government units would pass from corps tactical units to designated military government detachments, relieving tactical commanders of the responsibilities over "non-military activities" and instead placing them exclusively in the hands of military government officials.[70] A crucial step in the transfer of power, at least according to US military government doctrine, was thereby accomplished, albeit in rather chaotic circumstances, very unlike either Germany or Austria.

All the while, the lack of attention paid to Korea contributed to a scarcity of resources for the occupation, which in turn lowered the morale of the occupying force. The American experience in Korea was in stark contrast to that in Europe and Japan. In 1946 Frederick Silber from the Department of State's Office of Occupied Areas flew to Korea to determine the usefulness of efforts in political reorientation. Long before he left Japan for Korea he began to hear "repeated warnings about the horrors of the place." Silber recounted an end-of-the-line psychology from the highest to lowest ranks in military government. He noted that the military government suffered shortages of supplies and equipment—paper was so scarce that "every square inch [was] the subject of conflict between potential rival users."[71] Indeed, supply requirements were never met during the occupation. Maj. Gen. Orlando Ward, the commanding general of the Sixth Infantry Division, the other principal combat formation in the Twenty-Fourth, pointed out the complaints of a group of sergeants who had written to the press about shortages of critical items: "These men could not see why service of supply is, in their opinion, adequate in Japan and inadequate in Korea." Ward essentially agreed that property accountability was in a poor state and that for many important types of supply the system was fundamentally broken.[72]

The experiences of occupying commanders and soldiers revealed that the occupation was fraught with far more hardship than Germany's or Austria's. The travails of the 185th Regiment, a unit in the Fortieth Infantry Division, one of the Twenty-Fourth's principal combat formations, were common. It landed in Korea in September 1945 as part of the initial occupying force, with its mission to occupy the city of Taegu and surrounding areas. Its primary tasks were to accept the surrender of Japanese troops, take over all Japanese supplies, provide law and order, and administer the area until the arrival of military government teams. It also had the responsibility of conducting the military government mission until the arrival of trained military government units specifically designed to perform those duties, which involved a host of other complex political issues that went far beyond purely military tasks (and the 185th's own inherent capabilities). The difficulties were many. The regiment's history noted the Koreans' "hatred for the defeated Japanese, and the unfavorable political setup," as well as "threats and action by various groups" during the first months. Later, following the Moscow Conference in December 1945, Koreans in the regiment's occupied areas demonstrated throughout with placards denouncing the idea of trusteeship. As the regiment's history noted, the situation was "chaotic."[73]

Military government personnel elsewhere had more direct and immediate concerns. One soldier noted ominously the harassment that Koreans in the north inflicted by cutting off hydroelectric power to the south: "They do anything to agitate us. Every night, just like clockwork, the lights go out at 2100 hours and will stay off for 15 minutes. I think they want us to know that they could turn them off permanently if it [suits] them. They control the dam."[74] Many of the American occupiers apparently had a low opinion of their duties and of the Korean people themselves. The same soldier registered his disapproval at the Koreans for dumping garbage "out in front of the houses on the street" and also noted the lack of sanitary sewage.[75] Walter Simmons, a *Chicago Tribune* reporter, wrote that US soldiers told him that the "only things [Koreans] understand are the ball bat and pick handle" and that the soldiers unfavorably contrasted the Japanese with the Koreans: "The Japanese are friendly. The Koreans are hostile. You try to take a picture of a Korean child and he runs. You treat the Korean nice and he cheats you."[76] Hodge himself noted the poor treatment of the Koreans by the American troops: "There seems to be a let-down on the part of Americans everywhere in decency, standards of behavior, and in honesty," he wrote in late 1945.[77] Hodge felt compelled to send a letter to all his troop commanders, concerned about the feeling between his troops and the Koreans. He wrote: "This was not a conquered country, and an effort was to be made to understand [Koreans], to respect their customs, and to promote a friendly feeling. It was important to learn a few Korean phrases, so a pleasant greeting could be exchanged, and so on." Addressing the occupation forces in June 1946, he noted that when the American forces arrived in September, they were looked upon as heroes sent from the greatest nation in the world, but since that time many Koreans had changed their minds. Hodge also directed the troops to stop using demeaning terms such as "gook," to learn about Korean customs, and to "get over the idea that the Korean is servile. He isn't."[78]

If the occupation force structure proved inadequate in dealing with myriad political and social problems, the occupation's legal system made clear the dilemma of attempting to use US military government as the means to facilitate the move toward independence and democracy, especially in a nation that was liberated, not conquered, and that bore no blame for the war's conduct. The US military government, for example, issued hundreds of legal opinions on a wide variety of issues, from property and political rights to free speech. One opinion referred to a charge brought by US officials in the provost (military government) court against particular newspaper owners. The owners had published "false and defamatory statements" against the military government and were in violation of Military Government Ordinance No. 19. Specifically, articles in the papers had statements such as "People came to the city hall to ask for rice but got guns and beatings instead." The provost court ruled that the statements were false and deliberately intended to disturb the peace, and that the Korean newspaper editors were guilty. Upholding the court's decision, the military government's department of justice noted that Military Government Ordinance No. 19 recognized freedom of the press in Korean newspapers. The opinion went on to say, however, that the freedom was subject to restrictions necessary for the successful survival and operation of military government. Furthermore, the department pointed out that there were times when statements that could cause disorder or the imminent possibility of disorder could be prosecuted, because Military Government Proclamation No. 2 made such acts criminal.[79]

Looking at the requirements of occupation in relation to the "privileges and liberties recognized by America as being fundamental principles of civilized and progressive states," the department then attempted to square American notions of liberty with the requirements of military government. It noted that the statements made by the Korean newspapers did *not* rise to the level of subversion and that therefore the editors could not be criminally prosecuted for violating Military Government Proclamation No. 2. On the other hand, it noted that the requirements of military government *did* allow suppression of freedom of the press in this instance, and it ruled that the papers that published the statements could be suspended. The opinion stated, "In this entire matter, we must balance military necessity against privileges and liberties recognized by Americans as being fundamental principles of civilized and progressive states."[80] Particularly revealing was the opinion's use of the term "military necessity," the doctrinal standard for determining the requirement in an occupation. It was a difficult task for the American military occupiers to balance what seemed like competing interests—to ensure military government was obeyed without question and also to attempt to convey to Koreans that Americans were not hypocritical in facilitating the transition in Korea to an independent and democratic nation.

The gap between ideals and on-the-ground realities was nowhere more prominent than in efforts to return power to Koreans and to reconstitute political parties. Hodge opposed trusteeship altogether. He contended that it would be better to restore an independent Korean government as soon as practically possible, and therefore he sought to reinvigorate the political process by permitting the formation of political parties. But this standard military government approach played out rather badly. By early November, no fewer than 205 parties had formed in the south, and desperately searching for a way to control what looked like political chaos, Hodge fell victim to the inadequacies of the military government structure that he had on hand. His staff completely lacked the experience and even the basic language skills to evaluate and to determine which parties could best represent the Korean people across the political spectrum and also fruitfully work with the occupation force. Instead the Koreans who became most influential in the American military government were those whose mastery of the English language allowed them to best represent their interests—and to marginalize those who opposed them. Most of these had been educated by American missionaries and tended to follow Syngman Rhee, who had returned to the country in October and who saw himself as the presumptive leader of the Korean people. This "government of interpreters"—largely conservative landowners and businessmen, some of whom had a collaborative past with the Japanese—deliberately set themselves in sharp contrast to other political bodies, such as the moderate leftists under Yo Un-hyong. Prior to the arrival of the Americans, Yo and others had established the Committee for Preparation of Korean Independence, which soon became labeled by the American military government as a Soviet puppet organization.[81] Thus well-intentioned military government helped trigger polarization—which fomented unrest, protest, and violence.

The Soviet Occupation, the Moscow Conference, and the Joint Commission

The contrast between the American and Soviet occupations was significant. The Soviet Union entered the war against Japan in August 1945, virtually at the point of Japan's surrender, and was not included in any planning for postwar occupations. There were no wartime coalition organizations comparable to the Combined Chiefs of Staff or the European Advisory Commission to provide Allied strategic oversight. Accordingly, there was a complete absence of discussion before the occupation between the Americans and Soviets about control machinery, zonal division, and related topics.[82] While the Far Eastern Commission was established at the conclusion of the war and included the Soviet Union and other Western allies, its focus was on the occupation of Japan, and even there its role was greatly diminished, largely due to General MacArthur, who felt that the commission should not encroach upon his authority. In his words, it was reduced to not much more than a debating society.[83]

The Americans and Soviets in Korea therefore largely conducted their respective occupations as they saw fit, with almost no interaction between the military governments. The Soviets did not follow a doctrinal model such as the Americans and in many ways displayed a shrewder political understanding of postwar governance matters than the Americans did. Even though over 250,000 Soviet troops swept into the upper half of the Korean peninsula and even though the Soviets quickly lost their reputation as Korean liberators, given the widespread looting and raping that occurred, they did not establish much of a military government at all. Instead they simply empowered communist-controlled people's committees (which they had engineered to get into power) to run matters.[84] Furthermore, the Soviets quickly replaced Japanese administrators with Koreans, albeit those whom had returned from training and communist indoctrination in the Soviet Union.[85] A proclamation by the commander of the Twenty-Fifth Occupation Army stated that the objective of the Red Army was to "rid the area of all the plunderers" and that the Red Army had no "intentions of territorial gains or running the Government of Korea under a Russian system." Rather, the proclamation stated that a democratic system of government would be permitted, along with unions, and that religious freedom would be guaranteed.[86]

Recent scholarship has demonstrated that Soviet intentions and actions were not necessarily well intentioned, best indicated by the Koreans who fled the north.[87] Regardless, much of the Soviets' intentions, and much of the Soviet occupation generally, were unknown to the American military government. Efforts by Hodge to establish contact and to begin discussion with the Soviet commander during the first crucial weeks of the occupation in September failed.[88] The Soviet consulate in Seoul was a mysterious place—it was unknown what precisely the consul did there, though it was believed he ran an effective spy network. Accordingly, the information that American military government officials gained about the Soviets was vague and uncertain, and speculation ran wild.[89] Evidence of a communist-organized espionage system began to accumulate throughout 1945 and 1946. US military government officials came to see the Soviet occupation, rather inaccurately, though perhaps understandably, as part of a campaign of ultimate annexation of the entire peninsula. One such official later wrote that the actions of the Soviets indicated that their goal was to "take over North Korea and make of it a Soviet Socialist Republic for ultimate union with South Korea and incorporation in the Union of Soviet Socialist Republics."[90] Reports of the Soviets forcibly replacing local autonomous governments with "people's political committees" that marginalized or suppressed all others fit with other narratives of political parties in the south infiltrated with communist agents receiving support and direction from Moscow.[91] Some reports were no doubt true, but it became difficult to separate reality from fiction. At the same time, the thirty-eighth parallel quickly became a nonporous, militarized frontier. By November 1945, the border between the two zones prevented any significant interchange of information, goods, or persons.[92] By the following month, only one US convoy headed into the north per week.[93]

The result was a rapid establishment of two wholly dissimilar governmental systems. The first significant contacts between the occupiers did not occur until December 1945 in Moscow, in an attempt to work out a joint solution toward ending the occupation. The December Moscow Conference was the only detailed plan by the United

States and the Soviet Union regarding the future of Korea, though it occurred four months into the occupation itself. In retrospect, it is evident that the Moscow Conference moved the Korean occupation into the geopolitical calculation of the Cold War and the military, ideological, and cultural struggles that would define the world's politics for the next four and a half decades. Korea was only one topic among many in Moscow, which included efforts to obtain Allied recognition of Soviet-oriented governments in Romania and Bulgaria. The Moscow Conference also was almost exclusively conducted between the two superpowers. China and France were excluded, and the United Kingdom was not even consulted prior to calling the meeting.

As a result of the superpowers' meeting, military government in the two zones was to continue, though a US-Soviet military commission would attempt to move toward a jointly administered occupation. Under that joint arrangement, a host of political and logistical problems would presumably be solved through American and Soviet cooperation. After that, a trusteeship period of several years would follow.[94] However, this agreement by the United States to a trusteeship was a huge blow to Koreans in the south and a triumph for the Soviets, and it created a significant rift between Hodge and policymakers in Washington, though that should hardly have been surprising—trusteeship implied a lengthy occupation, not at all aligned with US military government doctrine.[95] Indeed, the Moscow Conference, perhaps because it operated so much in the geopolitical and strategic realm, looked to be a rare occasion during the early phase of the postwar occupations where US military interests *were* seemingly trumped by higher policy ones—though, as would be seen, the military mechanism was incapable of fulfilling those higher policy objectives, thereby dooming the policy to failure.

The Joint Commission followed the Moscow Conference, and there were procedural and substantive problems from the start. Split between five military commissioners and two foreign service officers on the Soviet side and five politically appointed commissioners, two foreign service officers, and three military officers on the American side, the Joint Commission had the underlying purpose, in the words of one of the participants, of "get[ting] a charter [for Korea] that might be part of a constitution."[96] But the mechanism of the Joint Commission proved to be grievously flawed, set into motion too late, and under the worst of circumstances. It met several times in the first months of 1946 but eventually deadlocked: the Soviets would not do anything but propose minimal administrative and economic changes; American policymakers wanted something more ambitious. An American goal was to remove the thirty-eighth parallel and to consider Korea as a single unit. The Soviet delegation wanted to discuss far more narrow economic and administrative matters, such as electrical power, rice delivery, and the evacuation of Japanese personnel.[97] But the US position put Hodge in a particularly difficult position. He was supposed to be making major policy decisions, but he felt that he should not approach the Soviets until he had clear understanding of what American policymakers wanted him to do. Honest to a fault and perhaps lacking both the confidence to act in civil-military matters as well as an explicit mandate to do so, he believed that he should not be approaching the Soviets on strategic issues at all and therefore suggested that political meetings be convened pursuant to intergovernmental communication rather than his own initiative. For Hodge, communication between military government officials could not get at the larger, political questions that transcended what he understood to be his ability to solve. Furthermore, Hodge believed that the trusteeship idea should be abandoned. He reported to MacArthur that "'trusteeship' connotes only one idea to Koreans, even after all efforts at reasoning. . . . Their idea stems from what the Japanese did to Korea starting from a 'trusteeship.'"[98] Hodge's acuity on the issue revealed the larger flaw in the American occupation. He clearly had empathy with the Korean people on the issue, and with better resources and with a more generous and imaginative vision on his part, the occupation might have taken a different turn. But the mismatch between American occupation leadership, doctrine, and organization and the overarching goals helped defeat the good intentions that he had.

As the Joint Commission stalled, distrust in the south continued to mount through the winter and spring of 1946. Koreans there were tired of being dictated to by the Allies, and continued trusteeship was the last straw. Kim Ku led a major demonstration in Seoul on the last day of 1945, and the city's streets were filled with flags and banners in protest.[99] A resolution of the Korean Congress of Political Parties, made up of groups across the ideological spectrum, addressed to the Allied powers and sent to the Department of State was quite clear: "We want our independence. . . . We demand our right to restore our territorial, political, and administrative prerogatives as a sovereign nation." The Korean Congress of Political Parties contended that while the Allies believed the Koreans were "unfit to be free" because they were divided among themselves, the truth was that Korea had been divided "by forces outside ourselves, like a body cut in half." The congress went on to contend that it could hold national elections after a provisional government had been fully recognized by the Allies and establish a completely autonomous government within a year.[100]

As an alternative, the State-War-Navy Coordinating Committee determined that the American military government should help to form independently a Korean "group to act in an advisory capacity to the United States members of the Joint Commission in matters relating to the creation of a provisional government."[101] This body, the Representative Democratic Council, quickly fell under the control of Rhee, who used it to increase his own power (and then later distanced himself from it as a way to continue his rise to the presidency of the Republic of Korea). Rhee, both strongly antitrusteeship and anticommunist, eventually successfully aligned himself with American interests and became president of the south's government in July 1948.[102] But Rhee only complicated any chance at unification. When the United States proposed making Rhee's rightist party part of a consulting body for the Joint Commission, the Soviets vehemently opposed such a move, claiming that antitrusteeship parties by their definition could not be included in negotiations in a future that presumably included trusteeship—which, to be fair, seemed on its face not completely unreasonable, since the United States had agreed at the Moscow Conference to trusteeship in the first place.[103] There was also political polarity in the south itself, with Rhee and his faction ostensibly representing "American-style" democracy (at least as preferred by the American occupiers), and others in the south who opposed him labeled as communists and therefore to be distrusted and even persecuted.

By the late spring and early summer of 1946, the Joint Commission had largely broken down as a vehicle for Korean unification. Rhee was on his way to ensuring that his political party would dominate

South Korean politics and would allow him to establish an autocratic government. Hodge correctly assumed that Moscow would push parties north of the thirty-eighth parallel even more fully into Moscow's sphere of influence. By then, the United States and the Soviet Union were also well into their Cold War trajectory in Korea. Edwin Pauley wrote to President Truman in June that it was in Korea "where a test will be made of whether a democratic competitive system can be adapted to meet the challenges of a defeated feudalism, or whether some other system, i.e. Communism, will become stronger." Pauley contrasted the systems starkly and put the occupation in ideological terms. The Americans and the Soviets had radically different meanings of democracy: for the Americans, it meant liberties such as freedom of the press, speech, and association. To the Soviets, US democracy was a "bourgeoisie illusion" exercised by corporate masters—true democracy, according to Soviet communist doctrine, meant "welfare of the masses."[104] While Pauley was accurate in his description, more important was his framing of the Korean occupation as a stark choice between the two superpowers. As articulated, the Koreans were at a crossroads that led to one hegemon or another. Any chance at setting their own course had faded away.

By August 1946 the American chief political adviser in Korea stated that the "basic job of the U.S. in Korea has been done." The Japanese had been disarmed and sent home, and the framework of administrative and judicial systems was in place: "communications have been restored, the school systems have been rebuilt, the currency has been saved, stark famine and distress have been overcome, and the change-over from the Japanese regime has been smoothly accomplished."[105] There had been some real accomplishment in the past year by the Americans, working in harsh conditions, undermanned and under-resourced as they were. Yet the adviser's assessment could not hide the very real failure of the Joint Commission, indicative of the larger failure to establish a unified government in Korea—an essentially political problem for which the structure of American military government provided no means to solve and that rather promoted the conditions for failure. Hodge was honest enough to recognize that further negotiations with the Soviets were pointless.[106] But moving to a higher political plane at this point would have only enmeshed the situation further into geopolitics. Locked into division, neither the Americans nor the Soviets could find any common agreement.[107]

The crucial first year of occupation was, in Bruce Cumings's words, the "crucible from which sprang the political and social forces that continue to play upon the Korean peninsula." Cumings notes how the division between north and south short-circuited indigenous ways to true Korean independence, autonomy, and democracy.[108] As sociologist Robert Schaeffer points out in his work on partitions, "because superpower states played important roles in partition and formed alliances with divided states, post-partition conflict . . . triggered superpower intervention."[109] That division and its hardening during and following the collapse of the Joint US-USSR Commission are often seen as a result of Cold War geopolitics. The troubles in Korea that exploded into full-scale conventional war in 1950 and then led to a superpower clash with the Chinese intervention in 1951 indeed do have their origins in the post–World War II superpower involvement, starting with the vague "trusteeship" formula that Roosevelt and others created in 1943. But in examining the work of the superpowers, especially the United States, it is also necessary to examine the *method* by which they occupied the country that they ostensibly liberated. South of the thirty-eighth parallel, the particular doctrine and subsequent actions of the US Army, which played a dominant role in constructing postwar governance planning and policy, bear much responsibility for what occurred during that first crucial year. The zonal occupation model, driven by military purposes, later hardened into permanent partition and not only denied Korea from fully participating in the international community but also dragged the occupying powers themselves into the midst of Korean political disputes, even as both nations sought exit from the peninsula as soon as possible.

The reality was that the Korean division was in fact exacerbated by a poorly resourced American military government model—one ill-suited to the complex realities on the ground. But by the fall of 1945, no alternative existed. The American postwar governance model, with all its advantages and disadvantages, was a template that called for a stable postwar context in which power would be turned over in relatively short order to an indigenous government that simply returned to power. That model had little relevance in Korea in 1945, and the strivings of the US military government officials, however well intentioned, were nonetheless wrongheaded, impractical, and ultimately counterproductive. The thirty-eighth parallel hardened into a permanent frontier, and civil conflict raged within and over that frontier after the American military government ended in 1948 and erupted into full-scale war in 1950.

Could Korea have been unified and neutralized, as what eventually occurred in Austria? Perhaps it could only have happened, if, as in Austria, a provisional government had been jointly recognized by both superpowers. Certainly an alternative in which the thirty-eighth parallel became porous, open to traffic, and demilitarized would have created a better chance for unification. So too would have a less militarized form of government in the south, such as a multinational commission or even a more robust, trained, and adept military government that had an awareness of Korean culture and politics, stressed Korean autonomy, made Japanese demobilization and disarmament the sole function of the Allied on-the-ground tactical leadership, and left the political decisions to those with more experience and knowledge. But none of this occurred or was even contemplated. And in June 1950, the US Army would return to Korea, this time to fight in a protracted and bloody conflict that would cost more than thirty thousand American and two million North and South Korean lives and leave the Korean peninsula divided to this day.

Conclusion

The Postwar Occupation Experience and Its Lessons for the Army

Military government did not end as rapidly as army or civilian leadership wanted. By 1947, both army and civilian leaders saw the need to do so. In July, Assistant Secretary of State John Peurifoy stated before the House Executive Expenditure Committee that while the army would maintain constabulary forces until peace treaties were signed with the occupied nations, all other occupation activities would be turned over to the State Department. Secretary of War Kenneth Royall told Lucius Clay that he was trying to "induce State to take over Military Government" and that he expected an answer from new secretary of state George Marshall by the early fall.[1] Secretary Marshall also believed that State should take over occupation responsibilities at the end of 1947.

In reality, even though two years had elapsed since the Axis defeat, planning for civilian-run governance was still very embryonic. Despite all the wartime and postwar discussion about the State Department and other civilian agencies taking the lead, fundamental questions remained. What would the size, composition, and mission of the force remaining in Europe be when State took over? What would the relationship be between the senior commander of military forces and the senior State Department representative? Who, in view of protocol and other considerations, would represent the United States at the various control councils? What was the timetable for the State Department's assumption of control? And what precisely would be the role of military forces in occupied territory once State had assumed complete occupational responsibility?[2]

The failure to have such questions answered at that late date highlighted how little postwar policy planning had been done and how much authority still remained with the army. The army's predominance in postwar governance had gradually waned, but there was no organization remotely comparable that could take over its role in the Cold War's first years. The Civil Affairs Division, though it was in matters of policy subordinate to the State Department's Office for Occupied Areas, still influenced the direction of postwar occupations. The division's Government Branch, for instance, initiated the various comprehensive directives for military government and continued to provide personnel to the State-War-Navy Coordinating Committee. That committee, in turn, approved the directives and sent them to the various military commanders who served as military governors in the field.[3] And while the army reduced its personnel involved in military government, it continued to provide the leadership for the occupations. Clay, the deputy military governor from 1945 to 1947 in the American zone in Germany (though de facto he was heading the occupation then), became the military governor outright in 1947 and remained in that position throughout the early implementation of the Marshall Plan and the Berlin Airlift. The civilian high commissioner who replaced him in 1949 was John McCloy, who, as assistant secretary of war, had done so much to protect and expand the army's prerogatives in postwar governance. Lt. Gen. Geoffrey Keyes replaced Gen. Mark Clark as the American high commissioner in Austria in 1947 and remained in that post likewise until 1949. General Hodge was the senior American in Korea until the creation of the South Korean state in 1948.

Nevertheless, the army wanted out of occupation duties. But it— and the US government as a whole—were still caught in an organizational dilemma, even if, admittedly, the army itself was somewhat responsible for it. Public pressure, particularly to demobilize troops, was immense after V-E Day and V-J Day, and while much work had been done on demobilization during the war, those efforts were not coordinated and synchronized with occupation planning.[4] Furthermore, senior leadership came to see that the army's role in the occupations was a drain and a distraction from its primary functions of deterrence and combat. The army had, only to a limited degree, institutionalized military government organizations. By 1949 seventy peacetime US Army Reserve civil affairs/military government units had been created.[5] But there was little done beyond this. The focus had shifted to warfighting itself, not on managing postconflict environments.

Thus while the army still had military government responsibility, it began institutionally to dispense with the organizational structures to oversee that responsibility. Despite its overall influence, the army's primary agency for occupation planning, the Civil Affairs Division, did not survive the decade and was dissolved in 1949.[6] In Eisenhower's final report as chief of staff to Royall (who had become the first secretary of the army), he wrote that while occupation was "worthy and necessary," it had to be seen as "preventive rather than positive security." Occupation, in other words, was not seen as forward-looking and as actively advancing American interests but as backward-looking and as simply preserving what had already been won. The magnitude and problems of occupation demanded such "concentrated efforts" that "relatively few men and little time are left for the Army's primary job." Eisenhower was clear about what that primary job was: "organizing, training, and sharpening for national defense." He was just as clear that, in his opinion, that job had "necessarily taken second place to the problems imposed by the defeat of Germany and Japan."[7]

A series of recommendations, reports, and studies prepared during the postwar period examined the successes and failures of the occupation efforts, and they highlighted the need to institutionalize the lessons of the postwar occupations. Former undersecretary of the army Karl Bendetsen (himself a civil affairs officer during the war) proposed that a "Special Assistant for Politico-Military and Civil Affairs" be established within the army in 1952. Another committee in 1953, led by Paul Davies, a prominent American corporate executive, proposed, among several organizational changes within the army, greater emphasis on civil affairs and military government.[8] A comprehensive study for the secretary of the army by special consultant Daniel Fahey Jr. looked not only at the army but also at postwar occupation policy in terms of civil-military integration. In certain respects, the Fahey Report validated the American approach to postwar governance. It concluded that future occupations should be run by the military, at least during the combat period and for a period until stability had been attained. Nonetheless, the Fahey Report pointed out several problems with the military approach to postwar governance. For example, the State Department and War Department (and other agencies) were often at cross-purposes. No single individual or agency had been in a position to "see and understand all of the broad forces, obstacles and controversies." The State Department had an "area desk" approach with insufficient focus on occupation policy, and it had not been involved in the day-to-day problems of administration in the occupied territories, in large part because State had lacked the personnel, training, and capability to perform such duties. In the absence of such overarching, integrated guidance, great authority and discretion had been given to military leaders on the ground. Troublesome problems were therefore resolved in accordance with a military point of view. The deficiency was only partially resolved by the creation of the State Department's Office of Occupied Areas, and that office had come about a year after the war had ended. The report therefore proposed a high-level interdepartmental committee to coordinate all US occupation policy, with both State and Defense having membership, though not to the exclusion of others. Other agencies participating in occupations should have members, and a secretariat should be authorized.[9]

But none of this took place. And it was not simply prejudice against performing the messy work of postwar occupation that made implementation of such recommendations difficult. The Fahey Report's proposed solutions revealed some of the tensions in civil-military relations, especially in defining political goals and determining military requirements. While providing more political direction would seem to cause an efficient application of the military to achieve those ends, the War Department leadership had feared that such politicization of the army during wartime would impede the accomplishment of the military mission. The immediate, exigent military end, in its view, was not consonant with the long-term political goal. The problem was temporal: the political end was vague, uncertain, contingent, and open to many possibilities and interpretations. Furthermore, assumptions made in wartime, especially about wartime allies, often were dubious or incorrect in a different context. Former secretary of war Henry Stimson pointed out in his postwar memoirs that giving greater weight to elusive long-term political goals over military goals that were precise, time-bound, and measurable would have been foolish in a conflict such as World War II, where military victory over Axis military forces was necessarily paramount.[10]

As for how well military government worked on the ground, researchers at Johns Hopkins University conducted a study, published in 1956. Over 4,700 questionnaires were sent out to former civil affairs/military government officers who had performed some sort of occupation duty (1,080 being returned). The results were mixed. Many respondents thought that certain aspects of training were effective, particularly the training at the School of Military Government in Charlottesville, Virginia, though some contended that it was excessively theoretical. Most respondents thought relevant country training was sufficient. On the other hand, despite the time and effort put into creating the hundreds of country manuals on a whole spectrum of topics, a majority of respondents found the manuals unhelpful, and nearly a third had never even heard of their existence. Unsurprisingly, many of the responses underscored the consequences of the narrow, militarily focused set of occupation goals. For example, personnel often did not understand the purpose of their duties and the occupation's relationship with the overall larger army mission. A majority of respondents noted that directives from higher headquarters were often not received in time, not clear in content, and of limited utility in the field. Overarching strategic objectives in programs such as denazification were, according to the majority of respondents, likewise seldom clearly defined, resulting in "confusion in the minds of both the [military government] personnel responsible for the conduct of the purge and in the minds of the occupied people." Equally unsurprising and in keeping with military government planning and doctrinal principles, respondents indicated that the most important responsibilities they undertook directly related to immediate military objectives, such as relieving tactical commanders by reestablishing order and obtaining supplies and services in direct support of military operations. Listed as less important were longer-range "political" goals such as "laying the basis for a democratic form of government" and "leaving friendly local people in control of a peaceful and stable community." Such views by respondents were virtually identical whether the interviewed personnel served in occupied or liberated nations.[11]

Despite the vast experience gained and the numerous studies conducted, the army's postwar history revealed that many lessons were not learned regarding postwar governance and, more generally, civilian pacification. The army in the Korean War demonstrated this lack of knowledge. Another Johns Hopkins study on civil affairs in Korea determined that the Eighth Army had done no substantive planning or organizing for civil affairs prior to the conflict's eruption in 1950. Within one year, however, the Eighth Army, as the major operational headquarters in Korea, was conducting civil affairs operations on such a scale that it required an organization of over four hundred personnel. The study further concluded that greater attention needed to be paid to civil affairs and to postconflict governance and that there should be greater stress on such matters at institutions such as West Point, the Army Command and General Staff College, and the Army War College. Like the Fahey Report, it concluded also that there needed to be a single focus of responsibility for civil affairs and military government functions and that the "vague locus of responsibility" for civil affairs in Korea, within the army and between it and other US and UN agencies, made it difficult for field commanders to obtain the complete picture required to conduct effective civil affairs.[12] The report clearly indicated that very little regarding military governance policy and practice, either during or after conflict, had been institutionalized within the army, even though southern Korea had been under American military occupation just two years prior.

As the Cold War lengthened into a protracted, highly political struggle, the army acknowledged that warfare had moved beyond the conventional, nation-state type. Accordingly, the World War II military government paradigm, premised on occupation of a nation-state following major conflict, lost much of its significance, though there was focus on civilian pacification in different contexts. The army's primary doctrinal manual for combat operations, *FM 100-5: Operations,* discussed in the 1954 version for the first time so-called limited wars.[13] In the early 1960s, counterinsurgency and civilian pacification efforts gained notice as the army began its mission in South Vietnam. In 1962, consistent with the Kennedy administration's flexible response strategy, the updated *FM 100-5* provided an analysis of counterinsurgency and unconventional warfare. As the 1954 manual had done, the 1962 *FM*

100-5 provided a definition of limited war in which military objectives were "subordinated to national objectives" and military operations were "conducted within the limits established by national policy," affirming the primacy of political, as opposed to purely military, ends. The manual also provided three chapters that dealt with unconventional warfare, military operations against irregular forces (including a brief discussion of civil affairs), and a chapter on "situations short of war" that discussed topics such as how to bolster a weak government threatened by insurgents. While much of the doctrinal language was vague or platitudinous at best, it did highlight the army's awareness of missions beyond conventional war.[14]

Yet despite its widespread experience in governance and perhaps because its energies were focused on combat operations, the army was not tasked with the overall pacification effort in Vietnam. Military government scholar Earl Ziemke has pointed out that the US military did not utilize military government concepts in South Vietnam, which, after all, was an autonomous nation with an existing government.[15] Instead, both the State Department and the Agency for International Development were initially given the primary roles in a war that did not follow the linear conflict model of defeat and occupation.[16] But having these agencies in the lead did not halt rampant organizational proliferation and subsequent chaos in command and control, similar to what occurred in the North Africa campaign. By the mid-1960s, there were some sixty disparate US agencies in the country with pacification responsibilities. In the words of Robert Komer, who would lead the effort to integrate those efforts, "the bureaucratic fact [was] that everybody and nobody was responsible for coping with [pacification] in the round."[17]

The major reasons for the slow response were bureaucratic and institutional. In contrast to the planning, doctrinal, and organizational development that had occurred between the world wars, there was little institutional depth to the army's understanding of pacification prior to Vietnam. As Komer pointed out, had the army begun in the 1950s or even early 1960s to think deeply about pacification and had seriously implemented organizational change based upon it, there could have been a more successful buildup and a more sophisticated approach taken. Instead the focus was on technological, not institutional, solutions, and that technological focus (such as the use of helicopters to carry out "search-and-destroy" missions) fit into pre-established practices.

A serious reorganizing of pacification efforts did not begin until the 1966 Honolulu Conference (primarily convened to discuss the political conditions in South Vietnam), well into major American combat in Vietnam.[18] The solution that followed for coordinating pacification efforts was one that the World War II military government planners would have heartily agreed with: control by the military. Komer himself, though not a member of the Department of Defense, concluded that the only way to break the interagency gridlock in Vietnam was to get rid of interagency competition altogether. He argued successfully to place the US pacification effort, termed Civil Operations and Revolutionary Development Support (CORDS), totally under Gen. William Westmoreland's command and control in 1967. As Komer put it, the military, and especially the army, had the assets, and the only way to make pacification work "was to get military resources . . . and the only way to do this was to put pacification under the military." The relative success of CORDS has been acknowledged, even by strong critics of US policy in Vietnam, though it was, as Komer noted, a mid-course correction and likely too late to stabilize the country sufficiently to allow for effective "Vietnamization" early enough in the war to make a significant difference.[19]

But this emphasis on unconventional warfare, pacification, and counterinsurgency was short-lived. Even while the CORDS pacification model began to yield some positive results and while the Vietnam War was raging at its height in 1968, the army began to distance itself from such matters. Instead it started to look to the conventional threat in Western Europe and became solely focused on conflict itself, not on its aftermath or conflict's collateral effects. In the fall of 1968, the army published a new *FM 100-5* that once more began to focus on conventional warfighting. The new version now had only a short chapter on unconventional warfare and another on the newly titled "stability operations."[20] In the 1970s and 1980s, the post-Vietnam army, battered and embittered by its Southeast Asia experience, completely dropped the focus on anything but so-called conventional, high-intensity conflict. Nowhere was this more evident than in its new doctrine. The 1976 *FM 100-5* was almost entirely focused on its "primary mission—winning the land battle."[21] The apex of this development occurred in the 1980s in the newly termed AirLand Battle concept. The 1982 *FM 100-5* was the summation of prescriptive, detail-oriented, and highly technical doctrine, singularly focused on the conventional high-intensity war paradigm in Central Europe against Warsaw Pact armies. In this doctrinal framework, discussions of unconventional war, limited war, or situations short of war were negligible. The overwhelming emphasis was on the army providing a powerful blow that would initially render the enemy off balance and then allow US and NATO forces to regain the initiative.[22] It was by implication a return to the depoliticized conflict model of World War II. But perhaps because there was no conflict imminent or ongoing, there was no similar effort to create doctrine and to organize for postconflict operations. Correspondingly, civil affairs units, though given a rather limited role during Vietnam, suffered from guilt-by-association with the "hearts and minds" approach of that conflict. By 1977 the army indicated it would no longer support the twelve civil affairs units it had in its contingency plans.[23]

By the end of the 1980s, following the American coup de main against Manuel Noreiga in Panama and, more important, following the collapse of the Soviet empire in Eastern Europe, the army moved beyond a nearly exclusive focus on high-intensity conventional warfare. While the Gulf War of 1991 appeared to validate AirLand Battle concepts, what had been the army's primary mission for two decades—defeating Warsaw Pact armies in Europe—no longer existed. And with the subsequent collapse of the bipolar order, the turbulent 1990s saw the army responsible for a broader range of missions than at any time in its recent history. Gen. Frederick Franks, who led the Army Training and Doctrine Command in the early 1990s, sought doctrine that would encompass a whole range of missions, from peacetime engagement to combat to postconflict resolution.[24] The doctrinal result was the notion of "operations other than war" (OOTW). *FM 100-5*'s 1993 incarnation depicted a continuum of "war," "conflict," and "peacetime," with the spectrum running from such missions as large-scale combat operations to antiterrorism to nation assistance and disaster relief.[25] Chapter 13 was actually devoted to operations other than war, briefly describing thirteen different responsibilities the army needed to be prepared to undertake.[26]

This approach brought criticism. Frederick Kagan contended that doctrine, and especially *FM 100-5* in its current form and proposed revision, had, by eliminating AirLand Battle as a centering concept, thereby eliminated substance. Doctrine had instead become excessively conceptual, reliant on a list of abstract and sometimes contradictory principles that were vague and cursory.[27] But with the army attempting to cover every sort of mission and situation, there was no turning back. When the army published its new operations doctrine under the series *FM 3-0* in June 2001, it once again provided a list of missions (slightly reduced from thirteen to ten) under the new term "stability operations," running from "peace operations" to "show of force." In attempting to cover all situations, *FM 3-0* barely touched upon the mission that would be the most demanding in the coming decade, counterinsurgency. The term was only mentioned in a few references and not even as a separate form of stability operations (the term that had replaced operations other than war) but under the larger concept of foreign defense. The coverage on terrorism was only slightly greater.

Consequently, when the United States began the so-called Global War on Terrorism, that doctrine "contributed little to understanding the army's role in planning, preparing, executing, and assessing missions related to terrorism."[28] And so, despite the fact that the army had spent the previous decade in conflicts short of war in Kosovo, Bosnia, Haiti, and Somalia, the army was criticized for being intellectually and institutionally unprepared for the postconflict and unconventional environments of Iraq and Afghanistan. The comment of Gen. Tommy Franks, commander of the American forces in the 2003 Iraq invasion, reflected this when he told his civilian superiors prior to the invasion, "You pay attention to the day *after* and I'll pay attention to the day *of*."[29] Franks's comment has drawn criticism for its alleged shortsightedness, but it was not that far removed from comments generals had always made about the primacy of immediate military goals—especially World War II generals. But the essential difference between the army in the early 1940s and the early 2000s was that during World War II, the army, at the peak of its power and influence in American government, had been developed (albeit imperfectly) an institutional culture to deal with eventual postconflict environments and, just as important, was fortunate enough to have in the post–World War I

Rhineland occupation a model that was somewhat usable in at least some of the post–World War II occupation locales.

Evidence of a lack of comprehensive planning of the Iraq War's "Phase IV," the postconflict, stability phase, was readily apparent. The war's military planners did in fact make long-range assumptions. The principal problem was that these assumptions were relatively unchallenged during planning and were often flawed, particularly the assumptions that the success of the initial combat phases of the operation would end decisively and would therefore lead to a safe and stable environment within Iraq, that government ministries would continue to function, and that therefore only minimal troop levels were needed in the country.[30] There was the further, more consequential erroneous assumption that civilian organizations such as the Organization for Reconstruction and Humanitarian Assistance (ORHA) would be able to take up the duties and responsibilities of postconflict stabilization. But no such organization—whether ORHA or other organizations such as the Defense Department's Office of Special Plans or the Executive Steering Group—was intellectually, institutionally, or organizationally capable of handling such a responsibility. ORHA was itself virtually created on the fly and was still being organized when it deployed to Kuwait in March 2003.[31]

When the realization came that the United States military was grappling with a full-blown insurgency in Iraq, significant and practical change came from the on-the-ground forces themselves, leading to a reexamination of doctrine, education, and organization. Though the history of the Iraq War in particular is still in its somewhat journalistic "first draft" stage (given that much of its planning and execution remain classified), there is evidence that the first and most important change was internal and institutional. Perhaps the most famous leader behind this effort, Gen. David Petraeus, was able to do so while located at the heart of the army's doctrinal center, commanding the Army Combined Arms Center at Fort Leavenworth, Kansas. While there, he orchestrated the creation of the counterinsurgency manual, *FM 3-24*.[32] Then, uniquely in military history, Petraeus was able to put those ideas into practice during the so-called surge of 2007 that, linked with the Sunni Awakening, appeared to halt the spiraling, out-of-control violence. While one can argue which leaders or what organization should take principal credit for the counterinsurgency "course correction" in mid-campaign, or even its long-term effectiveness, it was, as it were, an *institutional* turn—done primarily within the framework of the organization faced with the problem, the US military (and within it, predominantly the army).[33]

Problems of interagency cooperation persisted throughout the first decade of the twenty-first century in Iraq and to an even greater degree in Afghanistan, compounded and complicated in that latter country by the greater multinational effort there, where a slew of organizations and agencies loosely operated under the principle of "unity of effort."[34] Two documents published by the Department of Defense highlighted some of the difficulties. *DOD Instruction 3000.05,* published in September 2009, once again gave extremely vague and generic guidance, simply stating that stability operations "encompass various military missions, tasks, and activities conducted outside the United States in coordination with other instruments of national power to maintain or reestablish a safe and secure environment, provide essential governmental services, emergency infrastructure reconstruction, and humanitarian relief."[35] *Joint Publication 3-08: Interorganizational Coordination during Joint Operations,* published in June 2011, provided a more in-depth examination. It recognized the differences in military and civilian organizations, noting that the military focused on "reaching clearly defined and measurable objectives within given timelines under a [command-and-control] structure," whereas civilian organizations were "concerned with fulfilling changeable political, economic, social, and humanitarian interests using dialogue, bargaining, risk taking, and consensus building." It stated further that "while the ways and means between military and civilian organizations may differ, they share many purposes and risks, and the ultimate overall goal may be shared." But the publication did not define *what* the shared purposes and risks were. Instead, it offered various question-begging methods to overcome the gap, such as "forg[ing] a collective definition of the problem . . . [and] understand[ing] the objectives [and] end state." At other points, the doctrinal solution sounded simply hortatory and almost circular: "Unified action is promoted through close, continuous coordination and cooperation."[36]

These attempts to define stability operations and to establish coherent interagency processes pointed to the larger, more complex, and even paradoxical problems involved in postconflict governance. A criticism of the "American way of war" is that it is short-focused and lacks longer-range political ends and accordingly that the American method of war making is impatient, apolitical, astrategic, and ahistorical. Thus the argument is made that the 2003 Iraq invasion led to such a dismal state of affairs because, while a quick victory over Iraqi conventional military forces was achieved, decisive political success was not.[37] In contrast, some look to the post–World War II military governance doctrine, planning, and implementation and regard it as a "gold standard" that has not since been matched.[38]

It may appear that, in many ways, American military planners before and during World War II were more astute and thorough than their counterparts in 2003. The World War II planners created a doctrinal template that provided basic assumptions required to conduct everyday occupation duties; they created a relatively impressive, if not always properly implemented, training program; and they created organizational structures, both to promulgate policy at the strategic level and to implement it at the tactical level. But the comparison is somewhat misplaced. The World War II planners had the time, resources, and unity of purpose that their successors lacked. Furthermore, despite the praise often given to the World War II planners, they seemingly suppressed long-range "political" objectives in order to focus on military ones. Over and over, high- and lower-level military government officials bemoaned the utter lack of long-range policy goals. Yet the army was a victim of its own success in winning responsibility for postwar governance. Having done so, it caused the occupations to focus on immediate military objectives.

But history's contingencies are such that even the immediate suppression of political goals and the nearly exclusive focus on military ones yielded results that were both negative as well as positive. Dividing Korea, for example, for military purposes led to a partition that fostered conditions for war in 1950. At the same time, the apolitical militarized policies of the early years of the occupations in Austria and Germany sometimes worked to the advantage of both occupier and occupied, precisely because, in the absence of more sharply defined Cold War policy goals that included a forceful anticommunism, the initial occupation period allowed for a more pragmatic, nonideological discourse to be conducted. This localized, less "political" space in the first months after the war, for example, allowed Mark Clark to support Karl Renner, a socialist with communists in his cabinet. In the first year of occupation, Lucius Clay was seen as less a hardliner in Germany than most in the State Department, who far more quickly saw an emergent Soviet threat. Clay's federalist experiment, which helped realign the Western zones of Germany toward American interests and the American sphere of influence, was effective, while at the same time it did not disallow the communist or other leftist parties outright. Clay's actions provided a space for local authorities to regain control without resorting to excessive censorship or political prohibition.

Put in Clausewitzian terms, what the above reveals is that allowing civilian "political" decisions to be trumped by military decisions does not terminate politics. Rather, so doing militarizes politics. "Militarization" typically brings with it negative connotations. But militarization is not *necessarily* a bad method. Militarized decisions can sometimes be more pragmatic, less ideologically intense and polarizing, and more reflective of on-the-ground realities than those made at higher, purely civilian levels. When circumstances are right—a sophisticated and experienced senior military leader, an adequate and trained military force, a doctrine that makes sense in light of the on-the-ground conditions— militarized decisions may produce better results than apparently top-driven (civilian) ones. But if the military leader is not so sophisticated and experienced, the force not so adequate and trained, and the conditions not so conducive to the applicable doctrine, then the weaknesses in militarizing otherwise high policy decisions are readily apparent.

Postwar Governance and the Limits of Practice and Doctrine

It is tempting to search the historical record of the post–World War II occupations and to try to glean from it a better set of practices or a better doctrine or better institutional structures. But such attempts at "lessons learned" pose difficulties. In a RAND Corporation study published in 2003, titled *America's Role in Nation Building: From Germany to Iraq,* the authors attempted to "extract the best practices" from post–

World War II nation-building experiences, including Germany, Japan, Somalia, Kosovo, Iraq, and Afghanistan, noting that in particular the occupations of Germany and Japan "set a standard for postconflict nation building that has not been matched." In the study, the authors pulled together data ranging from military and police presence to total external assistance to postconflict deaths and, based on that information, further attempted to derive lessons from the nation-building experiences. One conclusion was that the occupation of Germany was "very successful," and the lessons learned were that "democracy can be transferred" and that "military forces can underpin democratic transformation."[39]

The RAND study was certainly not meant to be a comprehensive examination of postwar occupations and was, at the least, a useful and helpful way to frame some important issues in Iraq in 2003. Nonetheless, its selection of data and ultimate comparisons do prompt questions (which perhaps the authors intended). How, for example, can one compare Germany in the 1940s to Somalia and Kosovo in the 1990s or to Afghanistan in the 2000s? Even if the inputs for these different nation-building experiences are the same, do not their varied conditions in time and space potentially render empirical comparisons misleading? During the World War II occupations, experiences differed vastly, as comparisons of the European occupations of Germany and Austria with that of Korea should make evident. What does it mean to say, after all, that democracy can be "transferred?" What does it mean that military forces can "underpin" such a transference? The RAND study notes the lack of any substantial insurgency or residual Nazi resistance and that the massive occupation force "preempted" resistance. But clearly the predominant reason that there was no resistance was because the Germans did not seek to resist. Any efforts at "Werewolf" guerrilla movements were few and far between; the vast majority of Germans simply chose not to resist further.[40]

Another temptation is to find a text that provides a set of solutions that can be extrapolated to present problems. For the post–World War II occupation planners, the Hunt Report was such a document, though its maximum utility was in the locations—Austria and Germany— where the conditions most corresponded to the conditions that the report described. During the counterinsurgency period of the 2000s, one work looked upon as prescient and relevant was David Galula's *Pacification in Algeria, 1956–1958*. Galula was a French officer who had fought the Algerian insurgency. Some viewed his book as prophetic and considered it as having a "remarkable, almost timeless resonance nearly half a century later." There were numerous lessons that apparently could be drawn from Galula's work that had contemporary relevance. These included the need to recognize the signs of a budding insurgency, the need to emphasize policing rather than military tactics, the need to avoid a "decapitation strategy" as a means of defeating an insurgency, the critical need for information operations, the importance of sealing off borders, the importance of promoting women's rights, and the importance of according humane treatment to captured insurgents.[41] Such lessons implicitly underwrote the idea that the counterinsurgent force was the primary actor in the insurgency. It is noteworthy that not a single one of Galula's lessons mentioned the local populations themselves, except to be acted upon by the counterinsurgent. No lesson, for example, stated that a primary imperative was to listen to local actors, to adapt to local practices, or even to abandon, as required, doctrinal imperatives or lessons such as the above to fit with local cultural norms. Galula's book should give rise to caution in thinking of doctrine and practice as unilaterally imposed constructs in which an outside force imposes its will on a populace in order to fulfill a larger strategic imperative.

Historical failure has also been tied to organizational dysfunction, and many have looked to past examples to break through problems such as interagency disorder. Robert Komer has been cited as someone who saw the failure of bureaucracy in Vietnam quite clearly (and who took relatively successful steps to reform that bureaucracy): "The bureaucratic fact," he wrote, was "that below Presidential level everybody and nobody was responsible for coping with [the Vietnam War] in the round." Komer subsequently suggested a list of requirements to reorganize and overcome bureaucratic infighting and inherent conflict. These included selecting imaginative and flexible conflict managers at all levels, revising training and incentive systems to reward the adaptability rather than school solutions, and creating unified management at each organizational level. But Komer also grasped that the "greatest single constraint on the ability of the United States to achieve its aims in Vietnam was the sheer incapacity of the regimes we backed."

After all, Komer did reorganize CORDS and had a degree of considerable success. And yet Komer recognized that this had come about in the context of supporting an inept, corrupt government that could not be indefinitely sustained and that could not sustain itself. Even more penetratingly, he wrote: "It is too simple to conclude that the answer lies mostly in politically motivated or deceptive public statements designed to cloak our real purposes. We now know enough of the classified documents and message traffic to realize that we meant what we said. Instead what comes out so strongly . . . is the immense contrast between what high policy called for and what we actually did in Vietnam."[42] Policy statements and strategic intent can have limited to no meaning and can even be potentially harmful, if what is said and what is done are mismatched.

If anything, what the occupations reveal is that postwar governance, like counterinsurgency or pacification, is a highly complex, perhaps so-called wicked problem—a problem that resists definitive, doctrinal solutions, one that depends as much on the questions asked as about possible answers.[43] One promising way of approaching such problems is using "systemic operational design" theory that emerged in American military thinking in the 2000s. Design theory originates from a variety of sources, especially Austrian biologist Ludwig von Bertalaffsy's theories about universal systems, as well as from Soviet theories of deep operations in the 1930s and the research of Brig. Gen. Shimon Naveh of the Israel Defense Forces. In design theory, context is as important as doctrine and practice, and a particular context will trump doctrine and practice to adapt to existing situations.[44] Furthermore, design theory does not have a necessarily formulized way to resolve a wicked problem. Instead it recognizes a complexity that to some degree is irreducible. What exists is what design theorists call a *mess*: a complex web of conditions that only become a *problem* when someone attempts to understand the mess.[45]

Of course, military planning cannot be merely conceptual: it must lead to detailed, specified execution and therefore needs a heuristic model that can convert conception into reality. Doctrine is often used as a way to reduce complexity and also provide the conceptual starting-point. Design theory helps to overcome problems that come with an overreliance on doctrine, which serves great use but can be imprisoning. Design theory can conceptualize a variety of military efforts, including postconflict operations, specifically by defining problems and thereby sorting out solutions in postconflict "messes." Its theorists use seven sets of structured "discourse," ways of thinking though complex situations. Framing is the initial discourse, defined as a mental construct that attempts to rationalize the mess into a problem though what is called visual mapping, in which a swirl of actors are shown with connecting arrows.[46] For the Korean occupation in 1945, such a frame might have looked like this:

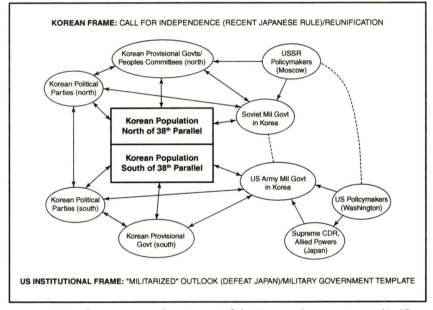

Figure C.1. A frame, or visual mapping, of the Korean Occupation, 1945. (Created by the author.)

Later actions can be added so the relationships indicated by the arrows become more apparent. What is also important in framing is breaking down what might be considered standard, hierarchical relationships and instead looking at on-the-ground reality and thus providing a new perspective on who or what is directing or influencing events. This conceptualizing also points out a major distinction between patterns of control and information flow in tightly bound organizations, such as the War Department in the 1940s, where hierarchies and one's place in them is a measure of one's influence, and a much more fluid environment in which highly dissimilar organizations are interacting with others in complex, competitive, and frequently contentious ways. Whereas, for example, the Civil Affairs Division's position in the War Department was a critical reason for its influence, the hierarchical position of, say, civilian policymakers in Washington during the actual Korean occupation accounts for something less than their positions in the US government hierarchy might lead one to believe. Furthermore, relationships are much more fluid and interactive in this environment. Most arrows shown in the above figure are "two-way"—in that both parties are seeking to influence the other. Some are dashed, to show limited or indirect influence. Finally, there is a self-conscious effort to view the frame—not just of, as in this instance, the Korean population itself but also one's own frame/point of view.

One essential feature in design theory is how much detailed planning is held initially in abeyance, in order to allow a freer flow of discourse to emerge.[47] A series of discourses follows framing that examine the enemy/rival system, the organizational system of friendly forces, and the resource systems available to solve the problem (as formulated in system framing). In the enemy/rival discourse, the enemy/rival's logic and behavior are mapped out and visualized in a way to interact with the overall system. An even more important step is to examine the friendly organizational system, to look at the possible combinations that could be brought to bear on the overall system, and to query whether or not alternative command systems exist. For the Korean occupation, an obvious question would have been whether military government as understood was really the right system in the first place. A "design" approach to post–World War II governance problems, for example, would have noted the utility of the Rhineland/*FM 27–5* military government construct in a nation such as Austria but further noted it needed to be drastically altered, if not dispensed with altogether, in Korea.

Design theory is problem *setting,* and, of course, it cannot hope to escape the prejudices and presumptions of the designers. Critics dismiss it as esoteric and unproven, with its most apparent application in the 2006 Second Lebanon War by the Israel Defense Forces being widely derided as a strategic failure.[48] Legitimate questions do exist about whether such a seemingly intuitive approach can ever be applied in the typically time- and resource-constrained environments of complex military operations. Design theory contends that all situations and problems are novel and therefore unique. This itself is an assumption, and it could force military planners back into rather conventional pathways all the same. Furthermore, if one remembers Komer's analysis of American strategy in Vietnam, one should realize that design is precisely—and only—an intellectual activity of provisional intentionality. Design theory cannot *do* anything. Komer's point should be remembered: the problem was not what the United States intended in Vietnam but rather that its intentions were not enough.

A useful clarification to design theory is found in the work of philosopher Hans-Georg Gadamer, whose ideas in many ways correspond, as well as provide context, to those of design theory (even if there is no indication of direct influence by him upon their work) and can perhaps provide a sense of greater historical perspective and humility to planners and policymakers. Gadamer recognized that one is bound by time and circumstance. As he stated in his magnum opus, *Truth and Method:* "History does not belong to us . . . we belong to it."[49] Before human beings can understand themselves through self-examination, they must understand themselves in the families, societies, and states in which they live.

The relational, historical experience of human beings interacting with other human beings is predicated on language and context. All people operate according to prejudices—literally prejudgments—that shape the narratives and understandings of situations in which human beings find themselves. Gadamer's approach is in this way decidedly not that of "deconstructionists" who see nefarious schemes and patterns of control behind apparently straightforward meanings in texts. Prejudices themselves, in Gadamer's account, are neither necessarily good nor bad. They are "biases of our opening to the world. They are simply conditions whereby we experience something." But human beings must understand that they are formed by them and also understand that they may pick out parts of these prejudices selectively.[50] Hermeneutical "interrogation" usually is thought of in terms of a literary past, but it can be extended outward into other domains—it "encompasses institutions and life-forms as well as texts."[51] Institutional traditions, as philosopher Alasdair MacIntyre points out, have their own language and culture, and those traditions are or are not internally intellectually coherent. Those traditions can be challenged and can absorb, refine, or reject outside influence. The larger point is that this occurs inevitably within those traditions' lives.[52] None of this means that we do not try to map out solutions, plan, synchronize efforts, or measure efforts toward progress. It does mean that since our understanding is limited, we can never fully enclose the subject within our own understanding of it. And similarly to design theorists, Gadamer insists that true understanding only occurs in actualizing and not simply contemplating, just as in design theory. John Schmitt states, "We cannot understand a wicked problem without proposing a solution."[53] Deriving a similar principle from legal hermeneutics, Gadamer points out that laws do not exist to be understood historically but to be put into concrete, contemporary application through interpretation: "Understanding here is always application."[54]

The Post–World War II Occupations as Models for Future Actions

Those who consider the post–World War II occupations as models or standards for the conduct of postconflict governance should realize how singular and contingent those particular occupations were. C. Wright Mills's notion of a "power elite" in Cold War America, of a system of maximum military power and prestige in the postwar era, it was during World War II when American military interests predominated over so-called political ones.[55] Events converged to the point where the US Army was at its apogee of power and influence. The ascendancy of the army in the federal bureaucracy, not to mention the skill within its bureaucracy of leaders such as Stimson and McCloy, and the bureaucratic and political skills of on-the-ground military commanders such as Clay and Clark—all those components were manifestations of a historical singularity that is unlikely to be repeated.

While touted as models for other postconflict efforts, what the post–World War II occupation experiences reveal is that notions of "on-high" strategic imperatives inadequately explain what actually occurs. Overstating these strategies' significance leads to the historical equivalent of the intentional fallacy—that history is simply a manifestation of the intentions of high-level policymakers, termed as "national interest." To quote Gadamer for a final time: "The interpreter of history always runs the risk of hypostasizing the connectedness of events when he regards their significance as that intended by the actual actors and planners. . . . The infinite web of motivations that constitutes history only occasionally and briefly acquires the clarity of what a single individual has planned."[56] "Interest" emerges from the crucible of imperatives, desires, and motivations of governmental agencies in particular. As the World War II occupations revealed, it was often a single agency within the US government, the army, that drove and shaped American strategic concepts during the early postwar years. The army's conceptions of postwar governance profoundly influenced US policymaking, especially the army's collective understanding of the primacy of military objectives. The army applied its intellectual construct for postwar governance, for good or ill, in the postwar occupations in different environments throughout the world. The doctrinal template set forth in *FM 27–5*, the decentralized decision-making authority provided to on-the-ground commanders, the decisions on troop placements and zonal divisions—all enabled the accomplishment of military objectives.

The most significant diplomacy during the first year of the Cold War was *army* diplomacy. Recent Cold War studies have looked beyond traditional bipolar explanations such as US-Soviet geopolitical competition and have examined the social, political, economic, technological, and ideological origins of the decades-long conflict. Curiously, relatively little attention has been focused on how military decisions determined the Cold War's early configuration. American military history has tended to stop at V-E Day and V-J Day, resuming five years later when the conventional "hot" Korean War broke out. But the very decision for military government meant that military commanders would have wide-ranging policy influence in postwar governance, whether in pushing for early elections in Germany, in advocating for recognition of a provisional government in Austria, or in aligning the military government with a political body that would eventually govern a partitioned half of the country in Korea. John Lewis Gaddis has recognized the military's influence in these contexts, pointing out that no one ordered Clay to do so much of what he did. (Gaddis points out, for example, that Clay, on his own initiative, allowed the German press to criticize the military government and even had the American Civil Liberties Union review his policies.)[57] Likewise Clay's decision to return authority to local German governments was actively criticized and resisted by civilians within his headquarters and higher. He carried it out nonetheless.

Just as important were the local conditions and local actors in the various occupied territories. In fact, such conditions and actors came to be more important than the army's doctrinal precepts: instead of local practices being successfully bent to fit such precepts, the reverse occurred. Where the doctrine fit in most neatly to the occupied territory, the US occupation was able to function relatively successfully, as in Austria. On the other hand, when the doctrinal template was applied in Korea, the local practices and conditions resisted it and refused to fit the doctrinal model.

It is in the thickness of history's structures—the organizations, institutions, bureaucracies, and resources of both friendly and rival systems and in these particular contexts in time and space—that the intentions of strategists become altered and reshaped into patterns that may not be intended or even fully understood. Restoring the postwar occupations to history in such complexity and contingency allows one to look differently at possible "solutions" to modern postconflict situations. Of course, one cannot simply say that history's singularities are such that trying to derive lessons is, for the most part, a futile exercise. Military professionals especially do not have the luxury of engaging in historical research for its own sake. But those professionals should look to the past with eyes fully open, particularly with an awareness that it is difficult to find textbook answers in the form of checklists or pseudoscientific models. Ultimately what a fuller understanding of the post–World War II occupations should reveal is that they were a culmination of past practice and a convergence of then-present power and authority. Those occupations were contingent and singular. They do not necessarily provide skeleton keys or roadmaps. But if studied closely, they can deepen our awareness of what occurs and what may be accomplished when war stops and something like peace begins.

Acknowledgments

I gratefully acknowledge the help and support of many people, and I note from the outset that the opinions expressed herein are entirely my own and are not those of the US Army or the US Department of Defense. Among those I would like to acknowledge include my faculty committee, Mark Parillo, Brent Maner, David Stone, and Robert Schaeffer from Kansas State University. I particularly benefited from taking classes from the first three of these scholars and from reading some of the work of the fourth. Sue Zschoche's Cold War course challenged me to look at the conflict and era in a new way, and Robert Baumann's course on military frontiers provided me insights about partitions and zonal divisions during postwar occupations. I also acknowledge in particular my adviser and mentor while attending the US Army War College from 2009 to 2010, Dick Sommers. Dick especially provided me with gracious amounts of his time and the benefit of his prodigious intellect while I researched and wrote. James Kievet and Brent Bankus, also from the Army War College, provided useful comments on my research into the development of the Civil Affairs Division. Steve Knott's Army War College elective on the 1944–1945 European campaign was especially helpful. Mike MacMahon provided insights into systematic operational design. Harry Leach provided me key texts on political constructivist theory. Traci Keegan provided me useful information on organizational theory. Conversations with Henry Gole were especially useful regarding the interwar years.

I also acknowledge the librarians and assistants of the libraries and archives where I researched, especially Jane Yates of the Citadel Archives, as well as the many librarians and archivists at the US Army

War College Library and the US Army Heritage and Education Center at Carlisle Barracks, Pennsylvania.

I would also like to thank Roger Cirillo from the Association of the United States Army for his great help in getting this book to publication, and Steve Wrinn and Allison Webster from the University Press of Kentucky for their always timely and courteous replies to my questions. Don McKeon and Ila McEntire also provided crucial advice during editing. Many thanks to David Rennie for his superb graphics.

I would be remiss if I failed to acknowledge the mentorship and friendship of Dave Diner in particular. Others have provided counsel and friendship, including seminar mates in classes at Kansas State University and at the US Army War College. Leaders, friends, teammates, and colleagues at I Corps in Fort Lewis, Washington, at the ISAF Joint Command in Afghanistan, and at US Central Command at MacDill Air Force Base, Florida, all provided support.

My family provided encouragement throughout, especially my mother, whose own father served as the military director of Bavaria following World War II (she herself lived in Munich during his service as director), and my late father. My father, a retired US Army infantry officer and veteran of both the Korean and Vietnam Wars, had a keen grasp of civil-military relations, and I am sure that the insights that he provided to me during my own career formed the basis for my interest in the topic. I dedicate this book in part to them. Last, and most important, I acknowledge my wonderful wife, Laura, to whom this work is also dedicated, and our beautiful daughter, Anna. Both daily bring joy and meaning to my life.

Notes

Abbreviations

AHEC	US Army Heritage and Education Center, Army War College, Carlisle Barracks, PA
Amherst Archives	Amherst College Archives and Special Collections, Amherst College Library, Amherst, MA
AWC	US Army War College, Carlisle Barracks, PA
CMH	US Army Center of Military History, Fort McNair, Washington, DC
Eisenhower Library	Dwight D. Eisenhower Library, Abilene, KS
FDR Library	Franklin D. Roosevelt Library, Hyde Park, NY
FRUS	*Foreign Relations of the United States*
GPO	US Government Printing Office
Hoover Institution	Hoover Institution on War, Revolution, and Peace, Stanford, CA
Hunt Report	*American Military Government of Occupied Germany, 1918–1920: Report of the Officer in Charge of Civil Affairs, Third Army and American Forces in Germany* (Washington, DC: GPO, 1943)
LOC	Library of Congress, Washington, DC
MGD	Military Government Division
NARA	National Archives and Records Administration, College Park, MD
OMGUS	Office of the Military Government for Germany (US)
OPM	Office of the Provost Marshal General
RG	Record Group
SHAEF	Supreme Headquarters, Allied Expeditionary Force

SMG   School of Military Government
Truman Library   Harry S. Truman Library, Independence, MO
UDF   Unclassified Decimal File

Introduction

1. Hajo Holborn, *American Military Government: Its Organization and Policies* (Washington, DC: Infantry Journal Press, 1947), xi.

2. Melvyn Leffler, *A Preponderance of Power: National Security, the Truman Administration, and the Cold War* (Palo Alto, CA: Stanford University Press, 1992), 11–12.

3. George Kennan, *American Diplomacy,* rev. ed. (Chicago: University of Chicago Press, 1984), 19.

4. Hiram Motherwell, "Military Occupation, and Then What?" *Harper's,* October 1943, 445.

5. John H. Hilldring, interview by Forrest Pogue, March 30, 1959, in Forrest Pogue, *George C. Marshall: Organizer of Victory, 1943–45* (New York: Viking, 1973), 458–59.

6. The literature on the postwar occupations is vast, and there are excellent works on specific occupations, including official histories and revisionist interpretations. For the occupation of Germany, see John Gimbel, *The American Occupation of Germany: Politics and the Military, 1945–1949* (Stanford, CA: Stanford University Press, 1968), and Earl F. Ziemke, *The U.S. Army in the Occupation of Germany, 1944–1946* (Washington, DC: CMH, 1975). For the occupation of Japan, see John Dower, *Embracing Defeat: Japan in the Wake of World War II* (New York: Norton, 1999), and Michael Schaller, *The American Occupation of Japan: The Origins of the Cold War in Asia* (New York: Oxford University Press, 1985). For the occupation of Austria, see Donald R. Whitnah and Edgar L. Erickson, *The American Occupation of Austria: Planning and Early Years* (Westport, CT: Greenwood, 1985), and James J. Carafano, *Waltzing into the Cold War: The Struggle for Occupied Austria* (College Station: Texas A&M Press, 2002). For the occupation of Korea, see Allan R. Millett, *The War for Korea, 1945–1950: A House Burning* (Lawrence: University Press of Kansas, 2005), and Bruce Cumings, *The Origins of the Korean War,* vols. 1 and 2 (Princeton, NJ: Princeton University Press, 1981, 1990).

7. For works on these conferences, see Herbert Feis, *Churchill, Roosevelt, Stalin: The War They Waged and the Peace They Sought* (Princeton, NJ: Princeton University Press, 1957); Lloyd C. Gardner, *Spheres of Influence: The Great Powers Partition Europe, from Munich to Yalta* (Chicago: Ivan Dee, 1993); Carolyn Eisenberg, *Drawing the Line: The American Decision to Divide Germany, 1944–*

1949 (Cambridge: Cambridge University Press, 1996); and most recently S. M. Plokhy, *Yalta: The Price of Peace* (New York: Viking, 2010). The papers of both conferences are found in the US government's Foreign Relations series: *FRUS: The Conferences at Malta and Yalta, 1945* (Washington, DC: GPO, 1955), and *FRUS: The Conference of Berlin, the Potsdam Conference, 1945* (Washington, DC: GPO, 1960).

8. Randolph Bourne, "The Collapse of American Strategy," in *War and the Intellectuals: Collected Essays, 1915–1919*, ed. with an introduction by Carl Resek (Indianapolis and Cambridge: Hackett, 1999 [Harper & Row, 1964]), 22.

9. Justin Kelly and Mike Brennan, *Alien: How Operational Art Devoured Strategy* (Carlisle Barracks, PA: Strategic Studies Institute, 2009), 6, 8.

10. Bruno Colson, *La culture strategique américaine: L'influence de Jomini* (Paris: FEDN, Economica, 1993), 183–84.

11. Command and General Staff School, *Principles of Strategy* vol. XLVI (Annapolis: US Naval Institute Press, 1920), 1615–1616, quoted in Samuel P. Huntington, *The Soldier and the State: The Theory and Politics of Civil-Military Relations* (New York: Vintage, 1957), 308.

12. See, e.g., Max Boot, *The Savage Wars of Peace: Small Wars and the Rise of American Power* (New York: Basic Books, 2002), 283. Boot correctly points out that the US Army ignored counterinsurgency and guerrilla warfare in its development of doctrine. It did *not* ignore, however, postconflict occupation operations that occurred after large-scale conventional conflicts.

13. US Marine Corps, *Small Wars Manual* (Washington, DC: GPO, 1940), para. 1–1c.

14. As Russell Weigley points out, "the idea that in 1941–45 the American government subordinated considerations of possible postwar advantage to the immediate requirements of military strategy in pursuit of military victory is familiar to the point of being a cliché." Russell Weigley, *The American Way of War: A History of United States Military Strategy and Policy* (Bloomington: Indiana University Press, 1973), xviii.

15. Henry L. Stimson and McGeorge Bundy, *On Active Service in Peace and War* (New York: Harper & Brothers, 1948), 565.

16. George Marshall to Dwight D. Eisenhower, April 25, 1945, in George Marshall, *The Papers of George C. Marshall*, vol. 5, January 1, 1945–January 7, 1947, ed. Forrest Pogue (Baltimore and London: Johns Hopkins University Press, 2003), 159.

17. Dwight D. Eisenhower, *Crusade in Europe* (Garden City, NY: Doubleday, 1948), 396. It should be noted that elsewhere in the same memoir, Eisenhower displays a Clausewitzian understanding of the meshing of warfare and politics, indicating perhaps that in the total war of World War II, for Eisenhower,

the political and military became inseparable, and the more immediate military aims, given postwar goals, became equivalent to political aims. Eisenhower, *Crusade*, 88, 367.

18. W. Averell Harriman, interview by Richard D. McKinzie and Theodore A. Wilson, 1971, 18–20, interview kept at the Truman Library. According to Harriman, Marshall and Eisenhower were "convinced that since Stalin kept his word on vital military commitments, he'd keep his word on the political matters." Ibid., 20.

19. See Lucius D. Clay for War Department, "CC 2135 (Secret) U.S. Aid for CDU and SPD," August 20, 1946, in Lucius Clay, *The Papers of Lucius D. Clay, Germany, 1945–1949*, vol. 1, ed. Jean Edward Smith (Bloomington: Indiana University Press, 1988), 256–57, and Jean Edward Smith, *Lucius D. Clay: An American Life* (New York: Henry Holt, 1990), 286, 290.

20. Dwight D. Eisenhower, "Demobilization Speech to Congress: Statement on Demobilization by General of the Army Dwight D. Eisenhower, Chief of Staff, U.S. Army, Supplementing His Remarks on Demobilization Made to Members of Congress in the Auditorium, Library of Congress, 1000 AM, EST, Tuesday, January 15, 1946" (Washington, DC: Army Information Branch, Information and Education Division, War Department, 1946).

21. John J. McCloy to General Distribution, including Hilldring, Acheson, and Clayton, for information to Generals Eisenhower and Clark, October 10, 1945, reference no. HX-55599, in box 10, Personal Papers of Lucius D. Clay, 1945–1949, RG 200, NARA.

22. J. A. Frank, "Organization for Administration of the Occupied Areas," January 1948, in box 2, Records of the Office of Secretary of State for Occupied Areas, RG 59, NARA.

23. Telephone Conference between Gen. Lucius D. Clay and Maj. Gen. John Hilldring, March 1, 1946, in box 6, Teleconference Transcripts, Personal Papers of Lucius D. Clay, 1945–1949, RG 200, NARA.

24. Isabel Hull, *Absolute Destruction: Military Culture and the Practices of War in Imperial Germany* (Ithaca, NY: Cornell University Press, 2005), 112–15, 117–30, 159–60, 206, and 324–28.

25. In the field of institutional sociology, a seminal work is Walter W. Powell and Paul J. DiMaggio, eds., *The New Institutionalism in Organizational Analysis* (Chicago: University of Chicago Press, 1991). In the field of political constructivism, especially as it relates to national security issues, see, e.g., Peter J. Katzenstein, ed., *The Culture of National Security* (New York: Columbia University Press, 1996), and Alexander Wendt, *Social Theory of International Politics* (Cambridge: Cambridge University Press, 1999).

26. Weber's most systematic writing on bureaucracy and on modes of author-

ity in organizations is in *The Theory of Social and Economic Organization*, ed. Talcott Parsons and trans. A. M. Henderson and Talcott Parsons (New York: Free Press, 1947), 124–35, 324–63. For discussion on bureaucracy's inevitability and pervasiveness in modernity, see also his essay "Parliament and Government in Germany," in Max Weber, *Political Writings*, ed. Peter Lassman and Ronald Speirs (Cambridge: Cambridge University Press, 1994), 146–47, 156–57.

27. Max Weber, "Socialism," in Weber, *Political Writings*, 281.

28. Weber, *Theory of Social and Economic Organization*, 135. See also Wolfgang Mommsen, "Max Weber's Political Sociology and His Philosophy of History," *International Social Science Journal*, 17 (1965): 35. Weber's alleged stressing of a rationalized military bureaucracy—based on his understanding of the German military model of the early twentieth century—has been criticized. Robert Miewald argues that Weber's stress on control, rationality, and order ignores in particular the dimensions of military existence in which those things are minimized. In particular, Miewald points out Weber's lack of appreciation of Clausewitz's understanding of war as an inherently chaotic and often irrational activity filled with uncertainty, friction, and fog. Robert D. Miewald, "Weberian Bureaucracy and the Military Model," *Public Administration Review* 30 (March–April 1970): 131–33. Yet this counterargument itself goes too far. As demonstrated by the US Army's planning and execution of *post*war policy (all of which occurred thousands of miles away from any actual fighting), much of what modern military organizations do never occurs in the chaotic environment of the battlefield.

29. Stephen Skowronek, *Building a New American State: The Expansion of National Administrative Capacities, 1877–1920* (Cambridge: Cambridge University Press, 1982), 8–9, 16. Skowronek specifically looks at the army as part of this process at 85–120 and 212–48. See also Louis Galambos, "By Way of Introduction" in *The New American State: Bureaucracies and Policies after World War II*, ed. Louis Galambos (Baltimore: Johns Hopkins University Press, 1987), 7–10.

30. See Huntington, *Soldier and State*, especially 350–54, 459–60.

31. Modern military sociology began during the early Cold War years. See, e.g., Edward A. Shils and Morris Janowitz, "Cohesion and Disintegration in the Wehrmacht in World War II," *Public Opinion Quarterly* 12 (1948): 280.

32. Powell and DiMaggio, *New Institutionalism*, 11. For an overview of new institutional theory, see the introduction, 1–38.

33. Institutional structures can shape how such institutions and even societies will align themselves politically. For an example of how an institutional structure will show whether a government will align more toward democracy or authoritarianism, see, e.g., James Mahoney, "Knowledge Accumulation in Comparative Historical Research: The Case of Democracy and Authoritarianism," in

Comparative Historical Analysis in Social Science, ed. James Mahoney and Dietrich Rueschemeyer (Cambridge: Cambridge University Press, 2003).

34. See, e.g., Don M. Snider, "The U.S. Army as Profession," in *The Future of the Army Profession,* 2nd ed., Don M. Snider, project director, and Lloyd J. Matthews, ed. (Boston: McGraw Hill, 2005), 13–16.

35. See Andrew Abbott, *The System of Professions: An Essay on the Division of Expert Labor* (Chicago: University of Chicago Press, 2001).

36. Kim S. Cameron and Robert E. Quinn, *Diagnosing and Changing Organizational Culture* (Reading, PA: Addison-Wesley, 1999), 14, 96.

37. Richard W. Scott, *Institutions and Organizations* (New York: Sage Publications, 2000), 169–70. As Scott writes, legal relationships in institutions are not only based upon the "external, objective, rational nature of law." Rather, "laws and regulations are socially interpreted and find their force and meaning in interactions between regulators and the regulated." Ibid., 169.

38. Typical "realist" versions of the Cold War include those by John Lewis Gaddis, whose most famous works include *Strategies of Containment: A Critical Appraisal of Postwar American National Security* (New York: Oxford University Press, 1982) and most recently, *The Cold War: A New History* (New York: Penguin, 2005). The more current school of realism, so-called neorealism, does account for institutional structures within nations. Neorealist works include Kenneth N. Waltz, *Theory of International Politics* (Reading, MA: Addison-Wesley, 1979), and Robert O. Keohane, *After Hegemony: Cooperation and Discord in the World Political Economy* (Princeton, NJ: Princeton University Press, 1984). The prominent Cold War historian Melvyn Leffler may be called a neorealist. His books include *A Preponderance of Power* and *For the Soul of Mankind: The United States, the Soviet Union, and the Cold War* (New York: Hill & Wang, 2007).

39. Peter Katzenstein, "Introduction," in Katzenstein, *Culture of National Security,* 23. Katzenstein says later in the same essay, "Behavior is shaped not only by goals, alternatives, and rules of maximization or satisficing central to rationalist models of politics. Behavior is shaped also by roles and norms that define standards of appropriateness." Ibid., 28.

40. As Kurt Burch states, "constructivism addresses central dilemmas of social theory: how does the *interplay* of actors and social structures and of material and ideational factors constitute, inform, and explain social life?" Kurt Burch, "Towards a Constructivist Comparative Politics," in *Constructivism and Comparative Politics,* ed. Daniel M. Green (London: M. E. Sharpe, 2002), 61. As Burch also emphasizes, "neither actors nor social structures can be the Archimedean point of social inquiry, since they mutually constitute each other in a continuous process of social construction." Ibid.

41. According to Katzenstein, "In the process of communication norms can emerge in a variety of ways; spontaneously evolving, as social practice; consciously promoted, as political strategies to further specific interests; deliberately negotiated, as a mechanism for conflict management; or as a combination, mixing these three types. State interests and strategies are thus shaped by a never-ending political process that generates understood standards for action." Katzenstein, *Culture of National Security,* 21.

42. Bill McSweeney, *Security, Identity, and Interests* (Cambridge: Cambridge University Press, 2000), 117.

43. Hans-Georg Gadamer, *Truth and Method,* 2nd rev. ed., translated by Joel Weinsheimer and Donald G. Marshall (New York: Continuum, 1989), 366.

44. Robert Komer, *Organization and Management of the "New Model" Pacification Program, 1966–1969* (Santa Monica, CA: RAND Corp., 1970), 232, and *Bureaucracy Does Its Thing: Institutional Constraints on US-GVN Performance in Vietnam* (Santa Monica, CA: RAND Corp., 1972), 7–10, 75.

45. Elizabeth Kier, "Culture and French Military Doctrine before World War II," in Katzenstein, *Culture of National Security,* 187. In both that essay and her related full-length book, Kier demonstrates how the adoption of interwar military strategy by the French army and the French government was not based on interest calculations but on domestic politics, competing subcultures within the army itself, and other cultural factors. See also Elizabeth Kier, *Imagining War: French and Military Doctrine between the Wars* (Princeton, NJ: Princeton University Press, 1997).

46. Kier, "Culture and French Military Doctrine," 187, 192, 203–4.

47. Michael C. Desch, *Civilian Control of the Military: The Changing Security Environment* (Baltimore: Johns Hopkins University Press, 1999), 25, 135–36.

48. Such appraisals include Robert Dallek, *Franklin D. Roosevelt and American Foreign Policy, 1932–1945,* with new afterword (New York: Oxford University Press, 1995), and Eric Larrabee, *Commander in Chief: Franklin Delano Roosevelt, His Lieutenants, and Their Wars* (New York: Simon & Schuster, 1987). For a more negative appraisal, see Thomas Fleming, *The New Dealers' War: Franklin D. Roosevelt and the War within World War II* (New York: Basic Books, 2001).

49. Huntington, *Soldier and State,* 80–97.

50. See, e.g., Richard Betts and Leslie Gelb, *The Irony of Vietnam: The System Worked* (Washington, DC: Brookings Institution Press, 1979). Bruce Kuklick contends that the Pentagon Papers were an example of governmental bureaucratic history, written as a way to absolve civilian defense policymakers of blame for the Vietnam War. Bruce Kuklick, *Blind Oracles: Intellectuals and War from Kennan to Kissinger* (Princeton, NJ: Princeton University Press, 2006), 168–81.

1. Military Government Planning prior to 1940

1. David Edelstein, *Occupational Hazards* (Ithaca, NY: Cornell University Press, 2008), 177–80.

2. For an overview, see Ralph H. Gabriel, "American Experience with Military Government," *American Historical Review* 49 (July 1944): 632–36.

3. Gabriel cites Scott's occupation of Mexico during and after the Mexican War as the first significant American occupation, noting that Scott was the first American commander to see civil and military matters as closely linked. He also credits Scott with astute public relations and viewed Scott's handling of martial law in the occupied territory as a "complete success." Ibid.

4. For a discussion of the origins of the Lieber code, see Richard Shelly Hartigan, *Lieber's Code and the Law of War* (Chicago: Precedent Publishing, 1983), 1–23.

5. See Frank Freidel, *Francis Lieber: Nineteenth Century Liberal* (Gloucester, MA: Peter Smith, 1968 [1947]), 323.

6. Francis Lieber to Henry Halleck, May 20, 1963, in *The Life and Letters of Francis Lieber*, ed. Thomas Sergeant Perry (London: Trübner, 1882), 334.

7. *General Orders 100: Instructions for the Government of Armies of the United States in the Field* (Washington, DC: War Department, April 24, 1863), reprinted by the House of Representatives, 43rd Congress, 1st Session, January 24, 1874, section I, paras. 1, 3, 11; section II, paras. 33, 37, 38, 39.

8. Geoffrey Best, *Humanity in Warfare* (London: Weidenfeld & Nicolson, 1980), 180. See also Garrard Glenn, *The Army and the Law*, rev. ed. by A. Arthur Schiller (New York: Columbia University Press, 1943), 43, 181.

9. Brian McAllister Linn, *The Echo of Battle: The Army's Way of War* (Cambridge, MA: Harvard University Press, 2007), 75–77.

10. Freidel, *Francis Lieber*, 336–40.

11. George B. Davis, *The Elements of International Law* (New York: Harper & Brothers, 1908), 504.

12. Best, *Humanity in Warfare*, 147–90.

13. See *The Hague Conventions of 1899 (II) and 1907 (IV) Respecting the Laws and Customs of War on Land* in *The Hague Conventions and Declarations of 1899 and 1907*, ed. James B. Scott (New York: Oxford University Press, 1918), section III, articles 42–56.

14. See US War Department, *Rules of Land Warfare: 1914, Corrected to April 15, 1915, Changes 1 and 2* (Washington DC, 1915), 7–8, 11, 15. See also Donald A. Wells, *The Laws of Land Warfare: A Guide to the U.S. Army Manuals* (Westport, CT: Greenwood, 1992), 5–11.

15. Samuel P. Huntington, *The Soldier and the State: The Theory and Politics of Civil-Military Relations* (New York: Vintage, 1957), 16–23. See also L. Michael

Allsep Jr., "New Forms of Dominance: How a Corporate Lawyer Created the American Military Establishment" (PhD. diss., University of North Carolina, 2008), 259–60.

16. See, e.g., Edward M. Coffman, *The Regulars: The American Army, 1898–1941* (Cambridge, MA: Harvard University Press, 2004), 142–43, and Huntington, *Soldier and State*, 237–69. See also, Timothy K. Nenninger, *The Leavenworth Schools and the Old Army: Education, Professionalism, and the Officer Corps of the United States Army, 1881–1918* (Westport, CT: Greenwood, 1978), 7.

17. Nenninger, *Leavenworth Schools*, 7.

18. Linn, *Echo of Battle*, 50–51.

19. William E. Birkhimer, *Military Government and Martial Law* (Washington, DC: James J. Chapman, 1892). Part 1 of Birkhimer's book consists of sixteen chapters that cover a variety of legal topics related to military government; part 2 has thirteen chapters and deals with martial law.

20. Quoted in Dan Campbell, "A Brief Sketch of the Life of William Edward Birkhimer, Colonel, 28th Infantry, United States Volunteers" (unpublished manuscript, circa 1943), 21–22, in Papers of William E. Birkhimer, AHEC.

21. Birkhimer, *Military Government*, 5–7, 28–36.

22. The army would officially recognize the distinction between military government and martial law in its 1928 *Manual for Courts-Martial* (subsequently updated in 1934 and 1943). Office of the Judge Advocate General, *A Manual for Courts-Martial, 1928* (effective April 1, 1928, corrected April 20, 1943) (Washington, DC: GPO, 1943), 1.

23. Birkhimer, *Military Government*, 1–36, 240.

24. Russell F. Weigley, "The Elihu Root Reforms and the Progressive Era," in *Command and Commanders in Modern Warfare: Proceedings of the Second Military History Symposium, United States Air Force Academy, 2–3 May 1968*, ed. William Geffen (Washington, DC: Office of Air Force History, Headquarters, US Air Force, 1971), 23–24; Allsep, "New Forms," 259–60. Works that discuss the managerial, educational and other reforms as part of the move toward the professionalization of the army during the late nineteenth and early twentieth centuries include Coffman, *Regulars*, 142–201; Huntington, *Soldier and State*, 222–69; Nenninger, *Leavenworth Schools*, 3–20; James E. Hewes Jr., *From Root to McNamara: Army Organization and Administration, 1900–1963* (Washington, DC: CMH, 1975), 3–21; and Russell F. Weigley, *History of the United States Army* (New York: Macmillan, 1967), 313–41.

25. Ronald J. Barr, *The Progressive Army: U.S. Army Command and Administration, 1870–1914* (London: Macmillan, 1998), 41–42, 55.

26. James Abrahamson, *America Arms for a New Century: The Making of a Great Military Power* (New York: Free Press, 1981), 34–35.

27. Linn, *Echo of Battle,* 64.

28. Allsep, "New Forms," 270

29. Charles E. Magoon, *The Law of Civil Government in Territory Subject to Military Occupation by the Military Forces of the United States* (Washington, DC: GPO, 1902), 20, 31, 35.

30. John R. Brooke, *Final Report of Major General John R. Brooke, Military Governor, On Civil Matters Concerning the Island of Cuba,* 1899, 7, on file at AHEC.

31. Leonard Wood, *The Military Obligation of Citizenship* (Princeton, NJ: Princeton University Press, 1915), 75.

32. John Biddle Porter, *The Geneva and the Hague Conventions: A Lecture Delivered to the Field Service School for Medical Officers, Class of 1914* (Fort Leavenworth, KS: Press of the Army Service Schools, 1914), 4, 8, 24.

33. For an account of the World War I Rhineland occupation, see Ernest Fraenkel, *Military Occupation and the Rule of Law: Occupation Government in the Rhineland, 1918–1923* (New York: Oxford University Press, 1944).

34. Morris Janowitz, *The Professional Soldier: A Social and Political Portrait* (New York: Free Press, 1960), 89–101.

35. Henry T. Allen, *The Rhineland Occupation* (Indianapolis: Bobbs-Merrill, 1927), 6.

36. I owe this understanding of the Hunt Report's origins to Dr. Henry Gole, who has written a biography of Smith (*Exposing the Third Reich: Colonel Truman Smith in Hitler's Army* [Lexington: University Press of Kentucky, 2013]). Smith would subsequently serve as assistant army attaché in Berlin and become well known in the army as an expert of Germany. Conversations with Dr. Henry Gole, April 8 and 15, 2010.

37. The German citizens of Coblenz also apparently experienced fewer problems with American troops than with German soldiers in garrison in peacetime. See John Curtis Rasmussen Jr., "The American Forces in Germany and Civil Affairs, July 1919–January 1923" (PhD diss., University of Georgia, 1971), 221–22.

38. For a brief account and comparison of life in the different Allied zones, see Margaret Pawley, *The Watch on the Rhine: The Military Occupation of the Rhineland* (London: I. B. Tauris, 2007), 25–50.

39. H. A. Smith, *Military Government* (Fort Leavenworth, KS: General Service Schools, General Staff School, 1920), 5, 8, 10, 16, 25–26.

40. Reprinted during World War II, the document's title is *American Military Government of Occupied Germany, 1918–1920: Report of the Officer in Charge of Civil Affairs, Third Army and American Forces in Germany* (Washington, DC: GPO, 1943), 6, 8 (hereinafter Hunt Report).

41. For a discussion on the Hunt Report's historical significance in dealing

with such matters for the first time in a comprehensive way, see Earl Ziemke, *The U.S. Army in the Occupation of Germany, 1944–46* (Washington, DC: CMH, 1975), 3. The Hunt Report is also cited as a primary source for military government policy in the compendium of US military government documents published by CMH. See Harry L. Coles and Albert K. Weinberg, eds., *Civil Affairs: Soldiers Become Governors* (Washington, DC: CMH, 1964), 6–7.

42. Hunt Report (citing Orders No. 1, Advance General Headquarters, Treves, France, December 13, 1918), 67, 79.

43. Thijs W. Brocades Zaalberg, *Soldiers and Civil Power: Supporting or Substituting Civil Authorities in Modern Peace Operations* (Amsterdam: Amsterdam University Press, 2006), 29.

44. Hunt Report, 64.

45. At the army's Combined Arms Center at Fort Leavenworth, Kansas, there is a Center for Army Lessons Learned (CALL), which publishes a number of products.

46. Hunt Report, III.

47. Ziemke, *U.S. Army in the Occupation*, 3.

48. *History of Military Government Division*, vol. 1 (1945), 4, in box No. 1, MGD, Decimal File 1942–1946, RG 389, NARA.

49. Hearings before the Committee on Military Affairs, House of Representatives, 78th Congress, 2nd Session, Part 2, January 21 and 24, 1944 (Washington, DC: GPO, Washington, 1944), 2.

50. Undated letter of Henry Stimson to Franklin D. Roosevelt (unsent), included in MGD, *History of Military Government Division*, vol. 1 (1945), in box no. 1, MGD, Decimal File 1942–1946, RG 389, NARA.

51. Max Boot, *The Savage Wars of Peace: Small Wars and the Rise of American Power* (New York: Basic Books, 2002), 283.

52. John A. Lejeune, *The Reminiscences of a Marine* (Philadelphia: Dorrance, 1930), 465.

53. US Marine Corps, *Small Wars Manual* (Washington DC: GPO, 1940), para. 1–1c. (emphasis added). See also, Boot, *Savage Wars*, 284–85. For a historical review of small wars doctrine and the *Small Wars Manual*, see Keith Bickel, *Mars Learning: The Marine Corps' Development of Small Wars Doctrine, 1915–1940* (Boulder, CO: Westview, 2001).

54. US Marine Corps, *Small Wars Manual*, para. 1–3c. See also, Boot, *Savage Wars*, 145.

55. US Marine Corps, *Small Wars Manual*, para. 1–1d.

56. Boot, *Savage Wars*, 284–85.

57. US Marine Corps, *Small Wars Manual*, para. 1–7.

58. It is noteworthy that while the *Small Wars Manual* had a section specifi-

cally devoted to military government, and while many of the fundamental principles discussed therein are similar to those of the subsequent army doctrinal statement on military government, there is no specific mention or theoretical understanding of "military necessity," a concept that would be critical for the army in defining its military government role in World War II. See *Small Wars Manual,* chapter 13.

59. See, e.g., Weigley, *American Way of War,* 400–402, and Huntington, *Soldier and State,* 292–94.

60. James A. Stever, "The Glass Firewall between Military and Civil Administration," *Administration and Society* 31 (March 1999): 40–41.

61. A. M. Carr-Saunders and P. A. Wilson, *The Professions* (London: Frank Cass, 1964 [1933]), 3.

62. Huntington, *Soldier and State,* 271–73.

63. It is noteworthy that Elihu Root, though a Republican, was a strong supporter of America's entry into the league, as was Henry L. Stimson, who would serve as Franklin D. Roosevelt's secretary of war in World War II. Clarence A. Berdahl, "The United States and the League of Nations," *Michigan Law Review* 27 (April 1929): 609, 620.

64. Huntington, *Soldier and State,* 290–94.

65. Quoted in Mark Stoler, *Allies and Adversaries: The Joint Chiefs of Staff, the Grand Alliance, and U.S. Strategy in World War II* (Chapel Hill and London: University of North Carolina Press, 2000), 2.

66. Ibid., 3, 15. See Stever, "Glass Firewall," 40–41.

67. This interwar isolation, and even segregation, should be distinguished from any alleged isolation that existed in the late nineteenth century. Historian John M. Gates disputes the characterization of the US Army as isolated on the frontier during that earlier period. See John M. Gates, "The Alleged Isolation of U.S. Army Officers in the Late 19th Century," in *The Military and Society: A Collection of Essays,* ed. Peter Karsten (New York: Garland, 1998), 178–91.

68. Huntington, *Soldier and State,* 298.

69. Hewes, *From Root to McNamara,* 50–56, 104–12.

70. Henry G. Gole, *The Road to Rainbow: Army Planning for Global War, 1934–1940* (Annapolis, MD: Naval Institute Press, 2003), xix.

71. Allan R. Millett and Peter Maslowski, *For the Common Defense: A Military History of the United States of America,* 2nd ed. (New York: Free Press, 1984), 407.

72. Stoler, *Allies and Adversaries,* 3.

73. See Harry P. Ball, *Of Responsible Command: A History of the U.S. Army War College* (Carlisle, PA: Alumni Association of US Army War College, 1984), 227–43.

74. Gole, *Road to Rainbow,* xix; ibid., 227–28.

75. A survey of the finding aids of the Army War College curricular files indicates that the topic was studied by committees six times in the 1920s and seven times in the 1930s. In addition, Colonel Hunt lectured on military government in 1933, and judge advocates analyzed the subject in 1926. AWC Curricular Archives Finding Aids, AHEC.

76. George S. Pappas, *Prudens Futuri: The U.S. Army War College, 1901–1967* (Carlisle Barracks, PA: Alumni Association of the US Army War College, 1967), 97.

77. *Basic Manual for Military Government by U.S. Forces,* in G1, Report of Committee, No. 6, Subj.: Provost Marshal General's Plan, Military Government, file 1–1935–6 (Date of Conference, November 1, 1934) AWC, Washington DC (AWC Curricular Files), file 1–1935–6, AHEC (hereinafter *1934 Basic Manual*). A subsequent, shorter manual was published in 1938 and was for the most part simply an abridged version of the 1934 manual.

78. Ira L. Hunt, "Some Principles of Military Government," Lecture Delivered at the Army War College, Washington DC, February 28, 1933, G-1 Course No. 7, 1932–1933 (AWC Curricular Files, file 391–A07, AHEC).

79. G1, Report of Committee, No. 6, Subj.: The Interest of G-1 in Civil Affairs; 2 (Date of Conference, December 19, 1924), AWC, Washington DC (AWC Curricular Files, number 287–6, AHEC) (hereinafter 1924 Committee).

80. G1, Report of Committee, No. 3, Subj.: Contributions by G-1 to the Various War Plans: Duties of G-1 at GHQ and on Higher Staffs; Problems of G-1 in War Games, Maneuvers and on Reconnaissance; Staff Administration of Civil Affairs in Occupied Territory (Date of Conference, September 23, 1925), AWC, Washington DC (AWC Curricular Files, file 311–3 AHEC) (hereinafter 1925 Committee).

81. G1, Report of Committee, No. 11, Subj.: Administration of Civil Affairs by Military Authority in Occupied Territory (Date of Conference, October 19, 1927), AWC, Washington DC (AWC Curricular Files, file 341–11 AHEC) (hereinafter 1927 committee).

82. 1924 Committee.

83. 1925 Committee.

84. 1927 Committee.

85. Ibid.

86. 1st Supplement to 1927 Committee, 1927 Committee.

87. Archibald King, 2nd Supplement to 1927 Committee, 1927 Committee. King would also play a role in drafting the field manual that would form the basis for US military government, *FM 27-5.* See Dan Allen, "Franklin D. Roosevelt and the Development of an American Occupation Policy in Europe" (PhD diss., Ohio State University, 1976), 4.

88. G1, Report of Committee, No. 6, Subj.: Provost Marshal General's Plan, Military Government (Date of Conference, November 1, 1934), AWC, Washington DC (AWC Curricular Files, file 1–1935–6, AHEC) (hereinafter 1934 Committee).

89. See G1, Report of Committee, No. 5, Subj.: Administration of Civil Affairs in Occupied Territory, Enemy Aliens, Prisoners of War, Draft Deserters, and Conscientious Objectors (Date of Conference, October 22, 1931), AWC, Washington DC (AWC Curricular Files, file 381–5, AHEC (hereinafter 1931 Committee); G1, Report of Committee, No. 6, Subj.: Provost Marshal General's Plan, Military Government (Date of Conference, October 23, 1933), AWC, Washington, DC (AWC Curricular Files, file 401–6, AHEC) (hereinafter 1933 Committee).

90. 1931 Committee, citing *U.S. v. Wallace* (20 Wallace 394).

91. See 1931 and 1933 Committees.

92. 1934 Committee; G1, Report of Committee, No. 7, Subj.: Military Government, Handling of Enemy Aliens, Prisoners of War, Draft Deserters and Conscientious Objectors (Date of Conference, November 19, 1937), AWC, Washington, DC (AWC Curricular Files, file 1–1938–7, AHEC) (hereinafter 1937 Committee).

93. 1933 Committee.

94. 1934 Committee.

95. 1934 and 1937 Committees.

96. *1934 Basic Manual,* 29, 30–33A, 34. See also Lieber Code, section IV, para. 85: "War-rebels are persons within an occupied territory who rise in arms against the occupying or conquering army, or against the authorities established by the same. If captured, they may suffer death, whether they rise singly . . . and whether called upon to do so by their own, but expelled, government or not."

97. *1934 Basic Manual,* 35–39, 41, and chart 1.

98. Gole, *Road to Rainbow,* 32, 122–27. Given the mandatory presence of all students at the committee sessions, it is a reasonable assumption that many planners on the army staff were familiar with military government principles set forth in them.

99. Earl Ziemke notes that the Army War College student committees frequently relied on the Hunt Report in the interwar years. He also points out that it was only in the 1930s, with the publication of a proposed handbook and the adoption of a less "legalistic" and more administrative and operational focus on military government, that work of practical value came from the committees. Ziemke, *U.S. Army in the Occupation,* 3.

100. For an analysis of the linkage between the Army War College and the War Plans Division, see Gole, *Road to Rainbow,* 113–21.

101. Gole, 32, *Road to Rainbow,* 122–27.

102. Edgar L. Erickson, "An Introduction to American Military Government–Civil Affairs in World War II" (Washington, DC: Office of the Chief of Military History, unpublished and incomplete, circa 1946). Multiple drafts of an official history of civil affairs in World War II were written by army historians after World War II, but an official history was never published. Copies of the drafts are located at CMH. In these drafts, official historians were the first to analyze and acknowledge the role the Army War College played in the planning for post–World War II military government.

103. A 1924 subcommittee was chaired by a Marine Corps colonel. The 1925 committee was chaired by a navy captain, with a subcommittee chaired by a Marine Corps colonel. The 1933 committee also had a navy captain on a subcommittee. 1924, 1925, 1933 Committees.

104. Quoted in G1, Report of Committee, No. 7, Subj.: Military Government, Handling of Enemy Aliens, Prisoners of War, Draft Deserters and Conscientious Objectors (Date of Conference, November 19, 1937), AWC, Washington DC (AWC Curricular Files, file 1–1938–7) at 34. Major Bonham was a 1935 War College graduate who stayed on the faculty until 1939.

2. Military Government Doctrine, Training, and Organization, 1940–1941

1. Mary Douglas, *How Institutions Think* (Syracuse, NY: Syracuse University Press, 1986), 47. See also W. Richard Scott, *Institutions and Organizations,* 2nd ed. (New York: Sage Publications, 2000), 66–68.

2. Barry Posen, *The Sources of Military Doctrine: France, Britain, and Germany between the World Wars* (Ithaca, NY: Cornell University Press, 1984), 38.

3. Samuel Huntington, "Inter-Service Competition and the Political Roles of the Armed Services," in *Problems of National Security,* ed. Henry Kissinger (New York: Praeger, 1965), 468.

4. *Field Manual 1-02: Operational Terms and Graphics* (Washington, DC: Headquarters, Department of the Army, September 2004), 1–65. For a contemporary discussion of doctrine, see *Field Manual 3-0: Operations* (Washington, DC: Headquarters, Department of the Army, February 2008), D-1, D-3.

5. William E. Birkhimer, *Military Government and Martial Law* (Washington, DC: James J. Chapman, 1892), title page; Virgil Ney, *Evolution of the United States Army Field Manual: Valley Forge to Vietnam* (Fort Belvoir, VA: US Army Combat Developments Command, 1966), 63, 70–71. See also Walter Edward Kretchik, "Peering through the Mist: Doctrine as a Guide for U.S. Army Operations, 1775–2000" (PhD diss., University of Kansas, 2001), 117–18.

6. Ney, *Evolution*, 75.

7. Posen, *Sources of Military Doctrine*, 13–33. See also Sten Rynning, *Changing Military Doctrine: Presidents and Military Power in Fifth Republic France, 1958–2000* (Westport, CT: Praeger, 2002), 2–4.

8. US War Department, *Basic Field Manual: Military Training; FM 21-5* (Washington, DC: GPO, 1941), para. 17. See also Posen, *Sources of Military Doctrine*, 13.

9. US War Department, *Basic Field Manual: Military Government; FM 27-5, July 30, 1940* (Washington, DC: GPO, July 1940).

10. Brig. Gen. William E. Shedd for Assistant Chief of Staff, G-3, January 18, 1940, in Harry L. Coles and Albert K. Weinberg, *Civil Affairs: Soldiers Become Governors* (Washington, DC: CMH, 1964), 7.

11. See Coles and Weinberg, *Civil Affairs*, 7n4.

12. Assistant Chief of Staff, G-1, for Assistant Chief of Staff, G-3, January 18, 1940, in Coles and Weinberg, *Civil Affairs*, 7.

13. US War Department, *Basic Field Manual: Rules of Land Warfare, 1934* (Washington, DC: GPO, 1934). Revealing the Army War College's significance in the process, faculty member Col. Edwin Glenn wrote the first revision of General Orders 100, which became the War Department's *Rules of Land Warfare* in 1914. See Donald A Wells, *The Laws of Land Warfare: A Guide to the U.S. Army Manuals* (Westport, CT: Greenwood, 1992), 5.

14. In both versions, international laws regarding military occupation are contained in chapter 10, paras. 271–344. US War Department, *Rules of Land Warfare, 1934;* US War Department, *Rules of Land Warfare, FM 27-10, October 1, 1940* (Washington, DC: GPO, 1940), paras. 271–344.

15. Coles and Weinberg, *Civil Affairs*, 7n4.

16. MGD, Office of the Provost Marshal General, "History of Military Government Training" (1945), 4, in box 1, entry 443, RG 389, NARA.

17. Dan Allen, "Franklin D. Roosevelt and the Development of American Occupation Policy in Europe" (PhD diss., Ohio State University, 1976), 4. Stimson himself indicated this in a letter he drafted to FDR but never sent. Henry L. Stimson to President Roosevelt (undated) in "History of Military Government Training," box 1, entry 443, RG 389, NARA.

18. Posen, *Sources of Military Doctrine*, 13–33

19. *FM 27-5, July 30, 1940*, para. 1.

20. *FM 27-5, July 30, 1940*, para. 3. Apart from a few stylistic differences, the definition of the War College's *Basic Manual* was identical: "Military Government is that form of Government which is established and maintained by a belligerent by force of arms over occupied territory of an enemy, and over the inhabitants thereof. 'Territory of the enemy' includes also domestic territory

recovered from rebels treated as belligerents." *Basic Manual for Military Government by U.S. Forces*, para. I.2, in G1, Report of Committee, No. 6, Subj.: Provost Marshal General's Plan, Military Government, file 1–1935–6, November 1, 1934, AWC Curricular Files, AHEC.

21. *FM 27-5, July 30, 1940*, para. 5.

22. *Basic Manual for Military Government by U.S. Forces*, para. I.3; *FM 27-10, October 1, 1940*, para. 6. Birkhimer, on the other hand, separated the commander's power from the sovereign's: "The character of government to be established over conquered territory depends entirely upon the laws of the dominant power, *or* the orders of the military commander." Birkhimer, *Military Government*, 33, emphasis added.

23. *FM 27-5, July 30, 1940*, para. 5. *General Orders 100: Instructions for the Government of Armies of the United States in the Field* (Washington, DC: War Department, April 24, 1863), reprinted by the House of Representatives, 43rd Congress, 1st Session, January 24, 1874, section I, paras. 3, 6. The War College Committee language stated: "During belligerent occupation, the power of the military commander flows directly from the laws of war, and is free from constitutional limitations on executive, legislative, and judicial powers. On the cessation of military operations, the military commander is subject to certain rules of law, of which the most important is the principle of 'immediate exigency' or 'necessity.'" Maj. John H. Van Vliet et al., Supplement No. 2 to Report of Committee, no. 6, Subj.: Military Government Plan, G1, Report of Committee, No. 6, Subject: Provost Marshal General's Plan, Military Government, file 401–6, October 23, 1933, AWC Curricular Files, AHEC.

24. See, e.g., James W. Riddleberger, "Impact of the Proconsular Experience on American Foreign Policy: A Reflective View," in *Americans as Proconsuls: United States Military Government in Germany and Japan, 1944–1952*, ed. Robert Wolfe (Carbondale: Southern Illinois University Press, 1984), 393.

25. *FM 27-5, July 30, 1940*, para. 9a.

26. Ibid., para. 10a.

27. *General Orders 100*, section I, paras. 14–15; *FM 27-10, Rules of Land Warfare, October 1, 1940*, para. 4a. See also Donald A. Wells, *The Laws of Land Warfare: A Guide to the U.S. Army Manuals* (Westport, CT: Greenwood, 1992), 34.

28. *General Orders 100*, section I, paras. 15–16.

29. See Mark Grimsley, *The Hard Hand of War: Union Military Policy toward Southern Civilians, 1861–1865* (Cambridge: Cambridge University Press, 1995), 149–51; Richard Shelly Hartigan, *Lieber's Code and the Law of War* (Chicago: Precedent, 1983), 16.

30. See *FM 27-10, Rules of Land Warfare, October 1, 1940*, para. 4b and c.

31. "Military necessity" was *not* defined in terms of occupation responsi-

bilities in the *Rules of Land Warfare*. There was a provision that discussed the "necessity of military government," but that related to the inability of a legitimate government to function and did not relate to the common understanding of military necessity. *FM 27-10, October 1, 1940*, para. 281.

32. *FM 27-10, October 1, 1940*, para. 9b.

33. *FM 27-5, July 30, 1940*, para. 9a.

34. Ibid., para. 33.

35. In the World War I Rhineland, occupation began only after fighting ceased, so there was no phase I for that occupation as subsequently defined by Colonel Hunt or in *FM 27-5*.

36. *FM 27-5, July 30, 1940*, para. 10d.

37. Ibid., paras. 10 c, d, and e.

38. *American Military Government of Occupied Germany, 1918–1920: Report of the Officer in Charge of Civil Affairs, Third Army and American Forces in Germany* (Washington, DC: GPO, 1943), 67, 333–45.

39. *United States Army and Navy Manual of Military Government and Civil Affairs, FM 27-5 and OpNav 50E-3, December 22, 1943* (Washington, DC: GPO, 1943). "The revised manual gains significance and presumably will command greater respect in the field because it is issued jointly by the Army and Navy." Maj. Frederick S. Simpich to Gen. Allen Gullion, Subject: Revision of FM 27-5, November 11, 1943, in box 716, OPMG, MGD, UDF 1942–1946, RG 389, NARA.

40. Col. Lewis K. Underhill, "Organization of Military Government" (SMG lecture, 1943), quoted in Merle Fainsod, "The Development of American Military Government Policy during World War II," in *American Experiences in Military Government in World War II*, ed. Carl J. Friedrich (New York: Rinehart, 1948), 27.

41. Hiram Motherwell, "Military Occupation, and Then What?," *Harper's*, October, 1943, 440.

42. Fainsod, "Development of American," 28–31.

43. Ibid. Ralph H. Gabriel praised the joint service cooperation that resulted in the 1943 version, saying that the revised manual "symbolized the close cooperation that has characterized the two services in the present conflict; it established identity of doctrine in an area of vast importance; and it made clear that thinking on the relation of war to civil populations had been made adequate to the complexities of modern civilization." Ralph H. Gabriel, "American Experience with Military Government," *American Historical Review* 49 (July 1944): 630.

44. Col. Frank Hastings to the Chief, Civil Affairs Division, Subject: Draft of Army and Navy Manual for Military Government and Civil Affairs, August 3,

1943, in box 716, OPMG, MGD, UDF 1942–1946, RG 389, NARA.

45. *FM 27-5 and OpNav 50E-3*, section I, para. 9n.

46. Ibid., paras. 1 and 8. Note paragraph 8 does, in contrast to the 1940 version of *FM 27-5*, make explicit the sovereign authority of the military governor by stating that the military commander/governor is "limited only by the laws and customs of war and by directives from higher authority." *FM 27-5 and OpNav 50E-3*, para. 8.

47. *FM 27-5 and OpNav 50E-3*, section I, paras. 1 and 8, emphasis added.

48. See also Fainsod, "Development of American," 31. Fainsod also points out a "marked hardening of attitude toward enemy populations" in that the "welfare of the governed" is no longer listed among basic objectives. Specifically, fraternizing with the local populace is discouraged. *FM 27-5 and OpNav 50E-3*, section I, para. 9i(10).

49. *FM 27-5 and OpNav 50E-3*, section I, para. 4.

50. Historians have noted that a distinction would be made between the terms "military government" and "civil affairs" in practical application during actual occupations. The former term would be used for conquered enemy territory and the latter, less imperialist-sounding, for administration in liberated territories. See, e.g., Thijs W. Brocades Zaalberg, *Soldiers and Civil Power: Supporting or Substituting Civil Authorities in Modern Peace Operations* (Amsterdam: Amsterdam University Press, 2006), 26–27.

51. See, e.g., the title of section III of the 1940 manual is "Civil Affairs Section of the Commanding General, Theater of Operations." *FM 27-5, July 30, 1940*, section III.

52. *FM 27-5 and OpNav 50E-3*, section I, para. 1c, emphasis added.

53. Ibid.

54. Adjutant General to Provost Marshal General, Subject: Establishment of School, March 13, 1942, in "History of Military Government Training," in box 1, entry no. 443, OPMG, MGD, UDF 1942–1946, RG 389, NARA. In an earlier memorandum from Jesse Miller to General Gullion, Miller states that the "express provisions of *FM 27-5* are that the civil affairs section of any army of occupation should be qualified, as a group, to function, with an adequate background, in a variety of civil activities, including public works, utilities, finance, health, safety and welfare, education, justice and communications." Jesse I. Miller to Maj. Gen. Allen Gullion, Subject: School of Military Government, January 10, 1942, in "History of Military Government Training," in box 1, entry no. 443, OPMG, MGD, UDF 1942–1946, RG 389, NARA.

55. Col. C. P. Stearns, "Civil Affairs Functions in the Present War," January 15, 1943, class III, remarks at opening exercises, SMG, in box 1, entry no. 443, OPMG, MGD, UDF 1942–1946, RG 389, NARA.

56. Earl Ziemke, *The U.S. Army in the Occupation of Germany, 1944–46* (Washington, DC: CMH, 1975), 3.

57. Col. Frank H. Hastings, Assistant Commandant, "Procedure for the Guidance of Student Officers in Connection with Civil Affairs Problems," January 22, 1943, in "History of Military Government Training," in box 1, entry no. 443, OPMG, MGD, UDF 1942–1946, RG 389, NARA.

58. Maj. Gen. J. A. Ulio, memorandum no. W350–91–42, Assignment of Graduates of the School of Military Government, September 16, 1942, in box no. 711, OPMG, MGD, UDF 1942–1946, RG 389, NARA.

59. Military Government Division, "Topical Outline of Military Government Handbooks" (undated, believed to be 1942), in "History of Military Government Training," in box 1, entry no. 443, OPMG, MGD, UDF 1942–1946, RG 389, NARA.

60. *U.S. Army Civil Affairs Handbooks: Austria, Army Service Forces Manual,* (Washington, DC: GPO, November 1943).

61. Military Government Division, Liaison and Studies Branch, "Checklist of Civil Affairs Handbooks, No. 2," May 30, 1944, in "History of Military Government Training," in box 1, entry no. 443, OPMG, Military Government Division, UDF 1942–1946, RG 389, NARA. In addition to Germany, the following countries also had handbooks prepared by May 1944 on a similar range of issues: Austria, Belgium, Bulgaria, Denmark, France, the French Indochina colonies, Hungary, Italy, Japan, Manchuria, the Netherlands, Norway, the Philippines, Poland, Rumania, Thailand, and Yugoslavia. Ibid.

62. *U.S. Army Civil Affairs Handbooks,* introduction.

63. E. H. Vernon, "Civil Affairs and Military Government," *Military Review* (January 1946): 25–32.

64. Supreme Headquarters, Allied Expeditionary Force, *Standard Policy and Procedure for Combined Civil Affairs Operations in Northwest Europe,* revised May 1, 1944.

65. Ibid., introduction, paras. 1 and 2.

66. Ibid., part 2, section 1, para. 25. See also Lt. Col. E. R. Blatzell, "Draft Notes Comprising Standard Policy and Procedure for Combined Civil Affairs Operations in North West Europe (SPP) and *FM 27-5,*" February 8, 1944, in box 31, SHAEF Policy, 1943–1945, Papers of Frank McSherry, AHEC.

67. *Standard Policy and Procedure for Combined Civil Affairs Operations in Northwest Europe,* part 2, section 1, para. 24a.

68. See C. Leonard Hoag, *American Military Government in Korea: War Policy and the First Year of Occupation, 1941–1946* (Washington, DC: CMH, 1970), 98–100.

69. Ibid., 98–99.

70. Earl Ziemke, "The Formulation and Initial Implementation of U.S. Occupation Policy in Germany," in *U.S. Occupation in Europe after World War II*, ed. Hans A. Schmitt (Lawrence: Regents Press of Kansas, 1978), 42.

71. *FM 27-5, July 30, 1940*, para. 6, stated that the Personnel Division (G-1) of the War Department "is responsible for the preparation of plans for and the determination of policies with respect to military government."

72. Brig. Gen. Wade H. Haislip to Chief of Staff of Army, Subject: Training of Personnel for Military Government and Liaison, December 3, 1941, in box 711, OPMG, MGD, UDF 1942–1946, RG 389, NARA.

73. The Judge Advocate General to Assistant Chief of Staff, G-1, Subject: Training of Personnel for Military Government, December 23, 1941, in box 711, OPMG, MGD, UDF 1942–1946, RG 389, NARA.

74. A short biography of Gullion is found in *The Army Lawyer: A History of the Judge Advocate General's Corps, 1774–1975* (Washington, DC: GPO, 1975), 154–57.

75. For a discussion of Gullion's involvement in the Japanese-American exclusion policy, as well as John J. McCloy's, see Kai Bird, *The Chairman: John J. McCloy and the Making of the American Establishment* (New York: Simon & Schuster, 1992), 149–51. McCloy would provide the chief civilian leadership for the Civil Affairs Division.

76. Brig. Gen. Harry L. Twaddle for Assistant Chief of Staff, G-1, Subject: Training of Personnel for Military Government and Liaison, December 9, 1941, in box 711, OPMG, MGD, UDF 1942–1946, RG 389, NARA.

77. Judge Advocate General for Assistant Chief of Staff, G-1, Subject: Training of Personnel for Military Government, December 23, 1941, in box 711, OPMG, MGD, UDF 1942–1946, RG 389, NARA.

78. Immediate Action by Order of Secretary of War to Provost Marshal General, Subject: Training of Personnel for Military Government and Liaison, February 9, 1942, in box 711, OPMG, MGD, UDF 1942–1946, RG 389, NARA.

79. Brig. Gen. H. R. Bull, Acting Assistant Chief of Staff, G-3 to Chief of Staff, Subject: Training of Personnel for Military Government and Liaison, March 5, 1942, box 711, OPMG, MGD, UDF 1942–1946, RG 389, NARA.

80. Adjutant General to Provost Marshal General, subject: Establishment of the School of Military Government, March 13, 1942, in box 711, OPMG, MGD, UDF 1942–1946, RG 389, NARA.

81. Col. Frank Hastings, "History of the School of Military Government," March 13, 1945, p. 3, in box 719, OPMG, MGD, UDF 1942–1946, RG 389, NARA.

82. Supplement to Administrative Log, Military Government Division, for Maj. Charles D. Hill, Assistant Executive Officer, June 4, 1945, in box 719,

OPMG, MGD, UDF 1942–1946, RG 389, NARA. Based on the log's record-ing, it appears that Miller served in a civilian capacity as acting director, Mili-tary Government Division, from August to November 1942, after which he was placed in an active military status at the rank of colonel and given the title of director. Ibid.

83. A short biography of Miller is found in *Who's Who in America,* vol. 22 (1942–1943).

84. Jesse I. Miller to Maj. Gen. Gullion, Subject: School of Military Govern-ment, January 10, 1942, in box 719, OPMG, MGD, UDF 1942–1946, RG 389, NARA.

85. Richard H. van Wagenen, "Class Notes, January–May 1943 School of Military Government," in Richard H. van Wagenen Papers, in box 1, AHEC.

86. Lt. Col. Paul S. Andrews, "Liaison-Preliminary," course VII, class IV, May 18, 1943, in box no. 840, OPMG, MGD, Liaison and Studies Branch File 1942–1946, RG 389, NARA.

87. Ralph H. Gabriel, "Preliminary Survey of American Experience with Mil-itary Government," course V, class VII, February 7, 1944, in box 840, OPMG, MGD, Liaison and Studies Branch File 1942–1946, RG 389, NARA.

88. Andrews, "Liaison-Preliminary."

89. Ralph H. Gabriel, "Military Government and the Civilian Population," course VI, class III, March 12, 1943, in box 840, OPMG, MGD, Liaison and Studies Branch File 1942–1946, RG 389, NARA.

90. Thomas H. Barber, "Functions of a Civil Affairs Staff Team," course IX, class IV, June 12, 1943, in box 840, OPMG, MGD, Liaison and Studies Branch File 1942–1946, RG 389, NARA.

91. Van Wagenen, "Class Notes."

92. Barber, "Functions of a Civil Affairs Staff Team."

93. MGD, "History of Military Government Training," 6–7.

94. Ibid.

95. Ibid.

96. Col. O. I. Nelson, Assistant Secretary, General Staff to Command-ing General, Services of Supply (SOS), Attention: Provost Marshal General, "Expansion of the School of Military Government and Military Government Division," August 14, 1942, in box 711, OPMG, MGD, UDF 1942–1946, RG 389, NARA.

97. Brig. Gen. J. F. Mee, Adjutant General to the Provost Marshal General, "Increase in Procurement Objectives, Army Specialist Corps," October 12, 1942, in box 711, RG 389, NARA; Maj. Gen. White to the Provost Marshal General (through Military Personnel Division, SOS), "Appointment of Persons Skilled in Military Government in the Specialist Reserve Section, Officer Reserve Corps,"

November 23, 1942, in box 711, OPMG, MGD, UDF 1942–1946, RG 389, NARA.

98. Maj. Gen. Myron Cramer, Judge Advocate General to Maj. Gen. Allen Gullion, April 10, 1943, in box 712, OPMG, MGD, UDF 1942–1946, RG 389, NARA.

99. Maj. Gen. Allen Gullion, Sample Letter to Possible Military Government Candidates (undated), in box 718, OPMG, MGD, UDF 1942–1946, RG 389, NARA.

100. Lt. Gen. Brehon Somervell to Provost Marshal General (3rd Endorsement), July 27, 1943, in box 711, OPMG, MGD, UDF 1942–1946, RG 389, NARA.

101. Col. Jesse Miller to Chief, Civil Affairs Division (Attention: Lt. Col. G. G. Berry), "A.U.S. Officers at Civil Affairs Training Schools," June 16, 1943, in box 711, OPMG, MGD, UDF 1942–1946, RG 389, NARA.

102. The following documents discuss the Civil Affairs Training Schools: Chief, Civil Affairs Division to Provost Marshal General, subject: Attendance of Officers Already in the Army at Civil Affairs Training Schools (CATS) for Military Government Training, June 26, 1943, in box 711, RG 389, NARA; Col. Jesse I. Miller for Director, Civil Affairs Division, subject: Disposition of Graduates of School of Military Government and Civil Affairs Training Schools (CATS), April 11, 1944, in box 711, OPMG, MGD, UDF 1942–1946, RG 389, NARA.

103. Robert P. Patterson to Cordell Hull, July 29, 1943, in box 711, OPMG, MGD, UDF 1942–1946, RG 389, NARA.

104. Director, Military Government Division, "Final Report of the Present Director, Military Government Division" (undated, but based on dates and the closure of the division in 1946, believed to be in 1946), in box 719, OPMG, MGD, UDF 1942–1946, RG 389, NARA.

105. George Fitzpatrick et al., *A Survey of the Experience and Opinions of U.S. Military Government Officers in World War II* (Chevy Chase, MD: Johns Hopkins University Operations Research Office, 1956), 3.

106. Col. O. I. Nelson, Assistant Secretary, General Staff to Commanding General, Service of Supply (SOS), Attention: Provost Marshal General, "Expansion of the School of Military Government and Military Government Division," August 14, 1942, in box 711, OPMG, MGD, UDF 1942–1946, RG 389, NARA.

107. Col. Jesse I. Miller to Maj. Gen. Allen Gullion, "Blue Printing for Military Government," October 7, 1942, in box 711, OPMG, MGD, UDF 1942–1946, RG 389, NARA.

108. Maj. Gen. Allen Gullion to Assistant Chief of Staff, G-3, Subject: Need for Civil Affairs Officers in Divisions, Corps and Armies, in box 711, OPMG, MGD, UDF 1942–1946, RG 389, NARA.

109. Ibid.

110. Vernon, "Civil Affairs and Military Government," 30.

111. "This Division [Civil Affairs Division] will perform the normal functions of a General Staff Division on all matters pertaining to Civil Affairs." Memorandum to Chief of Staff, Supreme Headquarters, Allied Expeditionary Force, Subject: Organization Civil Affairs, February 7, 1944, in box 29, SHAEF Organization, 1943–1945, Papers of Frank J. McSherry, AHEC.

112. Report of Maj. John Boettiger, provided by Maj. Gen. John H. Hilldring, to SHAEF Commander, March 2, 1944, in box 33, SHAEF Correspondence, Speeches, 1943–1945, Papers of Frank McSherry, AHEC.

113. The 1943 *FM 27-5* listed twenty-four separate functions (plus one "miscellaneous") for military government to perform, all of which fall into one of the SHAEF G-5 subdivisions listed in the G-5 figure reproduced above. *United States Army and Navy Manual of Military Government and Civil Affairs*, para. 12a-y.

114. Office of the Chief Historian, European Command, *Occupation Forces in Europe Series 1945–1946, Training Packet no. 51* (Frankfurt am Main, Germany: 1947), 16, 20–21, 36.

115. Philip H. Taylor, "The Administration of Occupied Japan," *Annals of the American Academy of Political and Social Science* 267 (January 1950): 141, 143.

116. *Occupation Forces in Europe Series 1945–1946, Training Packet no. 51,* 22–23.

117. Frank McSherry, Speech to the School on Demobilization and Disarmament, "Civil Affairs as It Pertains to Disarmament and Control Machinery," November 30, 1944, in box 33, SHAEF Correspondence, Speeches, 1943–1945, Papers of Frank McSherry, AHEC.

118. For a description of the inadequately trained US forces that first arrived in Korea, see E. Grant Meade, *American Military Government in Korea* (New York: King's Crown Press, 1951), 46–51. See also Hoag, *American Military Government in Korea,* 15. For an analysis of military government detachments, including their prior service in locations other than Korea or their intended assignment to locations other than Korea, see Statistical Research Division of the Office of Administration, Headquarters United States Army Military Government in Korea (USAMGIK), *History of the United States Army Military Government in Korea: Part I, Period of September 1945–30 June 1946,* October 1946, 21, 32, AHEC.

119. Col. Karl Bendetsen to Brig. Gen. Frank McSherry, December 30, 1943, in box 31, SHAEF Policy, 1943–1945, Papers of Frank McSherry, AHEC.

120. *United States Army and Navy Manual of Military Government and Civil Affairs,* para. 29b.

121. Hajo Halborn, *American Military Government: Its Organization and Policies* (Washington DC: Infantry Journal Press, 1947), 4.

122. Brig. Gen. Frank McSherry to Maj. Gen. Roger Lumley, "Organizational Standard Policy and Procedure for Combined Civil Affairs Operations in Northwest Europe," December 13, 1943, in box 31, SHAEF Policy, 1943–1945, Papers of Frank McSherry, AHEC.

123. Maj. Gen. Roger Lumley to Brig. Gen. Frank McSherry, January 13, 1944, in box 31, SHAEF Policy, 1943–1945, Papers of Frank McSherry, AHEC.

3. FDR, Interagency Conflict, and Military Government, 1941–1942

1. Randolph Bourne, "The State," in *War and the Intellectuals: Collected Essays, 1915–1919,* ed. with an introduction by Carl Resek (Indianapolis and Cambridge: Hackett, 1999 [Harper & Row, 1964]), 71, 89.

2. A relatively unflattering account of Wallace can be found in Thomas Fleming, *The New Dealers' War: Franklin D. Roosevelt and the War within World War II* (New York: Basic Books, 2001), 92–98, 456–57. A much more sympathetic account is found in John C. Culver and John Hyde, *American Dreamer: A Life of Henry A. Wallace* (New York: Norton, 2001). Ickes titled his memoir *The Autobiography of a Curmudgeon* (New York: Reynal & Hitchcock, 1943).

3. See Mark Stoler, "U.S. Civil-Military Relations in World War II," *Parameters* 21, no. 3 (Autumn 1991): 65. There are numerous accounts on FDR and his wartime cabinet. More detailed studies include James MacGregor Burns, *Roosevelt: The Soldier of Freedom* (New York: Harcourt, Brace, 1970), and Robert Dallek, *Franklin D. Roosevelt and American Foreign Policy, 1933–1945* (New York: Oxford University Press, 1995). For general overviews of FDR's entire administration, see Frank Freidel, *Franklin D. Roosevelt: A Rendezvous with Destiny* (Boston: Little, Brown, 1990), and David M. Kennedy, *Freedom from Fear: The American People in Depression and War, 1929–45* (New York: Oxford University Press, 1999).

4. Dallek, *Franklin D. Roosevelt and American Foreign Policy,* 359.

5. Dean Acheson, *Present at the Creation: My Years in the State Department* (New York: Norton, 1969), 47.

6. See Diaries of Henry L. Stimson, April 23, 1942, vol. 38, reel 7, p. 139; November 6, 1942, vol. 41, reel 8, p. 19; February 1, 1943, vol. 42, reel 8, p. 1; Yale University Library, New Haven, CT.

7. Kent Roberts Greenfield, *American Strategy in World War II: A Reconsideration* (Westport, CT: Greenwood, 1979 [1963]), 77.

8. See Kathryn McHale, General Director, American Association of University Women, to Franklin D. Roosevelt, June 25, 1942, Postwar Problems, Official Files (OF) 4351, FDR Library.

9. Burns, *Roosevelt,* 427.

10. Office of War Information, Bureau of Intelligence, "Attitudes toward Peace Planning," March 6, 1943, 2, 6, 7–8, Postwar Problems, OF 4351, FDR Library.

11. Hadley Cantril and Gerard B. Lambert, "Suggested Procedure to Make Administration's Post-War Policy Acceptable to American Public," Confidential Report for Samuel I. Rosenman, November 15, 1943, in box 329, Papers of Harry Hopkins, Sherwood Collection, FDR Library. See also Isador Lubin to Harry Hopkins, January 6, 1944, in box 329, Papers of Harry Hopkins, Sherwood Collection, FDR Library.

12. Cantril and Lambert, "Suggested Procedure."

13. M. H. Petit, "The Effect and Influence of War Department Policies and Procedures on the Readjustment of Our National Industrial Economy," submitted to Undersecretary of War Robert Patterson, April 23, 1943, in Papers of Robert Patterson (Postwar Planning Folder #1), LOC.

14. National Resources Planning Board, *Message from the President of the United States Transmitting Two Reports of the National Resources Planning Board: "National Resources Development Report for 1943" and "Security, Work, and Relief Policies"* (Washington, DC: GPO, January 1943).

15. Ibid.

16. Cordell Hull, *The Memoirs of Cordell Hull,* vol. 2 (New York: Macmillan, 1948), 1111.

17. See, e.g., Michael C. Desch, *Civilian Control of the Military: The Changing Environment* (Baltimore: Johns Hopkins University Press, 1999) 25; Greenfield, *American Strategy,* 50–51. For an account of the rise of the Joint Chiefs of Staff, see Stoler, "U.S. Civil-Military Relations," 60–73.

18. John J. McCloy, *The Challenge to American Foreign Policy* (Cambridge, MA: Harvard University Press, 1953).

19. Michael Beschloss, *The Conquerors: Roosevelt, Truman and the Destruction of Hitler's Germany, 1941–1945* (New York: Simon & Schuster, 2002), 88.

20. As an example, Andrew Roberts in his book *Masters and Commanders* remarks how Marshall "effectively removed from the War Secretary [the role of] being the president's principal military adviser and a central contributor to strategic decision making." *Masters and Commanders: How Four Titans Won the War in the West, 1941–1945* (New York: HarperCollins, 2009), 34. John McCloy also noted that it was Roosevelt's "habit to consult [Stimson] relatively infrequently and only on the broadest Army and Air Force Questions." McCloy, *Challenge to American Foreign Policy,* 37. Forrest Pogue, Marshall's definitive biographer, noted on the other hand that even on matters where he could go to FDR directly, Marshall sought Stimson's support in advance, recognizing the support and influence that Stimson provided. Forrest C. Pogue, "George C. Marshall on

Civil-Military Relationships in the United States," in *The United States Military under the Constitution of the United States, 1789–1989,* ed. Richard H. Kohn (New York: New York University Press, 1991), 201.

21. Diaries of Henry L. Stimson, December 18, 1942, vol. 41, reel 8, p. 101, Yale University Library.

22. For Stimson's influence on the postwar American foreign policy establishment, see Walter Isaacson and Evan Thomas, *The Wise Men: Six Friends and the World They Made* (New York: Simon & Schuster, 1986), 180–85. For a brief description of Stimson's senior War Department officials, see Geoffrey Perret, *There's a War to Be Won: The United States Army in World War II* (New York: Ballantine, 1991), 25–26. For a recent biography of Stimson, see David F. Schmitz, *Henry L. Stimson: The First Wise Man* (Wilmington, DE: Scholarly Resources, 2001).

23. Schmitz, *Henry L. Stimson,* 61–67.

24. Henry L. Stimson, "American Foreign Policy and the Spanish Situation," *New York University Contemporary Law Pamphlets,* series 1, no. 14 (1939): 5.

25. Henry L. Stimson and McGeorge Bundy, *On Active Service in Peace and War* (New York: Harper & Brothers, 1947), 48, 556.

26. Ibid., 48, 553, 556.

27. Ibid., 556.

28. For a brief discussion on the end of the New Deal, see Paul A. Koistinen, *Arsenal of World War II: The Political Economy of American Warfare, 1940–1945* (Lawrence: University Press of Kansas, 2004), 513–14.

29. Kennedy, *Freedom from Fear,* 457.

30. Office of Executive Director, Memorandum No. 10, Address by Vice President Henry Wallace, May 28, 1942, "The Price of Free World Victory," in box 11, Papers of Eleanor Lansing Dulles, Dwight D. Eisenhower Presidential Library, Abilene, KS.

31. Diaries of Henry L. Stimson, August 13, 1941, vol. 35, reel 7, p. 26, Yale University Library.

32. Harold L. Ickes to Henry L. Stimson, April 19, 1943, Secretary of Interior File, Harold L. Ickes Papers, LOC. Stimson subsequently replied in a slightly annoyed fashion, saying the charges had been thoroughly investigated and had no basis in fact. Henry L. Stimson to Harold L. Ickes, April 26, 1943, Secretary of Interior File, Harold L. Ickes Papers, LOC.

33. Ickes, *Autobiography of a Curmudgeon,* 331–32, 335–36.

34. Diaries of Harold L. Ickes, July 19, 1942, Harold L. Ickes Papers, reel 5, LOC.

35. Harold L. Ickes to Franklin D. Roosevelt, December 28, 1942, SMG File, OF 5136, FDR Library.

36. Diaries of Harold L. Ickes, July 19, 1942, reel 5, LOC.

37. Carl Grafton, "The Reorganization of Federal Agencies," *Administration and Society* 10, no. 4 (February 4, 1979): 441–43, 448.

38. James A. Stever, *The End of Public Administration: Problems of the Profession in the Post-Progressive Era* (Dobbs Ferry, NY: Transnational, 1988), 108.

39. For the view that FDR deliberately created such interagency competition, see, e.g., Donald G. Stevens, "Organizing for Economic Defense: Henry Wallace and the Board of Economic Warfare's Policy Initiatives, 1942," *Presidential Studies Quarterly* 26 (Fall 1996): 1127–28. For the view that it was poor management, see Acheson, *Present at the Creation*, 47.

40. Stever, *End of Public Administration*, 117.

41. Quentin M. Sanger, *Administrative History of the Foreign Economic Administration and Predecessor Agencies* (Washington, DC: Office of the Historian, Foreign Economic Administration, June 15, 1946), 10, 16. On file at AHEC.

42. FDR's preference for conducting foreign policy himself apparently began in his first term of office. See Freidel, *Franklin D. Roosevelt*, 106–9.

43. Hull, *Memoirs*, vol. 2, 1109–10.

44. Executive Order no. 8839, July 30, 1941, para. 3, Board of Economic Warfare File, 1941, OF 4226, FDR Library. For a list of board authorities, see also *Department of State Bulletin*, vol. 6 (Washington, DC: GPO, April 13, 1942), 337.

45. Culver and Hyde, *American Dreamer*, 271, 291.

46. Henry Wallace, March 4, 1942, diary entry in *The Price of Vision: The Diary of Henry Wallace, 1942–1946*, ed. John Morton Blum (Boston: Houghton Mifflin, 1973), 56.

47. As Wallace told Roosevelt, "the State Department should be informed at all times of action taken by the Board, but should not be in position of giving its specific approval before action can be taken." Henry Wallace, March 25, 1942, diary entry in ibid., 59.

48. Stevens, "Organizing for Economic Defense," 1129.

49. Sanger, *Administrative History*, 42.

50. Stimson noted in a diary entry the "good deal of friction" between Wallace and Jones at a board meeting. Diaries of Henry L. Stimson, April 23, 1942, vol. 18, reel 7, p. 139, Yale University Library. For an account of the Wallace-Jones feud as it related to the board, see Burns, *Roosevelt*, 341–42, and Fleming, *New Dealers' War*, 214–30.

51. Sanger, *Administrative History*, 126.

52. Acheson, *Present at the Creation*, 41; Stevens, "Organizing for Economic Defense," 1131.

53. Fleming, *New Dealers' War*, 229–30.

54. See Stuart L. Weiss, *The President's Man: Leo Crowley and Franklin Roo-*

sevelt in Peace and War (Carbondale: Southern Illinois University Press, 1996), 157, 216.

55. See Sanger, *Administrative History,* 166–203.

56. Ibid., 156.

57. Ibid., 189.

58. Eliot Janeway, "Trials and Errors: The Civilians Will Have Only Themselves to Blame if the Military Takes Over," *Fortune,* September 8, 1942, 14–18.

59. Ibid., 18.

60. Accounts of the controversy are found in two secondary sources. A narrative is found in Dan Allen, "Franklin D. Roosevelt and the Development of American Occupation Policy in Europe" (PhD diss., Ohio State University, 1976), 23–51. In *Civil Affairs: Soldiers Become Governors,* Harry L. Coles and Albert K. Weinberg provide a number of primary source documents as a guide to the controversy. Harry L. Coles and Albert K. Weinberg, *Civil Affairs: Soldiers Become Governors* (Washington, DC: CMH, 1964), 10–29. While these accounts and references are very valuable, I have interpreted the events relying on primary sources from the National Archives, the diaries of Harold Ickes and Henry Stimson, and documents found at the FDR Library (many though not all of which are in both of the above sources).

61. Presidential Memorandum to Robert P. Patterson, July 17, 1942, SMG File, OF 5136, CFWAR, FDR Library.

62. Robert P. Patterson to Franklin D. Roosevelt, July 20, 1942, SMG File, OF 5136, FDR Library.

63. For more on the meeting with Patterson, see Franklin D. Roosevelt to Marvin MacIntyre, August 8, 1942, SMG File, OF 5136, FDR Library. For FDR's direction to General Marshall, see Franklin D. Roosevelt to Army Chief of Staff, August 13, 1942, SMG File, OF 5136, FDR Library.

64. Gen. George C. Marshall to Franklin D. Roosevelt, Subject: School of Military Government, Charlottesville, VA, August 19, 1942, SMG File, OF 5136, FDR Library.

65. Ibid.

66. John J. McCloy to Harry Hopkins, September 10, 1942, SMG File, OF 5136, FDR Library.

67. Ibid.

68. Ibid.

69. Harry Hopkins to John J. McCloy, September 11, 1942, SMG File, OF 5136, FDR Library.

70. See, for example, Maj. Gen. Allen Gullion to Norman H. Davis, Chairman, American Red Cross, September 18, 1942, in box 711, OPMG, MGD, UDF 1942–1946, RG 389, NARA.

71. Harold L. Ickes to Henry L. Stimson, September 30, 1942, in box 711, OPMG, MGD, UDF 1942–1946, RG 389, NARA.

72. Harold L. Ickes to Franklin D. Roosevelt, October 27, 1942, SMG File, OF 5136, CFWAR, FDR Library.

73. Diaries of Harold L. Ickes, October 10, 1942, reel 5, LOC.

74. Franklin D. Roosevelt to Henry L. Stimson, October 29, 1942, SMG File, OF 5136, FDR Library.

75. Diaries of Harold L. Ickes, October 25, 1942, reel 5, LOC.

76. Francis Biddle, Cabinet Meeting Notes, October 29, 1942, container 1, Papers of Francis Biddle, FDR Library.

77. Knox's apparent willingness to let civilians have a major, even primary, role in postwar governance was spoken about between Gullion and Assistant Secretary of War Patterson. See Maj. Gen. Allen Gullion and Robert P. Patterson, transcribed telephonic conversation, 11:15 A.M., September 4, 1942, in Military Government Division, "History of Military Government Training," in box No. 1, entry no. 443, OPMG, MGD, UDF 1942–1946, RG 389, NARA.

78. Diaries of Henry L. Stimson, November 4, 1942, vol. 36, reel 8, p. 7, Yale University Library.

79. Diaries of Harold L. Ickes, October 25, 1942, reel 5, LOC; Francis Biddle, Cabinet Meeting Notes, October 29, 1942, container 1, Papers of Francis Biddle, FDR Library.

80. The copy of Daniels's report in the FDR Library is undated but is attached to memoranda from Daniels to FDR's secretary, Marvin McIntyre, dated December 2, 1942, and correspondence from Francis Biddle to FDR's personal secretary, Grace Tully, dated November 27, 1942. It is reasonable to surmise, therefore, that Daniels's report reached the president sometime in either late November or in December 1942. Jonathan Daniels to Franklin D. Roosevelt (undated), SMG File, OF 5136, FDR Library. For Padover's memorandum, see S. K. Padover to Harold J. Ickes, January 8, 1943, SMG File, OF 5136, FDR Library.

81. Jonathan Daniels to Franklin D. Roosevelt (undated).

82. Ibid.

83. "Plan for Coordinating the Economic Activities of U.S. Civilian Agencies in Liberated Areas," box 18, Records of the US Joint Chiefs of Staff, Central Decimal File, 1942–1945, RG 218, NARA.

84. S. K. Padover to Harold J. Ickes, January 8, 1943.

85. Ibid.

86. See, for example, the proposal by Michele Flournoy, "Training and Education for Post-Conflict Reconstruction," in *Winning the Peace: An American Strategy for Post-Conflict Reconstruction,* ed. Robert C. Orr (Washington, DC: Center for Strategic and International Studies, 2004), 126–37.

87. George F. Kennan, *Memoirs, 1925–1950* (New York: Pantheon Books, 1967), 23.

88. Henry L. Stimson to President Roosevelt (undated) in "History of Military Government Training," entry no. 443, box no. 1, OPMG, MGD, UDF 1942–1946, RG 389, NARA.

89. Ibid.

90. Stimson's account of the follow-up meeting is in Diaries of Henry L. Stimson, November 6, 1942, vol. 36, reel 8, p. 19, Yale University Library. The letter of February 1, 1943, references the problems encountered in North Africa, where the State Department had taken the lead in much civil affairs work (to be discussed in chapter 5). In that letter, Stimson pointed out the distinction between administrative duties, which are for the military to perform, and diplomatic responsibilities. He also provided FDR with four brief case studies on American military government in both US interventions in Cuba and those in the Philippines and Puerto Rico. Henry L. Stimson to Franklin D. Roosevelt, Memorandum on Military Government, February 1, 1943, in Diaries of Henry L. Stimson, vol. 42, reel 8.

91. Diaries of Henry L. Stimson, November 6, 1942, vol. 41, reel 8, p. 19, Yale University Library.

92. Diaries of Harold L. Ickes, November 8, 1942, reel 5, LOC.

93. Franklin D. Roosevelt to Gen. Edwin M. Watson, February 16, 1943, SMG File, OF 5136, FDR Library.

94. For the memorandum requiring the school to cease public relations, see Col. R. McDonald Gray to Col. Ralph Witamuth, May 29, 1943, in box 711, OPMG, MGD, UDF 1942–1946, RG 389, NARA. For an example of how the school was seen, ironically enough, as a tool of Wallace-driven global New Deal ambitions ("globaloney"), see Editorial, "Fantastic and Nuts," *New York Daily News,* April 9, 1943.

95. Stimson and Bundy, *On Active Service,* 48, 559.

96. Roosevelt to Stimson, November 10, 1943, in Coles and Weinberg, *Civil Affairs,* 108–9; European Relief Report on Supply and Administration in Event of Unconditional Surrender, to Commanding General, Army Service Forces, November 13, 1943, in Coles and Weinberg, 109.

97. Stimson and Bundy, *On Active Service,* 561.

98. See, e.g., Francis Biddle, *In Brief Authority* (Garden City, NY: Doubleday, 1962), 223.

99. For a discussion of military necessity as a principle invoked against enemy, and not friendly, forces and populations, see Nobuo Hayashi, "Contextualizing Military Necessity," *Emory International Law Review* 27 (2013): 247–50.

100. Franklin D. Roosevelt to Joseph P. Poindexter, December 9, 1941, telegram, in J. Garner Anthony, *Hawaii under Army Rule* (Stanford, CA: Stanford University Press, 1955). A chronology of events is provided at pages ix–x.

101. For an account of martial law in Hawaii, see generally, *Hawaii under Army Rule.*

102. Diaries of Harold L. Ickes, July 19, 1942, reel 5, LOC. Ickes later complained directly to Stimson about the Hawaii martial law situation. Harold L. Ickes to Henry L. Stimson, January 27, 1943, in box 57, General Correspondence of Assistant Secretary of War John J. McCloy, 1941–1945, RG 107, NARA.

103. Anthony, *Hawaii under Army Rule,* 101–18.

104. The Western Defense Zone included the states of Washington, Oregon, California, Montana, Idaho, Nevada, Utah, and Arizona and the then territory of Alaska. For an overview, see United States Army, Western Defense Command, "History of the Western Defense Command," September and October 1945, under the direction of Maj. Gen. H. G. Pratt, US Army, CG, Western Defense Command, AHEC.

105. "History of the Western Defense Command," 16–18. The proclamations, exclusion orders, and other relevant documents are contained in Office of Assistant Chief of Staff, Civil Affairs Division, *Proclamations, Exclusion, Restrictive Orders and Collateral Documents* (San Francisco: Wartime Civil Control Administration, 1942), AHEC.

106. Col. Joel F. Watson, Staff Judge Advocate to Commanding General, Western Defense Command and Fourth Army, Subject: Powers of the Commanding General of the Theater of Operations" (December 15, 1941), in annex 3 to chapter 19, "History of the Western Defense Command."

107. See Greg Robinson, *By Order of the President: FDR and the Internment of Japanese-Americans* (Cambridge, MA: Harvard University Press, 2001), 109–16. See also Biddle, *In Brief Authority,* 207–26.

108. *Final Report: Japanese Evacuation from the West Coast, 1942* (Washington, DC: GPO, 1943), 3.

109. Ibid., 4.

110. Lt. Gen. John DeWitt to Secretary of War Henry Stimson, Subject: Evacuation of Japanese and Other Subversive Persons from the Pacific Coast (February 14, 1942), in *Final Report,* 36.

111. Ibid., 37–67.

112. Kai Bird, *The Chairman: John J. McCloy and the Making of the American Establishment* (New York: Simon & Schuster, 1992), 150.

113. Ibid., 149–51.

114. Biddle, *In Brief Authority,* 216–19.

115. President, Executive Order 9066, "Authorizing the Secretary of War to Prescribe Military Areas" (February 19, 1942), in *Final Report,* 26–27.

116. See, e.g., Kennedy, *Freedom from Fear,* 757–58.

117. See *Final Report,* 8–18.

118. *Hirabayashi v. United States,* 320 U.S. 95 (1943).

119. *Korematsu v. United States,* 323 U.S. 218 (1944).

120. Ibid., 323 U.S. 223.

121. *Hirabayashi*, 320 U.S. 100.

122. Ibid., 320 U.S. 93.

123. For a discussion of professional expertise as the method to deal with problems in modern industrial societies, see Andrew Abbott, *The System of Professions: An Essay on the Division of Expert Labor* (Chicago: University of Chicago Press, 1988), 323–25.

4. North Africa and the Establishment of the Civil Affairs Division, 1943

1. Edwin J. Hayward, "Co-ordination of Military and Civilian Civil Affairs Planning," *Annals of the American Academy of Political and Social Science* 267 (January 1950): 19.

2. George F. Howe, *Northwest Africa: Seizing the Initiative in the West* (Washington, DC: CMH, 1985), 57.

3. Robert Murphy, *Diplomat among Warriors* (Garden City, NY: Doubleday, 1964), 145. Tellingly, Murphy titled the North Africa chapter of his memoirs "Everybody Gets into Eisenhower's Act." Ibid., 144.

4. Forrest Pogue, *George C. Marshall: Organizer of Victory, 1943–45* (New York: Viking, 1973), 457 (citing author interview with John H. Hilldring, March 30, 1959).

5. Ray S. Cline, *Washington Command Post: The Operations Division* (Washington, DC: CMH, 1951), 321.

6. Dwight D. Eisenhower to George C. Marshall, November 30, 1942, in *The Papers of Dwight D. Eisenhower, The War Years,* vol. 2, ed. Alfred D. Chandler Jr. (Baltimore: Johns Hopkins University Press, 1970), 781.

7. Eisenhower to Marshall, November 26, 1942, ibid., 772.

8. Diaries of Henry L. Stimson, March 28, 1943, vol. 42, reel 8, Yale University Library, New Haven, CT.

9. Ibid., February 11, 1943.

10. For a description of the various agencies, see "History of the Civil Affairs Division," War Department, Special Staff, World War II to March 1946" (Washington, DC: Office of the Chief of Military History, unpublished and incomplete), book 2, section 1, Civil Affairs Machinery, chapter 3, "Liaison Activities outside the United States Armed Forces," 1–9, call no. 2–3.7 AA.Q, part 2, copy 2, on file in the Historical Manuscript Collection at CMH. There are multiple versions of this incomplete and unpublished history (apparently planned to be official) in CMH's Historical Manuscript Collection, with different chapter titles and various forms of organization. To reduce confusion, I have provided the call number for the specific document that I cite. Many of the documents referred to

in this history were subsequently collected and published in Harry L. Coles and Albert K. Weinberg, *Civil Affairs: Soldiers Become Governors* (Washington, DC: CMH, 1964).

11. "History of the Civil Affairs Division," book 2, section 1, Civil Affairs Machinery, chapter 3, Liaison Activities outside the United States Armed Forces, 4–5.

12. Ibid., 6.

13. Ibid.

14. Ibid., 6–7.

15. George C. Marshall, "CCS-190: Planning for the Handling of Civil Affairs in Enemy Occupied Areas Which May Become Theaters of Operations," box 18, Records of the US Joint Chiefs of Staff, Central Decimal File, 1942–1945, RG 218, NARA.

16. Hayward, "Co-ordination of Military," 20.

17. "History of the Civil Affairs Division," book 2, Civilian Departments and Agencies, CAS- 4, quoting Roosevelt to Governor Lehman, March 19, 1943, call no. 2–3.7 AA.Q, part 2, copy 2, on file at CMH.

18. Ibid., CAS 5–6, call no. 2–3.7 AA.Q, part 2, copy 2, on file at CMH.

19. Ibid., CAS 7, quoting Henry L. Stimson to Herbert Lehman, June 2, 1943.

20. For an official history of the Office of Foreign Relief and Rehabilitation Operations, including its lack of a clear and authoritative mandate, see Quentin M. Sanger, *Administrative History of the Foreign Economic Administration and Predecessor Agencies* (Washington, DC: Office of the Historian, Foreign Economic Administration, June 15, 1946), 10 (on file at AHEC), 166–203.

21. Milo Perkins, "Plan for Coordinating the Economic Activities of U.S. Civilian Agencies in Liberated Areas" (attached to letter from Franklin D. Roosevelt to Cordell Hull, June 3, 1943), in box 18, Records of the US Joint Chiefs of Staff, Central Decimal File, 1942–1945, RG 218, NARA.

22. Roosevelt to Hull, June 3, 1943, in box 18, Records of the US Joint Chiefs of Staff, Central Decimal File, 1942–1945, RG 218, NARA.

23. "History of the Civil Affairs Division," book 2, section 1, Civil Affairs Machinery, 28, call no. 2–3.7 AA.Q, part 2, copy 2, on file at CMH.

24. Kenneth S. Davis, *FDR: The War President, 1940–1943* (New York: Random House, 2000), 720.

25. Hayward, "Co-ordination of Military," 23.

26. "History of the Civil Affairs Division," book 2, section 1, Civil Affairs Machinery, chapter 3, Liaison Activities outside the United States Armed Forces, 30, call no. 2–3.7 AA.Q, part 2, copy 2, on file at CMH.

27. "History of the Civil Affairs Division," book 2, chapter 1, Civil Affairs

Responsibility of the War Department, 8–9, call no. 2–3.7 AA.Q, part 1, copy 1, on file at CMH.

28. US War Department, *Military Government, FM 27-5, July 30, 1940* (Washington, DC: GPO, 1940), para. 6. See also "History of the Civil Affairs Division," book 2, chapter 1, Civil Affairs Responsibility of the War Department, 7, call no. 2–3.7 AA.Q, part 1, copy 1, on file at CMH.

29. Hayward, "Co-ordination of Military," 21.

30. "History of the Civil Affairs Division," book 2, chapter 1, Civil Affairs Responsibility of the War Department, 6, call no. 2–3.7 AA.Q, part 1, copy 1, on file at CMH.

31. See Otto L. Nelson Jr., *National Security and the General Staff* (Washington, DC: Infantry Journal Press, 1946) 335, 348–50. Nelson reprints Executive Order 9082 on pages 348–50. The order became effective on March 9, 1942, stating that it would remain in effect "during the continuance of the present war and for six months after the termination thereof." Ibid., 350.

32. Cline, *Washington Command Post*, 317.

33. JCS 202/3 and 202/7, "War Planning Agencies," March 25 and April 24, 1943, in Records of the US Joint Chiefs of Staff, CCS 300 (1-8-43), sec. 3. RG 218, NARA, quoted in Mark Stoler, *Allies and Adversaries: The Joint Chiefs of Staff, the Grand Alliance, and U.S. Strategy in World War II* (Chapel Hill and London: University of North Carolina Press, 2000), 107. Stoler discusses this in more depth as well. Ibid. 104–5.

34. The other newly created special divisions were the War Department Manpower Board, the Special Planning Division, the New Developments Division, Budget Division, and the Strength Accounting and Reporting Office. Nelson, *National Security*, 545–46.

35. Ibid.

36. Maj. Gen. Lucius Clay to Lt. Gen. Thomas Handy, February 11, 1943, in Diaries of Henry L. Stimson, vol. 42, reel 8, Yale University Library.

37. Ibid.

38. "History of the Civil Affairs Division," book 2, chapter 1, 9, call no. 2–3.7 AA.Q, part 1, copy 1, on file at CMH.

39. The official order came from the adjutant general of the army to the division's first director, Col. John H. F. Haskell: "By direction of the Secretary of War, a Civil Affairs Division of the War Department is established." Adjutant General to Colonel Haskell, March 1, 1943, in Coles and Weinberg, *Civil Affairs*, 68.

40. Seventy-fifth Joint Chiefs of Staff Meeting Minutes, April 20, 1943, box 18, Records of the US Joint Chiefs of Staff, Central Decimal File, 1942–1945, RG 218, NARA. See also see Cline, *Washington Command Post*, 317.

41. Diaries of Henry L. Stimson, February 11, 1943, vol. 42, reel 8, Yale University Library.

42. Ibid., March 28, 1943.

43. Ibid., February 11, 1943.

44. Ibid.

45. McCloy to Hopkins, September 10, 1942, and Hopkins to McCloy, September 11, 1942. SMG Files, Official Files (OF) 5136, FDR Library.

46. See generally Kai Bird, *The Chairman: John J. McCloy and the Making of the American Establishment* (New York: Simon & Schuster, 1992), 148–62.

47. For a chronology showing the gradual return to civil authority, see J. Garner Anthony, *Hawaii under Army Rule* (Stanford, CA: Stanford University Press, 1955), ix–x.

48. Diaries of Harold L. Ickes, July 7, 1942, Harold L. Ickes Papers, reel 5, LOC.

49. John J. McCloy, January 16 and January 30, 1943, diary entries in box DY 5, folder 45, John J. McCloy Papers, Amherst Archives.

50. Ibid.; McCloy, February 3, 1943, diary entry, in box DY 5, folder 45, Amherst Archives.

51. George C. Marshall to Lt. Gen. John E. Hull, February 26, 1943, in *The Papers of George Catlett Marshall,* vol. 3, December 7, 1941–May 31, 1943, ed. Larry I. Bland (Baltimore: Johns Hopkins University Press), 565.

52. Forrest Pogue, *George C. Marshall: Organizer of Victory, 1943–45* (New York: Viking, 1973), 457.

53. He served as chief of CAD from April 1943 to March 1946, and afterward became assistant secretary of state for occupied areas. John H. Hilldring biographical sheet, obtained from Official Files (OF), FDR Library.

54. "History of the Civil Affairs Division," book 2, Organizations, Functions, and Policy of the Civil Affairs Division, Civil Affairs Division Organization, 4, call no. 2–3.7 AA.Q, part 2, copy 2, on file at CMH.

55. Adjutant General to Col. John H. F. Haskell, March 1, 1943, in Coles and Weinberg, *Civil Affairs,* 68–69. Haskell served as acting chief of the Civil Affairs Division until April 1943, when he was replaced by Hilldring.

56. "History of the Civil Affairs Division," book 2, Organizations, Functions, and Policy of the Civil Affairs Division, Civil Affairs Division Organization, 6–9, call no. 2–3.7 AA.Q, part 2, copy 2, on file at CMH.

57. Nelson, *National Security,* 547–48.

58. "History of the Civil Affairs Division," book 2, Organizations, Functions, and Policy of the Civil Affairs Division, Civil Affairs Liaison Functions, 2–5, call no. 2–3.7 AA.Q, part 2, copy 2, on file at CMH.

59. Frank McSherry to General Holmes, July 2, 1944, in box 32, Papers of Frank McSherry, AHEC; John Hilldring to Frank McSherry, January 8, 1945, in box 33, Papers of Frank McSherry, AHEC.

60. John H. Hilldring to Lester D. Flory, February 16, 1945, in box 1, Papers of Lester D. Flory, AHEC.

61. Ibid.

62. Lester D. Flory to John H. Hilldring, May 3, 1945, in box 1, Papers of Lester D. Flory, AHEC.

63. Joint Chiefs of Staff (JCS) Paper 250/2, April 10, 1943, and JCS Paper 250/4, April 19, 1943, in box 18, Records of the US Joint Chiefs of Staff, Central Decimal File, 1942–1945, RG 218, NARA.

64. JCS 250/2. The two military departments agreed that the navy would assume responsibility for civil affairs and occupation duties in the Mariana, Caroline, Bonin, and Kurile Islands and Formosa in the Pacific Theater. JCS 250/5 Paper, August 25, 1943, in box 18, Records of the US Joint Chiefs of Staff, Central Decimal File, 1942–1945, RG 218, NARA. The navy later in the war would argue for the establishment of the Joint Civil Affairs Committee. After dispute between the services, the committee was established in April 1945. However, the Civil Affairs Division continued as before, and the committee was very inactive, with only six formal meetings held and no major decisions made by it. "History of the Civil Affairs Division," book 2, Organizations, Functions, and Policy of the Civil Affairs Division, Civil Affairs Liaison Functions, Joint Chiefs of Staff Agencies, 3–8, call no. 2–3.7 AA.Q, part 2, copy 2, on file at CMH.

65. "History of the Civil Affairs Division," book 2, Organizations, Functions, and Policy of the Civil Affairs Division, Civil Affairs Division Organization, 2, call no. 2–3.7 AA.Q, part 2, copy 2, on file at CMH.

66. McCloy, May 13, 1943, diary entry in box DY 5, folder 45, John J. McCloy Papers, Amherst Archives.

67. Adjutant General, "Coordinating Request for Civil Affairs Information from Civilian Agencies," June 21, 1943, in box 18, Records of the US Joint Chiefs of Staff, Central Decimal File, 1942–1945, RG 218, NARA.

68. "History of the Civil Affairs Division," book 2, Civilian Departments and Agencies, CCAS 3–6, call no. 2–3.7 AA.Q, part 2, copy 2, on file at CMH.

69. McCloy biographer Kai Bird has identified him as the State-War-Navy Coordinating Committee (SWNCC) chairman. Bird, *Chairman,* 229–30. Civil Affairs Division director Hilldring, while identifying himself as McCloy's primary military adviser on SWNCC, also identified Assistant Secretary of State James Clement Dunn as the SWNCC chairman in a January 1945 letter to SHAEF G-5 Frank McSherry. John Hilldring to Frank McSherry, January 24, 1945, in box 33, Papers of Frank McSherry, AHEC.

70. Draft, Joint Chiefs of Staff Memorandum for Information, circa 1945, "Composition of Governmental Committees (SWNCC, IPCOG, and ACC)

and Implementation of their Decisions," in War Department box 1, folder 3, Papers of John J. McCloy Files, Amherst Archives.

71. Hayward, "Co-ordination of Military," 26–27.

72. James W. Riddleburger to James F. Byrnes, June 20, 1945, with two attachments from the Department of Commerce ("Threatened Weakening of Potsdam Policy for Control of German Industry" and "Interest of Department of Commerce in Policy re: Industrialization of Germany"), in Department of State, box 1, Central European Division Files, RG 59, NARA.

73. Ibid.

74. C. Leonard Hoag, *American Military Government in Korea: War Policy and the First Year of Occupation, 1941–1946* (Washington DC: CMH, 1970), 29–30, available at AHEC.

75. F. S. V. Donnison, *Civil Affairs and Military Government Central Organization and Planning* (London: Her Majesty's Stationery Office, 1966), 67.

76. Charter of the CCAC (CCS 190/6/D), July 3, 1943 (approved by CCS June 25, 1943), in Coles and Weinberg, *Civil Affairs,* 124.

77. Donnison, *Civil Affairs,* 70–71.

78. Ibid., 67.

79. McCloy, November 2 and 9, 1943, diary entries in box DY 5, folder 45, John J. McCloy Papers, Amherst Archives.

80. Seventy-fifth Joint Chiefs of Staff Meeting Minutes, April 20, 1943. See also Donnison, *Civil Affairs,* 22–24.

81. Donnison, *Civil Affairs,* 22–24.

82. Diaries of Henry L. Stimson, June 1, 1943, vol. 42, reel 8, Yale Univesity Library.

83. Ibid., June 22, 1943.

84. "History of the Civil Affairs Division," part 3, chapter 1: Pre-invasion Relations with France and the French Civil Affairs Agreements, 1, call no. 2–3.7 AA.Q, part 3, copy 1, on file at CMH. This same volume has information regarding agreements for Belgium, the Netherlands, Luxembourg, Denmark, and Norway.

85. Ibid., 6–37.

86. Ibid., 28.

87. John G. Winant, "Summary Report of the Work of the European Advisory Commission," July 12, 1945, in Central European Division Files, box 1, RG 59, NARA; Lucius D. Clay, interview by Richard D. McKinzie, July 16, 1974, 7–8, Truman Library.

88. George Kennan, who served as Winant's political advisor for the European Advisory Commission, offers an account of the War Department's efforts to curtail the commission's influence. See George F. Kennan, *Memoirs, 1925–1950* (New York: Pantheon Books, 1967), 164–87.

89. Joint Chiefs of Staff to Secretary of State, January 4, 1944, OPD Files,

334.8, section 1, reprinted in part in Coles and Weinberg, *Civil Affairs,* 136. See also Bruce Kuklick, "The Genesis of the European Advisory Commission," *Journal of Contemporary History* 4 (October 1969): 197, 199.

90. Philip Mosely, "The Occupation of Germany: New Light on How the Zones Were Drawn," *Foreign Affairs* 28 (July 1950): 585–86.

91. "History of the Civil Affairs Division," book 2, section 1, chapter 5, Coordination with Allied Governments, 20–24, call no. 2–3.7 AA.Q, part 2, copy 1, on file at CMH.

92. Ibid., 24.

93. Kuklick, "Genesis of European Advisory Commission," 194.

94. John G. Winant to John J. McCloy, February 24, 1945, in box 1, State Department Central European Division Files, RG 59, NARA.

95. Brig. Gen. Cornelius Wickersham to Brig. Gen. Frank McSherry, "U.S. Policy Directives and Instructions," February 24, 1945, in box 29, Papers of Frank McSherry, AHEC.

96. Hayward, "Co-ordination of Military," 25.

97. Kennan, *Memoirs,* 172.

98. Mosely, "Occupation of Germany," 585–86.

99. See William M. Franklin, "Zonal Boundaries and Access to Berlin," *World Politics* 16 (October 1963): 15. For a specific history of the military occupation planning for Germany, see Office of the Chief Historian, European Command, *Planning for the Occupation of Germany, Special Text 41–10–62* (Frankfurt am Main, Germany: 1947).

100. See Mosely, "Occupation of Germany," 590–93; Franklin, "Zonal Boundaries," 11–12; and Diaries of Henry L. Stimson, July 31, 1944, vol. 42, reel 9, Yale University Library.

101. Henry L. Stimson and McGeorge Bundy, *On Active Service in Peace and War* (New York: Harper & Brothers, 1947), 560. For the letter of November 10, 1943, see Roosevelt to Stimson, in Coles and Weinberg, *Civil Affairs,* 108–9.

102. Diaries of Henry L. Stimson, November 12, 1943, vol. 15, reel 8, Yale University Library.

5. Planning and Implementing Military Government in Germany, 1943–1946

1. See Melvyn P. Leffler, *For the Soul of Mankind: The United States, the Soviet Union, and the Cold War* (New York: Hill & Wang, 2007), 64.

2. *FRUS: The Conferences at Malta and Yalta, 1945* (Washington, DC: GPO, 1955), 978. See also Herbert Feis, *Between War and Peace: The Potsdam Conference* (Westport, CT: Greenwood, 1960), 241.

3. The President to the Acting Secretary of State, February 21, 1944, in box 55, General Correspondence of the Assistant Secretary of War, John J. McCloy, 1941–1945, RG 107, NARA. See also James McAllister, *No Exit: America and the German Problem, 1943–1954* (Ithaca, NY: Cornell University Press, 2002), 42–47.

4. See John Gimbel, "Governing the American Zone of Germany," in *Americans as Proconsuls: United States Military Government in Germany and Japan,* ed. Robert Wolfe (Carbondale: Southern Illinois University Press, 1984), 92.

5. Charles Riddleberger, "The British Draft Policy Directives for Germany," November 1, 1944, in box 1, Central European Division, 1944–1953, RG 59, NARA.

6. See Richard Merritt, *Democracy Imposed: U.S. Occupation Policy and the German Public, 1945–1949* (New Haven: Yale University Press, 1995), 30.

7. See, e.g., Theodore A. Wilson, "Endgames: V-E Day and War Termination," in *Victory in Europe: 1945: From World War to Cold War,* ed. Arnold A. Offner and Theodore A. Wilson (Lawrence: University Press of Kansas, 2000), 18–21.

8. Ian Kershaw, *The End: The Defiance and Destruction of Hitler's Germany, 1944–1945* (New York: Penguin, 2011), 105–6, 120, 222, 256.

9. See, e.g., Max Hastings, *Armageddon: The Battle for Germany, 1944–1945* (New York: Vintage Books, 2005), 434; Richard Bessel, *Germany, 1945: From War to Peace* (New York: Harper Perennial, 2009) 125–32.

10. See Karl Bendetsen, Civil Affairs Division, SHAEF, "Comments on Political Guides for Areas of Probable Occupation," January 28, 1944, in box 31, SHAEF Policy, 1945–1945, Papers of Frank McSherry, AHEC.

11. See McAllister, *No Exit,* 70. See also Stephen Ambrose, *Eisenhower* (New York: Simon & Schuster, 1983), 401.

12. Dwight D. Eisenhower, *Crusade in Europe* (Garden City, NY: Doubleday, 1948), 367, 396.

13. Dwight D. Eisenhower, *The Eisenhower Diaries,* ed. Robert Ferrell (New York: Norton, 1981), passim, 118.

14. Letter to Milton S. Eisenhower, June 29, 1943, in *The Papers of Dwight David Eisenhower,* vol. 2, ed. Alfred D. Chandler (Baltimore and London: Johns Hopkins University Press, 1970), 1219.

15. Stephen Ambrose, *Eisenhower and Berlin, 1945: The Decision to Halt at the Elbe* (New York: Norton, 1967), 26–27, 31.

16. See George Marshall to Dwight D. Eisenhower, WAR 74256, April 28, 1945, in *The Papers of George C. Marshall, vol. 5, January 1, 1945–January 7, 1947,* ed. Forrest Pogue (Baltimore and London: Johns Hopkins University Press, 2003), 159; Cable to George C. Marshall, April 29, 1945, in Chandler, *Papers of Dwight David Eisenhower,* vol. 4, 2662.

17. Dwight D. Eisenhower to Harry S. Truman, October 26, 1945, in box 80, Marshall Correspondence, Prepresidential Papers, Papers of Dwight D. Eisenhower, Eisenhower Library.

18. Ambrose, *Eisenhower and Berlin, 1945,* 28.

19. Civil Affairs Division, Chief of Staff, Supreme Allied Commander, to All Civil Affairs Branch Directors and All Section Chiefs, Subject: High Level Policy Decisions, January 5, 1944, in box 31, SHAEF Policy, 1943–1945, Papers of Frank McSherry, AHEC.

20. Office of the Chief Historian, European Command, *Planning for the Occupation of Germany, Special Text 41–10–62* (Frankfurt am Main, Germany: Office of the Chief Historian, European Command, 1947), 4–26.

21. Ibid., 2–5.

22. Ibid., 35, quoting Maj. Gen. C. A. West, Deputy Assistant Chief of Staff, G-3 (Operations and Plans), Chief of Staff, Supreme Allied Command.

23. Ibid., 35, 58–62.

24. Supreme Headquarters, Allied Expeditionary Forces, Operation "ECLIPSE" Appreciation and Outline Plan, November 10, 1944, on file at the Combined Arms Research Library, Fort Leavenworth, KS, 3.

25. Ibid., section 1, para. 6.

26. Ibid., 1–2, 5.

27. James W. Riddleberger, Central European Division, Department of State, "American Policy for Treatment of Germany after Surrender," September 1, 1944, in box 1, Central European Division, 1944–1953, Department of State, RG 59, NARA.

28. Frederick H. Hartmann, *Germany between East and West: The Reunification Problem* (Englewood Cliffs, NJ: Prentice-Hall, 1965), 33.

29. Combined Chiefs of Staff, "Allocation of Zones of Occupation in Germany," September 16, 1944, in Papers and Minutes of Meetings, Octagon Conference (Office, US Secretary of the Combined Chiefs of Staff), 1944, in box 313, Combined Chiefs of Staff Conference Proceedings, 1941–1945, Eisenhower Library.

30. "Combined Chiefs of Staff Directive to the Supreme Commander, SHAEF (Mock Draft), Area: (1) Liberated Territory (2) Occupied Enemy Territory," undated, SHAEF Policy, 1943–1945, in box 31, Papers of Frank McSherry, AHEC.

31. "Conclusions of a Meeting Held on January 14, 1944," SHAEF Organization, 1943–1945, in box 29, Papers of Frank McSherry, AHEC.

32. Lt. Col. E. R. Baltzell, "Draft Notes Comprising Standard Policy and Procedure for Combined Civil Affairs Operations in North West Europe (SPP) and *FM 27-5*," February 8, 1944, SHAEF Policy, 1943–1945, in box 31, Papers of Frank McSherry, AHEC.

33. Subject Comments on Policies and Procedures to the Chief of Staff, February 7, 1944, SHAEF Policy, 1943–1945, in box 31, Papers of Frank McSherry, AHEC.

34. "Allied Military Government of Occupied Territory" (undated draft), SHAEF Policy, 1943–1945, in box 31, Papers of Frank McSherry, AHEC.

35. For a summary of the handbook controversy, see Earl Ziemke, *The U.S. Army in the Occupation of Germany, 1944–46* (Washington, DC: CMH, 1975), 83–89.

36. SHAEF, *Handbook of Military Government in Germany* (draft, 1944), introduction, paragraph 3; part 1, chapter 1, paragraphs 3, 7, 29, 38, 45; part 3, chapter 1, paragraphs 248, 250, on file at AHEC.

37. Ibid, part 1, chapter 1, paragraph 5; part 2, chapter 3, paragraphs 275, 276.

38. Franklin D. Roosevelt to Henry L. Stimson, August 26, 1944, in box 55, General Correspondence of Assistant Secretary of War, John J. McCloy, 1941–1945, EAC-Germany, RG 107, NARA.

39. "Suggested Recommendation on Treatment of Germany from the Cabinet Committee for the President," September 4, 1944, in Diaries of Henry L. Stimson, vol. 48, reel 9, Yale University Library, New Haven, CT.

40. See Earl F. Ziemke, "Improvising Stability and Change in Postwar Germany," in Wolfe, *Americans as Proconsuls,* 54; "Briefing Book Prepared in the Treasury Department," September 9, 1944, in US Department of State, *FRUS: The Conference at Quebec, 1944* (Washington, DC: GPO, 1972), 130.

41. Henry Morgenthau Jr., *Germany Is Our Problem* (New York and London: Harper & Brothers, 1945), 14, 48, 50.

42. Ibid., 192–93, 196.

43. Diaries of Henry L. Stimson, September 5, 1944, vol. 48, reel 9, Yale University Library.

44. David F. Schmitz, *Henry L. Stimson: The First Wise Man* (Wilmington, DE: Scholarly Resources, 2001), 167. Schmitz's biography touches on the many facets of Stimson's geopolitical thought.

45. JCS 1067 Series, in box 151, Prepresidential Papers, Papers of Dwight D. Eisenhower, Eisenhower Library.

46. Earl Ziemke, "The Formulation and Initial Implementation of U.S. Occupation Policy in Germany" in *U.S. Occupation in Europe after World War II,* ed. Hans A. Schmitt (Lawrence: Regents Press of Kansas, 1978), 29.

47. Ibid., 28–29.

48. Merritt, *Democracy Imposed,* 60.

49. John J. McCloy, interview by Jean Edward Smith, February 19, 1971, Columbia University Oral History Project, 9, Eisenhower Library.

50. See Bessel, *Germany 1945: From War to Peace* , 283–84; John Gimbel, *The American Occupation of Germany: Politics and the Military, 1945–1949* (Stanford, CA: Stanford University Press, 1968) 2, 5, 7–8.

51. See, e.g., "Interim Directive to SCAEF Regarding the Military Government of Germany in the Period Immediately Following the Cessation of Organized Resistance (Post-Defeat) [JCS 1067]," September 17, 1944, SHAEF Policy 1943–1945, in box 32, Papers of Frank McSherry, AHEC.

52. John J. McCloy, interview by Jean Edward Smith, February 19, 1971, Columbia University Oral History Project, 9.

53. Appendix D, Relief Directive to "Directive to SCAEF Regarding the Military Government in the Period Immediately Following the Cessation of Organized Resistance (Post-Defeat) [JCS 1067]," September 22, 1944 in *FRUS, 1945,* 143.

54. See John H. Backer, "From Morgenthau Plan to Marshall Plan," in Wolfe, *Americans as Proconsuls,* 156–57.

55. Ibid., 158.

56. Gimbel, *American Occupation of Germany,* 5.

57. Lucius D. Clay to John J. McCloy, June 16, 1945, in Lucius Clay, *The Papers of Lucius D. Clay,* vol. 1, ed. Jean Edward Smith (Bloomington: Indiana University Press, 1974), 23–24.

58. Lucius D. Clay to John H. Hilldring, December 2, 1945, ibid., 133; Lucius D. Clay to War Department, September 16, 1946, ibid., 263–64.

59. "Directive to SCAEF Regarding the Military Government in the Period Immediately Following the Cessation of Organized Resistance (Post-Defeat) [JCS 1067]," September 22, 1944 in *FRUS, 1945,* 144.

60. The document published and used immediately after the surrender was "Directive to the Commander in Chief of the United States Forces of Occupation Regarding the Military Government of Germany, May 10, 1945," in US Department of State, *Documents on Germany, 1944–1985* (Washington, DC: GPO, 1985), 17–18.

61. "The Principles to Govern the Treatment of Germany in the Initial Control Period," from "Protocol of the Proceedings of the Berlin (Potsdam) Conference," August 1, 1945, in US Department of State, *Documents on Germany, 1944–1985,* 56.

62. Clay, as deputy military governor, fell under the command of the military governor (initially Eisenhower), who was also "dual-hatted" as the European theater commander. He, in turn, reported to the Joint Chiefs of Staff in Washington. Clay took over as military governor and theater commander in 1947. See Ziemke, *U.S. Army in the Occupation,* 309, 426.

63. "Suggested Recommendations on Treatment of Germany from the Cabi-

net Committee for the President," September 4, 1944, in Diaries of Henry L. Stimson, vol. 48, reel 9, Yale University Library.

64. Oral history interview with Lucius Clay by Richard D. McKinzie, July 16, 1974, 15, Truman Library.

65. Oral history interview with John J. McCloy, no. 1 of 2 by John Luter, December 18, 1970, Columbia University Oral History Project, 14–15, Eisenhower Library.

66. Ibid., 15.

67. Ibid.

68. So recounted by McCloy in ibid.

69. Interview with Lucius D. Clay, 5.

70. Lucius D. Clay to John J. McCloy, June 29, 1945, Clay, *Papers,* vol. 1, 36.

71. Lucius D. Clay to John H. Hilldring, November 17, 1945, Clay, *Papers,* vol. 1, 119.

72. Hans Speier, *From the Ashes of Disgrace: A Journal from Germany* (Amherst: University of Massachusetts Press, 1981), 62.

73. Proclamation No. 1, Military Government: Germany, Supreme Commander's Area of Control, from OMGUS, *Military Government Gazette,* no. 5, June 1, 1946, AHEC.

74. Allied Military Government in Germany, *Army Service Forces Manual, Military Government Handbook, Germany, Section 2M: Proclamations, Ordinances, and Laws,* January 6, 1945, on file at AHEC.

75. "We Come as Conquerors," *Army Talks* 2, no. 7 (February 17, 1945), 1–4, Combined Arms Research Library, Fort Leavenworth, KS.

76. "Report of Military Government Detachment F-213 in Munich, Bavaria, May 1945–January 1946," in US Department of the Army, Civil Affairs Division, *Field Operation of Military Government Units* (Washington, DC: Civil Affairs Division, January 1949), 75–77.

77. Julian Bach, *America's Germany: An Account of the Occupation* (New York: Random House, 1946), 17.

78. Bessel, *Germany 1945,* 171–72.

79. Questionnaire: Sgt. Kalil Ayoob, Sixty-Fourth Mil. Gov. Company and Questionnaire: Charles Daniel Burge, Nutritional Survey Team, Bavaria, in box 1, World War II Veterans Collection, Civil Affairs, AHEC.

80. Maj. Richard J. Eaton, US Military Government Detachment, Leipzig, April 27, 1945, in box 1, World War II Veterans Collection, Civil Affairs, AHEC.

81. H. Price-Williams, SHAEF G-5 Division, to Mr. J. Beam, US Political Officer, SHAEF, et al., June 4, 1945, in box 1, General Records of Central Europe Division, 1944–1953, RG 59, NARA.

82. Bruce Harwood, *Bremerhaven: A Memoir of Germany, 1945–1947* (self-published, 2010), 17, 69.

83. Saul K. Padover, *Experiment in Germany: The Story of an American Intelligence Officer* (New York: Duell, Sloan & Pearce, 1946), 164, 166.

84. See Bessel, *Germany 1945*, 171, 175.

85. Lucius D. Clay to John H. Hilldring, July 5, 1945 in Clay, *Papers*, vol. 1, 47.

86. OMGUS, *Monthly Report of Military Governor, U.S. Zone, No. 7, Intelligence and Confidential Annexes*, February 20, 1946, AHEC.

87. OMGUS, *Monthly Report of Military Governor, U.S. Zone, No. 8, Intelligence and Confidential Annexes*, March 20, 1946, AHEC.

88. Merritt, *Democracy Imposed*, 259.

89. See Werner Müller, *Contesting Democracy: Political Ideas in Twentieth Century Europe* (New Haven: Yale University Press, 2011), 123, 128–29.

90. Konrad J. Jarausch, *After Hitler: Recivilizing Germans, 1945–1995* (Oxford: Oxford University Press, 2006), 109.

91. Lucius D. Clay, *Decision in Germany* (New York: Doubleday, 1950), 52.

92. Ibid., 52, 55.

93. General McNarney, Headquarters, U.S. Forces, European Theater, "Responsibility for Military Government in U.S. Zone in Germany," December 1945, in box 10, Papers of Walter B. Smith, General Correspondence, 1942–1961, Eisenhower Library.

94. John Lewis Gaddis, *The United States and the Origins of the Cold War, 1941–1947* (New York: Columbia University Press, 1972), 198.

95. Ibid., 199.

96. "Problems and Objectives of United States Policy," memorandum from William J. Donovan, Director Office of Strategic Services, to President Harry S. Truman, May 5, 1945, in box 9, Staff Member and Office Files: Rose Conway Files, Subject File 1949–1953, Department of State—Wireless Bulletins, November 19, 1946–January 31, 1947, Truman Library.

97. See Barbara Ann Chotiner and John W. Atwell, "Soviet Policy toward Germany, 1945–1949," in *U.S. Occupation in Europe after World War II*, ed. Hans Schmitt (Lawrence: Regents Press of Kansas, 1978), 45–49.

98. Harry S. Truman, *Memoirs*, vol. 1 (New York: Doubleday, 1955), 551.

99. Harry S. Truman, *Off the Record: The Private Papers of Harry S. Truman*, ed. Robert H. Ferrell (New York: Harper & Row, 1980), 80.

100. Gaddis, *United States and Origins of the Cold War*, 304–5.

101. W. Averell Harriman, oral history interview with Richard D. McKinzie and Theodore A. Wilson, Washington, DC, 1971, chapter 6, Truman Library.

102. For examples of the Eisenhower-Zhukov friendship, see the Eisenhower-Zhukov correspondence found in box 126, Prepresidential Papers, Papers of Dwight D. Eisenhower, Eisenhower Library.

103. Clay, *Decision in Germany*, 123.

104. Ibid., 278.

105. John Lukacs and George F. Kennan, *George F. Kennan and the Origins of Containment, 1944–1946: The Kennan-Lukacs Correspondence* (Columbia: University of Missouri Press, 1997), 36.

106. Jean Edward Smith, *Lucius D. Clay: An American Life* (New York: Holt, 1990), 290.

107. Ibid., 288, 290.

108. Merritt, *Democracy Imposed*, 264.

109. Rebecca Boehling, *A Question of Priorities: Democratic Reform and Economic Recovery in Postwar Germany* (Providence, RI: Berghahn Books, 1996) 154–55.

110. Smith, *Lucius D. Clay*, 286.

111. Lucius D. Clay for War Department, "CC 2135 (Secret) U.S. Aid for CDU and SPD," August 20, 1946, in Clay, *Papers*, vol. 1, 256–57.

112. See Office of Military Government, Bavaria (OMGB), *Weekly Detachment Report*, no. 53, May 16, 1946, RG 260.71, NARA.

113. Daniel E. Rogers, "Transforming the German Party System: The United States and the Origins of Political Moderation, 1945–1949," *Journal of Modern History* 65 (1993): 538.

114. "Directive to the Commander in Chief," 17–18.

115. "The Principles to Govern the Treatment of Germany in the Initial Control Period," 57.

116. "Directive to the Commander in Chief," 18.

117. Gimbel, *American Occupation of Germany*, 48.

118. Lucius D. Clay to O. P. Echols, "U.S. Policy in Germany," July 19, 1946, in Clay, *Papers*, vol. 1, 240.

119. Clay, "Proconsul of a People, by Another People, for Both Peoples," in Wolfe, *Americans as Proconsuls*, 108.

120. Lucius Clay to John J. McCloy, September 16, 1945, in box 56, General Correspondence of Assistant Secretary of War John J. McCloy, 1941–1945, Germany, RG 107, NARA.

121. H. H. Newman, "Administration of Military Government in the U.S. Zone in Germany," September 20, 1945, in box 15, Papers of Walter J. Muller, Hoover Institution.

122. "Notes for Statement of the Deputy Military Governor to the *Laenderrat* on 8 October 1946," in box 22, Records of the Executive Office, RG 260, NARA.

123. Gimbel, *American Occupation of Germany*, 49.

124. Newman, "Administration of Military Government."

125. Office of the Director, OMGUS, "Consolidation of Military Govern-

ment," in *Military Government Weekly Information Bulletin,* no. 13, October 20, 1945, in box 150, Prepresidential Papers, Eisenhower Library.

126. Special Report of the US Military Governor, "KPD-SPD Merger in the Soviet Zone," in J. Anthony Panuch Papers, Truman Library; OMGB, *Weekly Detachment Reports,* nos. 15 and 17, August 23 and September 6, 1945, RG 260.71, NARA.

127. Office of the Assistant Chief of Staff, G-5 Division, US Forces European Theater, *Military Government Weekly Information Bulletin,* no. 6, September 1, 1945, in box 150, Prepresidential Papers, Eisenhower Library.

128. R. B. Lovett (signed on behalf of General Eisenhower), "Administration of Military Government in the U.S. Zone in Germany," September 20, 1945, in box 15, Papers of Walter J. Muller, Hoover Institution.

129. C. L. Adcock, Director, OMGUS, to Offices of Military Governments, US Zones, Subject: Local Government Codes and Elections, November 23, 1945, in box 15, Papers of Walter J. Muller, Hoover Institution.

130. OMGB, *Weekly Detachment Report,* no. 17, September 6, 1945, RG 260.71, NARA.

131. OMGB, *Weekly Detachment Report,* no. 21, October 4, 1945, RG 260.71, NARA.

132. The CSU became the Bavarian counterpart of the conservative Christian Democratic Union (CDU) that came into existence in other German *Laender.*

133. OMGB, *Weekly Detachment Report,* no. 26, November 8, 1945, RG 260.71, NARA.

134. OMGB, Information Control Division, *Trend: A Weekly Report of Political Affairs and Public Opinion,* no. 9, July 25–31, 1946, RG 260.71, NARA.

135. Special Report of the US Military Governor, "KPD-SPD Merger in the Soviet Zone."

136. Rogers, "Transforming the German Party System," 530.

137. OMGB, *Weekly Detachment Report,* no. 39, February 8, 1946, RG 260.71, NARA.

138. OMGB, *Weekly Detachment Report,* no. 82, December 5, 1946, RG 260.71, NARA.

139. OMGB, *Weekly Detachment Report,* nos. 38 and 39, January 31 and February 8, 1946, RG 260.71, NARA.

140. Bruno Goldhammer quoted in OMGB, *Weekly Detachment Report,* no. 38, January 31, 1946, RG 260.71, NARA.

141. See, e.g., Walter J. Muller, "Constitutional Land-Assembly Elections, June 30, 1946, June 4, 1946," in box 15, Papers of Walter J. Muller, Hoover Institution.

142. OMGB, *Summary of Activities: Office of Military Government for Bavaria,* 1946, in box 15, Papers of Walter J. Muller, Hoover Institution.

143. OMGB, Information Control Division, "Special Brief of Political Affairs," December 2, 1946, in box 15, Papers of Walter J. Muller, Hoover Institution.

144. Arthur D. Kahn, *Experiment in Occupation: Witness to the Turnabout: Anti-Nazi War to Cold War, 1944–1946* (University Park: Pennsylvania State University Press, 2004), 141.

145. Harold Zink, *American Military Government in Germany* (New York: Macmillan, 1947), 185.

146. Ziemke, *U.S. Army in the Occupation*, 383.

147. Boyd L. Dastrup, "U.S. Military Occupation of Nuremberg, 1945–49" (PhD diss., Kansas State University, 1980), 48.

148. OMGUS, *Fragebogen*, Headquarters, OMGUS, 1945, in box 15, Papers of Walter J. Muller, Hoover Institution.

149. OMGB, *Summary of Activities: Office of Military Government for Bavaria*, 1946, 35.

150. "Report of Military Government Detachment F-213 in Munich, Bavaria, May 1945–January 1946," 75.

151. OMGB, *Weekly Detachment Report*, no. 3, June 4, 1945, RG 260.71, NARA.

152. OMGUS, *Denazification Monthly Report of the Military Governor*, no. 2, September 20, 1945, RG 260.71, NARA.

153. Gimbel, *American Occupation of Germany*, 102.

154. John Sparrow, *History of Personnel Demobilization in the United States Army, DA Pamphlet No. 20–210* (Washington, DC: GPO, 1952), 278.

155. See J. F. J. Gillen, *U.S. Military Government in Germany: American Influence on the Development of Political Institutions* (Karlsruhe: Historical Division, US Army European Command, 1950), 4–5.

156. "Germany: East and West," *New Republic*, June 18, 1945, 827.

157. See, e.g., Paul Bellamy, "A Trip through Hell: A Series of Articles Containing Observations on a Recent Trip through Central Europe," *Cleveland Plain Dealer*, 1946, 10.

158. OMGUS, *Denazification Monthly Report of the Military Governor*, no. 3, October 20, 1945, RG 260.71, NARA.

159. Ziemke, *U.S. Army in the Occupation*, 388.

160. OMGB, *Weekly Detachment Report*, no. 23, October 18, 1945, RG 260.71, NARA.

161. OMGUS, *Monthly Report of the Military Governor, U.S. Zone*, no. 6, January 20, 1946, RG 260.71, NARA.

162. Gimbel, *American Occupation of Germany*, 103.

163. OMGUS, *Monthly Report of the Military Governor, U.S. Zone*, no. 8, March 20, 1946, RG 260.71, NARA.

164. Robert A. Reese, "Elaboration of 17 May Denazification Directive," Headquarters OMGB, June 10, 1946, RG 260.71, NARA.

165. OMGB, *Weekly Detachment Report,* no. 54, May 23, 1946, RG 260.71, NARA.

166. "The Dreaded Follower: Embarrassing Occurrences in Connection with a *Spruchkammern* Proceeding at Augsburgland," *Schwabische Landeszeitung,* November 29, 1946, trans. by OMGB Intelligence Branch, in box 14, Papers of Walter J. Muller, 4, Hoover Institution; John Kormann, *U.S. Denazification Policy in Germany, 1944–1950* (Bonn: Historical Division, Office of the High Commission for Germany, 1952), 106–7.

167. Kormann, *U.S. Denazification Policy,* 107.

168. OMGUS, *Monthly Report of the Military Governor, U.S. Zone,* no. 24, January 1–30, 1947, RG 260.71, NARA.

169. William E. Griffith, "Notes on Nazism and Communism," Headquarters, OMGB, n.d., in box 14, Papers of Walter J. Muller, Hoover Institution.

170. See, e.g., James Dobbins et al., *America's Role in Nation Building from Germany to Iraq* (Santa Monica, CA: RAND Corp., 2003), xiii.

171. George Kennan, "American Diplomacy and the Military" (lecture at Grinnell College in 1950), in George Kennan, *American Diplomacy,* rev. ed. (Chicago: University of Chicago Press, 1984), 175–76.

6. Planning and Implementing Military Government in Austria, 1943–1946

1. "Declaration on Austria," in *FRUS, 1943, vol. I, General,* 761. See also Charles J. Simmons, "The United States in the Allied Occupation of Austria" (MA thesis, Columbia University, 1953), 6.

2. Simmons, "United States in the Allied Occupation," 7.

3. Hajo Holborn, *American Military Government: Its Organizations and Practices* (Washington, DC: Infantry Journal Press, 1947), 77.

4. See Milton Colvin, "Principal Issues in the U.S. Occupation of Austria, 1945–48," in *U.S. Occupation in Europe after World War II,* ed. Hans A. Schmitt (Lawrence: Regents Press of Kansas, 1978), 103–5.

5. See Edgar Erickson, "The Zoning of Austria," *Annals of the American Academy of Political and Social Science* (January 1950): 106.

6. Ibid., 107–10. The Joint Chiefs' expectation was that the occupation would only involve one US division.

7. Mark Clark, interview by Lt. Col. Forest S. Riggers Jr., October 1972, "Recollections and Reflections: Transcripts of the Debriefing of General Clark," section 3, 2, 24, 25, Mark W. Clark Papers, AHEC.

8. Fred L. Hadsel, "Epilogue: Reflections of the US Commanders in Austria and Germany," in Schmitt, *US Occupation in Europe,* 150–51.

9. Clark interview, section 3, 3, 25.

10. John Erhardt to General McNarney, April 13, 1945, in box 1, Papers of Lester Flory, AHEC.

11. Col. A. T. Maxwell, G-5, SHAEF, to Ambassador Phillips and Charles Peake, esq. (political advisers to SHAEF), "Austria," May 3, 1944, in box 42, Papers of Frank McSherry, AHEC.

12. "Interim Directive to AFHQ to Initiate Planning of Civil Affairs in Austria subject to Confirmation by the CCS," April 1944, in box 42, Papers of Frank McSherry, AHEC.

13. SHAEF Austrian Planning Section, "Planning Paper No. 2," May 27, 1944, in box 42, Papers of Frank McSherry, AHEC.

14. Col. T. R. Henn to Chief, Operations Branch, G-5, "Report on Visit to AFHQ," August 8, 1944, in box 42, Papers of Frank McSherry, AHEC.

15. Director, Civil Affairs Division, "Military Government in Austria Pre-Surrender Proclamations," November 24, 1944, in box 42, Papers of Frank McSherry, AHEC.

16. See Memorandum to Colonel Henn, Allied Force Headquarters, G-5 Section, December 30, 1944, "Resume of Austrian Planning," in box 1, Papers of Lester Flory, AHEC.

17. James Jay Carafano, *Waltzing into the Cold War: The Struggle for Occupied Austria* (College Station: Texas A&M Press, 2002), 11.

18. John H. Hilldring to Lester Flory, February 16, 1945, in box 1, Papers of Lester Flory, AHEC.

19. Joint Chiefs of Staff (JCS) Directive 1169/9, "Acceptance by the United States of America of Zone of Occupation in Austria," March 29, 1945, in box 42, Papers of Frank McSherry, AHEC.

20. Office of the Chief of Staff, Allied Force Headquarters [Allied Mediterranean Command], *Handbook for Military Government in Austria,* April 1945, introductory memorandum, chapter 1, paras. 1, 4, 5, AHEC (emphasis added).

21. Ibid., chapter 1, para. 5, chapter 2, paras. 1–2, and chapter 4, para. 4.

22. Ibid., chapter 1, para. 5, chapter 2, para. 7.

23. European Advisory Commission Agreement, "Authority on Control Machinery in Austria," July 4, 1945, in *FRUS: The Conference of Berlin (The Potsdam Conference), Vol. I, 1945* (Washington, DC: GPO, 1960), 351–52.

24. Gen. Mark Clark to Commanding General, Second Corps (Military District Commander), and Commanding General, Vienna Area Command, "Directive for Military Government in Austria," July 27, 1945, in box 42, Papers of Mark Clark, Citadel Archives.

25. "Military Government Instruction Number 7, Administration of Justice," September 7, 1945, in box 42, Papers of Mark Clark, Citadel Archives.

26. See, e.g., Carafano, *Waltzing,* 38.

27. For Clark's primary biography, see Martin Blumenson, *Mark Clark* (New York: Congdon & Weed, 1984).

28. Quoted in Fred L. Hadsel, "Reflections of the U.S. Commanders in Austria and Germany," 143–44.

29. See Donald R. Whitnah and Florentine E. Whitnah, *Salzburg under Siege: U.S. Occupation, 1945–1955* (New York: Greenwood, 1991), 111.

30. See Blumenson, *Mark Clark,* 251–52.

31. See Ralph W. Brown III, "A Cold War Army of Occupation? The U.S. Army in Vienna, 1945–1948" (PhD diss., University of Tennessee, Knoxville, 1995), 100–106.

32. Mark Clark, *From the Danube to the Yalu* (New York: Harper & Brothers, 1954), 5.

33. Henry Wallace contrasted Clark to Gen. Lucius Clay in August 1946, noting that Clark's attitude was much more "hard-boiled than that of Clay." August 14, 1946, diary entry in Henry Wallace, *The Price of Vision: The Diary of Henry Wallace, 1942–1946,* ed. John Morton Blum (Boston: Houghton Mifflin, 1973), 609–10.

34. Transmitting Memorandum of Conversation between Gen. Mark W. Clark and Dr. Karl Renner on September 28, 1945, October 1, 1945, memo from John G. Erhardt, in box 43, Papers of Mark Clark, Citadel Archives.

35. September 30, 1945, entry, quoting Message from Clark to Joint Chiefs of Staff, in Mark Clark Diaries, vol. 10, in box 66, Papers of Mark Clark, Citadel Archives.

36. November 29, 1945, entry, quoting Message from Clark to Eisenhower, in Mark Clark Diaries, vol. 10, in box 66, Papers of Mark Clark, Citadel Archives.

37. April 6, 1946, entry, quoting Message from Clark to Joint Chiefs of Staff, in Mark Clark Diaries, vol. 11, in box 66, Papers of Mark Clark, Citadel Archives.

38. August 6, 1945, entry in Mark Clark Diaries, vol. 10, in box 66, Papers of Mark Clark, Citadel Archives.

39. Mark Clark, "Austria" Speech Given to National War College, Washington, DC, September 10, 1946, in box 33, Papers of Mark Clark, Citadel Archives.

40. August 10, 1945, and September 1, 1945, entries in Mark Clark Diaries, vol. 10, in box 66, Papers of Mark Clark, Citadel Archives.

41. This official account is found in Headquarters, United States Forces Austria, *United States in Austria: A Review of Civil Affairs,* March 31, 1948, 27, AHEC.

42. See William Lloyd Stearman, *The Soviet Union and the Occupation of Austria* (Bonn: Siegler, 1964), 33.

43. United States Forces in Austria, *Military Government in Austria,* October 1, 1946, 8, AHEC.

44. See, e.g., the comments by Maj. Lloyd H. Landau that were made in an attachment to Brig. Gen. Lester Flory's report on his June 1945 mission to Vienna. Lester D. Flory, "Mission to Vienna: 3–13 June 1945," enclosure 1 (by Maj. Lloyd H. Landau), "Military Government," and enclosure 2, "Russian Occupation Troops" (by Col. F. T. Norcross), in box 1, Papers of Lester Flory, AHEC.

45. Wellington Samouche, "I Do Understand the Russians" (unpublished personal memoir), 13, in box 1, Papers of Wellington Samouche, AHEC.

46. See, e.g., Matthew Paul Berg, "Caught between *Iwan* and the *Weinhachtsmann:* Occupation, the Marshall Plan, and Austrian Identity," in *The Marshall Plan in Austria,* Contemporary Austrian Studies, vol. 8, ed. Günter Bischof, Anton Pelinka, and Dieter Stiefel (New Brunswick, NJ: Transaction, 2000), 157.

47. Samouche, "I Do Understand," 5.

48. Berg, "Caught between *Iwan,*" 159; Samouche, "I Do Understand," 5.

49. United States Forces in Austria, *Military Government in Austria,* October 1, 1946, 3–5, 7, AHEC.

50. Berg, "Caught between *Iwan,*" 157. See also "Austrian Reactions to Americans," in Whitnah and Whitnah, *Salzburg under Siege,* 93–104.

51. See Notes of Meeting, April 15, 1946, between Mark Clark, Political Adviser Erhardt, and Herbert Hoover, in box 41, Papers of Mark Clark, Citadel Archives.

52. August 15, 1945, entry in Mark Clark Diaries, vol. 10, in box 66, Papers of Mark Clark, Citadel Archives.

53. Petra Goedde, review of Ingrid Bauer, *"Welcome Ami, Go Home," Die Amerikanische Besatzung in Salzburg, 1945–1955,* in Bischof, Pelinka, and Stiefel, *Marshall Plan in Austria,* 575.

54. Diary of Clifton Lisle, May 20–21, 1945, entries in box 13, Papers of Clifton Lisle, AHEC.

55. Whitnah and Whitnah, *Salzburg under Siege,* 15, 106.

56. August 26, 1945, entry in Mark Clark Diaries, vol. 10, in box 66, Papers of Mark Clark, Citadel Archives.

57. January 25, 1946, entry in Mark Clark Diaries, vol. 11, in box 66, Papers of Mark Clark, Citadel Archives.

58. John H. Hilldring to Mark Clark, War Department Message, December 2, 1945, in box 40, Papers of Mark Clark, Citadel Archives.

59. "Organization for Military Government, U.S. Zone, Austria," April 10, 1946, in box 42, Papers of Mark Clark, Citadel Archives.

60. Eleanor Lansing Dulles, "U.S. Economic Policy, Austria," July 25, 1946,

in box 12, Papers of Eleanor Lansing Dulles, Eisenhower Library. Dulles was an economic adviser in the State Department.

61. JCS 1369/2, "Basic and Political Directive to Commander in Chief of U.S. Forces of Occupation Regarding the Military Government of Austria," June 26, 1945, in box 1, Papers of Lester Flory, AHEC.

62. See Erika Weinzierl, "The Origins of the Second Republic: A Retrospective View," in *Austria 1945–1995: Fifty Years of the Second Republic,* ed. Kurt Richard Luther and Peter Pulzer (Aldershot, UK: Ashgate, 1998), 9–10. See also Holborn, *American Military Government*, 78.

63. See Colvin, "Principal Issues," 106.

64. Weinzierl, "Origins of Second Republic," 22.

65. September 10, 1945, entry in Mark Clark Diaries, in vol. 10, box 66, Papers of Mark Clark, Citadel Archives.

66. Stanley J. Grogan, "Questions and Answers Written by Karl Renner and Forwarded to General Clark," in box 43, Papers of Mark Clark, Citadel Archives.

67. See Audrey Kurth Cronin, *Great Power Politics and the Struggle over Austria, 1945–1955* (Ithaca, NY: Cornell University Press, 1986), 36.

68. September 30, 1945, entry (quoting Clark's message to JCS) in Mark Clark Diaries, in vol. 10, box 66, Papers of Mark Clark, Citadel Archives.

69. Ibid.

70. November 30, 1945, entry (quoting Clark's message to JCS) in Mark Clark Diaries, in vol. 10, box 66, Papers of Mark Clark, Citadel Archives.

71. John G. Erhardt, "Transmitting Memorandum of Conversation between General Mark W. Clark and Dr. Karl Renner on September 28, 1945," October 1, 1945, in box 43, Papers of Mark Clark, Citadel Archives.

72. Ibid.

73. See *Monthly Report of the United States Commissioner, Military Government, Austria,* November, 1945, no. 1, 5–6, AHEC.

74. See the entries of October 20, October 31, and November 11, 1945 (Clark's messages to JCS) in Mark Clark Diaries, vol. 10, box 66, Papers of Mark Clark, Citadel Archives.

75. For the best American account of the remainder of the US occupation, see Carafano, *Waltzing.*

76. Stearman, *Soviet Union and Occupation,* 36.

77. *Monthly Report,* 1.

78. Department of State Press Release, "Statement on Recognition of Government of Austria, January 7, 1946," in *Documents on American Foreign Relations, Vol. VIII, July 1, 1945–December 31, 1946,* ed. Raymond Dennett and Robert K. Turner (Norwood, MA: Norwood Press, 1948), 311.

79. "Agreement between the Governments of the United Kingdom, the

United States of America, the Union of Socialist Soviet Republics, and the Government of the French Republic on the Machinery of Control in Austria," June 28, 1946, in Headquarters, United States Forces Austria, United States Forces in Austria, *A Review of Military Government,* January 1, 1947, AHEC.

80. "Report by the Secretary of State on the Latter Half of the Meeting of the Council of Foreign Ministers in Paris," June 15–July 12, 1946, in Dennett and Turner, *Documents on American Foreign Relations,* 248.

81. See Oliver Rathkopf, "International Perceptions of Austrian Neutrality," in *Neutrality in Austria,* Contemporary Austrian Studies, vol. 9, ed. Günter Bischof, Anton Pelinka, and Dieter Stiefel (New Brunswick, NJ: Transaction Publications, 2001), 69–71.

82. See Vojtechn Mastny, "The Soviet Godfathers of Austrian Neutrality," in *Neutrality in Austria,* 240.

83. For brief accounts of the Austrian Treaty in relation to larger Cold War political issues, see William G. Hyland, *The Cold War: Fifty Years of Conflict* (New York: Random House, 1991), 81–84, and David S. Painter, *The Cold War: An International History* (London: Routledge, 1999), 33–34.

84. David Edelstein, *Occupational Hazards: Success and Failure in Military Occupation* (Ithaca, NY: Cornell University Press, 2008), 184.

7. Planning and Implementing Military Government in Korea, 1943–1946

1. Bruce Cumings, *The Origins of the Korean War: Liberation and the Emergence of Separate Regimes, 1945–1947* (Princeton, NJ: Princeton University Press, 1981), 130.

2. Ibid., 124, 438.

3. See Hilary Conroy, *The Japanese Seizure of Korea, 1868–1910: A Study of Realism and Idealism in International Relations* (Philadelphia: University of Pennsylvania Press, 1960); Eugene C. I. Kim and Han-Kyo Kim, *Korea and the Politics of Imperialism, 1876–1910* (Berkeley: University of California Press, 1967); and Eugene C. I. Kim and Dorothea E. Mortimore, eds., *Korea's Response to Japan: The Colonial Period, 1910–1945* (Kalamazoo: Center for Korean Studies, Western Michigan University, 1975).

4. "Statement Released after the Cairo Conference by President Roosevelt, Generalissimo Chiang Kai-Shek and Prime Minister Churchill," December 1, 1943, in US Department of State, *The Record on Korean Unification, 1943–1960: Narrative Summary with Principal Documents* (Washington, DC: GPO, 1960), 42.

5. "The Potsdam Proclamation Defining Terms for the Surrender of Japan," July 26, 1945, in US Department of State, *Record on Korean Unification,* 43.

6. Cumings, *Origins of the Korean War,* 130.

7. Minutes of Roosevelt-Stalin Meeting, 3:30 P.M. at Livadia Palace, February 8, 1945, in *FRUS: The Conferences at Malta and Yalta, 1945* (Washington, DC: GPO, 1955), 770.

8. See E. Grant Meade, *American Military Government in Korea* (New York: King's Crown Press, 1951), 44–45.

9. William Stueck, "The Coming of the Cold War to Korea," in *Korea under the American Military Government, 1945–48,* ed. Bonnie Oh (Westport, CT: Praeger, 2002), 53.

10. See C. Leonard Hoag, *American Military Government in Korea: War Policy and the First Year of Occupation, 1941–1946* (Washington, DC: CMH, 1970), 2.

11. Memorandum of conversation by Assistant Secretary of State (Berle), May 12, 1943, *FRUS, 1943, Vol. III: The British Commonwealth, Eastern Europe, the Far East* (Washington, DC: GPO, 1963), 1092.

12. The Ambassador in China (Gauss) to the Secretary of State, May 19, 1944, *FRUS, 1944, Vol. V: The Near East, South Asia, and Africa, the Far East* (Washington, DC: GPO, 1965), 1292–93.

13. "Post War Status of Korea," Briefing Book Paper, Executive Secretariat Files (Preconference Document), Inter-Allied Consultation Regarding Korea, in *FRUS: Conferences at Malta and Yalta,* 358–61.

14. See Allan Millett, *The War for Korea, 1945–1950: A House Burning* (Lawrence: University Press of Kansas, 2005), 5.

15. See Pyung-choon Ham, *The Korean Political Tradition and Law: Essays in Korean Law and Legal History* (Seoul: Royal Asiatic Society, Korea Branch, 1967).

16. Hoag, *American Military Government,* 26.

17. Operations and Plans Division, War Department to Commander in Chief, Army Forces Pacific, Advance, Command Yokohama, September 9, 1945, in box 139, Records of the US Joint Chiefs of Staff, Geographic File, 1942–1945, RG 218, NARA.

18. The Joint Chiefs of Staff to the Secretary of State, "Assumptions for Planning for the Period of Military Occupation," May 14, 1944, in *FRUS, 1944, Vol. V,* 1261–62.

19. Hoag, *American Military Government,* 17.

20. See Millett, *War for Korea,* 53, and Hoag, *American Military Government,* 54.

21. Draft Memo to JCS from SWNCC, undated, in *FRUS, 1945, Vol. VI: The British Commonwealth, the Far East* (Washington, DC: GPO, 1969), 1038.

22. General Headquarters, US Army Forces, Pacific, Basic Outline Plan for Blacklist, August 8, 1945, para. 1a, AHEC.

23. Ibid., paras. 2a(4), 3a, 3c(1)(b), annex 5b.

24. Listed as "Japan Proper and Korea" or "Japan and Korea" in ibid., paras. 1a, 1d, 2a(8), 2b(7), 3, and 3c(1)(b).

25. See Message 121527/Z, General Headquarters, US Army Forces, Pacific, August 12, 1945 (with Basic Outline Plan for Blacklist), AHEC.

26. Basic Outline Plan for Blacklist, para. 2a.

27. "United States Initial Post-Surrender Policy for Japan, State-War-Navy Coordinating Committee (SWNCC)," approved by President Harry S. Truman, in Report of Government Section, Supreme Commander for the Allied Powers, *Political Reorientation of Japan, September 1945 to September 1948* (Washington DC: GPO, 1950), 423.

28. General Order No. 1, September 2, 1945, in *Political Reorientation of Japan*, 442.

29. Proclamation to the People of Korea Issued by Gen. Douglas MacArthur, September 7, 1945, in *Political Reorientation of Japan*, 453.

30. Memorandum for Imperial Japanese Government, Subject: Promotions of Civil Service Officials in Korea, October 2, 1945, in *Political Reorientation of Japan*, 472.

31. SWNCC 176/8, titled "Basic Initial Directive to the Commander-in-Chief, U.S. Army Forces Pacific, for the Administration of Civil Affairs in Those Areas of Korea Occupied by U.S. Forces," undated, in *FRUS, 1945, Vol. VI*, 1071, 1074–76.

32. The Acting Political Advisor in Korea (Langdon) to the Secretary of State, November 20, 1945, in *FRUS, 1945, Vol. VI*, 1131–32.

33. Robert Schaeffer, *Warpaths: The Politics of Partition* (New York: Hill & Wang, 1990), 8. For Schaeffer's discussion on the dividing of Korea, see 129–32.

34. See, e.g., George M. McCune, "Korea: The First Year of Liberation," *Pacific Affairs* 20 (March 1947): 4; Shannon McCune, "The Thirty-Eighth Parallel in Korea," *World Politics* 2 (January 1949): 232; and Arthur L. Grey Jr., "The Thirty-Eighth Parallel," *Foreign Affairs* 29 (April 1951): 482.

35. Grey, "Thirty-Eighth Parallel," 482.

36. William Stueck, *Rethinking the Korean War: A New Diplomatic and Strategic History* (Princeton, NJ: Princeton University Press, 2002), 12.

37. McCune, "Thirty-Eighth Parallel," 225.

38. Grey, "Thirty-Eighth Parallel," 486.

39. Edwin W. Pauley to Harry S. Truman and Secretary of State, August 11, 1945, in Papers of Harry Wolbers, box 1, AHEC.

40. James F. Byrnes, *Speaking Frankly* (New York: Harper, 1947), 221.

41. George Marshall to Molotov, April 8, 1948, in box 1, Papers of Harry L. Brown, AHEC.

42. John H. Hilldring, Speech to Economic Club of Detroit, March 10, 1947, in Hoag, *American Military Government,* 91.

43. Dean Rusk, *As I Saw It,* as told to Richard Rusk (New York: Norton, 1990), 124.

44. Jongsoo James Lee, *The Partition of Korea after World War II: A Global History* (New York: Palgrave Macmillan, 2006), 38.

45. Charles Bonesteel, interview by Lt. Col. Robert P. St. Louis, US Army Military History Institute, Project 73–2, 1973, on file at AHEC; Rusk, *As I Saw It,* 124; Grey, "Thirty-Eighth Parallel," 485.

46. Lee, *Partition of Korea,* 42.

47. General Headquarters, Supreme Commander, Allied Powers, *Summation of Non-Military Activities in Japan and Korea: 1945–46,* November 1945, 180.

48. Cumings, *Origins of the Korean War,* 123.

49. Hoag, *American Military Government,* 87.

50. Stueck, *Rethinking the Korean War,* 20.

51. Ibid.

52. Millett, *War for Korea,* 57.

53. Cumings, *Origins of the Korean War,* 440.

54. See, e.g., Undated Recollection by Mrs. Orlando Ward (wife of Maj. Gen. Orlando Ward, Commanding General of the Sixth Infantry Division, one of the occupying units in Korea), in box 5, Papers of Orlando Ward, AHEC.

55. Commander in Chief Army Forces, Advance, Tokyo, Japan, to War Department, Cable 52058, September 18, 1945 (containing Hodge's report), Records of the US Joint Chiefs of Staff, Geographic File, 1942–1945, in box 139, RG 218, NARA.

56. Secretary of State to Ambassador in Soviet Union, Telegram, November 3, 1945, *FRUS, 1945, Vol. VI,* 1106–7.

57. Commander in Chief, Pacific, Advance, Tokyo, Japan, to Joint Chiefs of Staff, Enclosure B to JCS 1483/12, October 1, 1945, Records of Joint Chiefs of Staff, Geographic File, 1942–1945, in box 140, RG 218, NARA.

58. Memorandum from Lt. Gen. John Hodge to General of the Army Douglas MacArthur, September 24, 1945, *FRUS, 1945, Vol. VI,* 1054–57.

59. Statistical Research Division of the Office of Administration, Headquarters US American Military Government in Korea, *History of United States Army Military Government in Korea Part I, Period of September 1945–30 June 1946,* October 1946, 27, 32, on file at AHEC.

60. William Stueck, *The Korean War: An International History* (Princeton, NJ: Princeton University Press, 1995), 20.

61. US Department of State, *Record on Korean Unification,* 27, 47–48.

62. See Meade, *American Military Government,* 46–51; Statistical Research

Division, *History of United States Army Military Government in Korea Part I,* 22–23, 82–83.

63. "Not Slave, Not Free," *Time,* October 8, 1945.

64. Meade, *American Military Government,* 49–51.

65. See résumé of Raymond A. Janowski in Papers of Raymond A. Janowski, AHEC.

66. General Headquarters, *Summation,* September–October 1945, 195, AHEC.

67. See US Department of State, *Record on Korean Unification,* 27; General Headquarters, *Summation,* September–October 1945, 176.

68. General Headquarters, *Summation,* April 1946, 1.

69. US American Military Government in Korea report no. 2, "Present Agricultural Position of South Korea," April 1947, AHEC.

70. General Headquarters, *Summation,* January 1946, 15.

71. Frederick Silber, Report on Survey Trip to Japan and Korea, November 25, 1946, in Records of Assistant Secretary of State for Occupied Areas, in box 5, RG 59, NARA.

72. Maj. Gen. Orlando W. Ward to Commanding General, Twenty-Fourth Corps, Subject: Letter to Hearst Syndicate by Group of Sergeants, Company I, Sixty-Third Infantry Regiment (March 23, 1947), and Maj. Gen. Orlando W. Ward, "To All Unit Commanders" (June 17, 1947), in box 5, Papers of Orlando Ward, AHEC.

73. *History of the 185th Infantry Regiment,* 1946, 72–74, 78–80, AHEC.

74. Military Journal of Tech. Sgt. James E. Hodges, November 25, 1940, to December 6, 1948, Summer 1947 entry, in box 1, Papers of James E. Hodges, AHEC.

75. Ibid.

76. Walter Simmons, "GIs Haven't a Kind Word to Say for Korea: Compared to It, Japan's Heaven, They Assert," *Chicago Tribune* Press Service, December 13, 1945, in United States Army in Korea Commandant's Office, General Correspondence, 1943–1946, in box 1, RG 554, NARA.

77. Hodge to Maj. Gen. Gilbert R. Cheeves, December 9, 1945, in United States Army in Korea Commandant's Office, General Correspondence, 1943–1946, in box 1, RG 554, NARA.

78. Message from the Commanding General, US Armed Forces in Korea, June 3, 1946, in United States Army in Korea (USAFIK) Commandant's Office, General Correspondence, 1943–1946, in box 1, RG 554, NARA.

79. See Opinion No. 239, Subject Defamation against Military Government, US Army Forces in Korea, in *Selected Legal Opinions of the Department of Justice, United States Army Military Government in Korea, Covering a Period from March 1946 to August 1948,* vol. 1. (Buffalo, NY: W.S. Hein, 1976 [1948]), 55, 57.

80. Ibid., 56–57.

81. For a description of the problem of the inadequacies of military government and the rise of the so-called government of interpreters, see "Labor Problems and Policies in Korea: Report of the Korean Subcommittee," Labor Advisory Mission, June 18, 1946, in United States Army Forces in Korea, US-USSR Joint Commission on Korea, Subject Files 1945–1947, Daily Radio Reports to News Conferences, in box 293, RG 554, NARA. For a description of Yo Un-hyong and the Committee for Preparation of Korean Independence, see Stueck, "Coming of the Cold War," 51–52, and Park Chan-Pyo, "The American Military Government and the Framework for Democracy in South Korea," in Oh, *Korea under the American Military Government,* 125–27.

82. Hoag, *American Military Government,* 2.

83. Douglas MacArthur, *Reminiscences* (New York: McGraw Hill, 1964), 293.

84. See Manduk Chung, "The United States in Korea: A Reluctant Participant, 1945–1948" (PhD diss., Michigan State University, 1975), 95–102.

85. Stueck, *Rethinking the Korean War,* 20.

86. "The Proclamation for Northern Korea by the Commander of the Twenty-Fifth Occupation Army," as reported by the Acting Political Adviser in Korea (Langdon) to the Secretary of State, November 18, 1945, in *FRUS, 1945, Vol. VI,* 1129.

87. Stueck, "Coming of the Cold War," 55. See also Kathryn Weathersby, "Soviet Policy toward Korea, 1944–1946" (PhD diss., Indiana University, 1990).

88. Political Advisor in Korea (H. Merrell Benninghof) to the Secretary of State, September 26, 1945, received October 9, in *FRUS, 1945, Vol. VI,* 1069.

89. See, e.g., Maj. Gen. Albert Brown, "The Communist Effort in Korea" (1951), 31, in Papers of Albert Brown, AHEC. Brown was the chief American commissioner in the US-USSR Joint Korean Commission. See also, Memorandum for G-2 Historian to Commander, Fourteenth Corps, Subject: Soviet Communist-Inspired Espionage in South Korea, in box 1, Papers of Harry J. Wolbers, AHEC.

90. Brown, 31.

91. H. Merrell Benninghof to the Secretary of State, October 1, 1945, in *FRUS, 1945, Vol. VI,* 1065; Political Adviser in Korea to Political Adviser in Japan, October 10, 1945, in *FRUS, 1945, Vol. VI,* 1070.

92. General Headquarters, *Summation,* November, 1945, 180.

93. General Headquarters, *Summation,* December, 1945, 190.

94. War Department General Staff Strategy and Policy Group, Strategic Policy, Korea, Colonel Dupuy, December 29, 1945, to Commander-in-Chief, Army Forces, Pacific, Advance Tokyo, War 90922, in box 140, Records of the US Joint Chiefs of Staff, Geographic File, 1942–1945, RG 218, NARA. See also Choi

Sang-Yong, "Trusteeship Debate and the Korean War," in Oh, *Korea under the American Military Government*, 13–14.

95. For a comprehensive account of both the conference and the joint commission, see Lee, *Partition of Korea*, 69–106.

96. Lawrence Lincoln interview by Lawrence Suid, "An Army Engineer: A Career and a Great Calling" (Fort Belvoir, VA: Office of History, US Army Corps of Engineers, 1993), in Papers of Lawrence J. Lincoln, AHEC.

97. Commanding General, US Army in Korea to War Department, January 23, 1946, TFGBI 153, in box 140, Records of the US Joint Chiefs of Staff, Geographic File, 1942–1945, RG 218, NARA; Political Advisor in Korea to Secretary of State, February 15, 1946, *FRUS, 1946, Vol. VIII, The Far East* (Washington, DC: GPO, 1971), 633.

98. Commanding General, US Army in Korea through Commander-in-Chief, Army Forces, Pacific, Advance, Tokyo, to War Department, TFGCG 206, December 30, 1945, in box 140, Records of the US Joint Chiefs of Staff, Geographic File, 1942–1945, RG 218, NARA.

99. General Headquarters, *Summation*, December 1945, 189.

100. "Resolution of the Korean Congress of Political Parties, Addressed to the Four Allied Powers and Sent to Department of State on December 4, 1945," *FRUS, 1945, Vol. VI*, 1110.

101. Policy Paper Adopted by State-War-Navy Coordinating Committee, SWNCC 176/18, adopted January 28, 1946, *FRUS, 1946, Vol. VIII*, 626.

102. Pyo, "American Military Government," 129–31; Millett, *War for Korea*, 81–83, 159.

103. Sang-Yong, "Trusteeship Debate," 28–30.

104. Edwin Pauley to Harry S. Truman, June 22, 1946, in box 1, Papers of Harry Wolbers, AHEC.

105. Political Advisor in Korea to Secretary of State, August 23, 1946, *FRUS, 1946, Vol. VIII*, 726.

106. Memorandum by State Department (Hilldring) of State-War-Navy Coordinating Committee to Secretary of Committee, July 25, 1946, *FRUS, 1946, Vol. VIII*, 718.

107. Stueck, "Coming of the Cold War," 41.

108. Cumings, *Origins of the Korean War*, 428.

109. Schaeffer, *Warpaths*, 7.

Conclusion

1. Kenneth Royall to Lucius Clay, Message W-84501, August 19, 1947, in box 7, Papers of Lucius D. Clay, December 1946–August 1948, RG 200, NARA.

2. See e.g., Clarence Huebner to War Department Plans and Operations, Message SX-1347, July 17, 1947, in box 7, Papers of Lucius D. Clay, December 1946–August 1948, RG 200, NARA.

3. See "Report on Factors Involved in Transfer from War to State of Economic and Financial Functions Relating to Administration of Germany, Austria, Japan, and Korea," June 19, 1947, in Office of Assistant Secretary of State for Occupied Areas, "Department of State Assumption of Operational Responsibilities in Occupied Areas," June 20, 1947, in box 2, Office of Assistant Secretary of State for Occupied Areas, RG 59, NARA.

4. John Sparrow, *History of Personnel Demobilization in the United States Army: DA Pamphlet No. 20–210, July 1952* (Washington, DC: GPO, 1952), 289.

5. See William R. Swarm, "Impact of the Proconsular Experience on Civil Affairs Organization and Doctrine" in *Americans as Proconsuls: United States Military Government in Germany and Japan, 1944–1952,* ed. Robert Wolfe (Carbondale: Southern Illinois University Press, 1984), 401–11.

6. The State Department's Office for Occupied Areas was similarly dissolved the same year. Edward N. Peterson, "The Occupation as Perceived by the Public, Scholars, and Policy Makers," in Wolfe, *Americans as Proconsuls,* 421.

7. *Final Report of the Chief of Staff, United States Army to the Secretary of the Army,* February 7, 1948 (Washington, DC: GPO, 1948).

8. See James E. Hewes Jr., *From Root to McNamara: Army Organization and Administration, 1900–1963* (Washington DC: CMH, 1975), 194–96.

9. Daniel H. Fahey Jr., Special Consultant to the Secretary of the Army, "Findings, Recommendations, and Conclusions Concerning U.S. Civil Affairs/ Military Government Organization," February 1951, 2, 3; analysis, part I, 2, 6; and analysis, part II, 3–5, on file at AHEC.

10. Henry L. Stimson and McGeorge Bundy, *On Active Service in Peace and War* (New York: Harper & Bros., 1948), 565.

11. George Fitzpatrick et al., September 1956, *A Survey of the Experience and Opinions of U.S. Military Government Officers in World War II* (Chevy Chase, MD: Operations Research Office, Johns Hopkins University), 3–4, 13–14, 21–27, 57, 66.

12. C. Darwin Stolzenbach and Henry Kissinger, *Civil Affairs in Korea, 1950–51* (Chevy Chase, MD: Johns Hopkins University Press, 1952), 1–3.

13. See Walter E. Kretchik, *U.S. Army Doctrine: From the American Revolution to the War on Terror* (Lawrence: University Press of Kansas, 2011), 176. Kretchik's book provides an excellent survey and understanding of modern army doctrine.

14. *Field Manual 100-5: Operations* (Washington DC: Headquarters, Department of the Army, February 1962), paras. 9, 10–12.

15. Earl Ziemke, "Conference of Scholars on the Administration of Occupied Areas, 1943–1955, April 10–11, 1970," 61, on file at the Truman Library.

16. Edward N. Peterson, Discussion of "The Occupation as Perceived by the Public, Scholars and Policy Makers," in Wolfe, *Americans as Proconsuls*, 433.

17. Robert W. Komer, *Bureaucracy Does Its Thing: Institutional Constraints on US-GVN Performance in Vietnam; Report Prepared for Defense Advanced Research Projects Agency, ARPA Order No. 189-1* (Santa Monica, CA: RAND Corp., 1972), 75. See also Robert W. Komer, *Organization and Management of the "New Model" Pacification Program, 1966–1969* (Santa Monica, CA: RAND Corp., 1970), 232–42. For an overview of efforts to overcome interagency difficulties in Vietnam, see Frank L. Jones, "Blowtorch: Robert Komer and the Making of Vietnam Pacification Policy," *Parameters* 35 (Autumn 2005): 103–18.

18. Komer, *Bureaucracy Does Its Thing*, 106–7.

19. Komer, *Organization and Management*, 20, 242. For a discussion of CORDS's success by a harsh critic of US policy and actions in Vietnam, see John Prados, *Vietnam: The History of an Unwinnable War* (Lawrence: University Press of Kansas, 2010), 320–21. See also Ronald Spector, *After Tet: The Bloodiest Year in Vietnam* (New York: Vintage, 1994), 279–94.

20. *Field Manual 100-5: Operations* (Washington, DC: Headquarters, Department of the Army, September 1968), chapters 11–13. See also Kretchik, *U.S. Army Doctrine*, 190–92.

21. *Field Manual 100-5: Operations* (Washington, DC: Headquarters, Department of the Army, July 1976), i.

22. *Field Manual 100-5: Operations* (Washington, DC: Headquarters, Department of the Army, August 1982). For a discussion of the development of AirLand Battle doctrine in the 1970s and 1980s, see John L. Romjue, *American Army Doctrine for the Post–Cold War* (Fort Monroe, VA: US Army Training and Doctrine Command, 1996), 16–19. See also Kretchik, *U.S. Army Doctrine*, 208.

23. Swarm, "Impact of the Proconsuls," 413.

24. Romjue, *American Army Doctrine*, 85.

25. *Field Manual 100-5: Operations* (Washington, DC: Headquarters, Department of the Army, June 1993), figure 2-1.

26. The thirteen activities were noncombatant evacuation operations, arms control, support to domestic civil authorities, humanitarian assistance and disaster relief, security assistance, nation assistance, support to counterdrug operations, combatting terrorism, peacekeeping operations, peace enforcement, show of force, support for insurgencies and counterinsurgencies, and attacks and raids. Ibid., 13-4–13-8.

27. Frederick Kagan, "Army Doctrine and Modern War: Notes toward a New Edition of *FM 100-5*," *Parameters* 37 (Spring 1997): 134–51.

28. *Field Manual 3-0: Operations* (Washington, DC: Headquarters, Department of the Army, June 2001), 9-18, 9-46. The ten types of stability operations listed were peace operations, foreign internal defense, security assistance, humanitarian and civic assistance, support to insurgencies, support to counterdrug operations, combating terrorism, noncombatant evacuation operations, arms control, and shows of force. See also Kretchik, *U.S. Army Doctrine,* 256.

29. The full quote is "While we at CENTCOM were executing the war plan, Washington should focus on policy-level issues. . . . I knew the President and Don Rumsfeld would back me up, so I felt free to pass the message along to the bureaucracy beneath them: You pay attention to the day *after* and I'll pay attention to the day *of.*" Tommy Franks, *American Soldier* (New York: HarperCollins, 2004), 441 (emphasis in the original).

30. See, e.g., Nora Bensahel et al., *After Saddam: Prewar Planning and the Occupation of Iraq* (Santa Monica, CA: RAND Corp., 2008), 234–35.

31. See Andrew Rathmell, "Planning Post-Conflict Reconstruction in Iraq: What Can We Learn?," *International Affairs* 81 (2005): 1021–27.

32. As a sign of the manual's influence among civilian intellectuals, it was eventually published by the prestigious University of Chicago Press. See *The U.S. Army/Marine Corps Counterinsurgency Field Manual: U.S. Army Field Manual 3-24* (Chicago: University of Chicago Press, 2007).

33. See, e.g., Bing West, *The Strongest Tribe: War, Politics, and the Endgame in Iraq* (New York: Random House, 2008). See also Kretchik, *U.S. Army Doctrine,* 260–67. For a critique of the Petraeus "surge" narrative, see Gian Gentile, *Wrong Turn: America's Deadly Embrace of Counterinsurgency* (New York: New Press, 2013), 85–111.

34. Henry Nuzum, *Shades of "CORDS" in the Kush* (Carlisle, PA: Strategic Studies Institute, 2010), 80–89.

35. US Department of Defense, *Department of Defense Instruction 3000.05* (September 16, 2009).

36. Joint Chiefs of Staff, *Joint Publication 3-08: Interorganizational Coordination during Joint Operations,* June 24, 2011, I-5, II-11–12.

37. Jeffrey Record, *Beating Goliath: Why Insurgencies Win* (Washington, DC: Potomac Books, 2009), 104–7, 110.

38. James Dobbins et al., *America's Role in Nation Building from Germany to Iraq* (Santa Monica, CA: RAND Corp., 2003), xiii.

39. Ibid., xiii, xv–xvi, xx (table S.1).

40. Ibid., 21. See, e.g., Ian Kershaw, *The End: The Defiance and Destruction of Hitler's Germany* (New York: Penguin, 2011), 279–80, and Frederick Taylor, *Exorcising Hitler: The Occupation and Denazification of Germany* (New York: Bloomsbury, 2011), 22–45.

41. Bruce Hoffman, foreword to David Galula, *Pacification in Algeria, 1956–1958* (Santa Monica, CA: RAND Corp., 2006 [1963]), v.

42. Komer, *Bureaucracy Does Its Thing,* 7–8, 10, *75.*

43. See, e.g., Jeff Conklin, "Wicked Problems and Social Complexity," in his *Dialogue Mapping: Building Shared Understanding of Wicked Problems* (Chichester, UK: John Wiley & Sons, 2005).

44. For an introduction to systematic operational design in military operations, see Huba Wass de Czege, "Systemic Operational Design: Learning and Adapting in Complex Missions," *Military Review* (January–February, 2009): 2–12.

45. J. F. Schmitt, "A Systemic Concept for Operational Design," 2006, available at http://www.au.af.mil/au/awc/awcgate/usmc/mcwl_schmitt_op_design.pdf, 3, 9, 12, 30.

46. Victor Delacruz, "Systemic Operational Design: Enhancing the Joint Planning Process," unpublished monograph, School of Advanced Military Studies, Fort Leavenworth, KS, 2007, 9, 30.

47. Ketti Davison, "From Tactical Planning to Operational Design," *Military Review* (September–October, 2008), 38.

48. A critique of design theory is found in Milan Vego, "A Case against Systemic Operational Design," *Joint Force Quarterly* 53 (2nd Quarter 2009): 69–75. General Naveh has responded forcefully to critics. See, e.g., Brig. Gen. (ret.) Shimon Naveh, interview by Matt Matthews, November 1, 2007, in *Operational Leadership Experience* (Fort Leavenworth, KS: Combat Studies Institute, 2007): 1–10.

49. Hans-Georg Gadamer, *Truth and Method,* 2nd rev. ed., trans. Joel Weinsheimer and Donald Marshall (New York: Continuum, 1989), 278.

50. Ibid., 9.

51. Hans-Georg Gadamer, *Philosophical Hermeneutics,* trans and ed. David E. Linge (Berkeley: University of California Press, 1976), 96.

52. See Alasdair MacIntyre, *Whose Justice? Which Rationality?* (Notre Dame, IN: University of Notre Dame Press, 1988), and *Three Rival Versions of Moral Inquiry: Encyclopedia, Genealogy, and Tradition* (Notre Dame, IN: University of Notre Dame Press, 1990).

53. Schmitt, "Systemic Concept," 9.

54. Gadamer, *Truth and Method,* 308.

55. See C. Wright Mills, *The Power Elite* (New York: Oxford University Press, 1956).

56. Gadamer, *Truth and Method,* 364–65.

57. John Lewis Gaddis, *We Now Know: Rethinking Cold War History* (Oxford: Oxford University Press, 1997), 199.

Bibliography

Primary Sources

Archival Materials

Amherst College Archives, Amherst, MA
    Papers and Diaries of John J. McCloy
The Citadel Archives, Charleston SC
    Papers and Diaries of Mark W. Clark
Dwight D. Eisenhower Presidential Library, Abilene, KS
    Combined Chiefs of Staff Conference Proceedings
    John J. McCloy Oral History
    Papers of C. D. Jackson
    Papers of Dwight D. Eisenhower
    Papers of Eleanor Lansing Dulles
    Papers of Oleg Patuhoff
    Papers of Walter Bedell Smith
    Prepresidential Papers
Franklin D. Roosevelt Presidential Library, Hyde Park, NY
    Official Files
    Papers of Francis Biddle
    Papers of Franklin D. Roosevelt
    Papers of Harry Hopkins
    Papers of Henry Wallace
    Presidential Personal Files
George C. Marshall Foundation, Lexington, VA
    Interviews and Reminiscences of George C. Marshall
Harry S. Truman Presidential Library, Independence, MO
    CIA Intelligence Files, 1946–53

Conference of Scholars on the Administration of Occupied Areas, 1943–1955,
   April 10–11, 1970
Dean Acheson Oral History
Lucius D. Clay Oral History
Papers of Abijah U. Fox
Papers of Dean Acheson
Papers of Harry S. Truman
Presidential Official Files
Presidential Secretarial Files
Staff Member and Office Files
Hoover Institution on War, Revolution, and Peace, Stanford, CA
   Papers of Walter J. Muller
Library of Congress, Washington, DC
   Papers and Diaries of Harold L. Ickes
   Papers of Robert Patterson
National Archives and Records Administration, College Park, MD
   Records Group 59, Records of the State Department
   Record Group 107, Records of the Office of the Secretary of War
   Records Group 165, Records of the War Department General and Special
      Staffs
   Records Group 200, Personal Papers of Lucius D. Clay
   Records Group 218, Records of the Joint Chiefs of Staff
   Records Group 260, Records of the Office of Military Government, Ger-
      many, United States
   Records Group 389, Records of the Provost Marshal General
   Records Group 554 Records of General Headquarters, Far East Command,
      Supreme Commander, Allied Powers and United Nations Command
US Army Center for Military History, Fort McNair, Washington DC
   Histories of the US Army Civil Affairs Division
US Army Heritage and Education Center, Carlisle Barracks, PA
   Papers of Albert Brown
   Papers of Charles H. Bonesteel III
   Papers of Clifton Lisle
   Papers of Frank McSherry
   Papers of Harry Wolbers
   Papers of James E. Hodges
   Papers of Lawrence Lincoln
   Papers of Lester D. Flory
   Papers of Mark W. Clark
   Papers of Orlando Ward

Papers of Raymond Janowski
Papers of Richard van Wagenen
Papers of Thomas H. Green
Papers of Wellington Samouche
Papers of William E. Birkhimer
US Army War College Curricular Files
Yale University Library, Manuscripts and Archives, New Haven, CT
Diaries of Henry L. Stimson

Official Documents

Allied Military Government in Germany. *Army Service Forces Manual, Military Government Handbook, Germany, Section 2M: Proclamations Ordinances and Laws.* January 6, 1945.

American Military Government of Occupied Germany, 1918–1920: Report of the Officer in Charge of Civil Affairs, Third Army and American Forces in Germany. Washington, DC: Government Printing Office, 1943.

Biennial Report of the Chief of Staff of the United States Army to the Secretary of War, July 1, 1943 to June 30, 1945. Washington, DC: Government Printing Office, 1945.

Eisenhower, Dwight D. "Demobilization Speech to Congress: Statement on Demobilization by General of the Army Dwight D. Eisenhower, Chief of Staff, US Army, Supplementing His Remarks on Demobilization Made to Members of Congress in the Auditorium, Library of Congress, 1000 AM, EST, Tuesday, January 15, 1946." Washington, DC: Army Information Branch, Information and Education Division, War Department, 1946.

Final Report, Japanese Evacuation from the West Coast, 1942. Washington, DC: Government Printing Office, 1943.

Final Report of the Chief of Staff, United States Army, to the Secretary of the Army. February 7, 1948. Washington, DC: Government Printing Office, 1948.

Foreign Relations of the United States: The Conferences at Malta and Yalta, 1945. Washington, DC: Government Printing Office, 1955.

Foreign Relations of the United States: The Conference at Quebec, 1944. Washington, DC: Government Printing Office, 1972.

Foreign Relations of the United States: The Conference of Berlin, the Potsdam Conference, 1945, Volume I. Washington, DC: Government Printing Office, 1960.

Foreign Relations of the United States, 1943, Volume I, General. Washington, DC: Government Printing Office, 1963.

Foreign Relations of the United States, 1943, Volume III: The British Common-

wealth, Eastern Europe, the Far East. Washington, DC: Government Printing Office, 1963.

Foreign Relations of the United States, 1944, Volume V: The Near East, South Asia, and Africa, the Far East. Washington, DC: Government Printing Office, 1965.

Foreign Relations of the United States, 1945, Volume VI: The British Commonwealth, the Far East. Washington, DC: Government Printing Office, 1969.

Foreign Relations of the United States, 1946, Volume VIII: The Far East. Washington, DC: Government Printing Office, 1971.

General Headquarters, Supreme Commander, Allied Powers. *Summation of Non-Military Activities in Japan and Korea:* 1945–46.

General Headquarters, US Army Forces, Pacific. Basic Outline Plan for BLACKLIST, August 8, 1945.

Headquarters, United States Forces, Austria. *A Review of Military Government,* January 1, 1947.

————. *United States in Austria: A Review of Civil Affairs.* Washington, DC: Headquarters, Department of the Army, March 31, 1948.

Field Manual 1-02: Operational Terms and Graphics. Washington, DC: Headquarters, Department of the Army, September 2004.

Field Manual 3-0: Operations. Washington, DC: Headquarters, Department of the Army, June 2001.

Field Manual 3-0: Operations. Washington, DC: Headquarters, Department of the Army, 27 February 2008.

Field Manual 100-5: Operations. Washington, DC: Headquarters, Department of the Army, February 1962.

Field Manual 100-5: Operations. Washington, DC: Headquarters, Department of the Army, September 1968.

Field Manual 100-5: Operations. Washington, DC: Headquarters, Department of the Army, July 1976.

Field Manual 100-5: Operations. Washington, DC: Headquarters, Department of the Army, August 1982

Field Manual 100-5: Operations. Washington, DC: Headquarters, Department of the Army, June 1993.

General Orders 100: Instructions for the Government of Armies of the United States in the Field. Washington, DC: War Department, April 24, 1863. Reprinted by the House of Representatives, 43rd Congress, 1st Session, January 24, 1874.

Gillen, J. F. J. *U.S. Military Government in Germany: American Influence on the Development of Political Institutions.* Karlsruhe: Historical Division, US Army European Command, 1950.

Hearings before the Committee on Military Affairs, House of Representatives,

78th Congress, 2nd Session, Part 2, January 21 and 24, 1944. Washington, DC: Government Printing Office, Washington, 1944.

History of the United States Army Military Government in Korea Part I, Period of September 1945–30 June 1946. Seoul: October 1946.

Information Branch, Civil Affairs Division. *The Impact of the War and Japanese Imperialism upon the Economic and Political Rehabilitation of Korea.* January 1947.

Joint Chiefs of Staff. *Joint Publication 3-08: Interorganizational Coordination during Joint Operations.* Washington, DC: June 24, 2011.

Kormann, John. *U.S. Denazification Policy in Germany, 1944–1950.* Bonn: Historical Division, Office of the High Commission for Germany, 1952.

Merrill, Dennis, ed. *Documentary History of the Truman Presidency, Volume 3: U.S. Policy in Germany after World War II: Denazification, Decartelization, Demilitarization, and Democratization.* Bethesda, MD: University Publications of America, 1995.

Monthly Report of the United States Commissioner. Vienna: US Military Government of Austria, November, 1945.

Office of Assistant Chief of Staff, Civil Affairs Division. *Proclamations, Exclusion, Restrictive Orders and Collateral Documents.* San Francisco: Wartime Civil Control Administration, 1942.

Office of the Chief Historian, European Command. *Occupation Forces in Europe Series 1945–1946, Training Packet No. 51.* Frankfurt am Main, Germany: 1947.

———. *Planning for the Occupation of Germany, Special Text 41–10–62.* Frankfurt am Main, Germany: 1947.

Office of the Chief of Staff, Allied Force Headquarters [Allied Mediterranean Command]. *Handbook for Military Government in Austria,* April 1945.

Office of Military Government (Bavaria). Information Control Division. *Trend: A Weekly Report of Political Affairs and Public Opinion,* no. 9, July 25–31, 1946. Munich: Office of Military Government (Bavaria), 1946.

———.*Summary of Activities: Office of Military Government for Bavaria, 1946.* Munich: Office of Military Government (Bavaria), 1946.

———.*Weekly Detachment Reports.* Munich: Office of Military Government (Bavaria), 1945–46.

Office of Military Government, US. *Monthly Reports of the Military Governor.* Berlin: Office of Military Government, US, 1945–46.

———. *US Zone, no. 1, Intelligence and Confidential Annexes,* August 20, 1945.

Office of the Director, Office of Military Government, US. "Consolidation of Military Government," in *Military Government Weekly Information Bulletin,* no. 13, October 20, 1945. Berlin: Office of Military Government, US, 1945.

Political Reorientation of Japan, September 1945 to September 1948. Washington DC: Government Printing Office, 1950.

Romjue, John L. *American Army Doctrine for the Post–Cold War.* Fort Monroe, VA: US Army Training and Doctrine Command, 1996.

Scott, James B., ed. *The Hague Conventions of 1899 (II) and 1907 (IV) Respecting the Laws and Customs of War on Land in The Hague Conventions and Declarations of 1899 and 1907.* New York: Oxford University Press, 1918.

Selected Legal Opinions of the Department of Justice, United States Army Government in Korea, Covering a Period from March 1946 to August 1948. Vol. 1. Buffalo, NY: W.S. Hein, 1976. First published 1948.

Sparrow, John. *History of Personnel Demobilization in the United States Army: DA Pamphlet No. 20–210, July 1952.* Washington, DC: Government Printing Office, 1952.

Supreme Headquarters, Allied Expeditionary Force. *Operation "ECLIPSE": Appreciation and Outline Plan.* November 10, 1944.

———. *Standard Policy and Procedure for Combined Civil Affairs Operations in Northwest Europe,* revised May 1, 1944.

United States Army and Navy Manual of Military Government and Civil Affairs, FM 27-5, and OpNav 50E-3, December 22, 1943. Washington, DC: Government Printing Office, 1943.

U.S. Army Civil Affairs Handbooks: Austria, Army Service Forces Manual, M 36–5, Section 5 Money and Banking. Washington, DC: Government Printing Office, November 1943.

US Army Military Government in Korea. *Report No. 2: Present Agricultural Position of South Korea.* April 1947.

US Department of Defense. *Department of Defense Instruction 3000.05.* September 16, 2009.

US Department of State. *American Policy in Occupied Areas: A Series of Article Reprinted from the Dept of State Bulletin of July 14, 1946, August 18, 1946, February 9, 1947, with Added New Material.* Washington, DC: Government Printing Office, 1947.

———. *Documents on Germany, 1944–1985.* Washington, DC: Government Printing Office, 1985.

———. *The Record on Korean Unification, 1943–1960: Narrative Summary with Principal Documents.* Washington, DC: Government Printing Office, 1960.

US Department of the Army, Civil Affairs Division. *Field Operation of Military Government Units.* Washington, DC: Civil Affairs Division, January 1949.

US Marine Corps. *Small Wars Manual.* Washington DC: Government Printing Office, 1940.

US War Department. *Basic Field Manual: Military Training; FM 21-5,* July 16, 1941. Washington, DC: Government Printing Office, 1941.

———. *Basic Field Manual, Rules of Land Warfare, 1934.* Washington, DC: Government Printing Office, 1934.

———. *Military Government: FM 27-5, July 30, 1940.* Washington, DC: Government Printing Office, 1940.

———. *Rules of Land Warfare: 1914, Corrected to April 15, 1915, Changes 1 and 2.* Washington, DC: Government Printing Office, 1915.

———. *Rules of Land Warfare, FM 27-10, October 1, 1940.* Washington, DC: Government Printing Office, 1940.

Official Website

US Department of State, Office of the Coordinator for Reconstruction and Stabilization. http://www.state.gov/s/crs/what/index.html (accessed October 1, 2010).

Unpublished Official Sources

Basic Manual for Military Government by U.S. Forces. In G1, Report of Committee, No. 6, Subj.: Provost Marshal General's Plan, Military Government, file 1–1935–6. Washington, DC: Army War College, 1934.

Brooke, John R. *Final Report of Major General John R. Brooke, Military Governor, On Civil Matters Concerning the Island of Cuba.* Havana: Headquarters, Division of Cuba, 1899.

Erickson, Edgar L. *An Introduction to American Military Government–Civil Affairs in World War II.* Washington, DC: Office of the Chief of Military History, circa 1946.

Fahey, Daniel H., Jr. Special Consultant to the Secretary of the Army. *Findings, Recommendations, and Conclusions Concerning U.S. Civil Affairs/Military Government Organization.* February 1951.

General Headquarters, US Army Forces, Pacific. *Basic Outline Plan for BLACK-LIST.* August 8, 1945.

History of the 185th Infantry Regiment, 1946.

History of the Civil Affairs Division, War Department, Special Staff, World War II to March 1946. Washington, DC: Office of the Chief of Military History, circa 1946–1947.

King, Archibald. *International Law in Its Bearing on Administration of Civil Affairs by Military Authority in Occupied Territory.* First supplement to *G1, Report of Committee, No. 11, Subj: Administration of Civil Affairs by Military Authority in Occupied Territory.* Washington, DC: Army War College, 1927.

———. *International Law in Its Bearing on Administration of Civil Affairs by Military Authority in Occupied Territory.* Second supplement to *G1, Report of*

Committee, No. 11, Subj: Administration of Civil Affairs by Military Authority in Occupied Territory. Washington, DC: Army War College, 1927.

Sanger, Quentin M. *Administrative History of the Foreign Economic Administration and Predecessor Agencies.* Washington, DC: Office of the Historian, Foreign Economic Administration, June 15, 1946.

Statistical Research Division of the Office of Administration Headquarters, US American Military Government in Korea. *History of United States Army Military Government in Korea, Part I: Period of September 1945–30 June 1946.* October 1946.

United States Army, Western Defense Command. *History of the Western Defense Command.* September–October 1945.

US Army General Staff, G1. *Report of Committee, No. 6, Subj.: The Interest of G-1 in Civil Affairs.* Washington, DC: Army War College, 1924.

———. *Report of Committee, No. 3, Subj.: Contributions by G-1 to the Various War Plans: Duties of G-1 at GHQ and on Higher Staffs; Problems of G-1 in War Games, Maneuvers and on Reconnaissance; Staff Administration of Civil Affairs in Occupied Territory.* Washington, DC: Army War College, 1925.

———. *Report of Committee, No. 5, Subj.: Administration of Civil Affairs in Occupied Territory, Enemy Aliens, Prisoners of War, Draft Deserters, and Conscientious Objectors.* Washington, DC: Army War College, 1931.

———. *Report of Committee, No. 6, Subj.: Provost Marshal General's Plan, Military Government.* Washington, DC: Army War College, 1934.

———. *Report of Committee, No. 7, Subj.: Military Government, Handling of Enemy Aliens, Prisoners of War, Draft Deserters and Conscientious Objectors.* Washington, DC: Army War College, 1937.

———. *Report of Committee, No. 11, Subj.: Administration of Civil Affairs by Military Authority in Occupied Territory.* Washington, DC: Army War College, 1927.

Cases

Hirabayashi v. United States, 320 U.S. 81 (1943).
Korematsu v. United States, 323 U.S. 214 (1944).

Secondary Sources

Books

Abbott, Andrew. *The System of Professions: An Essay on the Division of Expert Labor.* Chicago: University of Chicago Press, 1988.

———. *Time Matters: On Theory and Method.* Chicago: University of Chicago Press, 2001.

Abrahamson, James. *America Arms for a New Century: The Making of a Great Military Power*. New York: Free Press, 1981.

Acheson, Dean. *Present at the Creation: My Years in the State Department*. New York: Norton, 1969.

Allen, Henry T. *The Rhineland Occupation*. Indianapolis: Bobbs-Merrill, 1927.

Ambrose, Steven. *Eisenhower*. New York: Simon & Schuster, 1983.

———. *Eisenhower and Berlin, 1945: The Decision to Halt at the Elbe*. New York: Norton, 1967.

Anthony, J. Garner. *Hawaii under Army Rule*. Stanford, CA: Stanford University Press, 1955.

The Army Lawyer: A History of the Judge Advocate General's Corps, 1775–1975. Washington, DC: Government Printing Office, 1975.

Bach, Julian. *America's Germany: An Account of the Occupation*. New York: Random House, 1946.

Ball, Harry P. *Of Responsible Command: A History of the U.S. Army War College*. Carlisle, PA: Alumni Association of the US Army War College, 1984.

Barr, Ronald J. *The Progressive Army: U.S. Army Command and Administration, 1870–1914*. London: Macmillan, 1998.

Bensahel, Nora, Olga Oliker, Keith Crane, Rick Brennan Jr., Heather S. Gregg, Thomas Sullivan, and Andrew Rathmell. *After Saddam: Prewar Planning and the Occupation of Iraq*. Santa Monica, CA: RAND Corp., 2008.

Beschloss, Michael. *The Conquerors: Roosevelt, Truman and the Destruction of Hitler's Germany, 1941–1945*. New York: Simon & Schuster, 2002.

Bessel, Richard. *Germany 1945: From War to Peace*. New York: Harper Perennial, 2009.

Best, Geoffrey. *Humanity in Warfare*. London: Weidenfeld & Nicolson, 1980.

Betts, Richard, and Leslie Gelb. *The Irony of Vietnam: The System Worked*. Washington, DC: Brookings Institution Press, 1979.

Bickel, Keith. *Mars Learning: The Marine Corps' Development of Small Wars Doctrine, 1915–1940*. Boulder, CO: Westview, 2001.

Biddle, Francis. *In Brief Authority*. Garden City, NY: Doubleday, 1962.

Bird, Kai. *The Chairman: John J. McCloy and the Making of the America Establishment*. New York: Simon & Schuster, 1992.

Birkhimer, William E. *Military Government and Martial Law*. Washington, DC: James J. Chapman, 1892.

Bischof, Gunter, Anton Pelinka, and Dieter Stiefel, eds. *The Marshall Plan in Austria*. Contemporary Austrian Studies, vol. 8. New Brunswick, NJ: Transaction, 2000.

———. *Neutrality in Austria*. Contemporary Austrian Studies, vol. 9. New Brunswick, NJ: Transaction Publications, 2001.

Blumenson, Martin. *Mark Clark*. New York: Congdon & Weed, 1984.

Boehling, Rebecca. *A Question of Priorities: Democratic Reform and Economic Recovery in Postwar Germany*. Providence, RI: Berghahn Books, 1996.

Boot, Max. *The Savage Wars of Peace: Small Wars and the Rise of American Power*. New York: Basic Books, 2002.

Bourne, Randolph. *War and the Intellectuals: Collected Essays, 1915–1919*. Edited with an introduction by Carl Resek. Indianapolis and Cambridge: Hackett, 1999. First published by Harper & Row, 1964.

Burns, James MacGregor. *Roosevelt: The Soldier of Freedom*. New York: Harcourt, Brace, 1970.

Byrnes, James F. *Speaking Frankly*. New York: Harper, 1947.

Cameron, Kim S., and Robert E. Quinn. *Diagnosing and Changing Organizational Culture*. Reading, PA: Addison-Wesley, 1999.

Cameron, Robert S. *Mobility, Shock, and Firepower: The Emergence of the U.S. Army's Armor Branch, 1917–1945*. Washington, DC: Center of Military History, 2008.

Carafano, James J. *Waltzing into the Cold War: The Struggle for Occupied Austria*. College Station: Texas A&M Press, 2002.

Carr-Saunders, A. M., and P. A. Wilson. *The Professions*. London: Frank Cass, 1964. First published 1933.

Clark, Mark. *Calculated Risk*. New York: Harper & Brothers, 1950.

———. *From the Danube to the Yalu*. New York: Harper & Brothers, 1954.

Clay, Lucius. *Decision in Germany*. New York: Doubleday, 1950.

———. *The Papers of Lucius D. Clay: Germany, 1945–1949*. Vol. 1. Edited by Jean Edward Smith. Bloomington: Indiana University Press, 1988.

Cline, Ray S. *Washington Command Post: The Operations Division*. Washington, DC: Center of Military History, 1951.

Coffman, Edward M. *The Regulars: The American Army, 1898–1941*. Cambridge, MA: Harvard University Press, 2004.

Coles, Harry L., and Albert K. Weinberg, eds. *Civil Affairs: Soldiers Become Governors*. Washington, DC: Center of Military History, 1964.

Colson, Bruno. *La culture strategique américaine: L'influence de Jomini*. Paris: FEDN, Economica, 1993.

Conklin, Jeffrey. *Dialogue Mapping: Building Shared Understanding of Wicked Problems*. Chichester, UK: John Wiley & Sons, 2005.

Conroy, Hilary. *The Japanese Seizure of Korea, 1868–1910: A Study of Realism and Idealism in International Relations*. Philadelphia: University of Pennsylvania Press, 1960.

Cronin, Audrey, and Kurth Cronin. *Great Power Politics and the Struggle over Austria, 1945–1955*. Ithaca, NY: Cornell University Press, 1986.

Culver, John C., and John Hyde. *American Dreamer: A Life of Henry A. Wallace*. New York: Norton, 2001.

Cumings, Bruce. *The Origins of the Korean War*. Vols. 1 and 2. Princeton, NJ: Princeton University Press, 1981, 1990.

Dallek, Robert. *Franklin D. Roosevelt and American Foreign Policy, 1932–1945*. New York: Oxford University Press, 1995.

Davis, George B. *The Elements of International Law*. New York: Harper & Brothers, 1908.

Davis, Kenneth S. *FDR: The War President, 1940–1943*. New York: Random House, 2000.

Dennett, Raymond, and Robert K. Turner, eds. *Documents on American Foreign Relations: Vol. VIII, July 1, 1945–December 31, 1945*. Norwood, MA: Norwood Press, 1948.

Desch, Michael C. *Civilian Control of the Military: The Changing Security Environment*. Baltimore: Johns Hopkins University Press, 1999.

Dobbins, James, John G. McGinn, Keith Crane, Seth G. Jones, Rollie Lal, Andrew Rathmell, Rachel M. Swanger, and Anga R. Timilsina. *America's Role in Nation Building from Germany to Iraq*. Santa Monica, CA: RAND Corp., 2003.

Donnison, F. S. V. *Civil Affairs and Military Government Central Organization and Planning*. London: Her Majesty's Stationery Office, 1966.

Dorstal, Robert J., ed. *The Cambridge Companion to Gadamer*. New York: Cambridge University Press, 2002.

Douglas, Mary. *How Institutions Think*. Syracuse, NY: Syracuse University Press, 1986.

Dower, John. *Embracing Defeat: Japan in the Wake of World War II*. New York: Norton, 1999.

Echevarria, Antulio J., II. *Toward an American Way of War*. Carlisle, PA: Strategic Studies Institute, 2004.

Edelstein, David M. *Occupational Hazards: Success and Failure in Military Occupation*. Ithaca, NY: Cornell University Press, 2008.

Eisenberg, Carolyn. *Drawing the Line: The American Decision to Divide Germany, 1944–1949*. Cambridge: Cambridge University Press, 1996.

Eisenhower, Dwight D. *Crusade in Europe*. Garden City, NY: Doubleday, 1948.

———. *The Eisenhower Diaries*. Edited by Robert Ferrell. New York: Norton, 1981.

———. *The Papers of Dwight David Eisenhower*, vol. 2. Edited by Alfred D. Chandler. Baltimore and London: Johns Hopkins University Press, 1970.

Feis, Herbert. *Between War and Peace: The Potsdam Conference*. Westport, CT: Greenwood, 1960.

———. *Churchill, Roosevelt, Stalin: The War They Waged and the Peace They Sought.* Princeton, NJ: Princeton University Press, 1957.

Fisch, Arnold G. *Military Government in the Ryukyu Islands, 1945–1950.* Washington, DC: Center of Military History, 1988.

Fitzpatrick, George, et al. *A Survey of the Experiences and Opinions of U.S. Military Government Officers in World War II.* Chevy Chase, MD: Operations Research Office, Johns Hopkins University, 1956.

Fleming, Thomas. *The New Dealers' War: Franklin D. Roosevelt and the War within World War II.* New York: Basic Books, 2001.

Fraenkel, Ernest. *Military Occupation and the Rule of Law: Occupation Government in the Rhineland, 1918–1923.* New York: Oxford University Press, 1944.

Franks, Tommy. *American Soldier.* New York: HarperCollins, 2004.

Friedel, Frank. *FDR: Rendezvous with Destiny.* New York: Little, Brown, 1990.

———. *Francis Lieber: Nineteenth Century Liberal.* Gloucester, MA: Peter Smith, 1968. First published 1947.

Friedrich, Carl J. *American Experiences in Military Government in World War II.* New York: Rinehart & Sons, 1948.

Gadamer, Hans-Georg. *Philosophical Hermeneutics.* Translated and edited by David E. Linge. Berkeley: University of California Press, 1976.

———. *Truth and Method,* 2nd rev. ed. Translated by Joel Weinsheimer and Donald Marshall. New York: Continuum, 1989.

Gaddis, John Lewis. *The Cold War: A New History.* New York: Penguin, 2005.

———. *Strategies of Containment: A Critical Appraisal of Postwar American National Security.* New York: Oxford University Press, 1982.

———. *The United States and the Origins of the Cold War, 1941–1947.* New York: Columbia University Press, 1972.

———. *We Now Know: Rethinking Cold War History.* Oxford: Oxford University Press, 1997.

Galambos, Louis, ed. *The New American State: Bureaucracies and Policies after World War II.* Baltimore: Johns Hopkins University Press, 1987.

Galula, David. *Pacification in Algeria, 1956–1958.* Santa Monica, CA: RAND Corp., 2006. First published 1963.

Gardner, Lloyd C. *Spheres of Influence: The Great Powers Partition Europe, from Munich to Yalta.* Chicago: Ivan Dee, 1993.

Gentile, Gian. *Wrong Turn: America's Deadly Embrace of Counterinsurgency.* New York: New Press, 2013.

Geffen, William, ed. *Command and Commanders in Modern Warfare: Proceedings of the Second Military History Symposium, United States Air Force Academy, 2–3 May 1968.* Washington, DC: Office of Air Force History, Headquarters, United States Air Force, 1971.

Gilbert, Martin. *Churchill: A Life.* New York: Henry Holt, 1991.

Gimbel, John. *The American Occupation of Germany: Politics and the Military, 1945–1949.* Stanford, CA: Stanford University Press, 1968.

Glenn, Garrard. *The Army and the Law.* Revised by A. Arthur Schiller. New York: Columbia University Press, 1943.

Gole, Henry G. *The Road to Rainbow: Army Planning for Global War, 1934–1940.* Annapolis, MD: Naval Institute Press, 2003.

Green, Daniel M., ed. *Constructivism and Comparative Politics.* London: M. E. Sharpe, 2001.

Greenfield, Kent Roberts. *American Strategy in World War II: A Reconsideration.* Westport, CT: Greenwood, 1979. First published 1963.

Grimsley, Mark. *The Hard Hand of War: Union Military Policy toward Southern Civilians, 1861–1865.* Cambridge: Cambridge University Press, 1995.

Ham, Pyung-choon. *The Korean Political Tradition and Law: Essays in Korean Law and Legal History.* Seoul: Royal Asiatic Society, Korea Branch, 1967.

Hartigan, Richard Shelly. *Lieber's Code and the Law of War.* Chicago: Precedent, 1983.

Hartmann, Frederick H. *Germany between East and West: The Reunification Problem.* Englewood Cliffs, NJ: Prentice-Hall, 1965.

Harwood, Bruce. *Bremerhaven: A Memoir of Germany, 1945–1947.* Self-published, 2010.

Hastings, Max. *Armageddon: The Battle for Germany, 1944–1945.* New York: Vintage Books, 2005.

Herf, Jeffrey. *Divided Memory: The Nazi Past in Two Germanys.* Cambridge, MA: Harvard University Press, 1997.

Hewes, James E., Jr. *From Root to McNamara: Army Organization and Administration, 1900–1963.* Washington, DC: Center of Military History, 1975.

Hoag, C. Leonard. *American Military Government in Korea: War Policy and the First Year of Occupation, 1941–1946.* Washington, DC: Office of the Chief of Military History, 1970.

Holborn, Hajo. *American Military Government: Its Organization and Policies.* Washington, DC: Infantry Journal Press, 1947.

Howe, George F. *Northwest Africa: Seizing the Initiative in the West (United States Army in World War II, Mediterranean Theater of Operations).* Washington, DC: Center of Military History, 1985.

Hull, Cordell. *The Memoirs of Cordell Hull,* vol. 2. New York: Macmillan, 1948.

Hull, Isabel. *Absolute Destruction: Military Culture and the Practices of War in Imperial Germany.* Ithaca, NY: Cornell University Press, 2005.

Huntington, Samuel P. *The Soldier and the State: The Theory and Politics of Civil-Military Relations.* New York: Vintage, 1957.

Hyland, William G. *The Cold War: Fifty Years of Conflict*. New York: Random House, 1991.

Ickes, Harold L. *The Autobiography of a Curmudgeon*. New York: Reynal & Hitchcock, 1943.

Isaacson, Walter, and Evan Thomas. *The Wise Men: Six Friends and the World They Made*. New York: Simon & Schuster, 1986.

Janowitz, Morris. *The Professional Soldier: A Social and Political Portrait*. New York: Free Press, 1960.

Jarausch, Konrad J. *After Hitler: Recivilizing Germans, 1945–1995*. Oxford: Oxford University Press, 2006.

Kahn, Arthur D. *Experiment in Occupation: Witness to the Turnabout: Anti-Nazi War to Cold War, 1944–1946*. University Park: Pennsylvania State University Press, 2004.

Karsten, Peter, ed. *The Military in Society: A Collection of Essays*. New York: Garland, 1998.

Katzenstein, Paul J., ed. *The Culture of National Security*. New York: Columbia University Press, 1996.

Kelly, Justin, and Mike Brennan. *Alien: How Operational Art Devoured Strategy*. Carlisle, PA: Strategic Studies Institute, 2009.

Kennan, George. *American Diplomacy*. Rev. ed. Chicago: University of Chicago Press, 1984.

———. *Memoirs, 1925–1950*. New York: Pantheon, 1967.

Kennedy, David M. *Freedom from Fear: The American People in Depression and War, 1929–1945*. New York: Oxford University Press, 1999.

Keohane, Robert O. *After Hegemony: Cooperation and Discord in the World Economy*. Princeton, NJ: Princeton University Press, 1984.

Kershaw, Ian. *The End: The Defiance and Destruction of Hitler's Germany*. New York: Penguin, 2011.

Kier, Elizabeth. *Imagining War: French and British Military Doctrine between the Wars*. Princeton, NJ: Princeton University Press, 1997.

Kim, Eugene, and Han-kyo Kim. *Korea and the Politics of Imperialism, 1876–1910*. Berkeley: University of California Press, 1967.

Kim, Eugene, and Dorathea E. Mortimore, eds. *Korea's Response to Japan: The Colonial Period, 1910–1945*. Kalamazoo: Center for Korean Studies, Western Michigan University, 1975.

Kissinger, Henry, ed. *Problems of National Security*. New York: Praeger, 1965.

Kohn, Richard H., ed. *The United States Military under the Constitution of the United States, 1789–1989*. New York: New York University Press, 1991.

Koistinen, Paul A. C. *Arsenal of World War II: The Political Economy of American Warfare, 1940–1945*. Lawrence: University Press of Kansas, 2004.

Komer, Robert W. *Bureaucracy Does Its Thing: Institutional Constraints on US-GVN Performance in Vietnam; Report Prepared for Defense Advanced Research Projects Agency, DARPA Order No. 189–1.* Santa Monica, CA: RAND Corp., 1972.

———. *Organization and Management of the "New Model" Pacification Program, 1966–1969.* Santa Monica, CA: RAND Corp., 1970.

Kreger, Edward A., ed. *Cases on Martial Law.* Fort Leavenworth, KS: Army Service Schools, 1910.

Kretchik, Walter E. *U.S. Army Doctrine: From the American Revolution to the War on Terror.* Lawrence: University Press of Kansas, 2011.

Kuklick, Bruce. *Blind Oracles: Intellectuals and War from Kennan to Kissinger.* Princeton, NJ: Princeton University Press, 2006.

Lake, David A. *Entangling Relations: American Foreign Policy in Its Century.* Princeton, NJ: Princeton University Press, 1999.

Larrabee, Eric. *Commander in Chief: Franklin Delano Roosevelt, His Lieutenants, and Their Wars.* New York: Simon & Schuster, 1987.

Lee, Jongsoo James. *The Partition of Korea after World War II: A Global History.* Palgrave Macmillan: New York, 2006.

Leffler, Melvyn. *For the Soul of Mankind: The United States, the Soviet Union, and the Cold War.* New York: Hill & Wang, 2007.

———. *A Preponderance of Power: National Security, the Truman Administration and the Cold War.* Palo Alto, CA: Stanford University Press, 1992.

Lejeune, John A. *The Reminiscences of a Marine.* Philadelphia: Dorrance, 1930.

Linn, Brian McAllister. *The Echo of Battle: The Army's Way of War.* Cambridge, MA: Harvard University Press, 2007.

Lukacs, John, and George F. Kennan. *George F. Kennan and the Origins of Containment, 1944–1946: The Kennan-Lukacs Correspondence.* Columbia: University of Missouri Press, 1997.

Luther, Kurt Richard, and Peter Pulzer, eds. *Austria 1945–1995: Fifty Years of the Second Republic.* Aldershot, UK: Ashgate, 1998.

MacArthur, Douglas. *Reminiscences.* New York: McGraw Hill, 1964.

MacIntyre, Alasdair. *Three Rival Versions of Moral Inquiry: Encyclopaedia, Genealogy, and Tradition.* Notre Dame, IN: University of Notre Dame Press, 1990.

———. *Whose Justice? Which Rationality?* Notre Dame, IN: University of Notre Dame Press, 1988.

Magoon, Charles E. *The Law of Civil Government in Territory Subject to Military Occupation by the Military Forces of the United States.* Washington, DC: Government Printing Office, 1902.

Mahoney, James, and Dietrich Rueschemeyer, eds. *Comparative Historical Analysis in the Social Sciences.* Cambridge: Cambridge University Press, 2003.

Marshall, George. *The Papers of George C. Marshall.* Vol. 5, January 1, 1945–January 7, 1947. Edited by Forrest Pogue. Baltimore and London: Johns Hopkins University Press, 2003.

McAllister, James. *No Exit: America and the German Problem, 1943–1954.* Ithaca, NY: Cornell University Press, 2002.

McCloy, John J. *The Challenges to American Foreign Policy.* Cambridge, MA: Harvard University Press, 1953.

McSweeney, Bill. *Security, Identity, and Interests.* Cambridge: Cambridge University Press, 2000.

Meade, E. Grant. *American Military Government in Korea.* New York: King's Crown Press, 1951.

Melzer, Yehuda. *Concepts of Just War.* Leyden: A. W. Sitjhoff, 1975.

Merritt, Richard. *Democracy Imposed: U.S. Occupation Policy and the German Public, 1945–1949.* New Haven: Yale University Press, 1995.

Millett, Allan R. *The War for Korea, 1945–1950: A House Burning.* Lawrence: University Press of Kansas, 2005.

Millett, Allan R., and Peter Maslowski. *For the Common Defense: A Military History of the United States of America.* New York: Free Press, 1994.

Mills, C. Wright. *The Power Elite.* New York: Oxford University Press, 1956.

Morgenthau, Henry, Jr. *Germany Is Our Problem.* New York and London: Harper & Brothers, 1945.

Müller, Werner. *Contesting Democracy: Political Idea in Twentieth Century Europe.* New Haven: Yale University Press, 2011.

Murphy, Robert. *Diplomat among Warriors.* Garden City, NY: Doubleday, 1964.

Nelson, Otto L., Jr. *National Security and the General Staff.* Washington, DC: Infantry Journal Press, 1946.

Nenninger, Timothy K. *The Leavenworth Schools and the Old Army: Education, Professionalism, and the Officer Corps of the United States Army, 1881–1918.* Westport, CT: Greenwood, 1978.

Ney, Virgil. *Evolution of the United States Army Field Manual: Valley Forge to Vietnam.* Combat Operations Research Group (CORG) Memorandum. Fort Belvoir, VA: US Army Combat Developments Command, 1966.

Nuzum, Henry. *Shades of "CORDS" in the Kush.* Carlisle, PA: Strategic Studies Institute, 2010.

Offner, Arnold A., and Theodore A. Wilson, eds. *Victory in Europe: 1945: From World War to Cold War.* Lawrence: University Press of Kansas, 2000.

Oh, Bonnie, ed. *Korea under the American Military Government, 1945–48.* Westport, CT: Praeger, 2002.

Orr, Robert C., ed. *Winning the Peace: An American Strategy for Post-Conflict Reconstruction.* Washington, DC: Center for Strategic and International Studies, 2004.

Padover, Saul K. *Experiment in Germany: The Story of an American Intelligence Officer.* New York: Duell, Sloan & Pearce, 1946.

Painter, David S. *The Cold War: An International History.* London: Routledge, 1999.

Pappas, George S. *Prudens Futuri: The U.S. Army War College, 1901–1967.* Carlisle Barracks, PA: Alumni Association of the US Army War College, 1967.

Parrish, Thomas. *Roosevelt and Marshall: Partners in Politics and War: The Personal Story.* New York: William Morrow, 1989.

Pawley, Margaret. *The Watch on the Rhine: The Military Occupation of the Rhineland.* London: I. B. Tauris, 2007.

Perito, Robert M. *Guide for Participants in Peace, Stability, and Relief Operations.* Washington, DC: United States Institute of Peace, 2007.

Perret, Geoffrey. *There's a War to Be Won: The United States Army in World War II.* New York: Ballantine, 1991.

Perry, Thomas Sergeant, ed. *The Life and Letters of Francis Lieber.* London: Trübner, 1882.

Peterson, Edward. *The American Occupation of Germany: Retreat to Victory.* Detroit: Wayne State University Press, 1977.

Plokhy, S. M. *Yalta: The Price of Peace.* New York: Viking, 2010.

Pogue, Forrest. *George C. Marshall: Organizer of Victory, 1943–45.* New York: Viking, 1973.

Porter, John Biddle. *The Geneva and the Hague Conventions: A Lecture Delivered to the Field Service School for Medical Officers, Class of 1914.* Fort Leavenworth, KS: Press of the Army Service Schools, 1914.

Posen, Barry R. *The Sources of Military Doctrine: France, Britain, and Germany between the World Wars.* Ithaca, NY: Cornell University Press, 1984.

Powell, Walter W., and Paul J. DiMaggio, eds. *The New Institutionalism in Organizational Analysis.* Chicago: University of Chicago Press, 1991.

Prados, John. *Vietnam: The History of an Unwinnable War.* Lawrence: University Press of Kansas, 2010.

Record, Jeffrey. *Beating Goliath: Why Insurgencies Win.* Washington, DC: Potomac Books, 2009.

Roberts, Andrew. *Masters and Commanders: How Four Titans Won the War in the West, 1941–1945.* New York: HarperCollins, 2009.

Robinson, Greg. *By Order of the President: FDR and the Internment of Japanese-Americans.* Cambridge, MA: Harvard University Press, 2001.

Rusk, Dean. *As I Saw It.* As told to Richard Rusk. New York: Norton, 1990.

Rynning, Sten. *Changing Military Doctrine: Presidents and Military Power in Fifth Republic France, 1958–2000.* Westport, CT: Praeger, 2002.

Schaeffer, Robert. *Warpaths: The Politics of Partition.* New York: Hill & Wang, 1990.

Schaller, Michael. *The American Occupation of Japan: The Origins of the Cold War in Asia*. Oxford: Oxford University Press, 1985.

Schein, Edward. *The Corporate Culture Survival Guide*. San Francisco: Jossey-Bass, 1999.

———. *Organizational Culture and Leadership*. 3rd ed. San Francisco: Jossey-Bass, 2004.

Schmitt, Hans A., ed. *U.S. Occupation in Europe after World War II*. Lawrence: Regents Press of Kansas, 1978.

Schmitz, David F. *Henry L. Stimson: The First Wise Man*. Wilmington, DE: Scholarly Resources, 2001.

Schwartz, Thomas A. *America's Germany: John J. McCloy and the Federal Republic of Germany*. Cambridge, MA: Harvard University Press, 1991.

Scott, W. Richard. *Institutions and Organizations*. New York: Sage Publications, 2000.

Sherry, Michael. *In the Shadow of War: The United States since the 1930s*. New Haven: Yale University Press, 1995.

———. *Preparing for the Next War: American Plans for Postwar Defense, 1941–45*. New Haven: Yale University Press, 1977.

Skowronek, Stephen. *Building a New American State: The Expansion of National Administrative Capacities, 1877–1920*. Cambridge: Cambridge University Press, 1982.

Smith, H. A. *Military Government*. Fort Leavenworth, KS: General Service Schools, General Staff School, 1920.

Smith, Jean Edward. *Lucius D. Clay: An American Life*. New York: Henry Holt, 1990.

Snider, Don M., project director, and Lloyd J. Matthews, ed. *The Future of the Army Profession*, 2nd ed. Boston: McGraw Hill, 2005.

Spector, Ronald. *After Tet: The Bloodiest Year in Vietnam*. New York: Vintage, 1994.

Speier, Hans. *From the Ashes of Disgrace: A Journal from Germany*. Amherst: University of Massachusetts Press, 1981.

Stearman, William Lloyd. *The Soviet Union and the Occupation of Austria*. Bonn: Siegler, 1964.

Stever, James A. *The End of Public Administration: Problems of the Profession in the Post-Progressive Era*. Dobbs Ferry, NY: Transnational, 1988.

Stimson, Henry L. *American Foreign Policy and the Spanish Situation*. New York University Contemporary Law Pamphlets, series 1, 1939.

Stimson, Henry L., and McGeorge Bundy. *On Active Service in Peace and War*. New York: Harper & Brothers, 1948.

Stoler, Mark A. *Allies and Adversaries: The Joint Chiefs of Staff, the Grand Alliance, and U.S. Strategy in World War II*. Chapel Hill: University of North Carolina Press, 2000.

Stolzenbach, C. Darwin, and Henry Kissinger. *Civil Affairs in Korea, 1950–51.* Chevy Chase, MD: Johns Hopkins University Press, 1952.

Stueck, William. *The Korean War: An International History.* Princeton, NJ: Princeton University Press, 1995.

———. *Rethinking the Korean War: A New Diplomatic and Strategic History.* Princeton, NJ: Princeton University Press, 2002.

Taylor, Charles. *Dilemmas and Connections.* Cambridge, MA: Harvard University Press, 2011.

Taylor, Frederick. *Exorcising Hitler: The Occupation and Denazification of Germany.* New York: Bloomsbury, 2011.

Tierney, John J., Jr. *Chasing Ghosts: Unconventional Warfare in American History.* Washington, DC: Potomac Books, 2006.

Truman, Harry S. *Memoirs.* Vol. 1. New York: Doubleday, 1955.

———. *Off the Record: The Private Papers of Harry S. Truman.* Edited by Robert H. Ferrell. New York: Harper & Row, 1980.

The U.S. Army / Marine Corps Counterinsurgency Field Manual: U.S. Army Field Manual 3-24. Chi ago: University of Chicago Press, 2007.

Wallace, Henry. *The Price of Vision: The Diary of Henry Wallace, 1942–1946.* Edited by John Morton Blum. Boston: Houghton Mifflin, 1973.

Waltz, Kenneth N. *Theory of International Politics.* Reading, MA: Addison-Wesley, 1979.

Weber, Max. *Political Writings.* Edited by Peter Lassman and Ronald Speirs. Cambridge: Cambridge University Press, 1994.

———. *The Theory of Social and Economic Organization.* Edited by Talcott Parsons. Translated by A. M. Henderson and Talcott Parsons. New York: Free Press, 1947.

Weigley, Russell. *The American Way of War: A History of United States Military Strategy and Policy.* Bloomington: Indiana University Press, 1973.

———. *History of the United States Army.* New York: Macmillan, 1967.

Weiss, Stuart L. *The President's Man: Leo Crowley and Franklin Roosevelt in Peace and War.* Carbondale: Southern Illinois University Press, 1996.

Wells, Donald A. *The Rules of Land Warfare: A Guide to the U.S. Army Manuals.* Westport, CT: Greenwood, 1992.

Wendt, Alexander. *Social Theory of International Politics.* Cambridge: Cambridge University Press, 1999.

West, Bing. *The Strongest Tribe: War, Politics, and the Endgame in Iraq.* New York: Random House, 2008.

Whitnah, Donald R., and Edgar L. Erickson. *The American Occupation of Austria: Planning and Early Years.* Westport, CT: Greenwood, 1985.

Whitnah, Donald R., and Florentine E. Whitnah. *Salzburg under Siege: U.S. Occupation, 1945–1955.* New York: Greenwood, 1991.

Wiener, Frederick Bernays. *A Practical Manual of Martial Law*. Harrisburg, PA: Military Service Publishing Co., 1940.

Wolfe, Robert, ed. *Americans as Proconsuls: United States Military Government in Germany and Japan, 1944–1952*. Carbondale: Southern Illinois University Press, 1984.

Wood, Leonard. *The Military Obligation of Citizenship*. Princeton, NJ: Princeton University Press, 1915.

Zaalberg, Thijs W. Brocades. *Soldiers and Civil Power: Supporting or Substituting Civil Authorities in Modern Peace Operations*. Amsterdam: Amsterdam University Press, 2006.

Ziemke, Earl. *The U.S. Army in the Occupation of Germany, 1944–46*. Washington, DC: Center of Military History, 1975.

Zink, Harold. *American Military Government in Germany*. New York: Macmillan, 1947.

Articles

Bellamy, Paul. "A Trip through Hell: A Series of Articles Containing Observations on a Recent Trip through Central Europe." *Cleveland Plain Dealer,* 1946.

Berdahl, Clarence A. "The United States and the League of Nations." *Michigan Law Review* 26 (April 1929): 607–36.

Davison, Ketti. "From Tactical Planning to Operational Design." *Military Review* (September–October 2008): 33–39.

Erickson, Edgar. "The Zoning of Austria." *Annals of the American Academy of Political and Social Science* (January 1950): 106–13.

Fairman, Charles. "The Law of Martial Rule and the National Emergency." *Harvard Law Review* 55, no. 8 (June 1942): 1253–1302.

"Foreign News: Not Slave, Not Free." *Time,* October 8, 1945.

Franklin, William M. "Zonal Boundaries and Access to Berlin." *World Politics* 16 (October 1963): 1–31.

Gabriel, Ralph H. "American Experience with Military Government." *American Historical Review* 49 (July 1944): 632–36.

Grafton, Carl. "The Reorganization of Federal Agencies." *Administration and Society* 10, no. 4 (February 1979): 437–64.

Grey, Arthur L., Jr. "The Thirty-Eighth Parallel." *Foreign Affairs* 29, no. 3 (April 1951): 482–87.

Gunn, Damon M. "The Civil Affairs Detachment." *Military Review* (September 1945): 75–78.

Hayashi, Nobuo. "Contextualizing Military Necessity." *Emory International Law Review* 27 (2013): 189–283.

Hayward, Edwin J. "Co-ordination of Military and Civilian Civil Affairs Planning." *Annals of the American Academy of Political and Social Science* (January 1950): 19–27.

Jones, Frank L. "Blowtorch: Robert Komer and the Making of Vietnam Pacification Policy." *Parameters* 35 (Autumn 2005): 103–18.

Kagan, Frederick. "Army Doctrine and Modern War: Notes toward a New Edition of *FM 100-5*." *Parameters* 37 (Spring 1997): 134–51.

Kuklick, Bruce. "The Genesis of the European Advisory Commission." *Journal of Contemporary History* 4 (October 1969): 189–201.

McCune, George M. "Korea: The First Year of Liberation." *Pacific Affairs* 20, no. 1 (March 1947): 3–17.

McCune, Shannon. "The Thirty-Eighth Parallel in Korea." *World Politics* 2 (January 1949): 223–32.

Miewald, Robert D. "Weberian Bureaucracy and the Military Model." *Public Administration Review* 30 (March–April 1970): 129–33.

Mommsen, Wolfgang. "Max Weber's Political Sociology and His Philosophy of History." *International Social Science Journal* 17 (1965): 23–45.

Mosely, Philip. "The Occupation of Germany: New Light on How the Zones Were Drawn." *Foreign Affairs* 28 (July 1950): 580–604.

Motherwell, Hiram. "Military Occupation, and Then What?" *Harper's,* October 1943.

Naveh, Shimon. Interview by Matt Matthews, November 1, 2007, in *Operational Leadership Experience*. Fort Leavenworth, KS: Combat Studies Institute, 2007.

Rathmell, Andrew. "Planning Post-conflict Reconstruction in Iraq: What Can We Learn?" *International Affairs* 81 (2005), 1013–38.

Rogers, Daniel E. "Transforming the German Party System: The United States and the Origins of Political Moderation, 1945–1949." *Journal of Modern History* 65 (1993): 512–41.

Schmitt, J. F. "A Systemic Concept for Operational Design." 2006. http://www.au.af.mil/au/awc/awcgate/usmc/mcwl_schmitt_op_design.pdf.

Shils, Edward A., and Morris Janowitz. "Cohesion and Disintegration in the Wehrmacht in World War II." *Public Opinion Quarterly* 12 (1948): 280–315.

Stevens, Donald G. "Organizing for Economic Defense: Henry Wallace and the Board of Economic Warfare's Policy Initiatives, 1942." *Presidential Studies Quarterly* 26 (Fall 1996): 1126–39.

Stever, James A. "The Glass Firewall between Military and Civil Administration." *Administration and Society* 31 (March 1999): 28–49.

Stoler, Mark. "U.S. Civil-Military Relations in World War II." *Parameters* 21, no. 3 (Autumn 1991): 60–73.

Taylor, Philip H. "The Administration of Occupied Japan." *Annals of the American Academy of Political and Social Science* 267 (January 1950): 140–53.

Vego, Milan. "A Case against Systemic Operational Design." *Joint Force Quarterly* 53 (2nd Quarter 2009): 69–75.

Vernon, E. H. "Civil Affairs and Military Government." *Military Review* (January 1946): 25–32.

Wass de Czege, Huba. "Systemic Operational Design: Learning and Adapting in Complex Missions." *Military Review* (January–February 2009): 2–12.

"We Come as Conquerors." *Army Talks* 2, no. 7 (February 17, 1945): 1–4.

Unpublished Manuscripts and Dissertations

Adams, Thomas K. "Military Doctrine and the Organizational Culture of the United States Army." PhD diss., Syracuse University, 1990.

Allen, Dan. "Franklin D. Roosevelt and the Development of American Occupation Policy in Europe." PhD diss., Ohio State University, 1976.

Allsep, L. Michael, Jr. "New Forms of Dominance: How a Corporate Lawyer Created the American Military Establishment." PhD diss., University of North Carolina, 2008.

Brickman, James F. "The Development of the American General Staff: 1880–1920." US Army War College Military Studies Program Paper, 1993.

Brown, Ralph W, III. "A Cold War Army of Occupation? The U.S. Army in Vienna, 1945–1948." PhD diss., University of Tennessee, Knoxville, 1995.

Chung, Manduk. "The United States in Korea: A Reluctant Participant, 1945–1948." PhD diss., Michigan State University, 1975.

Dastrup, Boyd L. "U.S. Military Occupation of Nuremberg, 1945–49." PhD diss., Kansas State University, 1980.

Delacruz, Victor. "Systemic Operational Design: Enhancing the Joint Planning Process." Monograph, School of Advanced Military Studies, Fort Leavenworth, KS, 2007.

Groening, William H. "The Influence of the German General Staff on the American General Staff." US Army War College Military Studies Paper, 1985.

Kretchik, Walter E. "Peering through the Mist: Doctrine as a Guide for U.S. Army Operations, 1775–2000." PhD diss., University of Kansas, 2001.

Rasmussen, John Curtis, Jr. "The American Forces in Germany and Civil Affairs, July 1919–January 1923." PhD diss., University of Georgia, 1971.

Simmons, Charles J. "The United States in the Allied Occupation of Austria." MA thesis, Columbia University, 1953.

Weathersby, Kathryn. "Soviet Policy toward Korea, 1944–1946." PhD diss., Indiana University, 1990.

Williamson, Edward F. "A Comparison of the Post–Cold War Defense Budget Reductions to Prior Post-Conflict Reductions after World War II, Korea, and Vietnam." MA thesis, Naval Postgraduate School, 1993.

Index